Kaplan Publishing are constantly fir
ways to make a difference to your s
exciting online resources really do c
different to students looking for exa

CW00541160

This book comes with free MyKaplan online resources so that you can study anytime, anywhere. This free online resource is not sold separately and is included in the price of the book.

Having purchased this book, you have access to the following online study materials:

CONTENT	ACCA (including FFA,FAB,FMA)		FIA (excluding FFA,FAB,FMA)	
	Text	Kit	Text	Kit
iPaper version of the book	✓	✓	✓	✓
Interactive electronic version of the book	✓			
Check Your Understanding Test with instant answers	✓			
Material updates	✓	✓	✓	✓
Latest official ACCA exam questions*		✓		
Extra question assistance using the signpost icon**		✓		
Timed questions with an online tutor debrief using clock icon*		✓		
Interim assessment including questions and answers	✓		✓	
Technical answers	✓	✓	✓	✓

* Excludes F1, F2, F3, F4, FAB, FMA and FFA; for all other papers includes a selection of questions, as released by ACCA

** For ACCA P1-P7 only

How to access your online resources

Kaplan Financial students will already have a MyKaplan account and these extra resources will be available to you online. You do not need to register again, as this process was completed when you enrolled. If you are having problems accessing online materials, please ask your course administrator.

If you are already a registered MyKaplan user go to www.MyKaplan.co.uk and log in. Select the 'add a book' feature and enter the ISBN number of this book and the unique pass key at the bottom of this card. Then click 'finished' or 'add another book'. You may add as many books as you have purchased from this screen.

If you purchased through Kaplan Flexible Learning or via the Kaplan Publishing website you will automatically receive an e-mail invitation to MyKaplan. Please register your details using this email to gain access to your content. If you do not receive the e-mail or book content, please contact Kaplan Flexible Learning.

If you are a new MyKaplan user register at www.MyKaplan.co.uk and click on the link contained in the email we sent you to activate your account. Then select the 'add a book' feature, enter the ISBN number of this book and the unique pass key at the bottom of this card. Then click 'finished' or 'add another book'.

Your Code and Information

This code can only be used once for the registration of one book online. This registration and your online content will expire when the final sittings for the examinations covered by this book have taken place. Please allow one hour from the time you submit your book details for us to process your request.

Please scratch the film to access your MyKaplan code.

fmvY-48IH-NPm5-hqyZ

Please be aware that this code is case-sensitive and you will need to include the dashes within the passcode, but not when entering the ISBN. For further technical support, please visit www.MyKaplan.co.uk

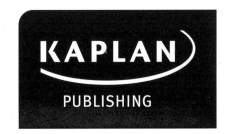

KAPLAN

PUBLISHING

Paper F9

Financial Management

EXAM KIT

KAPLAN
PUBLISHING

British Library Cataloguing-in-Publication Data

A catalogue record for this book is available from the British Library.

Published by:

Kaplan Publishing UK

Unit 2 The Business Centre

Molly Millar's Lane

Wokingham

Berkshire

RG41 2QZ

ISBN: 978-1-78415-698-5

Acknowledgements

The past ACCA examination questions are the copyright of the Association of Chartered Certified Accountants. The original answers to the questions from June 1994 onwards were produced by the examiners themselves and have been adapted by Kaplan Publishing.

We are grateful to the Chartered Institute of Management Accountants and the Institute of Chartered Accountants in England and Wales for permission to reproduce past examination questions. The answers have been prepared by Kaplan Publishing.

CONTENTS

Key features in this edition

In addition to providing a wide ranging bank of real past exam questions, we have also included in this edition:

- An analysis of all of the recent examination papers.

- Paper specific information and advice on exam technique.

- Our recommended approach to make your revision for this particular subject as effective as possible.

- This includes step by step guidance on how best to use our Kaplan material (Complete text, pocket notes and exam kit) at this stage in your studies.

- Enhanced tutorial answers packed with specific key answer tips, technical tutorial notes and exam technique tips from our experienced tutors.

- Complementary online resources including full tutor debriefs and question assistance to point you in the right direction when you get stuck.

You will find a wealth of other resources to help you with your studies on the following sites:

www.mykaplan.co.uk

www.kaplan-exam-tips.com

www.accaglobal.com/students/

Quality and accuracy are of the utmost importance to us so if you spot an error in any of our products, please send an email to mykaplanreporting@kaplan.com with full details, or follow the link to the feedback form in MyKaplan.

Our Quality Co-ordinator will work with our technical team to verify the error and take action to ensure it is corrected in future editions.

KAPLAN PUBLISHING

INDEX TO QUESTIONS AND ANSWERS

INTRODUCTION

Following the introduction of the revised exam format, all previous ACCA constructed response (long) exam questions within this kit have been adapted.

The specimen paper is included at the end of the kit.

KEY TO THE INDEX

PAPER ENHANCEMENTS

We have added the following enhancements to the answers in this exam kit:

Key answer tips

All answers include key answer tips to help your understanding of each question.

Tutorial note

Many answers include more tutorial notes to explain some of the technical points in more detail.

Top tutor tips

For selected questions, we 'walk through the answer' giving guidance on how to approach the questions with helpful 'tips from a top tutor', together with technical tutor notes.

These answers are indicated with the 'footsteps' icon in the index.

ONLINE ENHANCEMENTS

 Timed question with Online tutor debrief

For selected questions, we recommend that they are to be completed in full exam conditions (i.e. properly timed in a closed book environment).

In addition to the examiner's technical answer, enhanced with key answer tips and tutorial notes in this exam kit, online you can find an answer debrief by a top tutor that:

- works through the question in full

- points out how to approach the question

- shows how to ensure that the easy marks are obtained as quickly as possible, and

- emphasises how to tackle exam questions and exam technique.

These questions are indicated with the 'clock' icon in the index.

 Online question assistance

Have you ever looked at a question and not known where to start, or got stuck part way through?

For selected questions, we have produced 'Online question assistance' offering different levels of guidance, such as:

- ensuring that you understand the question requirements fully, highlighting key terms and the meaning of the verbs used

- how to read the question proactively, with knowledge of the requirements, to identify the topic areas covered

- assessing the detailed content of the question body, pointing out key information and explaining why it is important

- help in devising a plan of attack

With this assistance, you should then be able to attempt your answer confident that you know what is expected of you.

These questions are indicated with the 'signpost' icon in the index.

Online question enhancements and answer debriefs will be available on MyKaplan at:

www.MyKaplan.co.uk

ANALYSIS OF PAST PAPERS

The table below summarises the key topics that have been tested within the written test questions in the examinations to date. A much wider range of topics will now be examined following the introduction of objective test questions. Commencing September 2015, only selected questions will be released by ACCA every six months.

	J13	D13	J14	D14	J15	S15/ D15
Financial management function						
Nature and purpose of financial management						
Financial objectives and corporate strategy	✓	✓	✓			
Stakeholders and their impact on corporate strategy						
Not for profits						
Financial management environment						
Economic environment						
Financial markets and institutions						
Working capital management						
Elements and importance (including cash operating cycle)	✓		✓			
Inventories		✓				
Receivables	✓	✓			✓	✓
Payables						
Cash				✓		
Working capital needs and funding strategies		✓	✓	✓	✓	✓
Investment appraisal						
Appraisal process						
Non-discounted techniques						
NPV with tax						
NPV with tax and inflation	✓	✓	✓	✓	✓	✓
IRR						
Risk and uncertainty					✓	
Lease or buy			✓			
Asset replacement						
Capital rationing			✓			✓

	J13	D13	J14	D14	J15	S15/D15
Business finance and cost of capital						
Sources of short term finance						
Sources of long term finance	✓		✓	✓	✓	✓
Internal sources and dividend policy						
Gearing and capital structure	✓	✓			✓	✓
Small & medium enterprises						
Islamic financing		✓				
Sources and relative costs	✓					
Estimating cost of equity			✓	✓		
CAPM	✓	✓	✓			
Cost of debt						
Overall cost of capital	✓	✓	✓	✓		✓
Gearing theories						
Impact of cost of capital on investments		✓				
Business valuations						
Nature and purpose of valuation						
Models for valuing shares	✓		✓	✓	✓	
Valuing debt and other financial assets				✓		
Efficient markets hypothesis			✓			✓
Risk management						
Foreign exchange risk	✓		✓	✓	✓	✓
Interest rate risk					✓	✓
Forward contracts	✓			✓	✓	
Money market hedge	✓				✓	
Futures						
Hedging for interest rate risk					✓	✓

KAPLAN PUBLISHING

EXAM TECHNIQUE

GENERAL COMMENTS

- We recommend that you spend **15 minutes reading the paper** at the beginning of the exam:

    - read the questions and the examination requirements carefully, and

    - begin planning your answers.

    See the Paper Specific Information for advice on how to use this time for this paper.

- If 15 minutes are spent reading the examination paper, this leaves three hours to attempt the questions.

- **Divide the time** you spend on questions in proportion to the marks on offer:

    - one suggestion for this examination is to allocate 1.8 minutes to each mark available (180 minutes/100 marks), so a 20 mark question should be completed in approximately 36 minutes. If you plan to spend more or less time than 15 minutes reading the paper, your time allocation per mark will be different.

    - within that, try to allow time at the end of each question to review your answer and address any obvious issues.

    Whatever happens, always keep your eye on the clock and **do not over run on any part of any question!**

- If you **get completely stuck** with a question:

    - leave space in your answer book, and

    - **return to it later.**

- Stick to the question and **tailor your answer** to what you are asked.

    - Pay particular attention to the verbs in the question.

    - Try to apply your comments to the scenario where possible.

- If you do not understand what a question is asking, **state your assumptions**.

    Even if you do not answer in precisely the way the examiner hoped, you should be given some credit, if your assumptions are reasonable.

- You should do everything you can to make things easy for the marker.

    The marker will find it easier to identify the points you have made if your **answers are legible**.

OBJECTIVE TEST QUESTIONS

- Decide whether you want to attempt these at the start of the exam or at the end.

- No credit for working will be given in these questions, the answers will either be correct (2 marks) or incorrect (0 marks)

- Read the question carefully, as the alternative answer choices will be given based on common mistakes that could be made in attempting the question.

- If a question looks particularly difficult or time consuming, then miss it out first time through and come back to it later.

CONSTRUCTED RESPONSE (LONG) QUESTIONS

- **Written elements**:

  Your answer should have:

  - a clear structure

  - a brief introduction, a main section and a conclusion.

  Be concise.

  It is better to write a little about a lot of different points than a great deal about one or two points.

  Where possible, try to relate comments to the specific context given rather than your answer looking like it was simply copied out of the textbook.

- **Computations**:

  It is essential to include all your workings in your answers.

COMPUTER-BASED EXAMS – ADDITIONAL TIPS

- Do not attempt a CBE until you have completed all study material relating to it.

- On the ACCA website there is a CBE demonstration. It is ESSENTIAL that you attempt this before your real CBE. You will become familiar with how to move around the CBE screens and the way that questions are formatted, increasing your confidence and speed in the actual exam.

- Be sure you understand how to use the software before you start the exam. If in doubt, ask the assessment centre staff to explain it to you.

- Questions are displayed on the screen and answers are entered using keyboard and mouse.

- In addition to the traditional multiple choice question type, CBEs will also contain other types of questions, such as number entry questions, formulae entry questions, multiple correct answers (select two or more), matching labels to targets, stem questions with multiple parts and written questions requiring text entry.

- You need to be sure you know how to answer questions of these types before you sit the exam, through practice.

PAPER SPECIFIC INFORMATION

THE EXAM

FORMAT OF THE EXAM

From September 2016, the exam will be in **THREE sections**, and will be a mix of narrative and computational answers.

All questions are compulsory.

		Number of marks
Section A:	Fifteen objective test questions of 2 marks each	30
Section B:	Three objective test case studies	
	– five questions per case study of 2 marks each	30
Section C:	Two constructed response (long) questions:	
	Question 1: Any area of the syllabus	20
	Question 2: Any area of the syllabus	20
		‾‾‾‾
		100
		‾‾‾‾

Total time allowed: 3 hours and 15 minutes.

Note that:

- the F9 paper will have both a discursive and computational element. The objective test questions and the objective test case study questions will therefore include a mix of calculation-based and explanation-based questions.

- there is likely to be a discussion element included in the constructed response questions in Section C.

PASS MARK

The pass mark for all ACCA Qualification examination papers is 50%.

SECTION A QUESTIONS

Note that in the paper-based exam, all Section A questions will be multiple choice questions.

The computer-based exam will include different question styles, as described in the previous section on exam technique.

A mixture of these question types is included within this exam kit.

APPROACH TO THIS PAPER

F9 is divided into three different sections, requiring the application of different skills to be successful.

Section A

Stick to the timing principle of 1.8 minutes per mark. This means that the 15 OT questions in section A (30 marks) should take 54 minutes.

Work steadily. Rushing leads to careless mistakes and the OT questions are designed to include answers which result from careless mistakes.

If you don't know the answer, eliminate those options you know are incorrect and see if the answer becomes more obvious.

Remember that there is no negative marking for an incorrect answer. After you have eliminated the options that you know to be wrong, if you are still unsure, guess.

Section B

There is likely to be a significant amount of information to read through for each case. You should begin by reading the OT questions that relate to the case, so that when you read through the information for the first time, you know what it is that you are required to do.

Each OT question is worth two marks. Therefore you have 18 minutes (1.8 minutes per mark) to answer the five OT questions relating to each case. It is likely that all of the cases will take the same length of time to answer, although some of the OT questions within a case may be quicker than other OT questions within that same case.

Once you have read through the information, you should first answer any of the OT questions that do not require workings and can be quickly answered. You should then attempt the OT questions that require workings utilising the remaining time for that case.

All of the tips for section A are equally applicable to each section B question.

Section C

The constructed response questions in section C will require a written response rather than being OT questions. Therefore, different techniques need to be used to score well.

Unless you know exactly how to answer the question, spend some time planning your answer. Stick to the question and tailor your answer to what you are asked. Pay particular attention to the verbs in the question e.g. 'Calculate', 'State', 'Explain'.

As stated earlier, if you **get completely stuck** with a question, leave space in your answer book and return to it later.

If you do not understand what a question is asking, state your assumptions. Even if you do not answer in precisely the way the examining team hoped, you should be given some credit, provided that your assumptions are reasonable.

You should do everything you can to make things easy for the marker. The marker will find it easier to identify the points you have made if your answers are legible.

Computations: It is essential to include all your workings in your answers. Many computational questions require the use of a standard format. Be sure you know these formats thoroughly before the examination and use the layouts that you see in the answers given in this book and in model answers.

Adopt a logical approach and cross reference workings to the main computation to keep your answers tidy.

All sections

Don't skip parts of the syllabus. The F9 paper has 32 different questions so the examination can cover a very broad selection of the syllabus each sitting.

Spend time learning the rules and definitions.

Practice plenty of questions to improve your ability to apply the techniques and perform the calculations.

Spend the last five minutes reading through your answers and making any additions or corrections.

 Always keep your eye on the clock and do not over run on any part of any question!

DETAILED SYLLABUS

The detailed syllabus and study guide written by the ACCA can be found at:

www.accaglobal.com/students/

KAPLAN'S RECOMMENDED REVISION APPROACH

QUESTION PRACTICE IS THE KEY TO SUCCESS

Success in professional examinations relies upon you acquiring a firm grasp of the required knowledge at the tuition phase. In order to be able to do the questions, knowledge is essential.

However, the difference between success and failure often hinges on your exam technique on the day and making the most of the revision phase of your studies.

The **Kaplan complete text** is the starting point, designed to provide the underpinning knowledge to tackle all questions. However, in the revision phase, pouring over text books is not the answer.

MyKaplan knowledge check tests help you consolidate your knowledge and understanding and are a useful tool to check whether you can remember key topic areas.

Kaplan pocket notes are designed to help you quickly revise a topic area, however you then need to practise questions. There is a need to progress to full exam standard questions as soon as possible, and to tie your exam technique and technical knowledge together.

The importance of question practice cannot be over-emphasised.

The recommended approach below is designed by expert tutors in the field, in conjunction with their knowledge of the examiner and their recent real exams.

The approach taken for the fundamental papers is to revise by topic area. However, with the professional stage papers, a multi topic approach is required to answer the scenario based questions.

You need to practice as many questions as possible in the time you have left.

OUR AIM

Our aim is to get you to the stage where you can attempt exam standard questions confidently, to time, in a closed book environment, with no supplementary help (i.e. to simulate the real examination experience).

Practising your exam technique on real past examination questions, in timed conditions, is also vitally important for you to assess your progress and identify areas of weakness that may need more attention in the final run up to the examination.

In order to achieve this we recognise that initially you may feel the need to practise some questions with open book help and exceed the required time.

The approach below shows you which questions you should use to build up to coping with exam standard question practice, and references to the sources of information available should you need to revisit a topic area in more detail.

Remember that in the real examination, all you have to do is:

- attempt all questions required by the exam

- only spend the allotted time on each question, and

- get them at least 50% right!

Try and practice this approach on every question you attempt from now to the real exam.

Previously, the exam focus meant that students were able to attempt some form of 'question spotting' as there are a few large topic areas. Following the introduction of objective test questions, this will no longer be the case and to pass F9, students will need to understand information from the wide range of topics across the syllabus.

EXAMINER COMMENTS

We have included the examiner's comments to the specific new syllabus examination questions in this kit for you to see the main pitfalls that students fall into with regard to technical content.

However, too many times in the general section of the report, the examiner comments that students had failed due to:

- 'misallocation of time'

- 'running out of time' and

- showing signs of 'spending too much time on an earlier questions and clearly rushing the answer to a subsequent question'.

Good exam technique is vital.

THE KAPLAN PAPER F9 REVISION PLAN

Stage 1: Assess areas of strengths and weaknesses

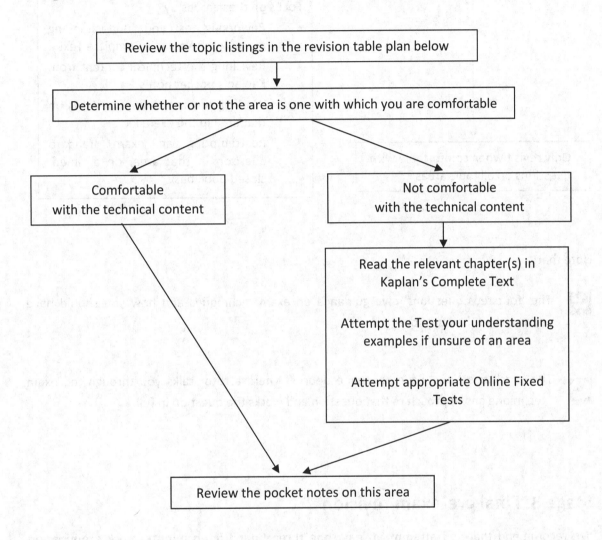

Review the topic listings in the revision table plan below

Determine whether or not the area is one with which you are comfortable

Comfortable
with the technical content

Not comfortable
with the technical content

Read the relevant chapter(s) in
Kaplan's Complete Text

Attempt the Test your understanding
examples if unsure of an area

Attempt appropriate Online Fixed
Tests

Review the pocket notes on this area

Stage 2: Practice questions

Follow the order of revision of topics as recommended in the revision table plan below and attempt the questions in the order suggested.

Try to avoid referring to text books and notes and the model answer until you have completed your attempt.

Try to answer the question in the allotted time.

Review your attempt with the model answer and assess how much of the answer you achieved in the allocated exam time.

Fill in the self-assessment box below and decide on your best course of action.

Note that:

 The 'footsteps questions' give guidance on exam techniques and how you should have approached the question.

 The 'clock questions' have an online debrief where a tutor talks you through the exam technique and approach to that question and works the question in full.

Stage 3: Final pre-exam revision

We recommend that you **attempt at least one three hour fifteen minute mock examination** containing a set of previously unseen exam standard questions.

It is important that you get a feel for the breadth of coverage of a real exam without advanced knowledge of the topic areas covered – just as you will expect to see on the real exam day.

Ideally this mock should be sat in timed, closed book, real exam conditions and could be:

* a mock examination offered by your tuition provider, and/or

* the pilot paper in the back of this exam kit, and/or

* the last real examination paper (available shortly afterwards on MyKaplan with 'enhanced walk through answers' and a full 'tutor debrief').

THE DETAILED REVISION PLAN

Topic	Complete Text Chapter	Pocket note Chapter	Questions to attempt	Tutor guidance	Date attempted	Self assessment
Investment appraisal	2 & 3	2 & 3	22 23	Start with the basics – remind yourself of the four techniques and ensure you can compare and contrast between them. Start with question 22 before attempting question 23 as an example of a recent past exam question in this area.		
– Further aspects of discounted cash flows	4	4	21 27	A popular exam topic, guaranteed to form part of the exam. There are many questions on this area. Start with questions 21 and 27 which are basic warm up questions. Build up to questions 24 and 25 which are slightly more complex questions on this area.		
– Risk and uncertainty	6	6	26 29	This is an aspect that is often examined alongside the more complex areas of discounted cash flow techniques. Question 30 is another good example of how this topic can be examined.		
– Asset investment decisions and capital rationing	5	5	32 33	This is an area that has not been widely examined within the recent exam diets. Despite this, it is worth having a quick recap of the techniques using these two questions.		

Topic	Complete Text Chapter	Pocket note Chapter	Questions to attempt	Tutor guidance	Date attempted	Self assessment
Working capital management	7	7	–	Begin by recapping on the key ratio calculations relating to working capital management and the calculation of the cash operating cycle.		
– Receivables and payables	9	9	14	Questions on working capital management will often draw upon several different elements.		
– Inventory	8	8	17	This question covers many aspects of working capital management and is a good illustration of the way the examiner tends to tackle this topic.		
– Cash and funding strategies	10	10	13 15	Question 13 contains good coverage of this chapter. Question 12 covers an area that has not been widely examined.		
Financial management function	1	1	1	Now is a good point to visit some of the less widely examined areas of the syllabus. Question 4 is a good example of how these more discursive elements are examined.		

KAPLAN PUBLISHING

KAPLAN'S DETAILED REVISION PLAN

Topic	Complete Text Chapter	Pocket note Chapter	Questions to attempt	Tutor guidance	Date attempted	Self assessment
The economic environment for business	11	11	6	Question 6 reflects how this topic could be examined.		
Financial markets and the treasury function	12	12	–	This is a fairly new area to the syllabus but it's worth covering this before you start reviewing the topics of business finance and risk management.		
Sources of finance	15	15	46	Question 46, taken from the June 07 exam, is an excellent illustration of the way the examiner will often pull from more than one syllabus area within his questions.		
Financial ratios	19	19	47	Questions involving the calculation and interpretation of financial ratios are very common. You must be able to calculate each of the key ratios as well as appreciate how they interrelate with each other.		
The cost of capital	17	17	52	This is another popular exam topic. As well as reviewing the complete text and the pocket notes, ensure you download and review the examiner's series of articles relating to CAPM.		

KAPLAN PUBLISHING

P.25

Topic	Complete Text Chapter	Pocket note Chapter	Questions to attempt	Tutor guidance	Date attempted	Self assessment
Capital structure	18	18	34	This is a tricky topic. Be sure to work carefully through the pocket notes, perhaps attempting the test your understandings within the complete text before attempting the exam standard questions.		
Business valuations and market efficiency	20	20	57 58 59	This is another popular exam topic and one which can be easily linked with other areas of the syllabus. You must be able to apply each of the main methods of business valuation and consider the impact that financing may have on a company's valuation.		
Dividend policy	16	16	42	This small topic is often examined alongside business valuations or sources of finance.		
Foreign exchange risk	13	13	62 63	Another topic that students often find difficult. Review the illustrations within the complete text but don't neglect the more discursive aspects, which are examined more frequently.		
Interest rate risk	14	14	65	This topic has not been extensively tested within recent exams.		

Note that not all of the questions are referred to in the programme above. We have recommended an approach to build up from the basic to exam standard questions.

The remaining questions are available in the kit for extra practice for those who require more questions on some areas.

MATHEMATICAL TABLES AND FORMULAE SHEET

Economic order quantity

$$= \sqrt{\frac{2C_oD}{C_H}}$$

Miller-Orr Model

Return point = Lower limit + ($\frac{1}{3}$ × spread)

$$\text{Spread} = 3 \left(\frac{\frac{3}{4} \times \text{Transaction cost} \times \text{Variance of cash flows}}{\text{Interest rate}} \right)^{\frac{1}{3}}$$

The Capital Asset Pricing Model

$$E(r)_j = R_f + \beta_j (E(r_m) - R_f)$$

The asset beta formula

$$\beta_a = \left(\frac{V_e}{(V_e + V_d(1-T))} \; \beta_e \right) + \left(\frac{V_d(1-T)}{(V_e + V_d(1-T))} \; \beta_d \right)$$

The Growth Model

$$P_0 = \frac{Do(1+g)}{(r_e - g)}$$

Gordon's growth approximation

$$g = br_e$$

The weighted average cost of capital

$$\text{WACC} = \left(\frac{V_e}{V_e + V_d} \right) k_e + \left(\frac{V_d}{V_e + V_d} \right) k_d(1-T)$$

The Fisher formula

$$(1 + i) = (1 + r)(1 + h)$$

Purchasing power parity and interest rate parity

$$S_1 = S_0 \times \frac{(1+h_c)}{(1+h_b)} \qquad F_0 = S_0 \times \frac{(1+i_c)}{(1+i_b)}$$

Present Value Table

Present value of 1 i.e. $(1 + r)^{-n}$

Where   r = discount rate

           n = number of periods until payment

Periods					*Discount rates (r)*						
(n)	**1%**	**2%**	**3%**	**4%**	**5%**	**6%**	**7%**	**8%**	**9%**	**10%**	
1	0.990	0.980	0.971	0.962	0.952	0.943	0.935	0.926	0.917	0.909	1
2	0.980	0.961	0.943	0.925	0.907	0.890	0.873	0.857	0.842	0.826	2
3	0.971	0.942	0.915	0.889	0.864	0.840	0.816	0.794	0.772	0.751	3
4	0.961	0.924	0.888	0.855	0.823	0.792	0.763	0.735	0.708	0.683	4
5	0.951	0.906	0.863	0.822	0.784	0.747	0.713	0.681	0.650	0.621	5
6	0.942	0.888	0.837	0.790	0.746	0.705	0.666	0.630	0.596	0.564	6
7	0.933	0.871	0.813	0.760	0.711	0.665	0.623	0.583	0.547	0.513	7
8	0.923	0.853	0.789	0.731	0.677	0.627	0.582	0.540	0.502	0.467	8
9	0.914	0.837	0.766	0.703	0.645	0.592	0.544	0.500	0.460	0.424	9
10	0.905	0.820	0.744	0.676	0.614	0.558	0.508	0.463	0.422	0.386	10
11	0.896	0.804	0.722	0.650	0.585	0.527	0.475	0.429	0.388	0.350	11
12	0.887	0.788	0.701	0.625	0.557	0.497	0.444	0.397	0.356	0.319	12
13	0.879	0.773	0.681	0.601	0.530	0.469	0.415	0.368	0.326	0.290	13
14	0.870	0.758	0.661	0.577	0.505	0.442	0.388	0.340	0.299	0.263	14
15	0.861	0.743	0.642	0.555	0.481	0.417	0.362	0.315	0.275	0.239	15

(n)	**11%**	**12%**	**13%**	**14%**	**15%**	**16%**	**17%**	**18%**	**19%**	**20%**	
1	0.901	0.893	0.885	0.877	0.870	0.862	0.855	0.847	0.840	0.833	1
2	0.812	0.797	0.783	0.769	0.756	0.743	0.731	0.718	0.706	0.694	2
3	0.731	0.712	0.693	0.675	0.658	0.641	0.624	0.609	0.593	0.579	3
4	0.659	0.636	0.613	0.592	0.572	0.552	0.534	0.516	0.499	0.482	4
5	0.593	0.567	0.543	0.519	0.497	0.476	0.456	0.437	0.419	0.402	5
6	0.535	0.507	0.480	0.456	0.432	0.410	0.390	0.370	0.352	0.335	6
7	0.482	0.452	0.425	0.400	0.376	0.354	0.333	0.314	0.296	0.279	7
8	0.434	0.404	0.376	0.351	0.327	0.305	0.285	0.266	0.249	0.233	8
9	0.391	0.361	0.333	0.308	0.284	0.263	0.243	0.225	0.209	0.194	9
10	0.352	0.322	0.295	0.270	0.247	0.227	0.208	0.191	0.176	0.162	10
11	0.317	0.287	0.261	0.237	0.215	0.195	0.178	0.162	0.148	0.135	11
12	0.286	0.257	0.231	0.208	0.187	0.168	0.152	0.137	0.124	0.112	12
13	0.258	0.229	0.204	0.182	0.163	0.145	0.130	0.116	0.104	0.093	13
14	0.232	0.205	0.181	0.160	0.141	0.125	0.111	0.099	0.088	0.078	14
15	0.209	0.183	0.160	0.140	0.123	0.108	0.095	0.084	0.074	0.065	15

Annuity Table

Present value of an annuity of 1 i.e. $\dfrac{1-(1+r)^{-n}}{r}$

Where   r = discount rate
           n = number of periods

Periods (n)	1%	2%	3%	4%	5%	6%	7%	8%	9%	10%	
1	0.990	0.980	0.971	0.962	0.952	0.943	0.935	0.926	0.917	0.909	1
2	1.970	1.942	1.913	1.886	1.859	1.833	1.808	1.783	1.759	1.736	2
3	2.941	2.884	2.829	2.775	2.723	2.673	2.624	2.577	2.531	2.487	3
4	3.902	3.808	3.717	3.630	3.546	3.465	3.387	3.312	3.240	3.170	4
5	4.853	4.713	4.580	4.452	4.329	4.212	4.100	3.993	3.890	3.791	5
6	5.795	5.601	5.417	5.242	5.076	4.917	4.767	4.623	4.486	4.355	6
7	6.728	6.472	6.230	6.002	5.786	5.582	5.389	5.206	5.033	4.868	7
8	7.652	7.325	7.020	6.733	6.463	6.210	5.971	5.747	5.535	5.335	8
9	8.566	8.162	7.786	7.435	7.108	6.802	6.515	6.247	5.995	5.759	9
10	9.471	8.983	8.530	8.111	7.722	7.360	7.024	6.710	6.418	6.145	10
11	10.37	9.787	9.253	8.760	8.306	7.887	7.499	7.139	6.805	6.495	11
12	11.26	10.58	9.954	9.385	8.863	8.384	7.943	7.536	7.161	6.814	12
13	12.13	11.35	10.63	9.986	9.394	8.853	8.358	7.904	7.487	7.103	13
14	13.00	12.11	11.30	10.56	9.899	9.295	8.745	8.244	7.786	7.367	14
15	13.87	12.85	11.94	11.12	10.38	9.712	9.108	8.559	8.061	7.606	15

(n)	11%	12%	13%	14%	15%	16%	17%	18%	19%	20%	
1	0.901	0.893	0.885	0.877	0.870	0.862	0.855	0.847	0.840	0.833	1
2	1.713	1.690	1.668	1.647	1.626	1.605	1.585	1.566	1.547	1.528	2
3	2.444	2.402	2.361	2.322	2.283	2.246	2.210	2.174	2.140	2.106	3
4	3.102	3.037	2.974	2.914	2.855	2.798	2.743	2.690	2.639	2.589	4
5	3.696	3.605	3.517	3.433	3.352	3.274	3.199	3.127	3.058	2.991	5
6	4.231	4.111	3.998	3.889	3.784	3.685	3.589	3.498	3.410	3.326	6
7	4.712	4.564	4.423	4.288	4.160	4.039	3.922	3.812	3.706	3.605	7
8	5.146	4.968	4.799	4.639	4.487	4.344	4.207	4.078	3.954	3.837	8
9	5.537	5.328	5.132	4.946	4.772	4.607	4.451	4.303	4.163	4.031	9
10	5.889	5.650	5.426	5.216	5.019	4.833	4.659	4.494	4.339	4.192	10
11	6.207	5.938	5.687	5.453	5.234	5.029	4.836	4.656	4.486	4.327	11
12	6.492	6.194	5.918	5.660	5.421	5.197	4.988	4.793	4.611	4.439	12
13	6.750	6.424	6.122	5.842	5.583	5.342	5.118	4.910	4.715	4.533	13
14	6.982	6.628	6.302	6.002	5.724	5.468	5.229	5.008	4.802	4.611	14
15	7.191	6.811	6.462	6.142	5.847	5.575	5.324	5.092	4.876	4.675	15

Section A

OBJECTIVE TEST QUESTIONS

Each question is worth two marks.

FINANCIAL MANAGEMENT FUNCTION

1   In relation to the financial management of a company, which of the following provides the best definition of a firm's primary financial objective?

    A   To achieve long-term growth in earnings

    B   To maximise the level of annual dividends

    C   To maximise the wealth of its ordinary shareholder

    D   To maximise the level of annual profits

2   Drag and drop to indicate whether the following objectives are financial or non-financial objectives of a company.

Objective	Financial	Non-financial
Maximisation of market share		
Earnings growth		
Sales revenue growth		
Achieving a target level of customer satisfaction		
Achieving a target level of return on capital employed		

3   Which THREE of the following are the main types of decision facing the financial manager in a company?

    A   Income decision

    B   Investment decision

    C   Dividend decision

    D   Financing decision

4 **Which of the following is an example of a financial objective that a company might choose to pursue?**

   A   Dealing honestly and fairly with customers on all occasions

   B   Provision of good working conditions and industrial relations

   C   Producing environmentally friendly products

   D   Restricting the level of gearing to below a specified target level

5 Value for money is an important objective for not-for-profit organisations.

   Which of the following actions is consistent with increasing value for money?

   A   Using a cheaper source of goods and thereby decreasing the quality of not-for-profit organisation services

   B   Searching for ways to diversify the finances of the not-for-profit organisation

   C   Decreasing waste in the provision of a service by the not-for-profit organisation

   D   Focusing on meeting the financial objectives of the not-for-profit organization

6 **Which of the following is LEAST likely to fall within financial management?**

   A   The dividend payment to shareholders is increased

   B   Funds are raised to finance an investment project

   C   Surplus assets are sold off

   D   Non-executive directors are appointed to the remuneration committee

7 **Drag and drop to indicate whether the following statements are true or false.**

Statement	True	False
Financial management is concerned with the long-term raising of finance and the allocation and control of resources.		
Management accounting is concerned with providing information for the more day-to-day functions of control and decision making.		
Financial accounting is concerned with providing information about the historical results of past plans and decisions		

8 **Which of the following tasks would typically be carried out by a member of the financial management team?**

   A   Evaluating proposed expansion plans

   B   Review of overtime spending

   C   Depreciation of non-current assets

   D   Apportioning overheads to cost units

9 **Which of the following is an example of an internal stakeholder in a firm?**

A   Company directors

B   Customers

C   Suppliers

D   Finance providers

10 **What is the main purpose of corporate governance?**

A   To separate ownership and management control of organisations

B   To maximise shareholder value

C   To facilitate effective management of organisations and to make organisations more visibly accountable to a wider range of stakeholders

D   To ensure that regulatory frameworks are adhered to

11 The agency problem is a driving force behind the growing importance attached to sound corporate governance.

In this context, who are the agents?

A   Customers

B   Shareholders

C   Managers

D   Auditors

12 **Which TWO of the following statements are correct?**

1   Maximising market share is an example of a financial objective

2   Shareholder wealth maximisation is the primary financial objective for a company listed on a stock exchange

3   Financial objectives should be quantitative so that their achievement can be measured

4   Three E's are used as a performance measure to assess value of money in not for profit organisations. The three E's stand for economy, efficiency and environment

13 **Which of the following is an 'efficiency' target that a not for profit organisation might put in place?**

A   Negotiation of bulk discounts

B   Pay rates for staff of appropriate levels of qualification

C   Staff utilisation

D   Customer satisfaction ratings

14 Managerial reward schemes should help ensure managers take decisions which are consistent with the objectives of shareholders.

   Which THREE of the following are characteristics of a carefully designed remuneration package?

   A   Linking of rewards to changes in shareholder wealth

   B   Matching of managers' time horizons to shareholders' time horizons

   C   Possibility of manipulation by managers

   D   Encouragement for managers to adopt the same attitudes to risk as shareholders

15 **Which of the following are typical criticisms of executive share option schemes (ESOPs)?**

   1   When directors exercise their options, they tend to sell the shares almost immediately to cash in on their profits

   2   If the share price falls when options have been awarded, and the options have no value, they cannot act as an incentive

   3   Directors may distort reported profits to protect the share price and the value of their share options

   A   1 only

   B   1 and 3 only

   C   2 and 3 only

   D   1, 2, and 3

16 The directors of Portico plc have recently engaged a firm of consultants to negotiate standard terms of trade for one of its strategic business units. This includes the agreement by Portico plc to pay a 5% penalty on any late invoice settlement.

   This policy is an illustration of the company's concern for which major stakeholder?

   A   Lenders

   B   Suppliers

   C   Customers

   D   Trade unions

17 **Under the terms of the UK Corporate Governance Code, what are the only type of directors permitted to sit on a company's audit committee?**

   A   Independent non-executive directors

   B   Non-executive directors

   C   Executive directors

   D   Directors with financial experience

FINANCIAL MANAGEMENT ENVIRONMENT

18   **Which of the following is (are) among the elements of fiscal policy?**

   1   Government actions to raise or lower taxes

   2   Government actions to raise or lower the size of the money supply

   3   Government actions to raise or lower the amount it spends

   A   1 only

   B   1 and 3 only

   C   2 and 3 only

   D   1, 2 and 3

19   **Which TWO of the following statements are correct?**

   1   Securitisation is the conversion of illiquid assets into marketable securities

   2   The reverse yield gap refers to equity yields being higher than debt yields

   3   Disintermediation arises where borrowers deal directly with lending individuals

   4   Demand-pull inflation will occur when there are increases in production costs independent to the state of demand

20   **Drag and drop to indicate whether the following statements are true or false.**

Statement	True	False
Coupon bearing securities have a fixed maturity and a specified rate of interest		
In the discount market, funds are raised by issuing bills at a discount to their eventual redemption or maturity value		

21   **The principal objectives of macroeconomic policy include which of the following?**

   1   Full employment of resources

   2   Price stability

   3   Economic growth

   4   Balancing the government budget

   A   1 and 2 only

   B   1 and 3 only

   C   1, 2 and 3 only

   D   1, 2, 3 and 4

22 Governments have a number of economic targets as part of their fiscal policy.

Which of the following government actions relate predominantly to fiscal policy?

1   Decreasing interest rates in order to stimulate consumer spending

2   Reducing taxation while maintaining public spending

3   Using official foreign currency reserves to buy the domestic currency

4   Borrowing money from the capital markets and spending it on public works

A   1 only

B   1 and 3

C   2 and 4 only

D   2, 3 and 4

23   Which THREE of the following are key roles played by money markets?

A   Providing short-term liquidity to companies, banks and the public sector

B   Providing short term trade finance

C   Allowing an organisation to manage its exposure to foreign currency risk and interest rate risk

D   Dealing in long-term funds and transactions

24   Which of the following are money market instruments?

1   Certificates of deposit

2   Corporate bond

3   Commercial paper

4   Treasury bill

A   1, 2 and 4 only

B   1 and 3 only

C   1, 3 and 4 only

D   1, 2 and 3 and 4

25   Which THREE of the following are common roles of the treasury function within a firm?

A   Short-term management of resources

B   Long-term maximisation of shareholder wealth

C   Long-term maximisation of market share

D   Risk management

26   **Which of the following is a difference between primary and secondary capital markets?**

A   Primary capital markets relate to the sale of new securities, while secondary capital markets are where securities trade after their initial offering

B   Both primary and secondary capital markets relate to where securities are traded after their initial offering

C   Both primary and secondary capital markets relate to the sale of new securities

D   Primary markets are where stocks trade and secondary markets are where loan notes trade

27   **Changes in monetary policy will influence which of the following factors?**

1   The level of exchange rates

2   The cost of finance

3   The level of consumer demand

4   The level of inflation

A   1 and 2 only

B   2 and 3 only

C   2, 3 and 4 only

D   1, 2 and 3 and 4

28   **Which of the following is/are usually seen as forms of market failure where regulation may be a solution?**

1   Imperfect competition

2   Social costs or externalities

3   Imperfect information

A   1 only

B   1 and 2 only

C   2 and 3 only

D   1, 2 and 3

29   There are two main types of financial market: capital and money markets, and within each of these are primary and secondary markets.

Which three of the following statements are true?

A   Primary markets allow the realisation of investments before their maturity date by selling them to other investors

B   Primary markets deal in new issues of loanable funds

C   Capital markets consist of stock-markets for shares and loan bond markets

D   Money markets provide short-term debt finance and investment

30 **Drag and drop to indicate whether the following statements are true or false.**

Statement	True	False
Interest rate smoothing is the policy of some central banks to move official interest rates in a sequence of relatively small steps in the same direction, rather than waiting until making a single larger step.		
If governments wish to influence the amount of money held in the economy or the demand for credit, they may attempt to influence the level of interest rates.		

31 **A variety of Corporate Governance rules have been introduced in different countries but what are the principles, common to all, that they typically include?**

1   The chairman and chief executive officer should not be the same individual

2   Non-executive directors on the board should prevent the board from being dominated by the executive directors

3   The audit committee should consist solely of executive directors

4   A remuneration committee should be established to decide on the remuneration of executive directors

A   1 and 2 only

B   1, 2 and 3 only

C   1, 2 and 4 only

D   1, 2, 3 and 4

32 **Which one of the following statements is correct?**

A   Direct taxes are levied on one set of individuals or organisations but may be partly or wholly passed on to others and are largely related to consumption not income

B   Indirect taxes are levied directly on income receivers whether they are individuals or organisations

C   A balanced budget occurs when total expenditure is matched by total taxation

D   A deficit budget occurs when total expenditure is less than total taxation income

33 **Drag and drop to indicate whether the following statements are true or false.**

Statement	True	False
Demand-pull inflation might occur when excess aggregate monetary demand in the economy and hence demand for particular goods and services enable companies to raise prices and expand profit margins		
Cost-push inflation will occur when there are increases in production costs independent of the state of demand e.g. rising raw material costs or rising labour costs		

34   Which THREE of the following are true, in relation to certificates of deposit?

    A   They are evidence of a deposit with an issuing bank

    B   They are not negotiable and therefore unattractive to the depositor as they do not ensure instant liquidity

    C   They provide the bank with a deposit for a fixed period at a fixed rate of interest

    D   They are coupon-bearing securities

35   Which of the following is least likely to be a reason for seeking a stock market listing?

    A   Enhancement of the company's image

    B   Transfer of capital to other users

    C   Improving existing owners' control over the business

    D   Access to a wider pool of finance

36   Which of the following is NOT typically a principal objective of macroeconomic policy?

    A   To achieve full employment of resources

    B   To achieve economic growth

    C   To achieve a balance of payments deficit

    D   To achieve an appropriate distribution of income and wealth

37   Which THREE of the following are advantages of having a centralised treasury department in a large international group of companies?

    A   No need for treasury skills to be duplicated throughout the group

    B   Necessary borrowings can be arranged in bulk, at keener interest rates than for smaller amounts

    C   The group's foreign currency risk can be managed much more effectively since they can appreciate the total exposure situation

    D   Local operating units should have a better feel for local conditions than head office and can respond more quickly to local developments

38   Investing in a small or medium sized business (SME) is inherently more risky than investing in a larger company due to lack of business history and a lower level of public scrutiny over accounts and records. What is the frequently used term to describe the difficulty SMEs can often face when raising finance?

    A   Maturity gap

    B   Funding gap

    C   Duration gap

    D   Equity gap

WORKING CAPITAL MANAGEMENT

39 Thrifty Plc's cash budget highlights a short-term surplus in the near future.

Which of the following actions would be appropriate to make use of the surplus?

A   Pay suppliers earlier to take advantage of any prompt payment discounts

B   Buy back the company's shares

C   Increase payables by delaying payment to suppliers

D   Invest in a long term deposit bank account

40 **Drag and drop to indicate whether the following statements are true or false.**

Statement	True	False
Working capital should increase as sales increase		
An increase in the cash operating cycle will decrease profitability		
Overtrading is also known as under-capitalisation		

41 **Which of the following might be associated with a shortening working capital cycle?**

A   Lower net operating cash flow

B   Increasing tax-allowable depreciation expenditure

C   Slower inventory turnover

D   Taking longer to pay suppliers

42 The following information has been calculated for D Co:

Trade receivables collection period	10 weeks
Raw material inventory turnover period	6 weeks
Work in progress inventory turnover period	2 weeks
Trade payables payment period	7 weeks
Finished goods inventory turnover period	6 weeks

What is the length of the working capital cycle?

☐ weeks

43 A company sells inventory for cash to a customer, at a selling price which is below the cost of the inventory items.

How will this transaction affect the current ratio and the quick ratio immediately after the transaction? Drag and drop to indicate whether each ratio will increase or decrease.

Ratio	Increase	Decrease
Current ratio		
Quick ratio		

44 A company has the following summarised Statement of Financial Position at 31 December 20X4:

	$000	$000
Non-current assets		1,000
Current assets		
Inventories	200	
Receivables	150	
Cash	100	
	450	
Current liabilities		
Payables	200	
Net current assets		250
		1,250

Over the next year the company should double its sales. The company does not plan to invest in any new non-current assets, but inventories, receivables and payables should all move in line with sales.

What cash balance in one year's time would this imply if the non-current assets were all land, no new capital was raised and all profits were paid out as dividends?

A $100,000 cash in hand

B $200,000 cash in hand

C $50,000 overdraft

D $100,000 overdraft

45 Goldstar has an accounts receivables turnover of 10.5 times, an inventory turnover of 4 times and payables turnover of 8 times.

What is Goldstar's cash operating cycle (assume 365 days in a year)?

A 80.38 days

B 6.50 days

C 22.50 days

D 171.64 days

46 The cash operating cycle is equal to which of the following?

A Receivables days plus inventory holding period minus payables days

B Inventory holding period minus receivables days minus payables days

C Receivables days plus inventory holding period plus payables days

D Receivables days minus payables days minus inventory holding period

47   A company has annual credit sales of $27 million and related cost of sales of $15 million. The company has the following targets for the next year:

Trade receivables days   50 days

Inventory days   60 days

Trade payables   45 days

Assume there are 360 days in the year.

What is the net investment in working capital required for the next year?

A $8,125,000

B $4,375,000

C $2,875,000

D $6,375,000

48   A cash budget was drawn up as follows:

	October	*November*	*December*
	$	$	$
Receipts			
Credit Sales	20,000	11,000	14,500
Cash Sales	10,000	4,500	6,000
Payments			
Suppliers	13,000	4,200	7,800
Wages	4,600	2,300	3,000
Overheads	3,000	1,750	1,900
Opening Cash	500		

What is the closing cash balance for December is budgeted to be?

A $20,550 overdraft

B $21,050 overdraft

C $22,450 deposit

D $24,950 deposit

49   **Which THREE of the following would be a key aspects of a company's accounts receivable credit policy?**

A   Assessing creditworthiness

B   Checking credit limits

C   Invoicing promptly and collecting overdue debts

D   Delaying payments to obtain a 'free' source of finance

50 A company is preparing its cash flow forecast for the next financial period.

Which THREE of the following items should be included in the calculations?

A   A corporation tax payment

B   A dividend receipt from a short term investment

C   The receipt of funding for the purchase of a new vehicle

D   A bad debt written off

51 For a retailer, let

S   = Sales

P   = Purchases

O   = Opening inventory

C   = Closing inventory

D   = Opening receivables

R   = Closing receivables

Which one of the following is the best expression for receivables days at the period end?

A $[D + R]/P \times 365$

B $[D + R]/S \times 365$

C $R/S \times 365$

D $D/S \times 365$

52 **Which of the following is not usually associated with overtrading?**

A   An increase in the current ratio

B   A rapid increase in revenue

C   A rapid increase in the volume of current assets

D   Most of the increase in current assets being financed by credit

53 Generally, increasing payables days suggests advantage is being taken of available credit but there are risks involved.

Which of the following is unlikely to be one of the risks involved in increasing payables days?

A   Customer bargaining power increasing

B   Losing supplier goodwill

C   Losing prompt payment discounts

D   Suppliers increasing the price to compensate

54 **Which of the following is an aim of a Just in Time system of inventory control?**

A   Increase in capital tied up in inventory

B   Creation of an inflexible production process

C   Elimination of all activities performed that do not add value

D   Lowering of inventory ordering costs

55 Although cash needs to be invested to earn returns, businesses need to keep a certain amount readily available.

Which THREE of the following are reasons for holding cash?

A   Movement motive

B   Transactions motive

C   Precautionary motive

D   Investment motive

INVESTMENT APPRAISAL

56 A company is considering investing in a two-year project. Machine set-up costs will be $125,000, payable immediately. Working capital of $4,000 is required at the beginning of the contract and will be released at the end.

Given a cost of capital of 10%, what is the minimum acceptable contract price (to the nearest thousand dollar) to be received at the end of the contract?

A $151,000

B $154,000

C $152,000

D $186,000

57 **Which of the following statements is correct?**

A   Tax allowable depreciation is a relevant cash flow when evaluating borrowing to buy compared to leasing as a financing choice

B   Asset replacement decisions require relevant cash flows to be discounted by the after-tax cost of debt

C   If capital is rationed, divisible investment projects can be ranked by the profitability index when determining the optimum investment schedule

D   Government restrictions on bank lending are associated with soft capital rationing

58 A company has 31 December as its accounting year end. On 1 January 20X5 a new machine costing $2,000,000 is purchased. The company expects to sell the machine on 31 December 20X6 for $350,000.

The rate of corporation tax for the company is 30%. Tax-allowable depreciation is obtained at 25% on the reducing balance basis, and a balancing allowance is available on disposal of the asset. The company makes sufficient profits to obtain relief for tax-allowable depreciation as soon as they arise.

If the company's cost of capital is 15% per annum, what is the present value of the tax-allowable depreciation at 1 January 20X5 (to the nearest thousand dollars)?

A $391,000

B $248,000

C $263,000

D $719,000

59 An investment project has a cost of $12,000, payable at the start of the first year of operation. The possible future cash flows arising from the investment project have the following present values and associated probabilities:

PV of Year 1 cash flow ($)	Probability	PV of Year 2 cash flow ($)	Probability
16,000	0.15	20,000	0.75
12,000	0.60	(2,000)	0.25
(4,000)	0.25		

What is the expected value of the net present value of the investment project?

A $11,850

B $28,700

C $11,100

D $76,300

60 A company has a 'money' cost of capital of 21% per annum. The inflation is currently estimated at 8% per annum.

What is the 'real' cost of capital?

 %

61 A company is considering a project which has an initial outflow followed by several years of cash inflows, with a cash outflow in the final year.

How many internal rates of return could there be for this project?

A   Either zero or two

B   Either one or two

C   Zero, one or two

D   Only two

62 A project consists of a series of cash outflows in the first few years followed by a series of positive cash inflows. The total cash inflows exceed the total cash outflows. The project was originally evaluated assuming a zero rate of inflation.

If the project were re-evaluated on the assumption that the cash flows were subject to a positive rate of inflation, what would be the effect on the payback period and the internal rate of return? Drag and drop to indicate whether the payback period and internal rate of return would increase or decrease.

Method	Increase	Decrease
Payback period		
Internal rate of return		

63 **The lower risk of a project can be recognised by increasing which one of the following?**

    A   The cost of the initial investment of the project

    B   The estimates of future cash inflows from the project

    C   The internal rate of return of the project

    D   The required rate of return of the project

64 A company has the following pattern of cash flow for a project:

Year	Cash flow
	$
0	(100,000)
1	40,000
2	20,000
3	30,000
4	5,000
5	40,000

The company uses a discount rate of 10%. In what year does discounted payback occur?

    A   Year 2

    B   Year 3

    C   Year 4

    D   Year 5

65 Sudan Co wishes to undertake a project requiring an investment of $732,000 which will generate equal annual inflows of $146,400 in perpetuity.

If the first inflow from the investment is a year after the initial investment, what is the IRR of the project?

    A   20%

    B   25%

    C   400%

    D   500%

66   **Which THREE of the following are advantages of the IRR?**

A   Considers the whole life of the project

B   Uses cash flows not profits

C   It is a measure of absolute return

D   It considers the time value of money

67   Jones Ltd plans to spend $90,000 on an item of capital equipment on 1 January 20X2. The expenditure is eligible for 25% tax-allowable depreciation, and Jones pays corporation tax at 30%. Tax is paid at the end of the accounting period concerned. The equipment will produce savings of $30,000 per annum for its expected useful life deemed to be receivable every 31 December. The equipment will be sold for $25,000 on 31 December 20X5. Jones has a 31 December year end and has a 10% post-tax cost of capital.

What is the present value at 1 January 20X2 of the tax savings that result from the tax-allowable depreciation?

A $13,170

B $15,828

C $16,018

D $19,827

68   Four projects, P, Q, R and S, are available to a company which is facing shortages of capital over the next year but expects capital to be freely available thereafter.

	P	Q	R	S
	$000	$000	$000	$000
Total capital required over life of project	20	30	40	50
Capital required in next year	20	10	30	40
Net present value of project at company's cost of capital	60	40	80	80

In what sequence should the projects be selected if the company wishes to maximise net present values?

A   P, R, S, Q

B   Q, P, R, S

C   Q, R, P, S

D   R, S, P, Q

69   Arnold is contemplating purchasing for $280,000 a machine which he will use to produce 50,000 units of a product per annum for five years. These products will be sold for $10 each and unit variable costs are expected to be $6. Incremental fixed costs will be $70,000 per annum for production costs and $25,000 per annum for selling and administration costs. Arnold has a required return of 10% per annum.

By how many units must the estimate of production and sales volume fall for the project to be regarded as not worthwhile?

A   2,875

B   7,785

C   8,115

D   12,315

70 The payback period is the number of years that it takes a business to recover its original investment from net returns. Which one of the following statements is true?

 A It is calculated before both depreciation and taxation

 B It is calculated before depreciation but after taxation

 C It is calculated after depreciation but before taxation

 D It is calculated after both depreciation and taxation

71 Data of relevance to the evaluation of a particular project are given below.

Cost of capital in real terms	10% per annum
Expected inflation	8% per annum
Expected increase in the project's annual cash inflow	6% per annum
Expected increase in the project's annual cash outflow	4% per annum

Which one of the following sets of adjustments will lead to the correct NPV being calculated?

	Cash inflow	Cash outflow	Discount percentage
A	Unadjusted	Unadjusted	10.0%
B	6% p.a. increase	4% p.a. increase	18.8%
C	6% p.a. increase	4% p.a. increase	10.0%
D	8% p.a. increase	8% p.a. increase	18.8%

72 Spotty Ltd plans to purchase a machine costing $18,000 to save labour costs. Labour savings would be $9,000 in the first year and labour rates in the second year will increase by 10%. The estimated average annual rate of inflation is 8% and the company's real cost of capital is estimated at 12%. The machine has a two year life with an estimated actual salvage value of £5,000 receivable at the end of year 2. All cash flows occur at the year end.

What is the NPV (to the nearest $10) of the proposed investment?

 A $50

 B $270

 C $376

 D $650

73 A company buys a machine for $10,000 and sells it for $2,000 at time 3. Running costs of the machine are: time 1 = $3,000; time 2 = $5,000; time 3 = $7,000.

If a series of machines are bought, run and sold on an infinite cycle of replacements, what is the equivalent annual cost of the machine if the discount rate is 10%?

 A $22,114

 B $8,892

 C $8,288

 D $7,371

74 A company has four independent projects available:

	Capital needed at time 0	NPV
	$	$
Project 1	10,000	30,000
Project 2	8,000	25,000
Project 3	12,000	30,000
Project 4	16,000	36,000

If the company has $32,000 to invest at time 0, and each project is infinitely divisible, but none can be delayed, what is the maximum NPV that can be earned?

A $85,000

B $89,500

C $102,250

D $103,000

75 A project has an initial outflow at time 0 when an asset is bought, then a series of revenue inflows at the end of each year, and then finally sales proceeds from the sale of the asset. Its NPV is £12,000 when general inflation is zero % per year.

If general inflation were to rise to 7% per year, and all revenue inflows were subject to this rate of inflation but the initial expenditure and resale value of the asset were not subject to inflation, what would happen to the NPV?

A The NPV would remain the same

B The NPV would rise

C The NPV would fall

D The NPV could rise or fall

76 Which of the following statements about the accounting rate of return (ARR) method and the payback method is true?

A Both methods are affected by changes in the cost of capital

B The ARR does not take account of returns over the entire life of the project

C The payback method is based on the project's cash flows

D A requirement for an early payback can reduce a company's liquidity

77 When considering investment appraisal under uncertainty, which of the following statements is true in relation to a simulation exercise?

A It considers the effect of changing one variable at a time

B It considers the impact of many variables changing at the same time

C It points directly to the correct investment decision

D It assesses the likelihood of a variable changing

78   **When considering standard deviation as a statistical measure, which of the following statements is true?**

   A   Standard deviation is a measure of the variability of a distribution around its mean

   B   The tighter the distribution, the higher the standard deviation will be

   C   The wider the dispersion, the less risky the situation

   D   Standard deviation is the weighted average of all the possible outcomes

BUSINESS FINANCE AND COST OF CAPITAL

79   The equity shares of Nice plc have a beta value of 0.80. The risk free rate of return is 6% and the market risk premium is 4%. Corporation tax is 30%.

   What is the required return on the shares of Nice plc (to one decimal place)?

   [   ] %

80   **Which of the following statements is correct?**

   A   A bonus issue can be used to raise new equity finance

   B   A share repurchase scheme can increase both earnings per share and gearing

   C   Miller and Modigliani argued that the financing decision is more important than the dividend decision

   D   Shareholders usually have the power to increase dividends at annual general meetings of a company

81   Four companies are identical in all respects, except for their capital structures, which are as follows:

	A plc	B plc	C plc	D plc
	%	%	%	%
Equity as a proportion of total market capitalisation	70	20	65	40
Debt as a proportion of total market capitalisation	30	80	35	60

The equity beta of A plc is 0.89 and the equity beta of D plc is 1.22.

   Within which ranges will the equity betas of B plc and C plc lie?

   A   The beta of B plc and the beta of C plc are both higher than 1.22.

   B   The beta of B plc is below 0.89 and the beta of C plc is in the range 0.89 to 1.22.

   C   The beta of B plc is above 1.22 and the beta of C plc is in the range 0.89 to 1.22.

   D   The beta of B plc is in the range 0.89 to 1.22 and the beta of C plc is higher than 1.22.

82   **Which TWO of the following statements concerning profit are correct?**

1   Accounting profit is not the same as economic profit

2   Profit takes account of risk

3   Accounting profit can be manipulated by managers

4   Gross profit margin is calculated as gross profit divided by shareholder's funds

83   A company issued its 12% irredeemable loan notes at 95. The current market price is 92. The company is paying corporation tax at a rate of 30%.

What is the current net cost of capital per annum of these loan notes (to one decimal place)?

[   ] %

84   **Ingham plc's capital structure is as follows:**

	$m
50c ordinary shares	12
8% $1 preference shares	6
12.5% loan notes 20X6	8
	26

The loan notes are redeemable at nominal value in 20X6. The current market prices of the company's securities are as follows.

50c ordinary shares	250c
8% $1 preference shares	92c
12.5% loan notes 20X6	$100

The company is paying corporation tax at the rate of 30%. The cost of the company's ordinary equity capital has been estimated at 18% pa.

What is the company's weighted average cost of capital for capital investment appraisal purposes?

A   9.71%

B   13.53%

C   16.29%

D   16.73%

85 **Which of the following statements is/are correct?**

1   An increase in the cost of equity leads to a fall in share price

2   Investors faced with increased risk will expect increased return as compensation

3   The cost of debt is usually lower than the cost of preference shares

A   2 only

B   1 and 3 only

C   2 and 3 only

D   1, 2 and 3

86 A company has just declared an ordinary dividend of 25.6p per share; the cum-div market price of an ordinary share is 280p.

Assuming a dividend growth rate of 16% per annum, what is the company's cost of equity capital (to one decimal place)?

[   ] %

87 **Which of the following would be implied by a decrease in a company's operating gearing ratio?**

A   The company is less profitable

B   The company is more risky

C   The company has a lower proportion of costs that are variable

D   The company has profits which are less sensitive to changes in sales volume

88 **Which of the following statements is part of the traditional theory of gearing?**

A   There must be taxes

B   There must exist a minimum WACC

C   Cost of debt increases as gearing decreases

D   Cost of equity increases as gearing decreases

89 **Which of the following statements is true of a scrip issue with perfect information?**

A   Decreases earnings per share

B   Decreases the debt/equity ratio of the company

C   Increases individual shareholder wealth

D   Increases the market price of the share

90   A company incorporates increasing amounts of debt finance into its capital structure, while leaving its operating risk unchanged.

Assuming that a perfect capital market exists, with corporation tax (but without personal tax), which of the following correctly describes the effect on the company's costs of capital and total market value? Drag and drop to indicate whether the cost of equity, weighted average cost of capital and total market value would increase or decrease.

	Increase	Decrease	Unaffected
Cost of equity			
Weighted average cost of capital			
Total market value			

91   **If for a given level of activity a firm's ratio of variable costs to fixed costs were to fall and, at the same time, its ratio of debt to equity were also to fall, what would be the effect on the firm's financial and operating risk? Drag and drop to indicate whether financial risk and operating risk would increase or decrease.**

	Increase	Decrease
Financial risk		
Operating risk		

92   A security's required return can be predicted using the CAPM using the formula:

$r_j = r_f + \beta_j (r_m - r_f)$

Security X has a beta value of 1.6 and provides a return of 12.0%

Security Y has a beta value of 0.9 and provides a return of 13.0%

Security Z has a beta value of 1.2 and provides a return of 13.2%

Security Z is correctly priced.

The risk free return is 6%.

What does this information indicate about the pricing of securities X, Y? Fill in the gaps in the statements below.

Security X is ....

Security Y is ....

Choose from the following:

underpriced

overpriced

93 The following are extracts from the statement of financial position of a company:

	$000	$000
Equity		
Ordinary shares	8,000	
Reserves	20,000	
		28,000
Non-current liabilities		
Bonds	4,000	
Bank loans	6,200	
Preference shares	2,000	
		12,200
Current liabilities		
Overdraft	1,000	
Trade payables	1,500	
		2,500
Total equity and liabilities		42,700

The ordinary shares have a nominal value of 50 cents per share and are trading at $5.00 per share. The preference shares have a nominal value of $1.00 per share and are trading at 80 cents per share. The bonds have a nominal value of $100 and are trading at $105 per bond.

What is the market value based gearing of the company, defined as prior charge capital/equity?

A   15.0%

B   13.0%

C   11.8%

D   7.3%

94 Fill in the gap in the statements below.
Risk that cannot be diversified away can be described as ....

Choose from the following:

Business risk

Financial risk

Systematic risk

Unsystematic risk

95   An all equity company issues some irredeemable loan notes to finance a project that has the same risk as existing projects. If the company operates in a tax free environment under conditions of perfect capital markets, what is the validity of the following statements?

Statement 1: The cost of equity will fall.

Statement 2: The weighted average cost of capital will rise.

	Statement 1	*Statement 2*
A	True	True
B	False	True
C	True	False
D	False	False

96   Which of the following is most likely to result in a company's financial gearing being high?

    A   Low taxable profits

    B   Low tax rates

    C   Inexpensive share issue costs

    D   Intangible assets being a low proportion of total assets

97   Compared to ordinary secured loan notes, which of the following statements is true when considering convertible secured loan notes?

    A   Likely to be more expensive to service because of their equity component

    B   Likely to be less expensive to service because of their equity component

    C   Likely to be more expensive to service because converting to equity requires the holders to make additional payments

    D   Likely to be less expensive to service because they must rank after ordinary secured loan stock

98   Which of the following is the best statement of the conclusion of Modigliani and Miller on the relevance of dividend policy?

    A   All shareholders are indifferent between receiving dividend income and capital gains

    B   Increase in retentions results in a higher growth rate

    C   Discounting the dividends is not an appropriate way to value the firm's equity

    D   The value of the shareholders' equity is determined solely by the firm's investment selection criteria

99 A company is going to take on a project using a mix of equity and debt finance in an economy where the corporation tax rate is 30%.

Assuming perfect markets, other than tax, which of the following statements is true about the project?

A β e > β a; WACC < Cost of equity calculated using β a; WACC < Cost of equity calculated using β e

B β e < β a; WACC > Cost of equity calculated using β a; WACC > Cost of equity calculated using β e

C β e > β a; WACC < Cost of equity calculated using β a; WACC > Cost of equity calculated using β e

D β e < β a; WACC > Cost of equity calculated using β a; WACC < Cost of equity calculated using β e

100 If a company that currently pays its workforce on a piece rate system were to automate its production line, which of the following responses would it expect of operating gearing?

A Decrease

B Increase

C Remain the same

D Increase or decrease depending on the nature of the production process

101 If a geared company's asset beta is used in the CAPM formula ($r_j = r_f + ß_j (r_m - r_f)$) what will r_j represent?

A The WACC of the company

B The ungeared cost of equity

C The geared cost of equity

D None of the above

102 Which of the following does NOT directly affect a company's cost of equity?

A Return on assets

B Expected market return

C Risk-free rate of return

D The company's beta

103 Which of the following ratios is used to measure a company's liquidity?

A Current ratio

B Interest cover

C Gross profit margin

D Return on capital employed

104 An analyst gathered the following data about a company:

	$
Current liabilities	300
Total debt	900
Working capital	200
Capital expenditure	250
Total assets	2,000
Cash flow from operations	400

Fill in the gaps in the statements below. If the company would like a current ratio of 2, it could .... current assets by 100 or .... current liabilities by 50

Choose from the following:

increase

decrease

105 **In relation to preference shares as a source of capital for a company, fill in the gaps below to complete the sentence.**

Preference shares are a form of .... capital which carry .... risk than ordinary shares.

Choose from the following:

equity

loan

lower

higher

106 **What is the dividend cover ratio a measure of?**

A   How many times the company's earnings could pay the dividend

B   The interest or coupon rate expressed as a percentage of the market price

C   The returns to the investor by taking about of dividend income and capital growth

D   How much of the overall dividend pay-out the individual shareholders are entitled to

107 **In relation to finance leases, which THREE of the following statements are true?**

A   The lease agreement cannot be cancelled.

B   One lease exists for the whole of useful life of the asset

C   The lessor retains the risks and rewards of ownership

D   The lessee is responsible for repairs and maintenance

BUSINESS VALUATIONS

108 Mr Mays has been left $30,000 which he plans to invest on the Stock Exchange in order to have a source of capital should be decide to start his own business in a few years' time. A friend of his who works in the City of London has told him that the London Stock Exchange shows strong form market efficiency.

If this is the case, which of the following investment strategies should Mr Mays follow?

   A   Study the company reports in the press and try to spot under-valued shares in which to invest

   B   Invest in two or three blue chip companies and hold the shares for as long as possible

   C   Build up a good spread of shares in different industry sectors

   D   Study the company reports in the press and try to spot strongly growing companies in which to invest

109 A company has 7% loan notes in issue which are redeemable in seven years' time at a 5% premium to their nominal value of $100 per loan note. The before-tax cost of debt of the company is 9% and the after-tax cost of debt of the company is 6%.

What is the current market value of each loan note (to two decimal places)?

   $ ☐

110 TKQ Co has just paid a dividend of 21 cents per share and its share price one year ago was $3.10 per share. The total shareholder return for the year was 19.7%.

What is the current share price (to two decimal places)?

   $ ☐

111 Compton plc has announced a 1 for 4 rights issue at a subscription price of $2.50. The current cum-rights price of the shares is $4.10.

What is the new ex-div market value of the shares?

   A $3.78
   B $2.82
   C $3.55
   D $1.32

112 An investor believes that they can make abnormal returns by studying past share price movements.

In terms of capital market efficiency, to which of the following does the investor's belief relate?

A   Fundamental analysis

B   Operational efficiency

C   Technical analysis

D   Semi-strong form efficiency

113 Supa plc has 50 million shares in issue, and its capital structure has been unchanged for many years.

Its dividend payments in the years 20X1 to 20X5 were as follows.

End of year	Dividends
	$000
20X1	2,200
20X2	2,578
20X3	3,108
20X4	3,560
20X5	4,236

Dividends are expected to grow at the same average rate into the future.

According to the dividend valuation model, what should be the market price per share at the start of 20X6 if the required return on the shares is 25% per annum?

A $0.96

B $1.10

C $1.47

D $1.39

114 The following data relates to an all equity financed company.

Dividend just paid	$50m
Earnings retained and invested	70%
Return on investments	15%
Cost of equity	25%

What is the market value of the company (to the nearest million dollars)?

A $381m

B $200m

C $221m

D $218m

115 The following information relates to two companies, Alpha plc and Beta plc.

	Alpha plc	*Beta plc*
Earnings after tax	$210,000	$900,000
P/E ra P/E ratio	16	21

Beta plc's management estimate that if they were to acquire Alpha plc they could save $100,000 annually after tax on administrative costs in running the new joint company. Additionally, they estimate that the P/E ratio of the new company would be 18.

On the basis of these estimates, what is the maximum that the shareholders of Beta plc should pay for the entire share capital of Alpha plc?

A $1.1m

B $2.9m

C $4.2m

D $2.0m

116 The shares of Fencer plc are currently valued on a P/E ratio of 8. The company is considering a takeover bid for Seed Limited, but the shareholders of Seed have indicated that they would not accept an offer unless it values their shares on a P/E multiple of at least 10.

Which three of the following are reasons which might justify an offer by Fencer plc for the shares of Seed on a higher P/E multiple?

A   Seed has better growth prospects than Fortunate

B   Seed has better-quality assets than Fortunate

C   Seed has a higher gearing ratio than Fortunate

D   Seed is in a different country from Fortunate, where average P/E ratios are higher

117 **Fill in the gap at the end of the following sentence.**

An investor, who bases all his investment decisions on information he has gathered from published statements and comments on company plans and performance, is acting as if he believed that the maximum level of efficiency of the capital market is .... form efficient.

Choose from the following:

Strong

Semi-strong

Weak

Zero

118 The following data relate to an all-equity financed company.

Dividend just paid	$200,000
Earnings retained and invested	40%
Return on investments	15%
Cost of equity	23%

What is the market value (to the nearest $1,000)?

A $922,000

B $1,247,000

C $1,176,000

D $1,784,000

119 **Drag and drop to indicate whether the following statements are true or false.**

Statement	True	False
The existence of projects with positive expected net present values contradicts the idea that the stock market is strong-form efficient.		
The existence of information content in dividends contradicts the idea that the stock market is strong-form efficient.		

120 Peter plc has made an offer of one of its shares for every three of Baker plc. Synergistic benefits from the merger would result in an increase in after-tax earnings of $4m per annum. Extracts from the latest accounts of both companies are as follows:

	Peter plc	Baker plc
Profit after tax	$120m	$35m
Number of shares	400 million	90 million
Market price of shares	250p	120p

Assume that the price of Peter plc's shares rises by 50c after the merger and that Peter issues new shares as consideration.

What will be the price-earnings ratio of the group?

A   6.76

B   8.11

C   9.07

D   10.75

121 Spanner Co has paid the following dividends per share in recent years:

Year	2013	2012	2011	2010
Dividend (cents per share)	36.0	33.8	32.8	31.1

The dividend for 2013 has just been paid and SKV Co has a cost of equity of 16%.

Using the historical dividend growth rate and the dividend growth model, what is the market price of Spanner Co shares to the nearest cent on an ex dividend basis?

A $4.67

B $5.14

C $3.44

D $6.97

122 **Asset-based business valuations using net realisable values are useful in which of the following situations?**

A   When the company is being bought for the earnings/cash flow that all of its assets can produce in the future.

B   For asset stripping

C   To identify a maximum price in a takeover

D   When the company has a highly-skilled workforce

123 For a company, let

EPS   = Earnings per share

PPS   = Price per share

VPS   = Value per share

EY   = Earnings yield

TE   = Total earnings

Which one of the following is the best expression for the value of the company?

A   TE × [1/EY]

B   EPS × [1/EY]

C   EPS/PPS

D   PPS/EPS

124 A company has just paid an ordinary share dividend of 32.0 cents and is expected to pay a dividend of 33.6 cents in one year's time. The company has a cost of equity of 13%.

What is the market price of the company's shares to the nearest cent on an ex dividend basis?

$ _____

125 Toggle Co has in issue 6% loan notes which are redeemable at their nominal value of $100 in three years' time. Alternatively, each loan may be converted on that date into 30 ordinary shares of the company.

The current ordinary share price of Toggle Co is $3.50 and this is expected to grow at 4% per year for the foreseeable future.

Toggle Co has a pre-tax cost of debt of 5% per year.

What is the current market value of each $100 convertible loan note?

A $102.12

B $107.06

C $115.74

D $118.46

RISK MANAGEMENT

126 What does the term 'matching' refer to?

A   The coupling of two simple financial instruments to create a more complex one

B   The mechanism whereby a company balances its foreign currency inflows and outflows

C   The adjustment of credit terms between companies

D   Contracts not yet offset by futures contracts or fulfilled by delivery

127 A company whose home currency is the dollar ($) expects to receive 500,000 pesos in six months' time from a customer in a foreign country. The following interest rates and exchange rates are available to the company:

Spot rate   15.00 peso per $

Six-month forward rate   15.30 peso per $

	Home country	Foreign country
Borrowing interest rate	4% per year	8% per year
Deposit interest rate	3% per year	6% per year

Working to the nearest $100, what is the six-month dollar value of the expected receipt using a money-market hedge?

A $32,500

B $33,700

C $31,800

D $31,900

128 Edted plc has to pay a Spanish supplier 100,000 euros in three months' time. The company's Finance Director wishes to avoid exchange rate exposure, and is looking at four options.

(1) Do nothing for three months and then buy euros at the spot rate

(2) Pay in full now, buying euros at today's spot rate

(3) Buy euros now, put them on deposit for three months, and pay the debt with these euros plus accumulated interest

(4) Arrange a forward exchange contract to buy the euros in three months' time

Which of these options would provide cover against the exchange rate exposure that Edted would otherwise suffer?

A   Option (4) only

B   Options (3) and (4) only

C   Options (2), (3) and (4) only

D   Options (1), (2), (3) and (4)

129 Drag and drop to indicate whether the following statements, concerning currency risk are true or false.

Statement	True	False
Leading and lagging is a method of hedging transaction exposure		
Matching receipts and payments is a method of hedging translation exposure		

130 A UK company has just despatched a shipment of goods to Sweden. The sale will be invoiced in Swedish kroner, and payment is to be made in three months' time. Neither the UK exporter nor the Swedish importer uses the forward foreign exchange market to cover exchange risk.

If the pound sterling were to weaken substantially against the Swedish kroner, what would be the foreign exchange gain or loss effects upon the UK exporter and the Swedish importer? Drag and drop to indicate your selection.

	Gain	Loss	No effect
UK exporter			
Swedish importer			

131 A UK company will purchase new machinery in three months' time for $7.5m. The forward exchange rate is $2.0383 – 2.0390/£.

What is the appropriate three month forward rate at which the company should hedge this transaction (to four decimal places)?

[   ]$/£

132 The current spot exchange rate between sterling and the euro is €1.4415/£. The sterling three month interest rate is 5.75% pa and the euro three month interest rate is 4.75% pa.

What should the three month €/£ forward rate be (to four decimal places)?

[   ]$/£

133 **Fill in the gap in the sentence below.**

The difference between the price of a futures contract and the spot price on a given date is known as ....

Choose from the following:

the initial margin

basis

hedge efficiency

the premium

134 **Which of the following statements is correct?**

A   Once purchased, currency futures have a range of close-out dates

B   Currency swaps can be used to hedge exchange rate risk over longer periods than the forward market

C   Banks will allow forward exchange contracts to lapse if they are not used by a company

D   Currency options are paid for when they are exercised

135 The following options are held by Frances plc at their expiry date:

(1) A call option on £500,000 in exchange for US$ at an exercise price of £1 = $1.90.

The exchange rate at the expiry date is £1 = $1.95.

(2) A put option on £400,000 in exchange for Singapore $ at an exercise price of £1 = $2.90.

The exchange rate at the expiry date is £1 = $2.95.

Which one of the following combinations (exercise/lapse) should be undertaken by the company?

Option

	Call	Put
	Call	*Put*
A	Exercise	Lapse
B	Exercise	Exercise
C	Lapse	Exercise
D	Lapse	Lapse

136 Eady plc is a UK company that imports furniture from a Canadian supplier and sells it throughout Europe. Eady plc has just received a shipment of furniture, invoiced in Canadian dollars, for which payment is to be made in two months' time. Neither Eady plc nor the Canadian supplier use hedging techniques to cover their exchange risk.

If the pound sterling were to weaken substantially against the Canadian dollar, what would be the foreign exchange gain or loss effects upon Eady plc and the Canadian supplier? Drag and drop to indicate your selection.

	Gain	Loss	No effect
Eady plc			
Canadian supplier			

137 What is the impact of a fall in the value of a country's currency?

(1) Exports will be given a stimulus

(2) The rate of domestic inflation with rise

A (1) only

B (2) only

C Both (1) and (2)

D Neither (1) or (2)

138 **Which of the following statements is true of a put option?**

A   It is the right to sell an asset at a fixed price

B   It is an obligation to sell an asset at a fixed price

C   It is the right to buy an asset at a fixed price

D   It is an obligation to buy an asset at a fixed price

139 **The following statements refer to interest rate risk. Are each of the following statements true or false?**

Statement 1: The aim of a forward rate agreement (FRA) is to lock the company into a target interest rate and hedge both adverse and favourable interest rate movements.

Statement 2: An interest rate guarantees (IRG) is more expensive than an FRA as one has to pay for the flexibility to be able to take advantage of favourable interest rate movements.

	Statement 1	*Statement 2*
A	True	True
B	False	True
C	True	False
D	False	False

140 **The following statements refer to interest rate futures. Are each of the following statements true or false?**

Statement 1: If you sell a futures contract you have a contract to lend money.

Statement 2: Each contract is for a standardised amount with a set maturity date. A whole number of contracts must be dealt with.

	Statement 1	*Statement 2*
A	True	True
B	False	True
C	True	False
D	False	False

141 The shape of the yield curve at any point in time is the result of three theories acting together.

Which of the following theories does not influence the yield curve?

A   Liquidity preference theory

B   Expectations theory

C   Flat yield theory

D   Market segmentation theory

142   Which of the following is shown by a yield curve?

A   The relationship between liquidity and bond interest rates

B   The relationship between time to maturity and bond interest rates

C   The relationship between risk and bond interest rates

D   The relationship between bond interest rates and bond prices

143   Which of the following measures will allow a UK company to enjoy the benefits of a favourable change in exchange rates for their Euro receivables contract while protecting them from unfavourable exchange rate movements?

A   A forward exchange contract

B   A put option for Euros

C   A call option for Euros

D   A money market hedge

144   Which of the following statements is correct?

A   Governments may choose to raise interest rates so that the level of general expenditure in the economy will increase

B   The normal yield curve slopes upward to reflect increasing compensation to investors for being unable to use their cash now

C   The yield on long-term loan notes is lower than the yield on short-term loan notes because long-term debt is less risky for a company than short-term debt

D   Expectations theory states that future interest rates reflect expectations of future inflation rate movements

145   Interest Rate Parity Theory generally holds true in practice. However it suffers from several limitations.

Which of the following is not a limitation of Interest Rate Parity Theory?

A   Government controls on capital markets

B   Controls on currency trading

C   Intervention in foreign exchange markets

D   Future inflation rates are only estimates

Section B

OBJECTIVE TEST CASE QUESTIONS

Each objective test case question is worth 15 marks.

FINANCIAL MANAGEMENT FUNCTION AND ENVIRONMENT

1   *This objective test case question contains question types which will only appear in a computer-based exam, but this question provides valuable practice for all students whichever version of the exam they are taking.*

The following are extracts from the last Board meeting at Y plc, a quoted high street retailer based in Country A. Y plc sources some products, such as food and clothing, from third party suppliers but also makes some of its own products, such as furniture. The context of the discussion is a plan to close a domestic furniture factory and build a new one in a cheaper country.

CEO: I think we should be more cautious about going ahead with plans to build a new factory in Country B as I've looked at their forecast inflation rates and they are higher than expected. This would send our costs sky high when the reason we want to build it is to save money. However, if we cannot boost profits, then I fear we will have to cut the next dividend, something that will be disastrous for our shareholders who will then sell our shares en masse.

Director A: Surely the exchange rate will move to compensate for the difference in inflation, so it won't make a huge difference?

Director B I think the key issue is improving reported profit – that is the main way we can keep our shareholders happy, which is, after all, our job. Sacking people in Country A will only result in a boost to the share price due to the cost savings – as long as we keep shareholders informed, that is.

Director C: I think we should be more worried about what is happening in our own country – the Government is talking about restricting the money supply to control excessive cost-push inflation.

Director D: I have some good news – the government has blocked a proposed merger between W plc and X plc (two rivals of Y plc) on competition grounds.

(a) **Which TWO dividend concepts/theories are consistent with the CEO's fears over the cut in dividend?**

    A   Modigliani and Miller dividend irrelevancy

    B   Clientele effect

    C   Residual theory

    D   Dividend signalling

(b) **What theory is consistent with Director A's view on exchange rates?**

    A   Interest rate parity

    B   Purchasing power parity

    C   Liquidity preference theory

    D   Market segmentation theory

(c) **Which TWO statements concerning Director B's comments are true?**

    A   Increasing profit is always in shareholders' best interests

    B   Directors have a fiduciary duty to put shareholder interests first

    C   Sacking staff will have no impact on the share price other than as a result of the cost savings that result

    D   In a semi-strong market the share price of Y plc will react when news about the new factory and any redundancies is made public

(d) **Which of the following statements concerning Director C's comments is/are true?**

    (i)   Restricting growth in the money supply will have more impact on 'demand pull' inflation than 'cost-push'.

    (ii)   Restricting the money supply may result in smaller businesses struggling to raise finance.

    (iii)   Restricting the money supply is part of a government's fiscal policy

    A   (i), (ii) and (iii)

    B   (i) and (ii) only

    C   (ii) and (iii) only

    D   (ii) only

(e) **Which one of the following is NOT a reason governments seek to limit monopoly power of companies?**

    A   Output is produced at a higher price than necessary

    B   Reduced incentive to innovate

    C   Reduced price discrimination

    D   High prices to limit new market entrants

WORKING CAPITAL MANAGEMENT

2   *This objective test case question contains question types which will only appear in a computer-based exam, but this question provides valuable practice for all students whichever version of the exam they are taking.*

Green Co is a furniture manufacturer whose auditors have pointed out that its working capital position is far from satisfactory. The main problem is the high level of inventory which has led to the company building up a larger and larger bank overdraft. Managers at Green Co have been to numerous public lectures discussing various types of inventory control systems and technologies, but have felt that most of them are impractical.

(a)   The following are assumptions or simplifications that may be made when considering calculations of economic order quantities.

(1)   Constant demand

(2)   Zero lead time

Which are assumptions behind the traditional economic order quantity formula,

EOQ $= \sqrt{(2 \times C_o \times D \div C_h)}$?

A   Both 1 and 2

B   1 only

C   2 only

D   Neither 1 nor 2

(b)   The production manager has established the following information about a major inventory item.

Purchase price per unit	$480
Annual demand	4,000
Supplier's delivery costs per order	$10
Chief buyer's salary per annum	$30,000
Total number of orders placed per annum*	1,000
Annual storage costs per unit	$2
Cost of capital	10% per annum

*Relates to all product lines, not just this one.

What is the economic order quantity for this inventory item?

A   40

B   80

C   200

D   400

(c)   Assume that Green Co adopts the EOQ as its order quantity for that item of inventory and that it takes one week for an order to be delivered.

How much inventory will Green Co have on hand when the order is placed? Assume there are 52 weeks in a year.

    _____ units

(d) The following statements refer to different types of inventory control systems and procedures.

(1) A just-in time system implies relatively low reorder costs

(2) Periodic review means ordering inventory when it falls below the designated safety inventory level.

(3) The two-bin system is effectively the same as a re-order level system

Which two of the above statements are correct?

A 1 only

B 1 and 3 only

C 2 and 3 only

D 1, 2 and 3

(e) The following possible benefits have been attributed to just-in-time systems.

(1) Reduced inventory levels

(2) Less waste

(3) Reduced production times

(4) Improved quality of output

Which of these claims can be justified?

A 1 only

B 1 and 2

C 1, 2 and 3

D 1, 2, 3 and 4

3 Hall Co is a retail organisation that buys goods from abroad for cash and sells them locally to both individuals and businesses. It has grown rapidly since its formation on 1 January 20X1 with results summarised below.

Year	20X1	20X2	20X3	20X4	20X5
					(forecast)
	$000	$000	$000	$000	$000
Sales	200	400	800	1,200	1,600
Cost of sales	(100)	(200)	(400)	(600)	(800)
Gross profit	100	200	400	600	800
Administration costs	(50)	(60)	(200)	(500)	(640)
Net profit ($000)	50	140	200	100	160

In the first year, sales were made on a purely cash basis, then credit sales were introduced for businesses. However Hall Co has now found that its working capital position has deteriorated as business customers take longer and longer to pay. When making decisions that affect the company's finances, a discount rate of 10% is used, which is the best estimate of the cost of capital. Assume credit sales equal business sales.

(a) For accounts receivable, Hall Co's credit policy will be influenced by which of the following:

(1) Competitor's terms

(2) Risk of irrecoverable debts

(3) Financing costs

(4) Supplier's terms

A   1 and 3 only

B   1 and 2 only

C   1, 2 and 3 only

D   1, 2, 3 and 4

(b) During the period up to and including 20X5, the expected receivables period has been maintained. However, by 20X5, the actual business proportion of sales has grown from 50% to 60%. Credit periods are as follows: 40 of customers take 1 month's credit, 40% of customers take 2 months' credit and 20% of customers take 3 months' credit.

What is the annual cost of financing 20X5 receivables?

A $7,200

B $12,000

C $14,400

D $24,000

(c) **If Hall were to offer customers 1.5% discount for payments within one month, what would be the annual cost of that in respect of receivables who currently take two months or three months to pay?**

	2-month receivables	3-month receivables
A	19.89%	9.49%
B	9.49%	4.64%
C	4.64%	9.49%
D	9.49%	19.89%

(d) Hall is considering the use of debt factoring or invoice discounting. The following statements have been made in relation to these services.

(1) It is apparent in both instances that someone else is collecting your debts

(2) The debts remain an asset of Hall Co under factoring

Which of these statements are correct?

A   1 only

B   Both 1 and 2

C   2 only

D   Neither 1 nor 2

(e) Which of the following is NOT a function of a credit control department?

    A   Advising existing customers on payment terms

    B   Determining whether to accept cash discounts

    C   Giving credit references to third parties

    D   Investigating potential customers' creditworthiness

4   Jeeps Co is concerned about its cash position and has taken to delaying payments to some suppliers in order to ease that problem. Each month the purchase ledger department splits the total value of invoices for that month into three categories, A, B and C depending on their importance.

Category A invoices, amounting to $2,000,000, are urgent and paid after 30 days

Category B invoices, amounting to $3,000,000, are less urgent and paid after 60 days; and

Category C invoices, amounting to $4,000,000, are least urgent and paid after 90 days.

Several suppliers have reacted to this by offering Jeeps Co a 2% cash discount if the accounts are settled within 15 days. Jeeps Co is currently considering whether or not to accept this. Another supplier, who Jeeps Co now waits 90 days to pay, has been threatening legal action over the $300,000 currently owed. Jeeps Co feels that some sort of compromise might be needed.

Jeeps Co's cost of capital is 12% per annum.

Assume that there are 30 days in a month and that purchases accrue evenly over the year.

(a)   Jeeps Co is considering the advantage of the early settlement discount from those it currently pays after:

    (1)   60 days

    (2)   90 days

    From which payables should Jeeps take the 2% cash discount?

    A   1 only

    B   Both 1 and 2

    C   2 only

    D   Neither 1 nor 2

(b)   What is Jeeps Co's payables period?

    A   60 days

    B   68 days

    C   70 days

    D   90 days

(c)   Which of the following is not a symptom of over-trading?

    A   Rapid increase in current assets

    B   Increase in shareholders' funds

    C   Increase in inventory and debtors receivables periods

    D   Rapid increase in revenue

(d)   To avoid a court action, Jeeps Co is thinking of offering to repay the creditor it owes $300,000 in instalments as follows (all figures in $000)

Now	1 month	2 months	3 months	4 months	5 months
75	45	45	45	45	45

How much will it cost or save Jeeps Co, in present value terms, if the creditor accepts the instalment offer?

A   save $2,227

B   save $2,114

C   cost $2,114

D   cost $2,227

(e)   A company can make decisions that affect its level of working capital. These can be described as either aggressive or conservative policies. Consider the following policies.

(1)   Both fluctuating and permanent current assets financed by short-term funds

(2)   Delay paying creditors (payables) for as long as possible

Which of these are aggressive policies?

A   1 only

B   Both 1 and 2

C   2 only

D   Neither 1 nor 2

5   This objective test case question contains question types which will only appear in a computer-based exam, but this question provides valuable practice for all students whichever version of the exam they are taking.

King Co is a decentralised organisation whose different divisions have approached the matter of cash control in different ways, partly because of their different circumstances.

The Western division is facing a two-year major capital investment programme for which significant funds need to be raised to meet the steady demand for cash. The division intends to use the 'Baumol model' to decide when to raise funds, which will be done by selling off investments currently earning 5% per annum. The transaction cost of these sales will be $500 per transaction and the total amount needed over the two years is $2,000,000.

The Alpine division has no significant investment plans but finds itself regularly having to either sell investments to make funds available or invest surplus cash. This is because of the considerable variation in weekly cash inflows which has been quantified as having a standard deviation of $50,000. As a result, the division uses the 'Miller-Orr model' to determine when to invest and when to make sales, using the same transaction cost and investment rate as the Western division.

The Southern division has just been created to manufacture a product used by other divisions but mainly sold to outside customers. The coming month, Month 1, will be spent converting and equipping existing corporate premises at a total cash cost of $800,000. Production will start in Month 2 and sales in Month 3. Planned sales volumes are as follows.

Month	3	4	5	6	7
Sales volume (000s)	10	11	13	16	20

The product will sell for $24 per unit. 20% of sales will be for cash. Of the credit sales, 25% of credit customers (including other divisions) pay in the month following the sale, 50% will pay one month later and 25% after another month.

(a) **How much finance should the Western division raise in a single tranche according to the Baumol model?**

    A $14,142

    B $20,000

    C $141,421

    D $200,000

(b) **What does the Miller-Orr model suggest is the spread between the upper and lower limits of cash levels that the Alpine division should maintain?**

    A $466

    B $2,163

    C $17,171

    D $79,699

(c) **What will be the Southern division's cash receipts from sales in Month 5?**

    A $211,200

    B $248,400

    C $292,800

    D $346,800

(d) **It is important to distinguish between a cash budget and a cash forecast. What is the validity of the following statements?**

Statement 1:   A cash forecast is an estimate of cash receipts and payments for a future period under existing conditions before taking account of possible actions to modify cash flows, raise new capital, or invest surplus funds.

Statement 2:   A cash budget is a commitment to a plan for cash receipts and payments for a future period after taking any action necessary to bring the preliminary cash forecast into conformity with the overall plan of the business.

Drag and drop the relevant statements to indicate whether they are true or false.

(e) **Which of the following is NOT an advantage to King Co of having a centralised treasury function?**

    A   Better foreign currency risk management

    B   Borrowing can be made at more advantageous rates

    C   Increases individual division's responsibility for cash

    D   The treasury function can be run as a profit centre to raise additional profits

6 Grumpy Co sells stress-relieving toys and, surprisingly perhaps, is happy with the progress it is making financially as it is growing and is profitable. There are issues however about cash flow.

An extract from the accounting records for the most recent financial period (a year) is as follows:

	$
Credit sales	480,000
Cash sales	80,000
Trade receivables	85,000
Other receivables	12,000
Credit purchases	212,000
Cash purchases	21,000
Trade payables	30,000
Other payables including VAT	26,000
Finished good inventory at start of year	45,000
Finished good inventory at end of year	52,000

In one typical cycle of trade (cycle X), goods were ordered on 17/1/15 and delivered 21 days later, the supplier was paid on 25/2/15. The goods remained in inventory for 62 days. At which point these goods were sold on credit terms of 60 days. Grumpy was eventually paid 68 days after the sale was made. Assume there are 365 days in the year.

(a) **What is the receivables period from the table data?**

    A   68 days

    B   65 days

    C   55 days

    D   74 days

(b) **What is the payables period from the table data?**

    A   52 days

    B   96 days

    C   47 days

    D   88 days

(c) **What is the inventory holding period?**

    A   81 days

    B   84 days

    C   90 days

    D   73 days

(d) **For cycle X, what is the cash operating cycle?**

    A   120 days

    B   31 days

    C   96 days

    D   130 days

(e)   **Which of the following statements about a cash operating cycle is true?**

(1)   A long operating cycle is more serious in a period of strong growth

(2)   Operating cycles tend to be longer in brand new businesses compared to established businesses

A   Both statements are true

B   Both statements are false

C   Only statement (1) is true

D   Only statement (2) is true

INVESTMENT APPRAISAL

7   *This objective test case question contains question types which will only appear in a computer-based exam, but this question provides valuable practice for all students whichever version of the exam they are taking.*

Bell Co has decentralised and divisional managers are allowed to make their own investment decisions subject to confirmation by the main company board. Because each of the three divisions (Ding, Dong and Merrily) are subject to different levels of risk, it has been thought appropriate to use different discount rates in each division.

Ding has been told that its real discount rate is 5%. The general rate of inflation, based on an index that uses a very wide range of prices, is 2%. In the industry in which Ding operates, a number of prices are seen to be inflating at 3%.

Dong is assessing a project in which the first of four annual lease payments has been agreed at $120,000. This is payable in one year's time and subsequent payments will rise by 4% per annum. Ding's proper money cost of capital is 8%.

Merrily is considering investing $1,000,000 in a project which will produce the following annual outflows and inflows.

Year	1	2	3
Outflows ($000)	1,800	2,500	1,500
Inflows ($000)	2,000	3,000	2,000

The cash flows, which arise at the end of each year, are stated in current year terms. It is expected that outflows will rise by 3% per annum and inflows by 2% per annum. The money cost of capital of the Merrily Division is 9%.

(a)   **What is Ding's money discount rate?**

A   7.1%

B   4.0%

C   1.9%

D   1.1%

b)   **What is the present value of Dong's last payment that will be made in four years' time (to the nearest $000)?**

$☐,000

(c) **What is the net present value of Merrily's project (to the nearest $000)?**

A $252,000

B $(10,000)

C $(39,000)

D $(61,000)

(d) **When considering risk in project appraisal, what is the main advantage of using simulations to assist the appraisal?**

A   A clear decision rule

B   More than one variable can change at a time

C   Statistically more accurate than other methods

D   Being diagrammatic is easier to understand

(e) **Is it possible to have a negative real discount rate to apply to the cash flow estimates made in current terms when making investment decisions?**

From the below, select yes or no and then select your reason

Answer:

Yes

No

Reason:

The calculation of a present value won't work if the discount rate is negative

Negative interest rates never happen in the real world

It will happen in deflationary times

It will happen if the rate of inflation exceeds the money cost of capital

8   *This objective test case question contains question types which will only appear in a computer-based exam, but this question provides valuable practice for all students whichever version of the exam they are taking.*

Care Co needs to replace a major piece of office equipment that is in constant use and for which there is expected to continue to be use for the foreseeable future. Two types of machine are available with different capital costs, useful lives, scrap values and annual running costs.

Machine 1 will initially cost $480,000, have a life of four years, scrap value of $60,000 and annual running costs of $72,000.

Machine 2 will initially cost $540,000, have a life of three years, scrap value of $120,000 and annual running costs of $47,000.

Care Co's cost of capital is 10%. Assume all cash flows, except the initial capital cost, occur at the end of the relevant year and assume that taxation and inflation can be ignored.

(a) **What is the equivalent annual cost of machine 2 (to the nearest $000)?**

A $142,000

B $179,000

C $189,000

D $228,000

(b) **Drag and drop the relevant statements to indicate whether they are true or false.**

(1) The equivalent annual cost calculation assumes the same type of machine is going to be used into the foreseeable future.

(2) The equivalent annual cost calculation assumes the capabilities of Machine 1 and Machine 2 are identical.

(c) It is now felt that the final scrap value of the machines depends on two factors: whether or not a new supplier enters the market (which would reduce the likely scrap value) and the strength of the dollar against other currencies (since sales of used machines will be made abroad). Adverse effects will each reduce the scrap value by 10% of the figure used in the investment appraisal. The relevant probabilities are as follows.

New supplier	Probability	Strong $	Probability
Yes	0.4	Yes	0.3
No	0.6	No	0.7

What is now the expected value of the scrap proceeds from machine 2?

A $106,800

B $109,000

C $111,600

D $113,000

(d) To overcome the difficulties of incorporating probabilities into the investment appraisal calculations, Care Co could perform a simulation exercise to help reach a decision.

Drag and drop to indicate whether the following statements, relating to simulation, are true or false.

(1) It eliminates the effects of risk associated with various estimates.

(2) It requires probabilities of estimates subject to risk to be known.

(e) **Which of the following statements about Care Co's replacement decision are true?**

(1) The decision between machine 1 and machine 2 could be found by calculating total NPV of each machine over a 12 year period.

(2) The replacement analysis model assumes that Care Co replaces like with like each time is needs to replace an existing asset.

A 1 only

B Both 1 and 2

C 2 only

D Neither 1 nor 2

9   Deacon Co is considering the manufacture of a new product to complement its existing range. The product will have a three-year life and new machinery will have to be bought for the manufacturing process. Annual costs and benefits of the product are as follows.

The equipment needed for making this product can be obtained in one of three ways.

Option 1 – Borrowing the money and making an outright purchase for a one-off cost of $1,280,000 payable on 31 December 20X0. After the project, the equipment could be sold for an estimated $290,000, receivable on 31 December 20X3.

Option 2 – Entering into a three-year finance lease for which an initial deposit of $300,000 is payable on 1 January 20X1 followed by three annual payments of $295,000 payable on 31 December 20X1 to 20X3.

Option 3 – Arranging three annual operating leases which require $375,000 to be paid on 1 January for each year of the project.

Deacon Co has a 31 December year end and pays corporation tax at 20% one year after the relevant year end. The equipment will qualify for 25% tax allowable depreciation, on a reducing balance basis. All lease payments are allowable against tax in the year of payment.

Deacon's post-tax cost of capital is 11%.

(a)   Under Option 1, what is the present value of the cash flow in respect of tax-allowable depreciation in 20X3 (to the nearest $000)?

      A $23,000

      B $26,000

      C $33,000

      D $37,000

(b)   Which of the following statements regarding leasing, as opposed to buying, capital assets are true?

      (1)   A lessor may be able to obtain capital assets more cheaply and some of this saving may be passed on to the lessee.

      (2)   Leasing may result in a business with cash flow problems being able to obtain use of a capital asset if raising finance for a purchase has proved difficult.

      A   1 only

      B   Both 1 and 2

      C   2 only

      D   Neither 1 nor 2

(c)   What is the present value of the tax saving in respect of the initial deposit associated with the finance lease in Option 2 (to the nearest $000)?

      A $24,000

      B $44,000

      C $49,000

      D $54,000

(d) **Which of the following statements regarding finance and operating leases are true?**

(1) In both types of lease, the lessee does not suffer or get benefit from the risks and rewards of ownership.

(2) Operating leases amount to a form of off balance sheet finance, whereas finance lease obligations need to be capitalised and shown on the balance sheet.

A 1 only

B Both 1 and 2

C 2 only

D Neither 1 nor 2

(e) **What is the negative NPV (to the nearest $000) of the cash flows associated with the operational lease?**

A 834

B 852

C 873

D 1,017

10 *This objective test case question contains question types which will only appear in a computer-based exam, but this question provides valuable practice for all students whichever version of the exam they are taking.*

Easter Co is about to hold its annual strategic planning meeting and a number of capital investment projects will be discussed. A summary of the projects' cash flows is shown below.

Project	NPV	Investment
	$000	$000
A	4,900	3,200
B	7,400	9,300
C	5,900	7,300
D	7,500	5,200
E	9,000	5,600

The investment will need to be made at the start of the coming year; no projects can be delayed and none are divisible. The funds available for these projects are limited to $10,000,000.

(a) **Which of the following statements about capital rationing is true?**

A Both hard and soft capital rationing are the result of external factors

B Both hard and soft capital rationing are the result of internal policies

C Hard rationing is the result of external factors, soft rationing is the result of internal policies

D Soft rationing is the result of external factors, hard rationing is the result of internal policies

(b) From the list below, select which projects should be accepted, based on the circumstances described?

Project A

Project B

Project C

Project D

(c) What projects would be accepted if it was found that projects A and E were mutually exclusive?

A   A and D

B   A and E

C   A, D and E

D   D and E

(d) What projects, and fractions of projects, would be accepted if a partner could be found to invest in a proportion of one of the projects making them effectively infinitely divisible (ignoring the mutually exclusive limitation)?

A   A, D and 2/7 E

B   A, E and 3/13 D

C   A, D and E

D   D and E

(e) A sixth project, Project F, is causing considerable confusion, particularly among those members of the board of Easter Co whose sole means of appraising projects is to find an internal rate of return (IRR) using the spreadsheet function on their computers. The summarised cash flows of Project F are as follows.

Time 0   Invest $4.00m

Time 1   Receive $8.80m

Time 2   Spend $4.83m

The spreadsheet function requires you to enter the cash flows of a project and also enter a guess for the IRR. The directors are struggling to guess the IRR for this sixth project.

What is the likely cause of the confusion over project F?

A   It has a single IRR between 5% and 10%

B   It has two positive IRRs

C   It has no real IRRs

D   It has one positive and one negative IRR

11 Ace Co is considering a new project. Ace currently installs burglar alarms, putting contact points on access portals and movement sensors in general areas of a property. The new project is in the fire alarm business, a business considered to be similar in many ways to what Ace currently does.

A junior member of the finance team has estimated the relevant cash flows for the project as follows:

Time	Description	Cash flow $
0	Loose tools	(6,000)
1-4	Contribution	25,000
1-4	Allocated overheads	(8,000)
2-5	Tax @ 25% of profit	(4,250)

No tax-allowable depreciation is available for loose tools.

Ace is entirely equity financed with a cost of equity correctly calculated as 12%.

(a) **What is the NPV of the above project to the nearest $100?**

A $28,700

B $53,000

C $58,400

D $34,100

(b) **The IRR of the above project has been correctly calculated as 26%. Which of the following statements are true?**

(1) The IRR is not a measure of absolute profitability and linear interpolation provides only an estimate of the IRR

(2) If the IRR of the project is higher than its cost of capital then the project is always acceptable regardless of the pattern of the cash flows

A Both statements are true

B Both statements are false

C Statement (1) only

D Statement (2) only

(c) **If the loose tools became allowable for tax-allowable depreciation which of the following statements would be true?**

(1) Profit before tax would rise

(2) The NPV of the project would rise

(3) Assuming that one of the answers to the NPV calculation above is correct then the decision to proceed would alter.

A (1) and (2)

B (2) and (3)

C (2) only

D (1) only

(d)   One of the directors thinks that calculating the payback period would be a useful addition. What is the projects payback period?

    A   3.8 months

    B   5.6 months

    C   3.5 months

    D   2.9 months

(e)   Which of the following statements are true of the payback period?

    (1)   It normally ignores time value

    (2)   It is a risk-focussed approach in decision-making

    (3)   There is clear advice once it is calculated

    A   All statements are true

    B   (1) and (3) only

    C   (1) and (2) only

    D   (2) and (3) only

BUSINESS FINANCE AND COST OF CAPITAL

12   Brash Co can buy a new piece of sophisticated machinery for $500,000 by borrowing under a secured loan at 8%. It has also researched the possibility of leasing the asset.

The company's finance director is a little rusty on leasing issues as the business has never leased before and he has worked in Brash Co for 20 years. He said 'I studied leasing years ago but I think leasing is always cheaper than borrowing because the lease company has access to greater amounts of finance and so benefits from economies of scale on that front'.

The managing director is sceptical, arguing that leasing companies are commercial and so each deal must be assessed on its merits. He commented: 'We have to careful here, I know the lease companies are always responsible for the maintenance but that can't be free!'

The lease offer is as follows:

The lease will be an operating lease over 5 years with lease payments of $146,000 annually in advance. Tax is payable 1 year after the accounting year-end and the corporation tax rate is 25%. Maintenance is payable by the lessor and costs $20,000 per annum payable at the end of each year, including the last year in preparation for sale. The residual value is expected to be $40,000 (the expected tax written down value at the end of the lease) and the lessor will retain that.

(a)   Which of the statements made by the finance director and the managing director are true?

    A   Both statements are true

    B   Both statements are false

    C   Only the finance director is correct

    D   Only the managing director is correct

(b)   **In a calculation to compare the cost of leasing with cost of borrowing to buy the asset above, which of the following costs are not relevant?**

A   The interest cash flows saved on borrowing

B   The saving on maintenance

C   The residual value

D   The tax-allowable depreciation

(c)   **What is the present value of the maintenance cash flows, after tax?**

A $19,870

B $29880

C $84,240

D $145,051

(d)   **What is the present of the tax relief on the lease payments, after tax?**

A $19,870

B $29,880

C $84,240

D $145,051

(e)   **Which of the following statements about the potential affect the lease would have on gearing are true?**

(1)   An operating lease is off balance sheet finance and so would never have an effect on traditional gearing ratios

(2)   If shareholders perceive that there is a significant operating lease in place then they may perceive an increase in risk

A   Both statements are true

B   Both statements are false

C   Only statement (1) is true

D   Only statement (2) is true

13   Kelvin Co is considering an extensive rights issue to raise new finance. It currently has 4 million shares and has been very successful over a prolonged period.

The terms of the deal are as follows:

•   One new share for every 4 held at a price of 90% of the existing market value per share

•   The existing market value is $20 per share (the cum rights price)

One of the directors is unhappy with offering any discounts to existing shareholders. He claims that the companies past success should be enough to encourage shareholders to increase their investment.

(a)   **What is the theoretical ex rights price (TERP) per share?**

   A $18.00

   B $19.60

   C $20.00

   D $24.50

(b)   **What would be the effect on the TERP value if the new shares were offered at a 20% discount level whilst raising the same total amount of finance?**

   A   The TERP value would not change since the total amount raised would be the same

   B   The TERP would increase

   C   The TERP would fall

   D   The TERP would fall to a level unacceptable to existing shareholders

(c)   **Which of the following statements about discounts on a rights issue are true?**

   (1)   The level of discount is simply not relevant to the wealth of a shareholder as long as they accept the right. It is ignorance of the theory that encourages the offer of a discount in most cases

   (2)   The bigger the discount the more likely a shareholder is to accept the rights offer in most cases

   A   Both statements are true

   B   Both statements are false

   C   Only statement (1) is true

   D   Only statement (2) is true

(d)   **Which of the following actions by shareholders would be the worst thing that they could do in relation to a rights issue as far as shareholder wealth is concerned?**

   A   Accept the rights offer without negotiation

   B   Renounce their rights and sell them on the open market

   C   Save their investment and do nothing

   D   Sell 50% of their rights on the open market whilst ignoring the rest

(e)   **Which of the following actions will result in the least dilution of control for existing shareholders?**

   A   Accept the rights offer without negotiation

   B   Renounce their rights and sell them on the open market

   C   Save their investment and do nothing

   D   Sell 50% of their rights on the open market

14 Dominance Co is considering raising some new finance but there is disagreement at board level how best to proceed.

The managing director thinks that the company should retain control in the hands of the existing and loyal shareholders. The finance director feels that the gearing level should be allowed to increase to benefit from the tax relief allowed on interest.

The existing equity is quoted at $4.20 cum div with an imminent dividend of 16c due any day. The company earnings have grown at a fairly steady rate of 8% over recent years, but expectations are for growth to be 2% points better in the future.

The company's debt is 4% irredeemable bonds, which were issued at a 5% discount of $95%. They have a nominal value of $100 but are currently quoted at $80 with the interest having just been paid. The corporation tax rate is 25%.

(a) **Assuming the business wants to retain control in the hands of the existing shareholders, how should it seek to raise the new finance?**

    A   A placing of new shares via a loyal broker

    B   A further public offering of shares

    C   A rights issue where it is expected that 95% of the existing shareholders will accept the offer

    D   Issue new debt

(b) **Assuming the business wants to maximise the tax shield on the new finance, how should it raise the money?**

    A   A placing of new shares and $10,000,000 of preference shares

    B   Accepting a VC offer which includes $5,000,000 of 4% redeemable bonds and some shares

    C   Sell redeemable debt with a market value $12,500,000 with interest at 5%. The redemption value will make up 25% of the market value

    D   Sell $12,000,000 irredeemable debt with interest at 5.25%

(c) **What is the cost of equity?**

    A   14.0%

    B   14.4%

    C   12.3%

    D   14.3%

(d) **What is the after tax cost of debt?**

    A   4.00%

    B   5.00%

    C   3.56%

    D   3.75%

(e) **In part (c) of this question, the cost of equity options for your answer are significantly greater than the cost of choices in part (d). The main reason for this is:**

    A   The total risk level in the business

    B   The specific risk in the business

    C   The tax shield

    D   The level of systematic risk in the business

15 The board of Empire Co are discussing their dividend policy and there have been various statements made by the directors.

Director A: Our shareholders rely on the level of dividend we pay and we cannot ignore that. We must pay out a dividend as expected otherwise our shareholders will be forced to sell shares or invest elsewhere.

Director B: I know that when I was young that if I got a rise in my allowance in a particular week then I was more likely to get it again. It was expected. We must pay what is expected.

Director C: What matters is the underlying value of the projects that we are doing now and we will do in the future. We should stop wasting time discussing this.

Director D: What matters is what we can afford in cash. If we are short of money then it should be discussion over – less dividend will have to be paid. What we could then do is issue more shares instead – I think that is called a scrip dividend.

(a) **Which director supports the dividend irrelevancy theory?**

    A   Director A

    B   Director B

    C   Director C

    D   Director D

(b) **Which director supports the signalling effect of dividends?**

    A   Director A

    B   Director B

    C   Director C

    D   Director D

(c) **Which director supports the dividend dependency theory?**

    A   Director A

    B   Director B

    C   Director C

    D   Director D

(d) **Which director is more concerned about company liquidity than dividend policy?**

    A   Director A

    B   Director B

    C   Director C

    D   Director D

(e)   Once the discussion about dividend policy was finalised there was another discussion about scrip issues. Which of the following statements are true?

(1)   In a scrip issue a shareholder will end up with more shares, this means there will be a gain to them.

(2)   Scrip issues serve the purpose of reducing market values in return for more shares. This can make the shares more marketable.

A   Both statements are true

B   Both statements are false

C   Only statement (1) is true

D   Only statement (2) is true

16   The board of a major bank is discussing their investment appraisal methodology as they have a new project under consideration. They have agreed that using the CAPM approach is sensible as they feel it likely that most of their shareholders will have a well-diversified shareholding in the stock market as a whole.

There has been some dispute about which risks constitute specific risks in the bank and which risks are more systematic in nature partly driven by the nature of the banks operations. Equally, no one seems quite sure what the required return derived from the CAPM formula actually represents.

The finance director has produced the following data relating to the bank itself, the financial market and the new project it is considering:

Data

Required return on existing debt	6.0%
Cost of existing debt to the bank	4.8%
Return on short dated government securities	5.2%
Return in the stock market	12.8%
Equity beta of the bank	1.35
Beta of the new project	1.52
Asset beta of the bank	1.15

(a)   Which one of the following risks could be correctly described as a systematic risk in this case?

A   The interest rates set by the bank

B   The risk of default by the banks customers on loans made

C   The recessionary pressures in the country in which the bank operates

D   The demand for loans made to the bank

(b)   In the CAPM what would be the value to use for the risk free rate of return (Rf), from the data above?

A   6.0%

B   4.8%

C   5.2%

D   4.16% (the after tax return on short dated government securities)

(c)   In the CAPM formula R = Rf + βj(Rm − Rf) what does the required return (R) represent? βj refers to the project beta.

A   The required return of the bank shareholders for their investment in the bank

B   The WACC of the bank

C   The marginal cost of new finance

D   The required return on the new project

(d)   What is the required return on the new project as derived from the CAPM formula above?

A   13.82%

B   13.94%

C   16.34%

D   16.75%

(e)   What is the meaning of a beta value of 1?

A   The investment is risk free

B   The investment has the same level of risk as the bank

C   The investments total risk is as risky as the market

D   The investment has the same level of systematic risk as the market

17   The board of Freedling Co are in discussion about the various risk types that face the business. It is evident that there is considerable confusion and disagreement.

Operating risk

Some of the directors feel that given the increasing volume of trade having fixed costs is the best thing to do. 'How can it be risky to have fixed costs when we know how much they are and that they don't change overly much from one year to the next' was one comment.

There was also a discussion about changing the cost structure. It was thought that this would be difficult as most staff, for example, were paid a salary and moving them on to an hourly rate would be opposed by them.

Gearing Risk

The directors were more aware in this area, with some favouring a more traditional view of gearing and others remembering Modigliani and Miller (M&M) fondly from their studies.

(a)   Which of the following statements are true of operating gearing?

(1)   Given the level of fixed costs do not change considerably from one year to the next, having a lot of fixed cost in Freedling's cost structure would mean that they had low levels of operating risk.

(2)   Variable costs are risky because they change as volume changes. Given Freedling is growing the year on year variable cost level has changed a lot as well.

A   Both statements are true

B   Both statements are false

C   Only statement (1) is true

D   Only statement (2) is true

(b) **In relation to changing the cost structure of Freedling which of the following statements are true?**

(1) Cost structures are very difficult to change. Once a business is set up the mix of variable and fixed cost is also set and changes are often simply not possible.

(2) If you change from a fixed cost to a variable cost dominated structure the variable cost per unit is often greater than the fixed cost per unit.

A Both statements are true

B Both statements are false

C Only statement (1) is true

D Only statement (2) is true

(c) **Assuming the board were considering raising more debt, under which circumstances would the assertion that the WACC of the business would fall hold true?**

(1) Under M&M no tax

(2) Under M&M with corporation tax

(3) At low levels of gearing under the traditional theory of gearing

A All statements are true

B Only statement (2) is true

C Only statement (3) is true

D Both statements (2) and (3) are true

(d) **Under M&M no tax which of the following statements are true?**

(1) It does not matter how a business raises finance.

(2) Shareholders, given the M&M assumptions, will recognise the level of risk inherent in any extra debt and compensate themselves by a commensurate increase in required return to leave the company WACC unaltered and without any inherent gain.

A Both statements are true

B Both statements are false

C Only statement (1) is true

D Only statement (2) is true

(e) In traditional theory diagrams the cost of debt line is often drawn with a slight tail, arcing upwards at very high levels of gearing. Which of the following statements about this feature are true?

(1) The rising tail represents an increased risk to debt holders

(2) Tax exhaustion can increase the cost of borrowing at high levels of gearing

(3) In practice businesses rarely reach this point as banks refuse to lend despite the high interests rates possible

A   All statements are true

B   Only statement (1) is true

C   Both statements (1) and (2) are true

D   Both statements (2) and (3) are true

BUSINESS VALUATIONS

18   *This objective test case question contains question types which will only appear in a computer-based exam, but this question provides valuable practice for all students whichever version of the exam they are taking.*

Kevin Dutton is an investor who specialises in buying corporate debt at discounted values and aims to make gains either by selling bonds at a higher value later or by receiving redemption payments. Kevin is currently evaluating the following investments:

Last year Kevin bought $1m nominal value of unquoted 4% bonds in Company A at a price of $500,000. The bonds are to be redeemed at par in 5 years' time but **Company A** is showing signs of financial distress. To value the bonds Kevin has estimated that a return of 30% is appropriate here to compensate for the risks of non-payment.

Company B, a forestry company, is looking to raise $5 million through the issue of 6 year deep discounted zero coupon bonds. The issue price has been set at a 40% discount. Kevin may invest but is looking for a return of 10% per annum to do so.

Kevin also owns fixed rate bonds in **Company C**. These bonds are traded on major bond markets. Kevin is thinking of selling them now as he believes that interest rates are going to increase shortly resulting in a drop in the bond price.

All three companies mentioned pay tax at 25%.

(a) What is the estimated current market value of Kevin's investment in the bonds in company A, to the nearest $1,000?

A $293,000

B $360,000

C $391,000

D $500,000

(b) Calculate the gross redemption yield on the deep discounted bonds. Give your answer as a percentage to 1 dp.

[   ] %

(c)   Calculate the minimum discount required so the deep discounted bonds give a return over 10%. Give your answer to the nearest whole percent.

    A   40%

    B   42%

    C   44%

    D   46%

(d)   Which of the following statements concerning deep discounted bonds are true?

    (i)   It is illegal for companies to issue bonds at a discount.

    (ii)   Deep discount bonds can help Company B's cash flow.

    (iii)   Investors' required returns will generally be lower with deep discounted bonds

    A   (i), (ii) and (iii)

    B   (i) and (ii) only

    C   (ii) only

    D   None of them

(e)   Which one of the following statements concerning bond prices is true?

    A   The price of bonds with fixed coupon rates will not be affected by changes in interest rates

    B   Changes in expected inflation levels will not affect bond prices

    C   Changes in bond values will result in changes in the return required by investors in those bonds

    D   Bond prices typically fall as interest rates rise

19   *This objective test case question contains question types which will only appear in a computer-based exam, but this question provides valuable practice for all students whichever version of the exam they are taking.*

Loki plc is a growing company specialising in making accessories for mobile phones and tablets. The company is currently all-equity financed with 2 million ordinary shares in issue. The existing shareholders are mainly family members and friends. The directors of Loki need to raise finance to fund a new factory and are considering a range of options including flotation and venture capital. Future growth is anticipated to be the following:

Earnings next year = $25m, expected to grow at 7% pa

Dividend next year = $14m, expected to grow at 4% pa

Flotation

Q plc, a listed company with similar business activities to Loki has a P/E ratio of 9, an equity beta of 1.2 and gearing, measured as Debt:Equity of 1:2. Loki is expected to grow faster than Q plc, at least in the short term.

If flotation is approved, then the issue share price would be set at a 15% discount to fair value. The directors of Loki do not believe that an asset valuation is of much use here.

Venture Capital

The directors of Loki have been in discussion with 4Ts, a listed venture capital company. As well as contributing equity, 4Ts would seek to spread the risk of their investment by also investing in the form of 4year 5%secured redeemable bonds and also convertible preference shares. The risk adjusted return on similar bonds has been estimated at 6%.

Corporation tax is currently 30%.

(a)   **Which one of the following statements, concerning the usefulness of asset based methods of business valuation, is correct?**

A   Replacement cost normally represents the minimum price which should be accepted for the sale of a business as a going concern

B   Break-up value should provide a measure of the maximum amount that any purchaser should pay for the business

C   Book value will normally be a meaningless figure as it will be based on historical costs

D   Asset based methods give consideration to non statement of financial position intangible assets such as a highly skilled workforce and a strong management team

(b)   **Calculate the value of Loki plc's equity beta to 2 dp**

(c)   **Calculate the issue price of Loki shares to the nearest cent using the dividend valuation model with a cost of equity of 14%.**

A $0.60

B $0.70

C $1.19

D $1.24

(d)   **What is the market value of the redeemable bonds?**

A $68.15%

B $91.91%

C $97.35%

D $100.00%

(e)   **Which TWO of the following statements concerning 4Ts' perspective are true?**

A   4Ts' investment in the preference shares will have the lowest risk out of the three methods of finance offered due to the option to convert.

B   4Ts will accept a lower level of dividends on the convertible preference shares compared to normal preference shares

C   4Ts are likely to prefer to use CAPM in valuing Loki shares

D   The current shareholders of Loki would be willing to sell a majority equity stake to 4Ts

20 David McNabb is a fund manager within M Inc, a global investment company. He has recently identified the following potential acquisition targets:

Company A is an unquoted, property development company with a portfolio of over two hundred houses at various stages of renovation. It has been loss making for the last two years due to the economic downturn. David believes that new government legislation will bring a welcome boost to the housing market.

Company B is an unquoted shoe manufacturer. It has also suffered in the recent recession but the directors are confident that the company is past the worst and growth lies ahead:

- Earnings are expected to be $12.5 million next year and expected to grow at 2% per annum

- Dividends will be $ 5million for each of the next three years and then expected to grow at 3% thereafter.

David has located a similar listed company that has an earnings yield of 12% and a cost of equity of 14%

Company C is a quoted fashion retailer. David believes that the current share price of $2.58 undervalues the company significantly, making it a suitable target. He is also interested in Company C as he feels it would have a good fit with his existing fund portfolio and would diversify away some risk.

(a)   **Which of the following valuation methods is most suitable for valuing Company A?**

   A   P/E ratio × earnings

   B   Dividend valuation model (DVM)

   C   Net realisable value of assets

   D   Market capitalisation

(b)   **Calculate the value of Company B by reference to its predicted earnings**

   A $104.2m

   B $106.3m

   C $125.0m

   D $127.5m

(c)   **Calculate the value of company B using the dividend valuation model.**

   A $42.3m

   B $43.2m

   C $46.8m

   D $47.3m

(d) **Which one of the following statements concerning David's opinion that Company C is undervalued is true?**

A   David believes that the stock market is strong form efficient and he has access to secret inside information

B   David believes that the stock market is semi-strong form efficient and he has access to secret inside information

C   David believes that the stock market is semi-strong form efficient and he has analysed financial statements and press releases to form his opinion

D   David believes that the stock market is weak form efficient and he has produced graphs of historic share prices to form his opinion

(e) **Which of the following statements concerning whether David should buy Company C to diversify away portfolio risk are true?**

(i)   The shareholders on M Inc are unlikely to value such diversification.

(ii)   David should always try to reduce the average beta of his portfolio.

(iii) David should seek to diversify away any systematic risk in his portfolio

A   (i), (ii) and (iii)

B   (i) and (ii) only

C   (i) only

D   None of them

21   *This objective test case question contains question types which will only appear in a computer-based exam, but this question provides valuable practice for all students whichever version of the exam they are taking.*

Pike Co, a listed conglomerate, is looking to buy Minnow Co, an advertising company owned and run by Fred Minnow. Fred has agreed to the sale and has insisted on cash consideration as he wishes to retire. Pike plc is considering issuing bonds to generate the cash required.

The following information is available:

Statement of financial position for Minnow Co

* Net book value of equity $10.3m
* Net realisable value $11.2m
* Replacement cost $15.3m
* Bank loan $2.5m

Statement of profit or loss

* Minnow Co made a profit after tax of $7m last year. This expected to grow by 3% per annum.

* Despite owning and running the company, Fred Minnow does not take a salary, preferring to take money out of the business via high dividends. Pike plc estimates that it will need to offer a salary of $100,000 to replace Fred when he leaves.

Cash flow

- Pike Co anticipates that, after making a number of changes, Minnow Co will generate free cash flow of $6m next year. This is expected to grow by 4% per annum thereafter.

Other information

- Trout and Co, a quoted advertising agency with similar gearing and growth prospects to Minnow Co, has a P/E ratio of 7, a WACC of 12% and a cost of equity of 15%.

- Minnow Co pays corporation tax at 30%.

(a)   **Based on asset values, what is the minimum amount Fred should accept for the equity of Minnow Co?**

      A $8.7m

      B $10.3m

      C $11.2m

      D $15.3m

(b)   **Calculate the market value of Minnow Co using earnings. Give your answer to the nearest $million.**

      $ ☐

(c)   **Calculate the market value of the equity of Minnow Co using discounted cash flows.**

      A $72.5m

      B $75.0m

      C $75.5m

      D $78.0m

(d)   **Which TWO of the following statements about the proposed acquisition are true?**

      A   Fred probably prefers to take dividends due to tax considerations

      B   A major risk faced by Pike Co is that customers will be loyal to Fred rather than the company, so may leave when he retires

      C   If the stock market that Pike Co is listed on is strong form efficient, then the share price of Pike plc will only react to the acquisition when the confirmation is published.

      D   The directors of Pike Co should only be concerned about the unsystematic risks of Minnow Co

(e) **Which of the following statements concerning the use of different valuation methods for Minnow Co is true?**

(i) Asset valuations are unlikely to give a good indicator of market value

(ii) Theoretically, discounted cash flow approaches are the best method

(iii) Dividend valuation model using historic dividend information would give a fair market valuation for the company.

A (i), (ii) and (iii)

B (i) and (ii) only

C (i) only

D (iii) only

22 *This objective test case question contains question types which will only appear in a computer-based exam, but this question provides valuable practice for all students whichever version of the exam they are taking.*

It is now 1/1/20X6. Predator Co is looking make a bid for entire share capital of Prey Co, a small family owned company that makes specialist gears for high performance racing bikes. Prey Co's products have had a niche but loyal customer base for many years but demand started to soar in late 20X3 when it was revealed that all the gold medal winners in the cycling events at the Olympics were using a new revolutionary gear type developed and patented by Prey Co. The sale has been agreed in principle but a valuation still needs to be agreed for Prey Co. The following information is available:

Prey Co – Statement of Financial Position

	Note	$000s
Non-current assets	1	400
Current assets	2	50
Total assets		**450**
Share capital (50 cent ords.)		100
Reserves		170
Bank Loans – repayable 20X8		140
Current liabilities		40
Total equity and liabilities		**450**

Note 1: Included in non-current assets is specialist machinery that has a NBV of $100,000, would cost $500,000 to replace but would only be able to be sold for scrap of $25,000 if disposed of.

Note 2: Current assets have a net realisable value of $40,000

Prey Co – Summary statements of financial position

$000s	20X1 (audited)	20X2 (audited)	20X3 (audited)	20X4 (audited)	20X5 (unaudited)	20X6 (forecast)
Profit after tax	(10)	20	60	130	140	156
Dividends paid	–	10	30	65	70	78

A similar quoted company has been found that has a cost of equity of 15% and a quoted P/E ratio of 10.

(a) Calculate the asset value of Prey Co's shares using net realisable value

   A   Zero

   B $185,000

   C $195,000

   D $270,000

(b) Calculate the asset value of Prey Co's shares using replacement cost.

   A $270,000

   B $500,000

   C $670,000

   D $770,000

(c) Which of the following statements concerning the use of asset valuations for Prey Co with the information given is true?

   (i)   The replacement cost valuation is a good indication of corporate value as Prey Co operates in a capital intensive industry

   (ii)   The replacement cost valuation is likely to be a poor indication of corporate value as Prey Co's most valuable asset is likely to be its brand name

   (iii) Net book value is an indicator of the minimum amount the current owners will want for their company.

   A   (i), (ii) and (iii)

   B   (i) only

   C   (ii) only

   D   (iii) only

(d) Calculate the share price of Prey Co using earnings

   A $7.00

   B $7.80

   C $14.00

   D $15.60

(e) What growth rate should be used if estimating the value of Prey Co using the dividend valuation model? Give your answer as a percentage to 1 dp.

   ☐ %

RISK MANAGEMENT

23   Mallett Co is an Australian firm currently manufacturing a large item of machinery which is due to be exported shortly to the United States. The sale has been priced in US dollars, the client is expected to pay 850,000 USD.

This is Mallett Co's first sale to an American client since most of its exports normally go to Asia. The client has agreed to pay Mallett Co three months from now. The following relevant additional information is available.

Spot rate   0.7233 US dollars to the Australian dollar

US dollar interest rate   3.3% per annum
Australian dollar interest rate   2.9% per annum

(a)   **What will be the Australian dollar receipt if the transaction is hedged using the money market?**

A   1,137,628 AUD

B   1,165,554 AUD

C   1,170,619 AUD

D   1,174,004 AUD

(b)   **Which of the following relationships suggests that current long-term interest rates can be used to predict future short-term interest rates?**

A   Expectations theory

B   Fisher effect

C   Interest rate parity

D   Purchasing power parity

(c)   **What is the 3-month forward exchange rate?**

A   0.7205 US dollars to the Australian dollar

B   0.7226 US dollars to the Australian dollar

C   0.7240 US dollars to the Australian dollar

D   0.7261 US dollars to the Australian dollar

(d)   One risk that a company which exports and imports may face is that of exchange losses when accounting results of its foreign branches or subsidiaries are converted into home currency.

What is the name usually given to this type of risk?

A   Economic risk

B   Political risk

C   Transaction risk

D   Translation risk

(e)   Why is a currency option a particularly suitable device to reduce exposure to currency movements when tendering for a contract priced in a foreign currency?

  A   Cheapest means of achieving a hedge

  B   Least risky means of achieving a hedge

  C   Least unfavourable effect in the published accounts

  D   You may not get the contract and therefore the currency

24   Noon Co, a company based in Centreland whose home currency is the Centreland Colon (CC), has been regularly buying components from and selling finished products to businesses in Flyland, where the currency is the Flyland Franc (FF).

One particular payment of 3,000,000 Flyland Francs has to be made by Noon Co to a supplier in Flyland in three months' time. The following information is available.

Spot rate	6.170 – 6.210 Flyland Francs to the Centreland Colon
Three-month forward rate	6.321 – 6.362 Flyland Francs to the Centreland Colon

Interest rates that can be used by Noon Co are as follows.

	Borrow	Deposit
Flyland Franc interest rate	18.0% per annum	13.5% per annum
Centreland Colon interest rate	8.1% per annum	6.3% per annum

(a)   What is the cost in Centreland Colons of a forward market hedge?

  A   471,550 CC

  B   474,608 CC

  C   483,092 CC

  D   486,224 CC

(b)   Which of the following relationships attempt to explain the difference between forward and spot rates of exchange between two currencies and the relative rates of interest in the countries of origin of the two currencies?

  A   Expectations theory

  B   Fisher effect

  C   Interest rate parity

  D   Purchasing power parity

(c)   What is the cost in Centreland Colons of a money market hedge?

  A   428,391 CC

  B   463,091 CC

  C   470,349 CC

  D   479,874 CC

(d) The following statements may refer to the characteristics of interest rate futures.

1 Amounts and periods are standardised

2 They are legally binding contracts

3 They can be bought and sold on a secondary market

4 They can be used both to hedge risks and to speculate on interest rate movements

Which of the above statements are true?

A 1 only

B 1 and 2 only

C 1, 2 and 3 only

D 1, 2, 3 and 4

(e) **If inflation is currently running at 3.8% per annum in Centreland, what (to the nearest 1%) is the implied inflation rate in Flyland?**

A 14% inflation

B 6% inflation

C 1% inflation

D 6% deflation

25 PZK Co, whose home currency is the dollar, trades regularly with customers in a number of different countries. The company expects to receive €1,200,000 in six months' time from a foreign customer. Current exchange rates in the home country of PZK Co are as follows:

Spot exchange rate: 4.1780 – 4.2080 euros per $

Six-month forward exchange rate: 4.2302 – 4.2606 euros per $

Twelve-month forward exchange rate: 4.2825 – 4.3132 euros per $

The interest rate in the home country of PZK Co is 4% per year.

As well as considering the use of derivatives to hedge the risk exposure presented by the receipt, the treasurer of PZK is looking at 'internal' methods such as invoicing in dollars and leading and lagging.

(a) **What type of risk exposure is PZK Co exposed to due to the foreign receipt?**

A Transaction risk

B Economic risk

C Translation risk

D Political risk

(b) **Calculate the loss compared to its current dollar value which PZK Co will incur by taking out a forward exchange contract on the future euro receipt.**

A $1,496

B $3,520

C $3,544

D $5,568

(c) **Calculate the annual interest rate in the foreign customer's country implied by the spot exchange rate and the twelve-month forward exchange rate.**

A   1.5%

B   3.9%

C   4.1%

D   6.6%

(d) **With reference to PZK making foreign currency purchases, which one of the following statements concerning whether PZK Co should 'lead' or 'lag' in its management of the anticipated receipt is true?**

A   The $ is expected to weaken against the €, so PZK should lead

B   The $ is expected to weaken against the €, so PZK should lag

C   The $ is expected to strengthen against the €, so PZK should lead

D   The $ is expected to strengthen against the €, so PZK should lag

(e) **Which of the following statements concerning whether PZK Co should invoice in dollars is/are true?**

(i)   Invoicing in dollars will eliminate all foreign exchange risk that PZK is exposed to.

(ii)   Invoicing in dollars will pass exchange rate risk to the customer.

(iii)   Invoicing in dollars may not be commercially acceptable to foreign customers

A   (i), (ii) and (iii)

B   (i) and (ii) only

C   (ii) and (iii) only

D   (ii) only

26 *This objective test case question contains question types which will only appear in a computer-based exam, but this question provides valuable practice for all students whichever version of the exam they are taking.*

H Company, a large manufacturer, is planning to sell an existing subsidiary and use the funds to buy land and build a new factory. The proceeds of the sale are likely to be delayed, so the directors have estimated that $10 million will be needed in 3 months' time for a period of 6 months. Given this, the directors have decided that a bank loan would be appropriate as a form of finance rather than equity sources.

After checking that interest rate yield curves in the financial press are normal rather than inverted, the treasurer is now looking to hedge the interest rate exposure. Traditionally H Company has used forward rate agreements (FRAs) for hedging interest rate risk exposure but the treasurer is now considering using interest rate futures, although she is concerned that futures will not be as good a hedge as the FRAs.

H Company's bank have offered an FRA on the following terms:

3v9 FRA 7.2- 7.8%

(a) **Which TWO of the following are possible reasons why the Directors decided that a bank loan was preferable to equity in this case?**

   A   The factory will act as security on the loan

   B   They believe Modigliani and Miller's theory of gearing with taxation.

   C   All equity sources have higher issue costs than the loan

   D   The servicing cost of the debt will be lower.

(b) **Which one of the following would NOT be a possible explanation for the normal yield curve observed?**

   A   Expectations theory

   B   Liquidity preference theory

   C   Market segmentation theory

   D   An expected rise in interest rates.

(c) **What is the payment/receipt payable on the FRA if the reference interest rate moves to 7.6% in 3 months' time?**

   A $10,000 payment

   B $10,000 receipt

   C $20,000 payment

   D $20,000 receipt

(d) **Which TWO of the following are reasons why futures are not always a perfect hedge?**

   A   Futures contracts are in standard sizes which may not coincide with how much H Company wants to borrow.

   B   Futures have standardised contract dates, which may not coincide with when H Company wants to take out the loan.

   C   Basis risk

   D   Interest rates are hard to predict

(e) **Which of the following statements concerning FRAs and interest rate futures is/are true?**

   (i)   In both cases Company H stills needs to borrow the money at the market rate in three months' time.

   (ii)   Both have standardised contract sizes.

   (iii) Both result in a net gain or loss that can be offset against the loss or gain on the associated real world borrowing.

   A   (i), (ii) and (iii)

   B   (i) and (ii) only

   C   (i) and (iii) only

   D   (i) only

27 *This objective test case question contains question types which will only appear in a computer-based exam, but this question provides valuable practice for all students whichever version of the exam they are taking.*

It is now the 31st of January. The treasurer of F Company is reviewing cash forecasts and funding requirements and has identified the need for the following transactions:

Transaction 1:

F Company will have a surplus of $1 million from 1st of May for 3 months, which will need to be deposited to earn additional interest. The treasurer has seen inverted interest rate yield curves in the financial press, so is considering using a 3v6 FRA quoted at 5%- 5.6% to hedge the interest rate risk exposure. He is also considering the use of interest rate options as an alternative strategy.

Transaction 2:

F Company also needs to borrow $20 million longer term debt to finance expansion. The treasurer would prefer to borrow at a floating rate but does not feel that the company can obtain competitive rates. He is thus considering the possibility of borrowing fixed and entering into a swap arrangement. F Company's advisors have identified G Company as a possible counter party. Details of the current borrowing rates that each company can achieve are as follows:

Company	Best fixed rate	Best variable rate
F	7%	LIBOR + 3%
G	6%	LIBOR + 1%

(a) **Which TWO predictions are normally associated with an inverted yield curve?**

    A   An expected fall in interest rates

    B   An expected rise in interest rates

    C   A fall in inflation

    D   A downturn of the economy into a recession.

(b) **What is the payment/receipt payable on the FRA if the reference interest rate moves to 5.5% on the 1st May?**

    A $250 payment

    B $250 receipt

    C $1,250 payment

    D $1,250 receipt

(c) **Which one of the following best describes an interest rate option?**

    A   A right but not an obligation to buy or sell interest rate futures

    B   An obligation to obtain a loan at an agreed interest rate at a future date

    C   A right but not an obligation to obtain a loan (or deposit) at a future date

    D   A right but not an obligation to an agreed interest rate on a notional loan or deposit

(d) **With reference to interest rate swaps, which of the following statements it true?**

A It allows the company a period of time during which it has the option to buy a forward rate agreement at a set price

B It locks the company into an effective interest rate

C It is an agreement whereby the parties to the agreement exchange interest rate commitments

D It involves the exchange of principle

(e) **Which of the following statements concerning the swap is / are true?**

(i) G company has been offered lower interest rates due to having a better credit rating.

(ii) Under the swap loan principals are exchanged.

(iii) If G defaults on the loan it has taken out, then F would also be liable under the swap.

A (i), (ii) and (iii)

B (i) and (ii) only

C (ii) and (iii) only

D (i) only

Section C

CONSTRUCTED RESPONSE PRACTICE QUESTIONS

FINANCIAL MANAGEMENT FUNCTION AND ENVIRONMENT

1   UUL CO

UUL Co is a public water supply company which was privatised a number of years ago. As the deputy Finance Director you are reviewing the draft financial statements which contain the following statement by the chairman:

'This company has delivered above average performance in fulfilment of our objective of maximising shareholder wealth. Earnings, dividends and the share price have all shown good growth. It is our intention to continue to deliver strong performance in the future'.

The following information has been extracted from the draft financial statements:

Year	20X6	20X2
Dividend per share	7.1c	4.2c
Earnings per share	41.3c	31.6c
Price/earnings ratio	22.0	17.0

You have obtained the following information regarding the water industry for the last 5 years:

Dividend growth	11% annually
Earnings growth	12% annually
Share price growth	18% annually

General inflation in the economy has averaged 2% per annum.

The number of shares in issue has remained unchanged over the last 5 years and the price/earnings ratios are calculated using year end share prices.

Required:

(a)   Calculate the equivalent annual growth in:

   (i)   Dividends per share

   (ii)   Earnings per share

   (iii)   Share price

   Critically comment on the views expressed by the chairman.   **(8 marks)**

(b)   Other than shareholders and directors, identify three other key stakeholders in a company such as UUL Co. Identify what financial and other objectives the company should aim to follow in order to satisfy each of these stakeholders.   **(6 marks)**

(c)   Identify what government intervention and other regulation UUL Co may suffer and how this will impact upon the company.   **(6 marks)**

(Total: 20 marks)

 Online question assistance

2   CCC

(a)   CCC is a local government entity. It is financed almost equally by a combination of central government funding and local taxation. The funding from central government is determined largely on a per capita (per head of population) basis, adjusted to reflect the scale of deprivation (or special needs) deemed to exist in CCC's region. A small percentage of its finance comes from the private sector, for example from renting out City Hall for private functions.

CCC's main objectives are:

- to make the region economically prosperous and an attractive place to live

- to provide service excellence in health and education for the local community.

DDD is a large listed entity with widespread commercial and geographical interests. For historic reasons, its headquarters are in CCC's region. This is something of an anomaly as most entities of DDD's size would have their HQ in a capital city, or at least a city much larger than where it is.

DDD has one financial objective: To increase shareholder wealth by an average 10% per annum. It also has a series of non-financial objectives that deal with how the entity treats other stakeholders, including the local communities where it operates.

DDD has total net assets of $1.5 billion and a gearing ratio of 45% (debt to debt plus equity), which is typical for its industry. It is currently considering raising a substantial amount of capital to finance an acquisition.

Required:

Discuss the criteria that the two very different entities described above have to consider when setting objectives, recognising the needs of each of their main stakeholder groups. Make some reference in your answer to the consequences of each of them failing to meet its declared objectives.   (10 marks)

(b)   MS is a private entity in a computer-related industry. It has been trading for six years and is managed by its main shareholders, the original founders of the entity. Most of the employees are also shareholders, having been given shares as bonuses. None of the shareholders has attempted to sell shares in the entity, so the problem of placing a value on them has not arisen. Dividends have been paid every year at the rate of 60 cents per share, irrespective of profits. So far, profits have always been sufficient to cover the dividend at least once but never more than twice.

MS is all-equity financed at present although $15 million new finance is likely to be required in the near future to finance expansion. Total net assets as at the last statement of financial position date were $45 million.

Required:

Discuss and compare the relationship between dividend policy, investment policy and financing policy in the context of the small entity described above, MS, and DDD, the large listed entity described in part (a). **(10 marks)**

(Total: 20 marks)

3   NEIGHBOURING COUNTRIES

(a)   Two neighbouring countries have chosen to organise their electricity supply industries in different ways.

In Country A, electricity supplies are provided by a nationalised industry. In Country B, electricity supplies are provided by a number of private sector companies.

Required:

Explain how the objectives of the nationalised industry in Country A might differ from those of the private sector companies in Country B.

Briefly discuss whether investment planning and appraisal techniques are likely to differ in the nationalised industry and private sector companies.   **(10 marks)**

(b)   Whilst the financial plans of a business are based on a single objective, it can face a number of constraints that put pressure on the company to address more than one objective simultaneously.

Required:

What types of constraints might a company face when assessing its long-term plans? Specifically refer in your answer to:

(i)   responding to various stakeholder groups, and   **(5 marks)**

(ii)   the difficulties associated with managing organisations with multiple objectives.   **(5 marks)**

(Total: 20 marks)

4   RZP CO

As assistant to the Finance Director of RZP Co, a company that has been listed on the London Stock Market for several years, you are reviewing the draft Annual Report of the company, which contains the following statement made by the chairman:

'This company has consistently delivered above-average performance in fulfilment of our declared objective of creating value for our shareholders. Apart from 20X2, when our overall performance was hampered by a general market downturn, this company has delivered growth in dividends, earnings and ordinary share price. Our shareholders can rest assured that my directors and I will continue to deliver this performance in the future'.

The five-year summary in the draft Annual Report contains the following information:

Year	20X4	20X3	20X2	20X1	20X0
Dividend per share	2.8¢	2.3¢	2.2¢	2.2¢	1.7¢
Earnings per share	19.04¢	14.95¢	11.22¢	15.84¢	13.43¢
Price/earnings ratio	22.0	33.5	25.5	17.2	15.2
General price index	117	113	110	105	100

A recent article in the financial press reported the following information for the last five years for the business sector within which RZP Co operates:

Share price growth   average increase per year of 20%
Earnings growth   average increase per year of 10%
Nominal dividend growth   average increase per year of 10%
Real dividend growth   average increase per year of 9%

You may assume that the number of shares issued by RZP Co has been constant over the five-year period. All price/earnings ratios are based on end-of-year share prices.

Required:

(a)   Analyse the information provided and comment on the views expressed by the chairman in terms of:

   (i)   growth in dividends per share

   (ii)   share price growth

   (iii) growth in earnings per share.

   Your analysis should consider both arithmetic mean and equivalent annual growth rates.   **(12 marks)**

(b)   Calculate the total shareholder return (dividend yield plus capital growth) for 20X4 and comment on your findings.   **(3 marks)**

(c)   Discuss FIVE factors that should be considered when deciding on a management remuneration package that will encourage the directors of RZP Co to maximise the wealth of shareholders. (Note: you do not have to give examples of management remuneration packages that might be appropriate for RZP Co.)   **(5 marks)**

                                                                    (Total: 20 marks)

5   **JJG CO (JUNE 09 - MODIFIED)**

 Timed question with Online tutor debrief

JJG Co is planning to raise $15 million of new finance for a major expansion of existing business and is considering a rights issue, a placing or an issue of bonds. The corporate objectives of JJG Co, as stated in its Annual Report, are to maximise the wealth of its shareholders and to achieve continuous growth in earnings per share.

Recent financial information on JJG Co is as follows

	20X8	20X7	20X6	20X5
Turnover ($m)	28.0	24.0	19.1	16.8
Profit before interest and tax ($m)	9.8	8.5	7.5	6.8
Earnings ($m)	5.5	4.7	4.1	3.6
Dividends ($m)	2.2	1.9	1.6	1.6
Ordinary shares ($m)	5.5	5.5	5.5	5.5
Reserves ($m)	13.7	10.4	7.6	5.1
8% Bonds, redeemable 2015 ($m)	20.0	20.0	20.0	20.0
Share price ($)	8.64	5.74	3.35	2.67

The par value of the shares of JJG Co is $1.00 per share. The general level of inflation has averaged 4% per year in the period under consideration. The bonds of JJG Co are currently trading at their par value of $100. The following values for the business sector of JJG Co are available:

Average return on capital employed	25%
Average return on shareholders' funds	20%
Average interest coverage ratio	20 times
Average debt/equity ratio (market value basis)	50%
Return predicted by the capital asset pricing model	14%

Required:

(a) **Evaluate the financial performance of JJG Co, and analyse and discuss the extent to which the company has achieved its stated corporate objectives of:**

   (i)   **Maximising the wealth of its shareholders**

   (ii) **Achieving continuous growth in earnings per share.**

   Note: up to 7 marks are available for financial analysis **(13 marks)**

(b) **Analyse and discuss the relative merits of a rights issue, a placing and an issue of bonds as ways of raising the finance for the expansion** **(7 marks)**

(Total: 20 marks)

6   NEWS FOR YOU

News For You operates a chain of newsagents and confectioner's shops in the south of a Northern European country, and are considering the possibility of expanding their business across a wider geographical area. The business was started in 20X2 and annual turnover grew to $10 million by the end of 20X6. Between 20X6 and 20X9 turnover grew at an average rate of 2% per year.

The business still remains under family control, but the high cost of expansion via the purchase or building of new outlets would mean that the family would need to raise at least $2 million in equity or debt finance. One of the possible risks of expansion lies in the fact that both tobacco and newspaper sales are falling. New income is being generated by expanding the product range stocked by the stores, to include basic foodstuffs such as bread and milk. News For You purchases all of its products from a large wholesale distributor which is convenient, but the wholesale prices leave News For You with a relatively small gross margin.

The key to profit growth for News For You lies in the ability to generate sales growth, but the company recognises that it faces stiff competition from large food retailers in respect of the prices that it charges for several of its products.

In planning its future, News For You was advised to look carefully at a number of external factors which may affect the business, including government economic policy and, in recent months, the following information has been published in respect of key economic data:

(i)   Bank base rate has been reduced from 5% to 4.5%, and the forecast is for a further 0.5% reduction within six months.

(ii) The annual rate of inflation is now 1.2%, down from 1.3% in the previous quarter, and 1.7% 12 months ago. The rate is now at its lowest for 25 years, and no further falls in the rate are expected over the medium/long term.

(iii)   Personal and corporation tax rates are expected to remain unchanged for at least 12 months.

(iv)   Taxes on tobacco have been increased by 10% over the last 12 months, although no further increases are anticipated.

(v)   The government has initiated an investigation into the food retail sector focusing on the problems of 'excessive' profits on certain foodstuffs created by the high prices being charged for these goods by the large retail food stores.

Required:

(a)   Explain the relevance of each of the items of economic data listed above to News For You. **(10 marks)**

(b)   Explain whether News For You should continue with their expansion plans. Clearly justify your arguments for or against the expansion. **(10 marks)**

(Total: 20 marks)

WORKING CAPITAL MANAGEMENT

7   GORWA CO (DEC 08 - MODIFIED)

The following financial information related to Gorwa Co:

	20X7	20X6
	$000	$000
Sales (all on credit)	37,400	26,720
Cost of sales	34,408	23,781
Operating profit	2,992	2,939
Finance costs (interest payments)	355	274
Profit before taxation	2,637	2,665

		20X7		20X6
	$000	$000	$000	$000
Non-current assets		13,632		12,750
Current assets				
Inventory	4,600		2,400	
Trade receivables	4,600		2,200	
	9,200		4,600	
Current liabilities				
Trade payables	4,750		2,000	
Overdraft	3,225		1,600	
	7,975		3,600	
Net current assets		1,225		1,000
		14,857		13,750
8% Bonds		2,425		2,425
		12,432		11,325

Capital and reserves		
Share capital	6,000	6,000
Reserves	6,432	5,325
	12,432	11,325

The average variable overdraft interest rate in each year was 5%. The 8% bonds are redeemable in ten years' time.

A factor has offered to take over the administration of trade receivables on a non-recourse basis for an annual fee of 3% of credit sales. The factor will maintain a trade receivables collection period of 30 days and Gorwa Co will save $100,000 per year in administration costs and $350,000 per year in bad debts. A condition of the factoring agreement is that the factor would advance 80% of the face value of receivables at an annual interest rate of 7%.

Required:

(a) **Discuss, with supporting calculations, the possible effects on Gorwa Co of an increase in interest rates and advise the company of steps it can take to protect itself against interest rate risk.** **(9 marks)**

(b) **Use the above financial information to discuss, with supporting calculations, whether or not Gorwa Co is overtrading.** **(11 marks)**

(Total: 20 marks)

8 **FLG CO (JUNE 08 - MODIFIED)**

FLG Co has annual credit sales of $4.2 million and cost of sales of $1.89 million. Current assets consist of inventory and accounts receivable. Current liabilities consist of accounts payable and an overdraft with an average interest rate of 7% per year. The company gives two months' credit to its customers and is allowed, on average, one month's credit by trade suppliers. It has an operating cycle of three months.

Other relevant information:

Current ratio of FLG Co	1.4
Cost of long-term finance of FLG Co	11%

Required:

(a) **Discuss the key factors which determine the level of investment in current assets.** **(4 marks)**

(b) **Briefly discuss the ways in which factoring can assist in the management of accounts receivable.** **(3 marks)**

(c) **Calculate the size of the overdraft of FLG Co, the net working capital of the company and the total cost of financing its current assets.** **(6 marks)**

(d) FLG Co wishes to minimise its inventory costs. Annual demand for a raw material costing $12 per unit is 60,000 units per year. Inventory management costs for this raw material are as follows:

Ordering cost:	$6 per order
Holding cost:	$0.5 per unit per year

The supplier of this raw material has offered a bulk purchase discount of 1% for orders of 10,000 units or more. If bulk purchase orders are made regularly, it is expected that annual holding cost for this raw material will increase to $2 per unit per year.

Required:

(i) Calculate the total cost of inventory for the raw material when using the economic order quantity. **(4 marks)**

(ii) Determine whether accepting the discount offered by the supplier will minimise the total cost of inventory for the raw material. **(3 marks)**

(Total: 20 marks)

9   PKA CO (DEC 07 - MODIFIED)   *Walk in the footsteps of a top tutor*

PKA Co is a European company that sells goods solely within Europe. The recently-appointed financial manager of PKA Co has been investigating the working capital management of the company and has gathered the following information:

Inventory management

The current policy is to order 100,000 units when the inventory level falls to 35,000 units. Forecast demand to meet production requirements during the next year is 625,000 units. The cost of placing and processing an order is €250, while the cost of holding a unit in stores is €0.50 per unit per year. Both costs are expected to be constant during the next year. Orders are received two weeks after being placed with the supplier. You should assume a 50-week year and that demand is constant throughout the year.

Accounts receivable management

Domestic customers are allowed 30 days' credit, but the financial statements of PKA Co show that the average accounts receivable period in the last financial year was 75 days. The financial manager also noted that bad debts as a percentage of sales, which are all on credit, increased in the last financial year from 5% to 8%.

Accounts payable management

PKA Co has used a foreign supplier for the first time and must pay $250,000 to the supplier in six months' time. The financial manager is concerned that the cost of these supplies may rise in euro terms and has decided to hedge the currency risk of this account payable. The following information has been provided by the company's bank:

Spot rate ($ per €):   1.998 ± 0.002

Six months forward rate ($ per €): 1.979 ± 0.004

Money market rates available to PKA Co:

	Borrowing	Deposit
One year euro interest rates:	6.1%	5.4%
One year dollar interest rates:	4.0%	3.5%

Assume that it is now 1 December and that PKA Co has no surplus cash at the present time.

Required:

(a)   Calculate the cost of the current ordering policy and determine the saving that could be made by using the economic order quantity model.   **(6 marks)**

(b)   Discuss ways in which PKA Co could improve the management of domestic accounts receivable.   **(6 marks)**

(c)   Evaluate whether a money market hedge, a forward market hedge or a lead payment should be used to hedge the foreign account payable.   **(8 marks)**

(Total: 20 marks)

10   KXP CO (DEC 12 - MODIFIED)

KXP Co is an e-business which trades solely over the internet. In the last year the company had sales of $15 million. All sales were on 30 days' credit to commercial customers.

Extracts from the company's most recent statement of financial position relating to working capital are as follows:

	$000
Trade receivables	2,466
Trade payables	2,220
Overdraft	3,000

In order to encourage customers to pay on time, KXP Co proposes introducing an early settlement discount of 1% for payment within 30 days, while increasing its normal credit period to 45 days. It is expected that, on average, 50% of customers will take the discount and pay within 30 days, 30% of customers will pay after 45 days, and 20% of customers will not change their current paying behaviour.

KXP Co currently orders 15,000 units per month of Product Z, demand for which is constant. There is only one supplier of Product Z and the cost of Product Z purchases over the last year was $540,000. The supplier has offered a 2% discount for orders of Product Z of 30,000 units or more. Each order costs KXP Co $150 to place and the holding cost is 24 cents per unit per year.

KXP Co has an overdraft facility charging interest of 6% per year.

Required:

(a)   Calculate the net benefit or cost of the proposed changes in trade receivables policy and comment on your findings.   **(6 marks)**

(b)   Calculate whether the bulk purchase discount offered by the supplier is financially acceptable and comment on the assumptions made by your calculation.   **(6 marks)**

(c)   Critically discuss the similarities and differences between working capital policies in the following areas:

(i)   Working capital investment

(ii)   Working capital financing.   **(8 marks)**

(Total: 20 marks)

11   ULNAD

Ulnad Co has annual sales revenue of $6 million and all sales are on 30 days' credit, although customers on average take ten days more than this to pay. Contribution represents 60% of sales and the company currently has no bad debts. Accounts receivable are financed by an overdraft at an annual interest rate of 7%.

Ulnad Co plans to offer an early settlement discount of 1.5% for payment within 15 days and to extend the maximum credit offered to 60 days. The company expects that these changes will increase annual credit sales by 5%, while also leading to additional incremental costs equal to 0.5% of sales revenue. The discount is expected to be taken by 30% of customers, with the remaining customers taking an average of 60 days to pay.

Required:

(a)   Evaluate whether the proposed changes in credit policy will increase the profitability of Ulnad Co.   (6 marks)

(b)   Renpec Co, a subsidiary of Ulnad Co, has set a minimum cash account balance of $7,500. The average cost to the company of making deposits or selling investments is $18 per transaction and the standard deviation of its cash flows was $1,000 per day during the last year. The average interest rate on investments is 5.11%.

Determine the spread, the upper limit and the return point for the cash account of Renpec Co using the Miller-Orr model and explain the relevance of these values for the cash management of the company.   (6 marks)

(c)   Discuss the key factors to be considered when formulating a working capital funding policy.   (8 marks)

(Total: 20 marks)

12   APX CO (DEC 09 - MODIFIED)

APX Co achieved a turnover of $16 million in the year that has just ended and expects turnover growth of 8.4% in the next year. Cost of sales in the year that has just ended was $10.88 million and other expenses were $1.44 million.

The financial statements of APX Co for the year that has just ended contain the following statement of financial position:

	$m	$m
Non-current assets		22.0
Current assets		
Inventory	2.4	
Trade receivables	2.2	
		4.6
Total assets		26.6

Equity finance:

	$m	$m
Ordinary shares	5.0	
Reserves	7.5	
		12.5
Long-term bank loan		10.0
		22.5
Current liabilities		
Trade payables	1.9	
Overdraft	2.2	
		4.1
Total liabilities		26.6

The long-term bank loan has a fixed annual interest rate of 8% per year. APX Co pays taxation at an annual rate of 30% per year.

The following accounting ratios have been forecast for the next year:

Gross profit margin:	30%
Operating profit margin:	20%
Dividend payout ratio:	50%
Inventory turnover period:	110 days
Trade receivables period:	65 days
Trade payables period:	75 days

Overdraft interest in the next year is forecast to be $140,000. No change is expected in the level of non-current assets and depreciation should be ignored.

Required:

(a) **Prepare the following forecast financial statements for APX Co using the information provided:**

    (i)   **an statement of profit or loss for the next year; and**

    (ii)   **a statement of financial position at the end of the next year.**   **(9 marks)**

(b) **Analyse and discuss the working capital financing policy of APX Co.**   **(6 marks)**

(c) **Analyse and discuss the forecast financial performance of APX Co in terms of working capital management.**   **(5 marks)**

         (Total: 20 marks)

13   HGR CO (JUNE 09 - MODIFIED)

 Timed question with Online tutor debrief

The following financial information relates to HGR Co:

Statement of financial position at the current date (extracts)

	$000	$000	$000
Non-current assets			48,965
Current assets			
Inventory		8,160	
Accounts receivable		8,775	
		16,935	
Current liabilities			
Overdraft	3,800		
Accounts payable	10,200		
		14,000	
Net current assets			2,935
Total assets less current liabilities			51,900

Cash flow forecasts from the current date are as follows:

	Month 1	Month 2	Month 3
Cash operating receipts ($000)	4,220	4,350	3,808
Cash operating payments ($000)	3,950	4,100	3,750
Six-monthly interest on traded bonds ($000)		200	
Capital investment ($000)			2,000

The finance director has completed a review of accounts receivable management and has proposed staff training and operating procedure improvements, which he believes will reduce accounts receivable days to the average sector value of 53 days. This reduction would take six months to achieve from the current date, with an equal reduction in each month. He has also proposed changes to inventory management methods, which he hopes will reduce inventory days by two days per month each month over a three-month period from the current date. He does not expect any change in the current level of accounts payable.

HGR Co has an overdraft limit of $4,000,000. Overdraft interest is payable at an annual rate of 6.17% per year, with payments being made each month based on the opening balance at the start of that month. Credit sales for the year to the current date were $49,275,000 and cost of sales was $37,230,000. These levels of credit sales and cost of sales are expected to be maintained in the coming year. Assume that there are 365 working days in each year.

Required:

(a)   Discuss the working capital financing strategy of HGR Co.   (6 marks)

(b)   For HGR Co, calculate:

   (i)   the bank balance in three months' time if no action is taken; and

   (ii)   the bank balance in three months' time if the finance director's proposals are implemented

   Comment on the forecast cash flow position of HGR Co and recommend a suitable course of action.   (9 marks)

(c)   Discuss how risks arising from granting credit to foreign customers can be managed and reduced.   (5 marks)

(Total: 20 marks)

 Calculate your allowed time, allocate the time to the separate parts

14   ANJO

Extracts from the recent financial statements of Anjo Inc are as follows:

Statement of profit or loss

	20X6	20X5
	$000	$000
Sales revenue	15,600	11,100
Cost of sales	9,300	6,600
Gross profit	6,300	4,500
Administration expenses	1,000	750
Profit before interest and tax	5,300	3,750
Interest	100	15
Profit before tax	5,200	3,735

Statements of financial position

	20X6		20X5	
	$000	$000	$000	$000
Non-current assets		5,750		5,400
Current assets				
Inventory	3,000		1,300	
Receivables	3,800		1,850	
Cash	120		900	
		6,920		4,050
Total assets		8,800		7,700

	$000	20X6 $000	$000	20X5 $000
Total equity		4,930		5,950
Current liabilities				
Trade payables	2,870		1,600	
Overdraft	1,000		150	
		3,870		1,750
Total equity and liabilities		8,800		7,700

All sales were on credit. Anjo Inc has no long-term debt. Credit purchases in each year were 95% of cost of sales. Anjo Inc pays interest on its overdraft at an annual rate of 8%. Current sector averages are as follows:

Inventory days: 90 days

Receivables days: 60 days

Payables days: 80 days

Required:

(a)   Calculate the following ratios for each year and comment on your findings.

   (i)   **Inventory days**

   (ii)   **Receivables days**

   (iii) **Payables days**   (8 marks)

(b)   Calculate the length of the cash operating cycle (working capital cycle) for each year and explain its significance.   (4 marks)

(c)   A factor has offered to take over sales ledger administration and debt collection for an annual fee of 0.5% of credit sales. A condition of the offer is that the factor will advance Anjo Inc 80% of the face value of its receivables at an interest rate 1% above the current overdraft rate. The factor claims that it would reduce outstanding receivables by 30% and reduce administration expenses by 2% per year if its offer were accepted.

   Evaluate whether the factor's offer is financially acceptable, basing your answer on the financial information relating to 20X6.   (8 marks)

                                                                  (Total: 20 marks)

15   ZSE CO (JUNE 10 - MODIFIED)

ZSE Co is concerned about exceeding its overdraft limit of $2 million in the next two periods. It has been experiencing considerable volatility in cash flows in recent periods because of trading difficulties experienced by its customers, who have often settled their accounts after the agreed credit period of 60 days. ZSE has also experienced an increase in bad debts due to a small number of customers going into liquidation.

The company has prepared the following forecasts of net cash flows for the next two periods, together with their associated probabilities, in an attempt to anticipate liquidity and financing problems. These probabilities have been produced by a computer model which simulates a number of possible future economic scenarios. The computer model has been built with the aid of a firm of financial consultants.

Period 1 cash flow $000	Probability	Period 2 cash flow $000	Probability
8,000	10%	7,000	30%
4,000	60%	3,000	50%
(2,000)	30%	(9,000)	20%

ZSE Co expects to be overdrawn at the start of period 1 by $500,000.

Required:

(a) Calculate the following values:

    (i)   the expected value of the period 1 closing balance

    (ii)   the expected value of the period 2 closing balance

    (iii) the probability of a negative cash balance at the end of period 2

    (iv) the probability of exceeding the overdraft limit at the end of period 2.

    Discuss whether the above analysis can assist the company in managing its cash flows. **(12 marks)**

(b) Identify and discuss the factors to be considered in formulating a trade receivables management policy for ZSE Co. **(5 marks)**

(c) Discuss whether profitability or liquidity is the primary objective of working capital management. **(3 marks)**

(Total: 20 marks)

16 PNP PLC (JUNE 07 - MODIFIED)

The following financial information relates to PNP plc, a UK-based firm, for the year just ended.

	£000
Sales revenue	5,242.0
Variable cost of sales	3,145.0
Inventory	603.0
Receivables	744.5
Payables	574.5

Segmental analysis of receivables

	Balance	Average payment period	Discount	Irrecoverable
Class 1	£200,000	30 days	1.0%	None
Class 2	£252,000	60 days	Nil	£12,600
Class 3	£110,000	75 days	Nil	£11,000
Overseas	£182,500	90 days	Nil	£21,900
	£744,500			£45,500

The receivables balances given are before taking account of irrecoverable debts. All sales are on credit. Production and sales take place evenly throughout the year. Current sales for each class of receivables are in proportion to their relative year-end balances before irrecoverable debts.

It has been proposed that the discount for early payment be increased from 1.0% to 1.5% for settlement within 30 days.

It is expected that this will lead to 50% of existing Class 2 receivables becoming Class 1 receivables, as well as attracting new business worth £500,000 in turnover. The new business would be divided equally between Class 1 and Class 2 receivables. Fixed costs would not increase as a result of introducing the discount or by attracting new business. PNP finances receivables from an overdraft at an annual interest rate of 8%.

Required:

(a) Calculate the net benefit or cost of increasing the discount for early payment and comment on the acceptability of the proposal. **(9 marks)**

(b) Calculate the current cash operating cycle and the revised cash operating cycle caused by increasing the discount for early payment. **(4 marks)**

(c) Identify and explain the key elements of a receivables management system suitable for PNP plc. **(7 marks)**

(Total: 20 marks)

 Online question assistance

17 PLOT CO (DEC 13 - MODIFIED)

Plot Co sells both Product P and Product Q, with sales of both products occurring evenly throughout the year.

Product P

The annual demand for Product P is 300,000 units and an order for new inventory is placed each month. Each order costs $267 to place. The cost of holding Product P in inventory is 10 cents per unit per year. Buffer inventory equal to 40% of one month's sales is maintained.

Product Q

The annual demand for Product Q is 456,000 units per year and Plot Co buys in this product at $1 per unit on 60 days credit. The supplier has offered an early settlement discount of 1% for settlement of invoices within 30 days.

Other information

Plot Co finances working capital with short-term finance costing 5% per year. Assume that there are 365 days in each year.

Required:

(a) Calculate the following values for Product P:

    (i) The total cost of the current ordering policy **(3 marks)**

    (ii) The total cost of an ordering policy using the economic order quantity **(3 marks)**

    (iii) The net cost or saving of introducing an ordering policy using the economic order quantity. **(1 mark)**

(b) Calculate the net value in dollars to Plot Co of accepting the early settlement discount for Product Q. **(5 marks)**

(c) Identify the objectives of working capital management and discuss the central role of working capital management in financial management. **(8 marks)**

(Total: 20 marks)

18   WQZ CO (DEC 10 - MODIFIED)

WQZ Co is considering making the following changes in the area of working capital management:

Inventory management

It has been suggested that the order size for Product KN5 should be determined using the economic order quantity model (EOQ).

WQZ Co forecasts that demand for Product KN5 will be 160,000 units in the coming year and it has traditionally ordered 10% of annual demand per order. The ordering cost is expected to be $400 per order while the holding cost is expected to be $5.12 per unit per year. A buffer inventory of 5,000 units of Product KN5 will be maintained, whether orders are made by the traditional method or using the economic ordering quantity model.

Receivables management

WQZ Co could introduce an early settlement discount of 1% for customers who pay within 30 days and at the same time, through improved operational procedures, maintain a maximum average payment period of 60 days for credit customers who do not take the discount. It is expected that 25% of credit customers will take the discount if it were offered.

It is expected that administration and operating cost savings of $753,000 per year will be made after improving operational procedures and introducing the early settlement discount.

Credit sales of WQZ Co are currently $87.6 million per year and trade receivables are currently $18 million. Credit sales are not expected to change as a result of the changes in receivables management. The company has a cost of short-term finance of 5.5% per year.

Required:

(a)   Calculate the cost of the current ordering policy and the change in the costs of inventory management that will arise if the economic order quantity is used to determine the optimum order size for Product KN5.   **(6 marks)**

(b)   Briefly describe the benefits of a just-in-time (JIT) procurement policy.   **(3 marks)**

(c)   Calculate and comment on whether the proposed changes in receivables management will be acceptable. Assuming that only 25% of customers take the early settlement discount, what is the maximum early settlement discount that could be offered?   **(6 marks)**

(d)   Discuss the factors that should be considered in formulating working capital policy on the management of trade receivables.   **(5 marks)**

(Total: 20 marks)

INVESTMENT APPRAISAL

19   ARMCLIFF CO

 Timed question with Online tutor debrief

Armcliff Co is a division of Shevin Inc which requires each of its divisions to achieve a rate of return on capital employed of at least 10% pa. For this purpose, capital employed is defined as fixed capital and investment in inventories. This rate of return is also applied as a hurdle rate for new investment projects. Divisions have limited borrowing powers and all capital projects are centrally funded.

The following is an extract from Armcliff's divisional accounts:

Statement of profit or loss for the year ended 31 December 20X4

	$m
Sales revenue	120
Cost of sales	(100)

Operating profit	20

Assets employed as at 31 December 20X4

	$m	$m
Non-current assets (NBV)		75
Current assets (including inventories $25m)	45	
Current liabilities	(32)	

		13

Net capital employed		88

Armcliff's production engineers wish to invest in a new computer-controlled press. The equipment cost is $14m. The residual value is expected to be $2m after four years operation, when the equipment will be shipped to a customer in South America.

The new machine is capable of improving the quality of the existing product and also of producing a higher volume. The firm's marketing team is confident of selling the increased volume by extending the credit period.

The expected additional sales are:

Year 1	2,000,000 units
Year 2	1,800,000 units
Year 3	1,600,000 units
Year 4	1,600,000 units

Sales volume is expected to fall over time due to emerging competitive pressures. Competition will also necessitate a reduction in price by $0.50 each year from the $5 per unit proposed in the first year. Operating costs are expected to be steady at $1 per unit, and allocation of overheads (none of which are affected by the new project) by the central finance department is set at $0.75 per unit.

Higher production levels will require additional investment in inventories of $0.5m, which would be held at this level until the final stages of operation of the project. Customers at present settle accounts after 90 days on average.

Required:

(a)   **Determine whether the proposed capital investment is attractive to Armcliff, using the average rate of return on capital method, as defined as average profit-to-average capital employed, ignoring receivables and payables.**

  Note: Ignore taxes. (10 marks)

(b)   (i)   **Suggest three problems which arise with the use of the average return method for appraising new investment.** (3 marks)

  (ii)   **In view of the problems associated with the ARR method, why do companies continue to use it in project appraisal?** (3 marks)

(c)   **Briefly discuss the dangers of offering more generous credit.** (4 marks)

(Total: 20 marks)

 Calculate your allowed time, allocate the time to the separate parts

20   WARDEN CO (DEC 11 - MODIFIED)

Warden Co plans to buy a new machine. The cost of the machine, payable immediately, is $800,000 and the machine has an expected life of five years. Additional investment in working capital of $90,000 will be required at the start of the first year of operation. At the end of five years, the machine will be sold for scrap, with the scrap value expected to be 5% of the initial purchase cost of the machine. The machine will not be replaced.

Production and sales from the new machine are expected to be 100,000 units per year. Each unit can be sold for $16 per unit and will incur variable costs of $11 per unit. Incremental fixed costs arising from the operation of the machine will be $160,000 per year.

Warden Co has an after-tax cost of capital of 11% which it uses as a discount rate in investment appraisal. The company pays profit tax one year in arrears at an annual rate of 30% per year. Tax allowable depreciation and inflation should be ignored.

Required:

(a)   **Calculate the net present value of investing in the new machine and advise whether the investment is financially acceptable.** (7 marks)

(b)   **Calculate the internal rate of return of investing in the new machine and advise whether the investment is financially acceptable.** (4 marks)

(c) (i)   Explain briefly the meaning of the term 'sensitivity analysis' in the context of investment appraisal   (2 marks)

     (ii) Calculate the sensitivity of the investment in the new machine to a change in selling price and to a change in discount rate, and comment on your findings.

                                                                                      (7 marks)

                                                                              (Total: 20 marks)

21   DAIRY CO

After securing an extension to an existing contract, the directors of Dairy Co are reviewing the options relating to a machine that is a key part of the company's production process.

Option 1 – Replace the machine

The cost of a new machine would be $450,000, payable immediately.

Maintenance costs would be payable at the end of each year of the project. The first maintenance payment for the new machine is $25,000 although this is expected to rise by 7.5% per year.

Option 2 – Overhaul the existing machine

The alternative to replacement is a complete overhaul of an existing machine, the cost of which would be $275,000, also payable immediately. This would be classified as capital expenditure.

However, under this option, the annual maintenance costs will be higher at $40,000 in year 1 with expected annual increases of 10.5%.

As the new machine is likely to reduce the variable cost, the contribution will be different depending on which machine is used. The contribution from each machine (excluding maintenance costs) is tabulated as follows, with the inflow of funds assumed to be at the end of each year:

Year	Year 1	Year 2	Year 3	Year 4	Year 5
Contribution with new machine ($)	150,000	170,000	190,000	210,000	220,000
Contribution with overhauled machine ($)	130,000	145,000	155,000	160,000	160,000

The financial manager is unsure of the cost of capital, but expects it is around 12%. Taxation can be ignored.

Required:

(a)   Calculate the net present value of each option.   (7 marks)

(b)   Estimate the internal rate of return of each plan.   (5 marks)

(c)   Interpret the results that you have obtained in parts (a) and (b) above, and recommend which alternative should be chosen.   (3 marks)

(d)   Explain the different roles of a treasury department and a finance department in the context of a new investment, and discuss the need for close liaison between the two departments.   (5 marks)

                                                                              (Total: 20 marks)

22   INVESTMENT APPRAISAL

(a)   Explain and illustrate (using simple numerical examples) the Accounting Rate of Return and Payback approaches to investment appraisal, paying particular attention to the limitations of each approach.   **(7 marks)**

(b)   (i)   Explain the differences between NPV and IRR as methods of Discounted Cash Flow analysis.   **(5 marks)**

(ii)   A company with a cost of capital of 14% is trying to determine the optimal replacement cycle for the laptop computers used by its sales team. The following information is relevant to the decision:

The cost of each laptop is $2,400. Maintenance costs are payable at the end of *each full year* of ownership, but not in the year of replacement, e.g. if the laptop is owned for two years, then the maintenance cost is payable at the end of year 1.

Interval between replacement (years)	Trade-in value ($)	Maintenance cost
1	1,200	Zero
2	800	$75 (payable at end of Year 1)
3	300	$150 (payable at end of Year 2)

Required:

Ignoring taxation, calculate the equivalent annual cost of the three different replacement cycles, and recommend which should be adopted. What other factors should the company take into account when determining the optimal cycle?   **(8 marks)**

(Total: 20 marks)

23   DARN CO (DEC 13 - MODIFIED)

Darn Co has undertaken market research at a cost of $200,000 in order to forecast the future cash flows of an investment project with an expected life of four years, as follows:

Year	1	2	3	4
Sales revenue ($000)	1,250	2,570	6,890	4,530
Costs ($000)	500	1,000	2,500	1,750

These forecast cash flows are before taking account of general inflation of 4.7% per year. The capital cost of the investment project, payable at the start of the first year, will be $2,000,000. The investment project will have zero scrap value at the end of the fourth year. The level of working capital investment at the start of each year is expected to be 10% of the sales revenue in that year.

Tax allowable depreciation would be available on the capital cost of the investment project on a 25% reducing balance basis. Darn Co pays tax on profits at an annual rate of 30% per year, with tax being paid one year in arrears. Darn Co has a nominal (money terms) after-tax cost of capital of 12% per year.

Required:

(a)   Calculate the net present value of the investment project in nominal terms and comment on its financial acceptability.   **(12 marks)**

(b)   Explain ways in which the directors of Darn Co can be encouraged to achieve the objective of maximisation of shareholder wealth.   **(8 marks)**

(Total: 20 marks)

24   CHARM INC

Charm Inc, a software company, has developed a new game, 'Fingo', which it plans to launch in the near future. Sales of the new game are expected to be very strong, following a favourable review by a popular PC magazine. Charm Inc has been informed that the review will give the game a 'Best Buy' recommendation. Sales volumes, production volumes and selling prices for 'Fingo' over its four-year life are expected to be as follows:

Year	1	2	3	4
Sales and production (units)	150,000	70,000	60,000	60,000
Selling price ($ per game)	$25	$24	$23	$22

Financial information on 'Fingo' for the first year of production is as follows:

Direct material cost	$5.40 per game
Other variable production cost	$6.00 per game
Fixed costs	$4.00 per game

Advertising costs to stimulate demand are expected to be $650,000 in the first year of production and $100,000 in the second year of production. No advertising costs are expected in the third and fourth years of production. Fixed costs represent incremental cash fixed production overheads. 'Fingo' will be produced on a new production machine costing $800,000. Tax allowable depreciation will be claimed on a reducing balance basis at a rate of 25%. The machine will have a useful life of four years at the end of which no scrap value is expected.

Charm Inc pays tax on profit at a rate of 30% per year and tax liabilities are settled in the year in which they arise. Charm Inc uses an after-tax discount rate of 10% when appraising new capital investments. Ignore inflation.

Required:

(a)   Calculate the net present value of the proposed investment and comment on your findings.   **(11 marks)**

(b)   Discuss the reasons why the net present value investment appraisal method is preferred to other investment appraisal methods such as payback, return on capital employed and internal rate of return.   **(9 marks)**

(Total: 20 marks)

25   PLAY CO

Play Co manufactures safety surfacing for children's playgrounds. The main raw material required is rubber particles and these are currently purchased from an outside supplier for $3.50 per tonne. This price is contractually guaranteed for the next four years. If the contract is terminated within the next two years, Play Co will be charged an immediate termination penalty of $150,000 which will not be allowed as a tax deductible expense.

The directors are considering investing in equipment that would allow Play Co to manufacture these particles in house by using recycled tyres.

The machine required to process the tyres will cost $400,000, and it is estimated that at the end of year four the machine will have a second-hand value of $50,000.

The costs associated with the new venture are as follows:

Variable costs (per tonne produced) $0.80

Fixed costs (per annum) $192,500

The additional fixed costs include maintenance costs of $40,000 and the additional depreciation charge (calculated on a straight-line basis over the life of the asset) relating to the machine.

All of the above are quoted in current price terms. Inflationary increases are expected as follows:

Variable costs: 3% per annum

Maintenance costs: 5% per annum

Other fixed costs: 2% per annum

The annual demand for the particles (based on the sales forecasts of the company) is:

	Year 1	Year 2	Year 3	Year 4
Demand (in tonnes)	100,000	110,000	130,000	160,000

Profit tax of 30% per year will be payable one year in arrears. Tax allowable depreciation on a 25% reducing balance basis could be claimed on the cost of the equipment, with a balancing allowance being claimed in the fourth year of operation when the machine is disposed of.

Required:

(a)   Using 15% as the after-tax discount rate, advise Play Co on the desirability of purchasing the equipment. (Your workings should be shown to the nearest $000)
(12 marks)

(b)   Identify and briefly discuss FOUR limitations of Net Present Value techniques when applied to investment appraisal. (4 marks)

(c)   Comment on how the project would affect the different stakeholders of Play Co.
(4 marks)

(Total: 20 marks)

26   DUO CO (DEC 07 - MODIFIED) *Walk in the footsteps of a top tutor*

Duo Co needs to increase production capacity to meet increasing demand for an existing product, 'Quago', which is used in food processing. A new machine, with a useful life of four years and a maximum output of 600,000 kg of Quago per year, could be bought for $800,000, payable immediately. The scrap value of the machine after four years would be $30,000. Forecast demand and production of Quago over the next four years is as follows:

Year	1	2	3	4
Demand (kg)	1.4 million	1.5 million	1.6 million	1.7 million

Existing production capacity for Quago is limited to one million kilograms per year and the new machine would only be used for demand additional to this.

The current selling price of Quago is $8.00 per kilogram and the variable cost of materials is $5.00 per kilogram. Other variable costs of production are $1.90 per kilogram. Fixed costs of production associated with the new machine would be $240,000 in the first year of production, increasing by $20,000 per year in each subsequent year of operation.

Duo Co pays tax one year in arrears at an annual rate of 30% and can claim tax allowable depreciation (tax-allowable depreciation) on a 25% reducing balance basis. A balancing allowance is claimed in the final year of operation.

Duo Co uses its after-tax weighted average cost of capital when appraising investment projects. It has a cost of equity of 11% and a before-tax cost of debt of 8.6%. The long-term finance of the company, on a market-value basis, consists of 80% equity and 20% debt.

Required:

(a) Calculate the net present value of buying the new machine and advise on the acceptability of the proposed purchase (work to the nearest $1,000).   **(13 marks)**

(b) Explain the difference between risk and uncertainty in the context of investment appraisal, and describe how sensitivity analysis and probability analysis can be used to incorporate risk into the investment appraisal process.   **(7 marks)**

(Total: 20 marks)

27   OKM CO (JUNE 10 - MODIFIED)

The following draft appraisal of a proposed investment project has been prepared for the finance director of OKM Co by a trainee accountant. The project is consistent with the current business operations of OKM Co.

Year	1	2	3	4	5
Sales (units/yr)	250,000	400,000	500,000	250,000	
	$000	$000	$000	$000	$000
Contribution	1,330	2,128	2,660	1,330	
Fixed costs	(530)	(562)	(596)	(631)	
Depreciation	(438)	(438)	(437)	(437)	
Interest payments	(200)	(200)	(200)	(200)	
Taxable profit	162	928	1,427	62	
Taxation		(49)	(278)	(428)	(19)
Profit after tax	162	879	1,149	(366)	(19)
Scrap value				250	
After-tax cash flows	162	879	1,149	(116)	(19)
Discount at 10%	0.909	0.826	0.751	0.683	0.621
Present values	147	726	863	(79)	(12)

Net present value = 1,645,000 – 2,000,000 = ($355,000) so reject the project. The following information was included with the draft investment appraisal:

(1)   The initial investment is $2 million

(2)   Selling price: $12/unit (current price terms), selling price inflation is 5% per year

(3)   Variable cost: $7/unit (current price terms), variable cost inflation is 4% per year

(4)   Fixed overhead costs: $500,000/year (current price terms), fixed cost inflation is 6% per year

(5) $200,000/year of the fixed costs are development costs that have already been incurred and are being recovered by an annual charge to the project

(6)   Investment financing is by a $2 million loan at a fixed interest rate of 10% per year

(7)   OKM Co can claim 25% reducing balance tax allowable depreciation on this investment and pays taxation one year in arrears at a rate of 30% per year

(8)   The scrap value of machinery at the end of the four-year project is $250,000 9. The real weighted average cost of capital of OKM Co is 7% per year

(10) The general rate of inflation is expected to be 4.7% per year

Required:

(a)   Identify and comment on any errors in the investment appraisal prepared by the trainee accountant.   (5 marks)

(b)   Prepare a revised calculation of the net present value of the proposed investment project and comment on the project's acceptability.   (10 marks)

(c)   Discuss the problems faced when undertaking investment appraisal in the following areas and comment on how these problems can be overcome:

(i)   an investment project has several internal rates of return

(ii)   the business risk of an investment project is significantly different from the business risk of current operations.   (5 marks)

(Total: 20 marks)

28   BRT CO (JUNE 11 - MODIFIED)

BRT Co has developed a new confectionery line that can be sold for $5·00 per box and that is expected to have continuing popularity for many years. The Finance Director has proposed that investment in the new product should be evaluated over a four-year time-horizon, even though sales would continue after the fourth year, on the grounds that cash flows after four years are too uncertain to be included in the evaluation. The variable and fixed costs (both in current price terms) will depend on sales volume, as follows.

Sales volume (boxes)	less than 1 million	1–1.9 million	2–2.9 million	3–3.9 million
Variable cost ($ per box)	2.80	3.00	3.00	3.05
Total fixed costs ($)	1 million	1.8 million	2.8 million	3.8 million

Forecast sales volumes are as follows.

Year	1	2	3	4
Demand (boxes)	0.7 million	1.6 million	2.1 million	3.0 million

The production equipment for the new confectionery line would cost $2 million and an additional initial investment of $750,000 would be needed for working capital. Tax allowable depreciation (tax-allowable depreciation) on a 25% reducing balance basis could be claimed on the cost of equipment. Profit tax of 30% per year will be payable one year in arrears. A balancing allowance would be claimed in the fourth year of operation.

The average general level of inflation is expected to be 3% per year and selling price, variable costs, fixed costs and working capital would all experience inflation of this level. BRT Co uses a nominal after-tax cost of capital of 12% to appraise new investment projects.

Required:

(a)   Assuming that production only lasts for four years, calculate the net present value of investing in the new product using a nominal terms approach and advise on its financial acceptability (work to the nearest $1,000).   **(13 marks)**

(b)   Discuss THREE ways of incorporating risk into the investment appraisal process.

                                                                                                    (7 marks)

                                                                                         (Total: 20 marks)

29   UMUNAT INC

Umunat Inc is considering investing $50,000 in a new machine with an expected life of five years. The machine will have no scrap value at the end of five years. It is expected that 20,000 units will be sold each year at a selling price of $3.00 per unit. Variable production costs are expected to be $1.65 per unit, while incremental fixed costs, mainly the wages of a maintenance engineer, are expected to be $10,000 per year. Umunat Inc uses a discount rate of 12% for investment appraisal purposes and expects investment projects to recover their initial investment within two years.

Required:

(a)   Explain why risk and uncertainty should be considered in the investment appraisal process.   **(4 marks)**

(b)   Evaluate the sensitivity of the project's net present value to a change in the following project variables:

(i)   sales volume

(ii)   sales price

(iii) variable cost

and discuss the use of sensitivity analysis as a way of evaluating project risk.

                                                                                                    (10 marks)

(c)   Upon further investigation it is found that there is a significant chance that the expected sales volume of 20,000 units per year will not be achieved. The sales manager of Umunat Inc suggests that sales volumes could depend on expected economic states that could be assigned the following probabilities:

Economic state	Poor	Normal	Good
Probability	0.3	0.6	0.1
Annual sale volume (units)	17,500	20,000	22,500

Required:

Calculate and comment on the expected net present value of the project. **(6 marks)**

                                                                                         (Total: 20 marks)

30 VICTORY

Victory Co is considering the purchase of new equipment which would enable the company to expand its operations. The equipment will cost $1.2 million and have a three-year life, at the end of which it will have a scrap value of $600,000.

The equipment will mean Victory requires further factory space at an annual rental of $80,000, payable in advance, with the first payment being made on the day the equipment is purchased.

Further annual fixed costs charged to the project will be $715,000 in total. Amongst other things, this includes:

- $86,000 of bank interest payable on the loan to cover the cost of the equipment.

- $74,000 of costs allocated out of head office overheads.

- A depreciation charge for the new machinery that has been calculated using the straight-line method over the life of the machine.

Additional annual sales are expected to be 60,000 units per annum in each of the three years. Each unit will sell for $40 and has a variable production cost of $25.

A further investment of $340,000 will be required for working capital. This will need to be in place at the start of the year. This will increase to $400,000 in the following year and $450,000 in the year after that. This working capital investment will be fully recovered at the end of the project.

If Victory Co buys the new equipment it can claim tax allowable depreciation on the investment on a 25% reducing balance basis. The company pays taxation in the year to which it relates at an annual rate of 30%. Victory Co uses a cost of capital of 10% per annum for appraising its investments.

Required:

(a) **Prepare a forecast of the annual after-tax cash flows of the investment and calculate and comment on its net present value**   **(11 marks)**

(b) **Calculate the sensitivity of your answer to part (a) to changes in the expected annual sales (in units) and discuss the implications of your findings to Victory Co**

(5 marks)

(c) **Describe two other methods (excluding sensitivity analysis) that a company can use to incorporate either risk or uncertainty when appraising investments**   **(4 marks)**

(Total: 20 marks)

 Online question assistance

31 CJ CO (DEC 10 - MODIFIED)

CJ Co is a profitable company which is financed by equity with a market value of $180 million and by debt with a market value of $45 million. The company is considering an investment project, as follows.

Project A

This project is an expansion of existing business costing $3·5 million, payable at the start of the project, which will increase annual sales by 750,000 units. Information on unit selling price and costs is as follows:

Selling price: $2.00 per unit (current price terms)

Selling costs: $0.04 per unit (current price terms)

Variable costs: $0.80 per unit (current price terms)

Selling price inflation and selling cost inflation are expected to be 5% per year and variable cost inflation is expected to be 4% per year. Additional initial investment in working capital of $250,000 will also be needed and this is expected to increase in line with general inflation.

Other information

CJ Co has a nominal weighted average after-tax cost of capital of 10% and pays profit tax one year in arrears at an annual rate of 30%. The company can claim tax allowable depreciation (tax-allowable depreciation) on a 25% reducing balance basis on the initial investment in both projects.

Risk-free rate of return: 4%

Equity risk premium: 6%

General rate of inflation: 4.5% per year

Directors' views on investment appraisal

The directors of CJ Co require that all investment projects should be evaluated using either payback period or return on capital employed (accounting rate of return). The target payback period of the company is two years and the target return on capital employed is 20%, which is the current return on capital employed of CJ Co. A project is accepted if it satisfies either of these investment criteria.

The directors also require all investment projects to be evaluated over a four-year planning period, ignoring any scrap value or working capital recovery, with a balancing allowance (if any) being claimed at the end of the fourth year of operation.

Required:

(a) Calculate the net present value of Project A and advise on its acceptability if the project were to be appraised using this method.   **(12 marks)**

(b) Critically discuss the directors' views on investment appraisal.   **(8 marks)**

     (Total: 20 marks)

32 BASRIL

Basril Inc is reviewing investment proposals that have been submitted by divisional managers. The investment funds of the company are limited to $800,000 in the current year. Details of three possible investments, none of which can be delayed, are given below.

Project 1

An investment of $300,000 in work station assessments. Each assessment would be on an individual employee basis and would lead to savings in labour costs from increased efficiency and from reduced absenteeism due to work-related illness. Savings in labour costs from these assessments in money terms are expected to be as follows:

Year	1	2	3	4	5
Cash flows (£000)	85	90	95	100	95

Project 2

An investment of $450,000 in individual workstations for staff that is expected to reduce administration costs by $140,800 per annum in money terms for the next five years.

Project 3

An investment of $400,000 in new ticket machines. Net cash savings of $120,000 per annum are expected in current price terms and these are expected to increase by 3.6% per annum due to inflation during the five-year life of the machines.

Basril Inc has a money cost of capital of 12% and taxation should be ignored.

Required:

(a) Determine the best way for Basril Inc to invest the available funds and calculate the resultant NPV:

    (i)   on the assumption that each of the three projects is divisible

    (ii)   on the assumption that none of the projects are divisible.   **(10 marks)**

(b) Explain how the NPV investment appraisal method is applied in situations where capital is rationed.   **(4 marks)**

(c) Discuss the reasons why capital rationing may arise.   **(6 marks)**

         (Total: 20 marks)

33 ASOP CO (DEC 09 - MODIFIED)

ASOP Co is considering an investment in new technology that will reduce operating costs through increasing energy efficiency and decreasing pollution. The new technology will cost $1 million and have a four-year life, at the end of which it will have a scrap value of $100,000.

A licence fee of $104,000 is payable at the end of the first year. This licence fee will increase by 4% per year in each subsequent year.

The new technology is expected to reduce operating costs by $5.80 per unit in current price terms. This reduction in operating costs is before taking account of expected inflation of 5% per year.

Forecast production volumes over the life of the new technology are expected to be as follows:

Year	1	2	3	4
Production (units per year)	60,000	75,000	95,000	80,000

If ASOP Co bought the new technology, it would finance the purchase through a four-year loan paying interest at an annual before-tax rate of 8.6% per year.

Alternatively, ASOP Co could lease the new technology. The company would pay four annual lease rentals of $380,000 per year, payable in advance at the start of each year. The annual lease rentals include the cost of the licence fee.

If ASOP Co buys the new technology it can claim tax allowable depreciation on the investment on a 25% reducing balance basis. The company pays taxation one year in arrears at an annual rate of 30%. ASOP Co has an after-tax weighted average cost of capital of 11% per year.

Required:

(a)   Based on financing cash flows only, calculate and determine whether ASOP Co should lease or buy the new technology.   **(11 marks)**

(b)   Using a nominal terms approach, calculate the net present value of buying the new technology and advise whether ASOP Co should undertake the proposed investment.   **(6 marks)**

(c)   Discuss and illustrate how ASOP Co can use equivalent annual cost or equivalent annual benefit to choose between new technologies with different expected lives.
                                                                      (3 marks)

                                                                      (Total: 20 marks)

BUSINESS FINANCE AND COST OF CAPITAL

34   FMY

FMY Co manufactures glass bottles for the drinks industry. It has been trading for 15 years. The company at present has no long-term debt although it does have an overdraft facility that is used for short-term financing needs.

The company is forecasting post-tax earnings of $4.5 million on revenue of $32 million for the current year. These sales and earnings levels are expected to continue unless new investment is undertaken. The Managing Director (MD), who is also a significant shareholder, is planning a major expansion programme that will require raising $5 million of new finance for capital investment.

This investment yields a positive net present value of $1.2 million when evaluated at the company's post-tax cost of capital of 12%, and is expected to increase post-tax earnings by $1m per annum (before considering the method of financing the expansion).

The Board is considering two alternative methods of financing this expansion:

(1)   A 1 for 4 rights issue to existing shareholders. There are currently 10 million shares in issue, each of which is trading at $2.20.

(2)   Medium-term (five years) debt, interest rate fixed at 8.6%, secured on the company's non-current assets, mainly land and buildings.

The company pays tax one year in arrears at 30%.

Required:

(a) Comment on the effect of each suggested method of financing on the valuation of the company. Your answer should refer to capital structure theories amongst other things. **(12 marks)**

(b) Explain the major differences between Islamic finance and other conventional forms of finance such as those being considered by FMY Co. Identify, and briefly discuss, two Islamic financial instruments that would be of use to FMY Co in the above situation. **(8 marks)**

(Total: 20 marks)

35   FENCE CO (JUNE 14 - MODIFIED)

The equity beta of Fence Co is 0.9 and the company has issued 10 million ordinary shares. The market value of each ordinary share is $7.50. The company is also financed by 7% bonds with a nominal value of $100 per bond, which will be redeemed in seven years' time at nominal value. The bonds have a total nominal value of $14 million. Interest on the bonds has just been paid and the current market value of each bond is $107.14.

Fence Co plans to invest in a project which is different to its existing business operations and has identified a company in the same business area as the project, Hex Co. The equity beta of Hex Co is 1.2 and the company has an equity market value of $54 million. The market value of the debt of Hex Co is $12 million.

The risk-free rate of return is 4% per year and the average return on the stock market is 11% per year. Both companies pay corporation tax at a rate of 20% per year.

Required:

(a) Calculate the current weighted average cost of capital of Fence Co. **(7 marks)**

(b) Calculate a cost of equity which could be used in appraising the new project. **(4 marks)**

(c) Explain the difference between systematic and unsystematic risk in relation to portfolio theory and the capital asset pricing model. **(4 marks)**

(d) Discuss the significance of the efficient market hypothesis (EMH) for the financial manager. **(5 marks)**

(Total: 20 marks)

36   RWF

RWF Co has stated the following corporate objectives:

–   Maintain gearing (debt/equity) at or below 60%

–   Provide real growth in earnings per share

RWF Co is considering a potential project which should expand sales and automate production but is unsure how to fund the $9 million required. It can either carry out a rights issue at $6 per share or issue additional debt at a pre-tax cost of 10%.

The most recent statement of profit or loss and forecasts which include the impact of the project and financing alternatives are shown below:

Statement of profit or loss:	$000	$000	$000
	Current	Forecast Debt issue	Forecast Rights issue
Sales	70,000	85,000	85,000
Variable cost of sales	32,000	34,000	34,000
Fixed cost of sales	9,000	16,000	16,000
Gross profit	29,000	35,000	35,000
Administration costs	16,000	17,000	17,000
Profit before interest and tax	13,000	18,000	18,000
Interest	4,000	4,900	4,000
Profit before tax	9,000	13,100	14,000
Taxation	2,700	3,930	4,200
Profit after tax	6,300	9,170	9,800
Dividends	2,000	2,500	3,000
Retained earnings	4,300	6,670	6,800

At the end of the most recent year RWF Co had 12 million shares, share capital and reserves totalling $90 million and $50 million of 8% debentures. General inflation is currently 5%.

Required:

(a)   **Evaluate the two finance options being considered and recommend which option RWF Co should accept. You should consider the impact each finance option will have on the ability of the company to achieve its stated objectives. The impact on two other key ratios of the business (including operating gearing) should also be considered.** **(15 marks)**

(b)   **Provide a critical discussion of the corporate objectives which have been stated by RWF Co and recommend how the company could improve its corporate objectives.** **(5 marks)**

(Total: 20 marks)

 Online question assistance

37   BAR CO (DEC 11 - MODIFIED)

Bar Co is a stock exchange listed company that is concerned by its current level of debt finance. It plans to make a rights issue and to use the funds raised to pay off some of its debt. The rights issue will be at a 20% discount to its current ex-dividend share price of $7.50 per share and Bar Co plans to raise $90 million. Bar Co believes that paying off some of its debt will not affect its price/earnings ratio, which is expected to remain constant.

Statement of profit or loss information

	$m
Turnover	472
Cost of sales	423
Profit before interest and tax	49
Interest	10
Profit before tax	39
Tax	12
Profit after tax	27

Statement of financial position information

	$m
Equity	
Ordinary shares ($1 nominal)	60
Reserves	80
	140
Long-term liabilities	
8% bonds ($100 nominal)	125
	265

The 8% bonds are currently trading at $112.50 per $100 bond and bondholders have agreed that they will allow Bar Co to buy back the bonds at this market value. Bar Co pays tax at a rate of 30% per year.

Required:

(a)   Calculate the theoretical ex rights price per share of Bar Co following the rights issue. **(3 marks)**

(b)   Calculate and discuss whether using the cash raised by the rights issue to buy back bonds is likely to be financially acceptable to the shareholders of Bar Co, commenting in your answer on the belief that the current price/earnings ratio will remain constant. **(7 marks)**

(c)   Compare and contrast the financial objectives of a stock exchange listed company such as Bar Co and the financial objectives of a not-for-profit organisation such as a large charity. **(10 marks)**

(Total: 20 marks)

38   NUGFER (DEC 10 - MODIFIED)

The following financial position statement as at 30 November 2010 refers to Nugfer Co, a stock exchange-listed company, which wishes to raise $200m in cash in order to acquire a competitor.

	$m	$m	$m
Assets			
Non-current assets			300
Current assets			211
Total assets			511
Equity and liabilities			
Share capital		100	
Retained earnings		121	
Total equity			221
Non-current liabilities			
Long-term borrowings		100	
Current liabilities			
Trade payables	30		
Short-term borrowings	160		
Total current liabilities		190	
Total liabilities			290
Total equity and liabilities			511

The recent performance of Nugfer Co in profitability terms is as follows:

Year ending 30 November	2007	2008	2009	2010
	$m	$m	$m	$m
Revenue	122.6	127.3	156.6	189.3
Operating profit	41.7	43.3	50.1	56.7
Finance charges (interest)	6.0	6.2	12.5	18.8
Profit before tax	35.7	37.1	37.6	37.9
Profit after tax	25.0	26.0	26.3	26.5

Notes:

(1)   The long-term borrowings are 6% bonds that are repayable in 2012

(2)   The short-term borrowings consist of an overdraft at an annual interest rate of 8% 3. The current assets do not include any cash deposits

(4)   Nugfer Co has not paid any dividends in the last four years

(5)   The number of ordinary shares issued by the company has not changed in recent years

(6)   The target company has no debt finance and its forecast profit before interest and tax for 2011 is $28 million

Required:

(a)   Evaluate suitable methods of raising the $200 million required by Nugfer Co, supporting your evaluation with both analysis and critical discussion.   **(16 marks)**

(b)   Briefly explain the factors that will influence the rate of interest charged on a new issue of bonds.   **(4 marks)**

(Total: 20 marks)

39   SPOT CO (DEC 13 - MODIFIED)

Spot Co is considering how to finance the acquisition of a machine costing $750,000 with an operating life of five years. There are two financing options.

Option 1

The machine could be leased for an annual lease payment of $155,000 per year, payable at the start of each year.

Option 2

The machine could be bought for $750,000 using a bank loan charging interest at an annual rate of 7% per year. At the end of five years, the machine would have a scrap value of 10% of the purchase price. If the machine is bought, maintenance costs of $20,000 per year would be incurred.

Taxation must be ignored.

Required:

(a)   Evaluate whether Spot Co should use leasing or borrowing as a source of finance, explaining the evaluation method which you use.   **(10 marks)**

(b)   Discuss the attractions of leasing as a source of both short-term and long-term finance.   **(5 marks)**

(c)   In Islamic finance, explain briefly the concept of riba (interest) and how returns are made by Islamic financial instruments.   **(5 marks)**

(Total: 20 marks)

40   ECHO CO (DEC 07 - MODIFIED) *Walk in the footsteps of a top tutor*

The following financial information relates to Echo Co:

Statement of profit or loss information for the last year

	$m
Profit before interest and tax	12
Interest	3
Profit before tax	9
Income tax expense	3
Profit for the period	6
Dividends	2
Retained profit for the period	4

Statement of financial position information as at the end of the last year

	$m	$m
Ordinary shares, par value 50c	5	
Retained earnings	15	
Total equity		20
8% loan notes, redeemable in three years' time		30
Total equity and non-current liabilities		50

Average data on companies similar to Echo Co:

Interest coverage ratio	8 times
Long-term debt/equity (book value basis)	80%

The board of Echo Co is considering several proposals that have been made by its finance director. Each proposal is independent of any other proposal.

Proposal A

The current dividend per share should be increased by 20% in order to make the company more attractive to equity investors.

Proposal B

A bond issue should be made in order to raise $15 million of new debt capital. Although there are no investment opportunities currently available, the cash raised would be invested on a short-term basis until a suitable investment opportunity arose. The loan notes would pay interest at a rate of 10% per year and be redeemable in eight years time at par.

Proposal C

A 1 for 4 rights issue should be made at a 20% discount to the current share price of $2.30 per share in order to reduce gearing and the financial risk of the company.

Required:

(a) Analyse and discuss Proposal A. (5 marks)

(b) Evaluate and discuss Proposal B. (8 marks)

(c) Calculate the theoretical ex rights price per share and the amount of finance that would be raised under Proposal C. Evaluate and discuss the proposal to use these funds to reduce gearing and financial risk. (7 marks)

(Total: 20 marks)

41 ZIGTO CO (JUNE 2012 - MODIFIED)

Zigto Co is a medium-sized company whose ordinary shares are all owned by the members of one family. It has recently begun exporting to a European country and expects to receive €500,000 in six months' time. The prospect of increased exports to the European country means that Zigto Co needs to expand its existing business operations in order to be able to meet future orders. All of the family members are in favour of the planned expansion, but none are in a position to provide additional finance. The company is therefore seeking to raise external finance of approximately $1 million. At the same time, the company plans to take action to hedge the exchange rate risk arising from its European exports.

Zigto Co could put cash on deposit in the European country at an annual interest rate of 3% per year, and borrow at 5% per year. The company could put cash on deposit in its home country at an annual interest rate of 4% per year, and borrow at 6% per year. Inflation in the European country is 3% per year, while inflation in the home country of Zigto Co is 4.5% per year.

The following exchange rates are currently available to Zigto Co:

Current spot exchange rate	2.000 euro per $
Six-month forward exchange rate	1.990 euro per $
One-year forward exchange rate	1.981 euro per $

Required:

(a) Discuss the factors that Zigto Co should consider when choosing a source of debt finance and the factors that may be considered by providers of finance in deciding how much to lend to the company. (7 marks)

(b) Explain the nature of a *mudaraba* contract and discuss briefly how this form of Islamic finance could be used to finance the planned business expansion. (5 marks)

(c) Calculate whether a forward exchange contract or a money market hedge would be financially preferred by Zigto Co to hedge its future euro receipt. (5 marks)

(d) Calculate the one-year expected (future) spot rate predicted by purchasing power parity theory and explain briefly the relationship between the expected (future) spot rate and the current forward exchange rate. (3 marks)

(Total: 20 marks)

42 PAVLON

(a) Pavlon Inc has recently obtained a listing on the Stock Exchange. 90% of the company's shares were previously owned by members of one family but, since the listing, approximately 60% of the issued shares have been owned by other investors.

Pavlon's earnings and dividends for the five years prior to the listing are detailed below:

Years prior to listing	Profit after tax ($)	Dividend per share (cents)
5	1,800,000	3.6
4	2,400,000	4.8
3	3,850,000	6.16
2	4,100,000	6.56
1	4,450,000	7.12
Current year	5,500,000(estimate)	

The number of issued ordinary shares was increased by 25% three years prior to the listing and by 50% at the time of the listing. The company's authorised capital is currently $25,000,000 in 25¢ ordinary shares, of which 40,000,000 shares have been issued. The market value of the company's equity is $78,000,000.

The board of directors is discussing future dividend policy. An interim dividend of 3.16 cents per share was paid immediately prior to the listing and the finance director has suggested a final dividend of 2.34 cents per share.

The company's declared objective is to maximise shareholder wealth.

Required:

(i) Comment upon the nature of the company's dividend policy prior to the listing and discuss whether such a policy is likely to be suitable for a company listed on the Stock Exchange. **(5 marks)**

(ii) Discuss whether the proposed final dividend of 2.34 cents is likely to be an appropriate dividend:

– If the majority of shares are owned by wealthy private individuals; and

– If the majority of shares are owned by institutional investors.

(10 marks)

(b) The company's profit after tax is generally expected to increase by 15% per year for three years, and 8% per year after that. Pavlon's cost of equity capital is estimated to be 12% per year. Dividends may be assumed to grow at the same rate as profits.

Required:

Use the dividend valuation model to give calculations to indicate whether Pavlon's shares are currently under- or over-valued. **(5 marks)**

(Total: 20 marks)

43 ARWIN

Arwin plans to raise $5m in order to expand its existing chain of retail outlets. It can raise the finance by issuing 10% loan stock redeemable in ten years' time, or by a rights issue at $4.00 per share. The current financial statements of Arwin are as follows:

Statement of profit or loss for the last year

	$000
Sales revenue	50,000
Cost of sales	30,000
Gross profit	20,000
Administration costs	14,000
Profit before interest and tax	6,000
Interest	300
Profit before tax	5,700
Taxation at 30%	1,710
Profit after tax	3,990

Changes in equity

	$000
Dividends	2,394
Net change in equity (retained profits)	1,596

Statement of financial position

	$000
Net non-current assets	20,100
Net current assets	4,960
	25,060
Ordinary shares, par value 25¢	2,500
Retained profit	20,060
12% loan stock (redeemable in six years)	2,500
	25,060

The expansion of business is expected to increase sales revenue by 12% in the first year. Variable cost of sales makes up 85% of cost of sales. Administration costs will increase by 5% due to new staff appointments. Arwin has a policy of paying out 60% of profit after tax as dividends and has no overdraft.

Required:

(a) For each financing proposal, prepare the forecast statement of profit or loss after one additional year of operation. **(5 marks)**

(b) Evaluate and comment on the effects of each financing proposal on the following:

    (i)   **Financial gearing**

    (ii)   **Operational gearing**

    (iii) **Interest cover**

    (iv) **Earnings per share.**   **(12 marks)**

(c) Comment on the view that businesses are unlikely to have high financial gearing and high operating gearing **(3 marks)**

(Total: 20 marks)

44 ASSOCIATED INTERNATIONAL SUPPLIES CO

The following are summary financial statements for Associated International Supplies Co.

	20X4	20X9
	$000	$000
Non-current assets	115	410
Current assets	650	1,000
Total assets	765	1,410
Capital and reserves	210	270
Non-current liabilities	42	158
Current liabilities	513	982
	765	1,410
Sales revenue	1,200	3,010
Cost of sales, expenses and interest	1,102	2,860
Profit before tax	98	150
Tax and distributions	33	133
Retained earnings	65	17

Notes: Cost of sales was $530,000 for 20X4 and $1,330,000 for 20X9.

Trade receivables are 50% of current assets; trade payables 25% of current liabilities for both years.

Required:

(a)   You are a consultant advising Associated International Supplies Co. Using suitable financial ratios, and paying particular attention to growth and liquidity, write a report on the significant changes faced by the company since 20X4.

The report should also comment on the capacity of the company to continue trading, together with any other factors considered appropriate. An appendix to the report should be used to outline your calculations.   **(15 marks)**

(b)   Explain and evaluate the sources of equity finance available to small businesses for non-current assets.   **(5 marks)**

                                                                                             (Total: 20 marks)

45   AMH CO (JUNE 13 MODIFIED)

 Timed question with online tutor debrief

AMH Co wishes to calculate its current cost of capital for use as a discount rate in investment appraisal. The following financial information relates to AMH Co:

Financial position statement extracts as at 31 December 2012

	$000	$000
Equity		
Ordinary shares (nominal value 50 cents)	4,000	
Reserves	18,000	22,000
Long-term liabilities		
4% Preference shares (nominal value $1)	3,000	
7% Bonds redeemable after six years	3,000	
Long-term bank loan	1,000	7,000
		29,000

The ordinary shares of AMH Co have an ex div market value of $4.70 per share and an ordinary dividend of 36.3 cents per share has just been paid. Historic dividend payments have been as follows:

Year	2008	2009	2010	2011
Dividends per share (cents)	30.9	32.2	33.6	35.0

The preference shares of AMH Co are not redeemable and have an ex div market value of 40 cents per share. The 7% bonds are redeemable at a 5% premium to their nominal value of $100 per bond and have an ex interest market value of $104.50 per bond. The bank loan has a variable interest rate that has averaged 4% per year in recent years.

AMH Co pays profit tax at an annual rate of 30% per year.

Required:

(a)   Calculate the market value weighted average cost of capital of AMH Co.   **(12 marks)**

(b)   Discuss how the capital asset pricing model can be used to calculate a project-specific cost of equity for AMH Co, referring in your discussion to the key concepts of systematic risk, business risk and financial risk.   **(8 marks)**

(Total: 20 marks)

 Calculate your allowed time, allocate the time to the separate parts

46   GTK INC (JUNE 07 - MODIFIED) *Walk in the footsteps of a top tutor*

The finance director of GTK Inc is preparing its capital budget for the forthcoming period and is examining a number of capital investment proposals that have been received from its subsidiaries. Details of these proposals are as follows:

Proposal 1

Division A has requested that it be allowed to invest $500,000 in solar panels, which would be fitted to the roof of its production facility, in order to reduce its dependency on oil as an energy source.

The solar panels would save energy costs of $700 per day but only on sunny days. The Division has estimated the following probabilities of sunny days in each year.

	Number of sunny days	Probability
Scenario 1	100	0.3
Scenario 2	125	0.6
Scenario 3	150	0.1

Each scenario is expected to persist indefinitely, i.e. if there are 100 sunny days in the first year, there will be 100 sunny days in every subsequent year. Maintenance costs for the solar panels are expected to be $2,000 per month for labour and replacement parts, irrespective of the number of sunny days per year. The solar panels are expected to be used indefinitely.

Proposal 2

Division C has requested approval and funding for a new product which it has been secretly developing, Product RPG. Product development and market research costs of $350,000 have already been incurred and are now due for payment. $300,000 is needed for new machinery, which will be a full scale version of the current pilot plant. Advertising takes place in the first year only and would cost $100,000. Annual cash inflow of $100,000, net of all production costs but before taking account of advertising costs, is expected to be generated for a five-year period. After five years Product RPG would be retired and replaced with a more technologically advanced model. The machinery used for producing Product RPG would be sold for $30,000 at that time.

Other information

GTK Inc is a profitable, listed company with several million dollars of shareholders' funds, a small overdraft and no long-term debt. For profit calculation purposes, GTK Inc depreciates assets on a straight-line basis over their useful economic life. The company can claim tax-allowable depreciation on machinery on a 25% reducing balance basis and pays tax on profit at an annual rate of 30% in the year in which the liability arises. GTK Inc has a before-tax cost of capital of 10%, an after-tax cost of capital of 8% and a target return on capital employed of 15%.

Required:

(a)   For the proposed investment in solar panels (Proposal 1), calculate:

(i)   the net present value for each expected number of sunny days

(ii)   the overall expected net present value of the proposal

Comment on your findings. Ignore taxation in this part of the question.   **(10 marks)**

(b)   Assuming GTK Inc wishes to raise $1.1 million, discuss how equity finance or traded debt (bonds) might be raised, clearly indicating which source of finance you recommend and the reasons for your recommendation.   **(10 marks)**

(Total: 20 marks)

47   TFR (JUNE 07 - MODIFIED)

TFR is a small, profitable, owner-managed company which is seeking finance for a planned expansion. A local bank has indicated that it may be prepared to offer a loan of $100,000 at a fixed annual rate of 9%. TFR would repay $25,000 of the capital each year for the next four years.

Annual interest would be calculated on the opening balance at the start of each year. Current financial information on TFR is as follows:

Current turnover:	$210,000
Net profit margin:	20%
Annual taxation rate:	25%
Average overdraft:	$20,000
Average interest on overdraft:	10% per year
Dividend payout ratio:	50%
Shareholders' funds:	$200,000
Market value of non-current assets	$180,000

As a result of the expansion, turnover would increase by $45,000 per year for each of the next four years, while net profit margin would remain unchanged. No tax allowable depreciation would arise from investment of the amount borrowed.

TFR currently has no other debt than the existing and continuing overdraft and has no cash or near-cash investments. The non-current assets consist largely of the building from which the company conducts its business. The current dividend payout ratio has been maintained for several years.

Required:

(a) Assuming that TFR is granted the loan, calculate the following ratios for TFR for each of the next five years:

    (i)   interest cover

    (ii)   medium to long-term debt/equity ratio

    (iii) return on equity

    (iv) return on capital employed.   **(12 marks)**

(b) Comment on the financial implications for TFR of accepting the bank loan on the terms indicated above.   **(8 marks)**

      (Total: 20 marks)

48 GXG CO (JUNE 13 - MODIFIED)

GXG Co is an e-business which designs and sells computer applications (apps) for mobile phones. The company needs to raise $3,200,000 for research and development and is considering two financing options.

Option 1

GXG Co could suspend dividends for two years, and then pay dividends of 25 cents per share from the end of the third year, increasing dividends annually by 4% per year in subsequent years. Dividends in recent years have grown by 3% per year.

Option 2

GXG Co could issue $3,200,000 of bonds paying annual interest of 6%, redeemable after ten years at par.

Recent financial information relating to GXG Co is as follows:

	$000
Operating profit	3,450
Interest	200
Profit before taxation	3,250
Taxation	650
Profit after taxation	2,600
Dividends	1,600
	$000
Ordinary shares (nominal value 50 cents)	5,000

Under options 2 and 3, the funds invested would earn a before-tax return of 18% per year.

The profit tax rate paid by the company is 20% per year.

GXG Co has a cost of equity of 9% per year, which is expected to remain constant.

Required:

(a) Using the dividend valuation model, calculate the value of GXG Co under option 1, and advise whether option 1 will be acceptable to shareholders. **(6 marks)**

(b) Calculate the effect on earnings per share and interest cover of the proposal to raise finance by issuing new debt (option 2), and comment on your findings.

(5 marks)

(c) Discuss the factors to be considered in choosing between traded bonds, new equity issued via a placing and venture capital as sources of finance. **(9 marks)**

(Total: 20 marks)

49 ILL COLLEAGUE

A colleague has been taken ill. Your managing director has asked you to take over from the colleague and to provide urgently needed estimates of the discount rate to be used in appraising a large new capital investment. You have been given your colleague's working notes, which you believe to be numerically accurate.

Working notes

Estimates for the next five years (annual averages)

Stock market total return on equity	16%
Own company dividend yield	7%
Own company share price rise	14%
Own company equity Beta	1.4
Growth rate of own company earnings	12%
Growth rate of own company dividends	11%
Growth rate of own company sales	13%
Treasury bill yield	12%

The company's gearing level (by market values) is 1:2 debt to equity, and after-tax earnings available to ordinary shareholders in the most recent year were $5,400,000, of which $2,140,000 was distributed as ordinary dividends. The company has 10 million issued ordinary shares, which are currently trading on the Stock Exchange at 321 cents. Corporate debt may be assumed to be risk-free. The company pays tax at 35% and personal taxation may be ignored.

Required:

(a) Estimate the company's weighted average cost of capital using:

(i) the dividend valuation model

(ii) the capital asset pricing model.

State clearly any assumptions that you make.

Under what circumstances would these models be expected to produce similar values for the weighted average cost of capital? **(9 marks)**

(b)   You are now informed that the proposed investment is a major diversification into a new industry, and are provided with the following information about the new industry:

Average industry gearing level (by market value)	1:3 debt to equity
Average β equity	1.50

Using any relevant information from parts (a) and (b), recommend which cost of equity should be used for the investment. Any relevant calculations not included in your answer to part (a) should form part of your answer.   **(6 marks)**

(c)   Discuss the problems estimating the appropriate data inputs for using the capital asset pricing model in investment appraisal.   **(5 marks)**

(Total: 20 marks)

50   AQR CO (JUNE 11 - MODIFIED)

The finance director of AQR Co has heard that the market value of the company will increase if the weighted average cost of capital of the company is decreased. The company, which is listed on a stock exchange, has 100 million shares in issue and the current ex div ordinary share price is $2·50 per share. AQR Co also has in issue bonds with a book value of $60 million and their current ex interest market price is $104 per $100 bond. The current after-tax cost of debt of AQR Co is 7% and the tax rate is 30%.

The recent dividends per share of the company are as follows.

Year	2006	2007	2008	2009	2010
Dividend per share (cents)	19.38	20.20	20.41	21.02	21.80

The finance director proposes to decrease the weighted average cost of capital of AQR Co, and hence increase its market value, by issuing $40 million of bonds at their par value of $100 per bond. These bonds would pay annual interest of 8% before tax and would be redeemed at a 5% premium to par after 10 years.

Required:

(a)   Calculate the market value after-tax weighted average cost of capital of AQR Co in the following circumstances:

   (i)   before the new issue of bonds takes place

   (ii)   after the new issue of bonds takes place.

   Comment on your findings.   **(12 marks)**

(b)   Discuss the director's view that issuing traded bonds will decrease the weighted average cost of capital of AQR Co and thereby increase the market value of the company.   **(8 marks)**

(Total: 20 marks)

51 CARD CO (DEC 13 - MODIFIED)

Card Co has in issue 8 million shares with an ex dividend market value of $7.16 per share. A dividend of 62 cents per share for 2013 has just been paid. The pattern of recent dividends is as follows:

Year	2010	2011	2012	2013
Dividends per share (cents)	55.1	57.9	59.1	62.0

Card Co also has in issue 8.5% bonds redeemable in five years' time with a total nominal value of $5 million. The market value of each $100 bond is $103.42. Redemption will be at nominal value.

Card Co is planning to invest a significant amount of money into a joint venture in a new business area. It has identified a proxy company with a similar business risk to the joint venture. The proxy company has an equity beta of 1.038 and is financed 75% by equity and 25% by debt, on a market value basis.

The current risk-free rate of return is 4% and the average equity risk premium is 5%. Card Co pays profit tax at a rate of 30% per year and has an equity beta of 1.6.

Required:

(a) Calculate the cost of equity of Card Co using the dividend growth model. **(3 marks)**

(b) Discuss whether the dividend growth model or the capital asset pricing model should be used to calculate the cost of equity. **(5 marks)**

(c) Calculate a project-specific cost of equity for Card Co for the planned joint venture.

(4 marks)

(d) Discuss whether changing the capital structure of a company can lead to a reduction in its cost of capital and hence to an increase in the value of the company. **(8 marks)**

(Total: 20 marks)

52 IRQ CO

IRQ Co has recently taken out a new variable rate bank loan to fund an expansion programme into the Middle East. The capital structure of the company is now as follows:

$400m par value of 50c shares trading at $2.30 – IRQ Co has an equity beta of 1.1.

$600m par value of 6% irredeemable loan notes trading at $107.

$100m variable rate bank loan – the current interest charge is 5%.

The directors of IRQ Co are keen to know what the weighted average cost of capital has now become in order to evaluate projects the company is considering.

Interest rates have risen in recent times and the company is paying more interest on the variable rate bank loan than was originally expected. The directors of IRQ Co are keen to understand how interest rates are determined and how they could hedge the interest rate risk on any future borrowings.

The expansion into the Middle East is progressing well and further expansion in the future is likely. During their trips to the Middle East a number of key clients and contacts have suggested that IRQ Co should consider the use of Islamic Finance for any future expansion.

The risk free rate is 4% and the market premium is 7%. Corporation tax is 28%.

Required:

(a) Calculate the WACC of IRQ Co. (8 marks)

(b) Explain briefly the over-the-counter and exchange traded methods that IRQ Co could use to hedge against future interest rate risk. Provide illustrative calculations of how a forward rate agreement could be used to protect the cost of future borrowings. (8 marks)

(c) Explain the key principles of Islamic Finance and describe how any future variable rate bank loan could be structured under the principles of Islamic Finance. (4 marks)

(Total: 20 marks)

BUSINESS VALUATIONS

53 KFP CO (JUNE 09 - MODIFIED)

KFP Co, a company listed on a major stock market, is looking at its cost of capital as it prepares to make a bid to buy a rival unlisted company, NGN. Both companies are in the same business sector. Financial information on KFP Co and NGN is as follows:

	KFP Co		NGN	
	$m	$m	$m	$m
Non-current assets		36		25
Current assets	7		7	
Current liabilities	3		4	
Net current assets		4		3
Total assets less current liabilities		40		28

	KFP Co		NGN	
	$m	$m	$m	$m
Ordinary shares, par value 50c	15		5	
Retained earnings	10		3	
Total equity		25		8
7% bonds, redeemable at par in seven years' time		15		
9% bonds, redeemable at par in two years' time				20
Total equity and non-current liabilities		40		28

Other relevant financial information:
Risk-free rate of return	4.0%
Average return on the market	10.5%
Taxation rate	30%

NGN has a cost of equity of 12% per year and has maintained a dividend payout ratio of 45% for several years. The current earnings per share of the company is 80c per share and its earnings have grown at an average rate of 4.5% per year in recent years.

The ex div share price of KFP Co is $4.20 per share and it has an equity beta of 1.2. The 7% bonds of the company are trading on an ex interest basis at $94.74 per $100 bond. The price/earnings ratio of KFP Co is eight times.

The directors of KFP Co believe a cash offer for the shares of NGN would have the best chance of success. It has been suggested that a cash offer could be financed by debt.

Required:

(a) Calculate the weighted average cost of capital of KFP Co on a market value weighted basis. **(9 marks)**

(b) Calculate the total value of the target company, NGN, using the following valuation methods:

  (i) Price/earnings ratio method, using the price/earnings ratio of KFP Co; and

  (ii) Dividend growth model. **(5 marks)**

(c) Comment on the suggestion that debt could be used to finance a cash offer for NGN. **(6 marks)**

(20 marks)

54 CLOSE CO (DEC 11 MODIFIED)

 Timed question with online tutor debrief

Recent financial information relating to Close Co, a stock market listed company, is as follows.

	$m
Profit after tax (earnings)	66.6
Dividends	40.0

Statement of financial position information:

	$m	$m
Non-current assets		595
Current assets		125
		────
Total assets		720
		────
Current liabilities		70
Equity		
Ordinary shares ($1 nominal)	80	
Reserves	410	
	────	
		490
Non-current liabilities		
6% Bank loan	40	
8% Bonds ($100 nominal)	120	
	────	
		160
		────
		720
		────

Financial analysts have forecast that the dividends of Close Co will grow in the future at a rate of 4% per year. This is slightly less than the forecast growth rate of the profit after tax (earnings) of the company, which is 5% per year. The finance director of Close Co thinks that, considering the risk associated with expected earnings growth, an earnings yield of 11% per year can be used for valuation purposes.

Close Co has a cost of equity of 10% per year and a before-tax cost of debt of 7% per year. The 8% bonds will be redeemed at nominal value in six years' time. Close Co pays tax at an annual rate of 30% per year and the ex-dividend share price of the company is $8·50 per share.

Required:

(a)   Calculate the value of Close Co using the following methods:

     (i)   net asset value method

     (ii)   dividend growth model

     (iii)   earnings yield method.   **(5 marks)**

(b)   Calculate the weighted average after-tax cost of capital of Close Co using market values where appropriate.   **(8 marks)**

(c)   Discuss the circumstances under which the weighted average cost of capital (WACC) can be used as a discount rate in investment appraisal. Briefly indicate alternative approaches that could be adopted when using the WACC is not appropriate.   **(7 marks)**

                                                   (Total: 20 marks)

 Calculate your allowed time, allocate the time to the separate parts

55   MFZ CO (JUNE 14 - MODIFIED)

The following financial information relates to MFZ Co, a listed company:

Year	2014	2013	2012
Profit before interest and tax ($m)	18.3	17.7	17.1
Profit after tax ($m)	12.8	12.4	12.0
Dividends ($m)	5.1	5.1	4.8
Equity market value ($m)	56.4	55.2	54.0

MFZ Co has 12 million ordinary shares in issue and has not issued any new shares in the period under review. The company is financed entirely by equity, and is considering investing $9.2 million of new finance in order to expand existing business operations. This new finance could be either long-term debt finance or new equity via a rights issue. The rights issue price would be at a 20% discount to the current share price. Issue costs of $200,000 would have to be met from the cash raised, whether the new finance was equity or debt.

The annual report of MFZ Co states that the company has three financial objectives:

Objective 1: To achieve growth in profit before interest and tax of 4% per year

Objective 2: To achieve growth in earnings per share of 3.5% per year

Objective 3: To achieve total shareholder return of 5% per year

MFZ Co has a cost of equity of 12% per year.

Required:

(a) **Analyse and discuss the extent to which MFZ Co has achieved each of its stated objectives.** **(7 marks)**

(b) **Calculate the total equity market value of MFZ Co for 2014 using the dividend growth model and briefly discuss why the dividend growth model value may differ from the current equity market value.** **(5 marks)**

(c) **Discuss the sources and characteristics of long-term debt finance which may be available to MFZ Co.** **(8 marks)**

(Total: 20 marks)

56 NN CO (DEC 10 - MODIFIED)

The following financial information refers to NN Co:

Current statement of financial position

	$m	$m	$m
Assets			
Non-current assets			101
Current assets			
Inventory		11	
Trade receivables		21	
Cash		10	
			42
Total assets			143
Equity and liabilities			
Ordinary share capital		50	
Preference share capital		25	
Retained earnings		19	
Total equity			94
Non-current liabilities			
Long-term borrowings		20	
Current liabilities			
Trade payables	22		
Other payables	7		
Total current liabilities		29	
Total liabilities			49
Total equity and liabilities			143

NN Co has just paid a dividend of 66 cents per share and has a cost of equity of 12%. The dividends of the company have grown in recent years by an average rate of 3% per year. The ordinary shares of the company have a par value of 50 cents per share and an ex div market value of $8.30 per share.

The long-term borrowings of NN Co consist of 7% bonds that are redeemable in six years' time at their par value of $100 per bond. The current ex interest market price of the bonds is $103.50.

The preference shares of NN Co have a nominal value of 50 cents per share and pay an annual dividend of 8%. The ex div market value of the preference shares is 67 cents per share.

NN Co pay profit tax at an annual rate of 25% per year.

Required:

(a)   Calculate the equity value of NN Co using the following business valuation methods:

    (i)   the dividend growth model

    (ii)   net asset value.   **(5 marks)**

(b)   Calculate the after-tax cost of debt of NN Co.   **(4 marks)**

(c)   Calculate the weighted average after-tax cost of capital of NN Co.   **(6 marks)**

(d)   Explain the concept of market efficiency and distinguish between strong form efficiency and semi-strong form efficiency.   **(5 marks)**

        (Total: 20 marks)

57   CORHIG CO (JUNE 2012 - MODIFIED)

Corhig Co is a company that is listed on a major stock exchange. The company has struggled to maintain profitability in the last two years due to poor economic conditions in its home country and as a consequence it has decided not to pay a dividend in the current year. However, there are now clear signs of economic recovery and Corhig Co is optimistic that payment of dividends can be resumed in the future. Forecast financial information relating to the company is as follows:

Year	1	2	3
Earnings ($000)	3,000	3,600	4,300
Dividends ($000)	nil	500	1,000

The company is optimistic that earnings and dividends will increase after Year 3 at a constant annual rate of 3% per year.

Corhig Co currently has a before-tax cost of debt of 5% per year and an equity beta of 1.6. On a market value basis, the company is currently financed 75% by equity and 25% by debt.

During the course of the last two years the company acted to reduce its gearing and was able to redeem a large amount of debt. Since there are now clear signs of economic recovery, Corhig Co plans to raise further debt in order to modernise some of its non-current assets and to support the expected growth in earnings. This additional debt would mean that the capital structure of the company would change and it would be financed 60% by equity and 40% by debt on a market value basis. The before-tax cost of debt of Corhig Co would increase to 6% per year and the equity beta of Corhig Co would increase to 2.

The risk-free rate of return is 4% per year and the equity risk premium is 5% per year. In order to stimulate economic activity the government has reduced profit tax rate for all large companies to 20% per year.

The current average price/earnings ratio of listed companies similar to Corhig Co is 5 times.

Required:

(a) Estimate the value of Corhig Co using the price/earnings ratio method and discuss the usefulness of the variables that you have used.   **(4 marks)**

(b) Calculate the current cost of equity of Corhig Co and, using this value, calculate the value of the company using the dividend valuation model.   **(6 marks)**

(c) Calculate the current weighted average after-tax cost of capital of Corhig Co and the weighted average after-tax cost of capital following the new debt issue, and comment on the difference between the two values.   **(6 marks)**

(d) Discuss how the shareholders of Corhig Co can assess the extent to which they face business risk, explaining the nature of the risk being assessed.   **(4marks)**

(Total: 20 marks)

58   MAT CO

MAT Co operates a chain of stores selling furniture. It has a successful business model and is seeking to raise additional finance in order to grow further. MAT Co is currently listed on AIM (a secondary market) but the shares in the company are only traded infrequently. The following information refers to MAT Co:

Most recent statement of financial position

	$m	$m
Assets		
Non-current assets		71
Current assets		
Inventory	8	
Trade receivables	11	
Cash	15	
		34
Total assets		105
Equity and liabilities		
Ordinary share capital		40
Retained earnings	27	
Total equity		67
Non-current liabilities		
Long-term borrowings		18
Current liabilities		
Trade payables	20	
Total liabilities		38
Total equity and liabilities		105

MAT Co has paid the following dividends in recent years:

2008 – 4.1 cents

2009 – 4.3 cents

2010 – 4.7 cents

Since the most recent statement of financial position the company has declared a dividend of 5.0 cents and this will be paid shortly. The ordinary shares of the company have a par value of 25 cents and a market value of 66 cents per share. The equity beta of the company is estimated to be 1.15.

Prior to considering potential sources of finance the directors of MAT Co are keen to gain a better understanding of the value of the company.

The return on government bonds is currently 5% and the equity risk premium is 8%.

Required:

(a) **Calculate the total equity value of MAT Co using the dividend growth model'**

(6marks)

(b) **Comment on the relevance of the total equity value calculated when compared to the total market value of the equity of the company.** (5 marks)

(c) **Explain the factors the directors of MAT Co should take into account when considering how to raise additional finance.** (9 marks)

(Total: 20 marks)

59 THP CO (JUNE 08 - MODIFIED) *Walk in the footsteps of a top tutor*

THP Co is planning to buy CRX Co, a company in the same business sector, and is considering paying cash for the shares of the company. The cash would be raised by THP Co through a 1 for 3 rights issue at a 20% discount to its current share price.

The purchase price of the 1 million issued shares of CRX Co would be equal to the rights issue funds raised, less issue costs of $320,000. Earnings per share of CRX Co at the time of acquisition would be 44.8c per share. As a result of acquiring CRX Co, THP Co expects to gain annual after-tax savings of $96,000.

THP Co maintains a payout ratio of 50% and earnings per share are currently 64c per share. Dividend growth of 5% per year is expected for the foreseeable future and the company has a cost of equity of 12% per year.

Information from THP Co's statement of financial position:

Equity and liabilities	$000
Shares ($1 par value)	3,000
Reserves	4,300
	7,300
Non-current liabilities	
8% loan notes	5,000
Current liabilities	2,200
Total equity and liabilities	14,500

Further information:

THP Co

THP Co dividend per share = 32c per share

Share price of THP Co = $4.80

Market capitalisation of THP Co = $14.4m

Price earnings ratio of THP Co = 7.5

Required:

(a) Assuming the rights issue takes place and ignoring the proposed use of the funds raised, calculate:

(i) the rights issue price per share

(ii) the cash raised

(iii) the theoretical ex rights price per share; and

(iv) the market capitalisation of THP Co. **(5 marks)**

(b) Using the price/earnings ratio method, calculate the share price and market capitalisation of CRX Co before the acquisition. **(3 marks)**

(c) Assuming a semi-strong form efficient capital market, calculate and comment on the post acquisition market capitalisation of THP Co in the following circumstances:

(i) THP Co does not announce the expected annual after-tax savings; and

(ii) the expected after-tax savings are made public. **(5 marks)**

(d) Discuss the factors that THP Co should consider, in its circumstances, in choosing between equity finance and debt finance as a source of finance from which to make a cash offer for CRX Co. **(7 marks)**

(Total: 20 marks)

60   DARTIG CO (DEC 08 - MODIFIED) *Walk in the footsteps of a top tutor*

Dartig Co is a stock-market listed company that manufactures consumer products and it is planning to expand its existing business. The investment cost of $5 million will be met by a 1 for 4 rights issue. The current share price of Dartig Co is $2.50 per share and the rights issue price will be at a 20% discount to this. The finance director of Dartig Co expects that the expansion of existing business will allow the average growth rate of earnings per share over the last four years to be maintained into the foreseeable future.

The earnings per share and dividends paid by Dartig over the last four years are as follows:

	2003	2004	2005	2006	2007
Earnings per share (cents)	27.7	29.0	29.0	30.2	32.4
Dividend per share (cents)	12.8	13.5	13.5	14.5	15.0

Dartig Co has a cost of equity of 10%. The price/earnings ratio of Dartig Co has been approximately constant in recent years. Ignore issue costs.

Required:

(a)   Calculate the theoretical ex rights price per share prior to investing in the proposed business expansion. `

(3 marks)

(b)   Calculate the expected share price following the proposed business expansion using the price/earnings ratio method.

(3 marks)

(c)   Discuss whether the proposed business expansion is an acceptable use of the finance raised by the rights issue, and evaluate the expected effect on the wealth of the shareholders of Dartig Co.

(5 marks)

(d)   At a recent board meeting of Dartig Co, a non-executive director suggested that the company's remuneration committee should consider scrapping the company's current share option scheme, since executive directors could be rewarded by the scheme even when they did not perform well. A second non-executive director disagreed, saying the problem was that even when directors acted in ways which decreased the agency problem, they might not be rewarded by the share option scheme if the stock market were in decline.

Required:

Explain the nature of the agency problem and discuss the use of share option schemes as a way of reducing the agency problem in a stock-market listed company such as Dartig Co.

(9 marks)

(Total: 20 marks)

61 PHOBIS (DEC 07 - MODIFIED)

(a) Phobis Co is considering a bid for Danoca Co. Both companies are stock-market listed and are in the same business sector. Financial information on Danoca Co, which is shortly to pay its annual dividend, is as follows:

Number of ordinary shares	5 million
Ordinary share price (ex div basis)	$3.30
Earnings per share	40.0c
Proposed payout ratio	60%
Dividend per share one year ago	23.3c
Dividend per share two years ago	22.0c
Equity beta	1.4
Other relevant financial information	
Average sector price/earnings ratio	10
Risk-free rate of return	4.6%
Return on the market	10.6%

Required:

Calculate the value of Danoca Co using the following methods:

(i)   price/earnings ratio method

(ii)   dividend growth model

and discuss the significance, to Phobis Co, of the values you have calculated, in comparison to the current market value of Danoca Co.   (10 marks)

(b) Phobis Co has in issue 9% bonds which are redeemable at their par value of $100 in five years' time. Alternatively, each bond may be converted on that date into 20 ordinary shares of the company. The current ordinary share price of Phobis Co is $4.45 and this is expected to grow at a rate of 6.5% per year for the foreseeable future. Phobis Co has a cost of debt of 7% per year.

Required:

Calculate the following current values for each $100 convertible bond:

(i)   market value

(ii)   floor value

(iii)   conversion premium.   (6 marks)

(c) **Discuss the significance to a listed company if the stock market on which its shares are traded is shown to be semi-strong form efficient.   (4 marks)**

(Total: 20 marks)

 Online question assistance

RISK MANAGEMENT

62 NEDWEN

Nedwen Co is a UK-based company which has the following expected transactions..

One month: Expected receipt of $240,000

One month: Expected payment of $140,000

Three months: Expected receipts of $300,000

The finance manager has collected the following information:

Spot rate ($ per £):   1.7820 ± 0.0002

One month forward rate ($ per £):   1.7829 ± 0.0003

Three months forward rate ($ per £): 1.7846 ± 0.0004

Money market rates for Nedwen Co:

	Borrowing	Deposit
One year sterling interest rate:	4.9%	4.6
One year dollar interest rate:	5.4%	5.1

Assume that it is now 1 April.

Required:

(a)   Discuss the differences between transaction risk, translation risk and economic risk.

(6 marks)

(b)   Calculate the expected sterling receipts in one month and in three months using the forward market.

(3 marks)

(c)   Calculate the expected sterling receipts in three months using a money-market hedge and recommend whether a forward market hedge or a money market hedge should be used.

(5 marks)

(d)   Discuss how sterling currency futures contracts could be used to hedge the three-month dollar receipt.

(6 marks)

(Total: 20 marks)

63 BOLUJE CO (DEC 08 - MODIFIED)

Three years ago Boluje Co built a factory in its home country costing $3.2 million. To finance the construction of the factory, Boluje Co issued peso-denominated bonds in a foreign country whose currency is the peso. Interest rates at the time in the foreign country were historically low. The foreign bond issue raised 16 million pesos and the exchange rate at the time was 5.00 pesos/$.

Each foreign bond has a par value of 500 pesos and pays interest in pesos at the end of each year of 6.1%. The bonds will be redeemed in five years' time at par. The current cost of debt of peso-denominated bonds of similar risk is 7%.

In addition to domestic sales, Boluje Co exports goods to the foreign country and receives payment for export sales in pesos. Approximately 40% of production is exported to the foreign country.

The spot exchange rate is 6.00 pesos/$ and the 12-month forward exchange rate is 6.07 pesos/$. Boluje Co can borrow money on a short-term basis at 4% per year in its home currency and it can deposit money at 5% per year in the foreign country where the foreign bonds were issued. Taxation may be ignored in all calculation parts of this question.

Required:

(a) Briefly explain the reasons why a company may choose to finance a new investment by an issue of debt finance. **(7 marks)**

(b) Calculate the current total market value (in pesos) of the foreign bonds used to finance the building of the new factory. **(4 marks)**

(c) Assume that Boluje Co has no surplus cash at the present time:

  (i) Explain and illustrate how a money market hedge could protect Boluje Co against exchange rate risk in relation to the dollar cost of the interest payment to be made in one year's time on its foreign bonds. **(4 marks)**

  (ii) Compare the relative costs of a money market hedge and a forward market hedge. **(2 marks)**

(d) Briefly describe other methods, excluding derivatives, that Boluje Co could use to hedge against exchange rate risk. **(3 marks)**

(Total: 20 marks)

 Online question assistance

64 **EXPORTERS PLC** *Walk in the footsteps of a top tutor*

Exporters plc, a UK company, is due to receive 500,000 Northland dollars in 6 months' time for goods supplied. The company decides to hedge its currency exposure by using the forward market. The short-term interest rate in the UK is 12% per annum and the equivalent rate in Northland is 15%. The spot rate of exchange is 2.5 Northland dollars to the pound.

Required:

(a) Calculate how much Exporters plc actually gains or losses as a result of the hedging transaction if, at the end of the six months, the pound, in relation to the Northland dollar, has:

  (1) gained 4%,

  (2) lost 2% or

  (3) remained stable.

  You may assume that the forward rate of exchange simply reflects the interest differential in the two countries (i.e. it reflects the Interest Rate Parity analysis of forward rates) **(8 marks)**

    (b)   **Compare a forward market currency hedge with:**

        (1)   **a currency futures hedge,**

        (2)   **a currency options hedge.**

        Indicate in each of the three cases how the hedging facility is actually provided, the nature of the costs and the potential outcomes of the hedge.

                (12 marks)

                (Total: 20 marks)

65   ELECT CO

Elect Co is a stock-market listed manufacturing company that is seeking additional finance of $5m to undertake a new project. The finance director of Elect Co is currently considering whether to raise the capital via debt or equity finance.

The capital structure of the company (before the new finance has been raised) is as follows:

	$m	$m
Equity		
Ordinary shares (par value 50c per share)	10	
Reserves	30	
	——	40
Debt		
Bond A (par value $100)	10	
Bank loan	5	
	——	15
		——
		55
		——

The ordinary shares are currently trading at $1.70 each. The company's cost of equity has been estimated at 15%.

Bond A will be redeemed at par in six years' time and pays a fixed annual interest of 8%. The pre-tax cost of this finance has been estimated at 10%.

The bank loan is repayable in two years' time. It is a floating rate loan at LIBOR + 1%. LIBOR is currently at 3%.

Some initial enquiries made by the finance director have indicated that further fixed rate debt finance could be raised at an annual post-tax cost of 7%. Floating rate debt finance could be obtained for LIBOR + 2%. Market experts are divided over the expectations of future interest rates with some expecting rates to remain steady for the foreseeable future and others predicting an increasing of up to 4%.

Elect Co pays corporation tax at a rate of 30%.

Required:

    (a)   **Calculate the current market value of Bond A**   **(2 marks)**

    (b)   **Calculate the current weighted average cost of capital of Elect Co**   **(6 marks)**

(c) Evaluate the impact on the weighted average cost of capital of raising the new finance via:

(i) Equity

(ii) Fixed rate debt

State any assumptions that you make. (4 marks)

(d) Discuss the factors affecting the choice between fixed and floating rate debt and describe three methods of hedging interest rate risk that may be appropriate for Elect Co. (8 marks)

(Total: 20 marks)

66 CC CO

CC Co is considering launching a new product. Relevant financial information includes:

Selling price (current price terms)	$12 per unit
Variable costs (current price terms)	$7 per unit
Incremental fixed overhead costs	$250,000 per year

General price inflation is expected to average 4.7% per year over the period. However, the selling price is expected to inflate at 5% per annum, the variable costs to inflate by just 4% per annum, and the fixed costs by 6% per year.

Production and sales are expected to be at the following levels:

Year	1	2	3	4
Units	250,000	500,000	400,000	200,000

To manufacture the new product CC Co will need to purchase a new machine. The only suppliers of this machine are located overseas. If the machine was ordered immediately it would cost €1.5m. Payment must be made in Euros and would be due upon delivery of the machine in three month's time.

CC Co will be able to claim tax allowable depreciation on the investment on a straight line basis over the estimated four-year life of the asset. The company pays tax one year in arrears at a rate of 30% and the asset is not expected to have any scrap value at the end of the project.

The real weighted average cost of capital of CC Co is 5.1%.

The spot exchange rate is 0.70 €/$ and the three-month forward exchange rate is 0.698 €/$. CC Co can earn 2.9% per year on short-term euro deposits and can borrow short term in dollars at 5.5%.

Required:

(a) Calculate the expected dollar payment in three months' time using both a forward market hedge and a money market hedge and recommend whether a forward market hedge or a money market hedge should be used to mitigate the exchange risk on the potential purchase of the machine. (6 marks)

(b) Based on your recommendation in part (b,) calculate the net present value of the proposed investment in three months' time and comment on the project's acceptability. (10 marks)

(c) Discuss the impact inflation has on exchange rates. (4 marks)

(Total: 20 marks)

Section A

ANSWERS TO OBJECTIVE TEST QUESTIONS

FINANCIAL MANAGEMENT FUNCTION

1   **C**

2   **Statements 2, 3 and 5 are financial objectives**

Achieving market share (a relative measure), or customer satisfaction (a qualitative measure), are non-financial objectives.

3   **B, C and D**

Financial management aims to ensure that the money is available to finance profitable projects and to select those projects which the company should undertake. Once profits have been made the decision then needs to be made about how much to distribute to the owners and how much to re-invest for the future. Income decisions are really sub-divisions of the investment decision.

4   **D**

This is a financial objective that relates to the level of financial risk that the company is prepared to accept. The other objectives are non-financial.

5   **C**

6   **D**

7   **All three statements are true**

8   **A**

A review of overtime spending and apportioning overheads to cost units is typically carried out by a member of the management accounting team. Depreciation of non-current assets is typically carried out by a member of the financial accounting team.

9   **A**

B, C and D are examples of connected stakeholders.

10   **C**

11   **C**

The separation of ownership and control creates a situation where managers act as the agents of the owners (shareholders).

12   Statements 2 and 3 are correct. The three E's in statement 4 should be economy, efficiency and effectiveness.

13   **C**

Negotiation of bulk discounts is an 'economy target' (A).   Paying rates for staff of appropriate levels of qualification is also an 'economy' target (B).   Customer satisfaction rating is an 'effectiveness' target (D).

14   **A, B and D**

Managerial reward schemes should be clearly defined and impossible to manipulate.

15   **D**

16   **B**

Invoices are received from suppliers, not any of the other three stakeholders.

17   **A**

The Code clearly states that the requirement is for independent non-executive directors, but only one member of the committee (as a minimum) needs have recent and relevant financial experience, not all of them.

FINANCIAL MANAGEMENT ENVIRONMENT

18   **B**

Fiscal policy is implemented through the raising and lowering of taxes and through the raising and lowering of government spending.   1 only is not correct because there is another aspect to fiscal policy other than just taxation.   2 and 3 is not correct because government actions to raise or lower the size of the money supply is an aspect of monetary policy, not fiscal policy.   1, 2, and 3 is not correct because government actions to raise or lower the size of the money supply is an aspect of monetary policy, not fiscal policy.

19   **Statements 1 and 3 are correct**

20   **Both statements are true**

21   **C**

22   **C**

23   **A, B and C** Statement 4 describes cost-push inflation.

24   C

Money markets focus on short term financial instruments. A corporate bond is a long-term source of finance, hence is a capital market instrument.

25   A, B and D

26   A

27   D

Monetary policy which increases the level of domestic interest rates is likely to raise exchange rates as capital is attracted into the country (statement1). Any restrictions on the stock of money, or restrictions on credit, will raise the cost of borrowing, making fewer investment projects worthwhile and discouraging expansion by companies (statement 2). Periods of credit control and high interest rates reduce consumer demand (statement 3). Monetary policy is often used to control inflation (statement 4).

28   D

29   B, C and D

It is the secondary market, not the primary market, that deals in 'second-hand' securities

30   Both statements are true

31   C

The audit committee should consist of non-executive directors.

32   C

33   Both statements are true

34   A, C and D

Certificates of deposits are fully negotiable and hence attractive to the depositor since they ensure instant liquidity if required.

35   C

A stock market listing is likely to involve a significant loss of control to a wider circle of investors.

36   C

One of the principal objectives of macroeconomic policy will typically be to achieve balance of payments equilibrium, not a deficit.

37   A, B and C

Local operating units (decentralised treasury function) should have a better feel for local conditions than head office and can respond more quickly to local developments. This is an advantage of decentralisation.

38   B

> A funding gap often arises when SMEs want to expand beyond their available funds but are not yet ready for a listing on the stock market.

WORKING CAPITAL MANAGEMENT

39   A

40   All three statements are correct

41   D

> Taking longer to pay trade payables would shorten the cash cycle as cash stays with company possession for a longer period of time. Lower net operating cash flows and slower inventory turnovers are signs of a lengthening cash cycle. Depreciation expenditure is a non-cash item and does not affect the cash cycle.

42   17 weeks

	Weeks
Raw materials	6
Payables	(7)
Production	2
Finished goods	6
Receivables	10
	17

43   Current ratio: decrease   Quick ratio: increase

The current liabilities figures used as the denominator will stay the same in both cases. The total of the current assets will decrease because the reduction in the inventory value will be greater than the increase in cash. Therefore the current ratio will decrease. The total of the liquid assets will increase because of the higher cash balance. Therefore the quick ratio will increase.

44 C

	$000	$000		$000	$000
			Next year		
Non-current assets		1,000	⟶		1,000
Current assets					
Inventories	200			400	
Receivables	150			300	
Cash	100			Nil	
	450			700	
Current liabilities					
Overdraft				(50)	
Payables	(200)			(400)	
Net current assets		250			250
		1,250			1,250
Capital		1,250			1,250

45 A

The cash operating cycle = receivables days + inventory holding period – payables days.

The receivables days = 365/average receivables turnover or 365/10.5 = 34.76.   The inventory holding period = 365/inventory turnover or 365/4 = 91.25. The payables days = 365/payables turnover ratio = 365/8 = 45.63.

Putting it all together: cash operating cycle = 34.76 + 91.25 – 45.63 = 80.38.

46 A

47 B

Inventory = 15,000,000 × 60/360 = $2,500,000

Trade receivables = 27,000,000 × 50/360 = $3,750,000

Trade payables = 15,000,000 × 45/360 = $1,875,000

Net investment required = 2,500,000 + 3,750,000 – 1,875,000 = $4,375,000

48 D

	Jan	Feb	March
	$	$	$
Total receipts	30,000	15,500	20,500
Total payments	(20,600)	(8,250)	(12,700)
Net cash flow	9,400	7,250	5,800
Balance b/f	500	9,900	17,150
Balance c/f	9,900	17,150	24,950

'Credit sales' under 'Receipts' implies receipts from credit customers.

49   A, B and C

Delaying payments to obtain a 'free' source of finance would be a key aspect of a company's accounts payable policy, not accounts receivable.

50   A, B AND C

51   C

Closing receivables days = closing receivables balance/sales × 365 days

52   A

While overtrading can result in higher inventory and receivables (and payables) resulting in the current ratio increasing in the short term, over the longer term the inevitable drain on cash will result in falling liquidity ratios.

53   A

Customer bargaining power increasing is associated with increased receivables days, not payables days.

54   C

A Just in Time inventory control system aim to reduce capital tied up in inventory, not increase it (A). The system aims to create a flexible production process which is responsive to the customer's requirements, not an inflexible process (B). With a Just in Time system, although inventory holding costs are close to zero, inventory ordering costs are high, not low (D).

55   B, C and D

INVESTMENT APPRAISAL

56   C

Time	Flow	DF@10%	PV
0	(125,000)	1	(125,000)
0	(4,000)	1	(4,000)
2	4,000	0.826	3,304
			————
			125,696
			————

Therefore, contract price @ time 2 × 0.826 = 125,696

Price = 125,696/0.826 = $152,174

57   C

58   A

The investment is made on 1 January 20X5, so tax-allowable depreciation can first be set off against profits for the accounting period ended 31 December 20X5. The tax cash saving will therefore be at 31 December 20X5. i.e. time 1.

Time	Date	$	Tax saved ($)	Payment time
0	1 January 20X5	2,000,000		
1	Tax-allowable depreciation	(500,000)	@ 30% = 150,000	1
		1,500,000		
2	31 December 20X6	(350,000)		
		1,150,000	@ 30% = 345,000	2

Present value = ($150,000 × 0.870) + ($345,000 × 0.756) = $391,320

59   C

Total cash flow	Joint probability	EV of cash flow
$		$
36,000	0.1125	4,050
14,000	0.0375	525
32,000	0.4500	14,400
10,000	0.1500	1,500
16,000	0.1875	3,000
(6,000)	0.0625	(375)
		23,100
	Less initial investment	(12,000)
	EV of the NPV	11,100

60   12%

(1 + money rate) = (1 + real rate) × (1 + inflation rate)

1.21 = (1 + real rate) × 1.08

Real rate= 12%

61   C

In general, it is possible for a project to have up to as many IRRs as there are sign changes in the cash flows. Since the project's cash flows have two sign changes there can be up to two IRRs. The NPV profile could take various forms depending on the relative magnitudes of the cash flows.

62   Payback period: decrease   Internal rate of return: increase

The payback period will decrease and the IRR increase, because the outflow at time 0 is unaffected by inflation.

Consider a simple project.

Time	Cash flow	Inflation at, say, 10%	Revised cash flow
	$		$
0	(100)	1	(100)
1	(100)	1.1	(110)
2	100	1.12	121
3	100	1.13	133
4	100	1.14	146

Payback period 3 years to 2.7 years

IRR = approx 17% to approx 30%

63   B

The internal rate of return (C) and the cost of the initial investment (A) are independent of the risk of the project. The lower the risk of the project, the less (not greater) is the required rate of return (D).

64   D

To work out discounted payback, cash flows must first be discounted at the company rate.

Year	Cash flow	Discount factor	Present value	Cumulative present value
	$		$	$
0	(100,000)	1	(100,000)	(100,000)
1	40,000	0.909	36,360	(63,640)
2	20,000	0.826	16,520	(47,120)
3	30,000	0.751	22,530	(24,590)
4	5,000	0.683	3,415	(21,175)
5	40,000	0.621	24,840	3,665

Discounted payback occurs in year 5.

65   A

Net initial investment = $732,000

The IRR is the interest rate at which the NPV of the investment is zero.

PV of perpetuity = $146,400/r

The IRR is where $146,400/r = $732,000

IRR = $146,400/$732,000 × 100% = 20%

If you selected 25% you in fact assumed that the first inflow is coterminous with the initial investment. If you selected 500% you calculated the $732,000 net investment correctly but your final calculation was 'upside-down'. If you selected 400% you made both of these errors.

66   A, B and D

IRR is based on discounted cash flow principles. It therefore considers all of the cash flows in a project (A), does not include notional accounting costs such as depreciation (B) and it considers the time value of money (D). It is not an absolute measure of return, however, as IRR is expressed as a percentage. Two projects can have the same IRR but very different cash flows. C is therefore an incorrect statement.

67   B

Tax period	Narrative		Tax saved @30%	Timing	DF@10%	PV
		$	$			$
y/e 31/12/X2	Cost of asset	90,000				
	Tax allowable depreciation	(22,500)	6,750	1	0.909	6,136
		67,500				
y/e 31/12/X3	Tax allowable depreciation	(16,875)	5,063	2	0.826	4,182
		50,625				
y/e 31/12/X4	Tax allowable depreciation	(12,656)	3,797	3	0.751	2,852
		37,969				
y/e 31/12/X5	Disposal	(25,000)				
	Balancing allowance	12,969	3,891	4	0.683	2,658
		NIL				15,828

68   B

	P	Q	R	S
NPV/$ of capital in restricted period	60/20	40/10	80/30	80/40
	= 3	= 4	= 2.67	= 2

The optimal sequence is QPRS

69   B

	Cash flow	10% factor	PV
	$000		$
Time 0 machine	(280)	1	(280,000)
Time 1 – 5 contribution	200	3.791	758,200
Time 1 – 5 fixed costs	(95)	3.791	(360,145)
Positive NPV			118,055

PV of contribution must fall by $118,055

Sales volume must fall by $118,055/758,200 = 15.57%

Fall in sales volume   = 0.1557 × 50,000

= 7,785

70 B

The payback is most likely to take post-tax cash flows.

71 B

As there are different rates of inflation the 'money approach' must be used, i.e. the cash flows must be inflated at their specific rates and discounted at the money cost of capital.

(1 + Money rate) = (1 + Real rate) × (1 + Inflation rate) = 1.1 × 1.08 = 1.188

72 C

Money cost of capital = [(1.08 × 1.12) − 1] × 100 = 20.96%

Time	t0	t1	t2
	$	$	$
Outlay	(18,000)		
Labour		9,000	9,900
Salvage			5,000
			14,900
20.96% discount factor	1	0.8267	0.6835
Present value	(18,000)	7,440	10,184

NPV = $376

73 C

	$	Discount factor	$
Time 0	(10,000)	1.000	(10,000)
Time 1	(3,000)	0.909	(2,727)
Time 2	(5,000)	0.826	(4,130)
Time 3	(5,000)	0.751	(3,755)
NPV	(20,612)		

Equivalent annual cost = 20,612/2.487 = $8,288

74 B

	Capital needed at time 0	NPV	NPV/£ needed at time 0	Rank	Invested	NPV
	$	$	$		$	$
Project 1	10,000	30,000	3.0	2	10,000	30,000
Project 2	8,000	25,000	3.125	1	8,000	25,000
Project 3	12,000	30,000	2.5	3	12,000	30,000
Project 4	16,000	36,000	2.25	4 (1/8)	2,000	4,500

75 C

The NPV impact of the initial outflow is unaffected.

The revenue flows will be subject to inflation, but then should be discounted at a money rate. The net effect is no change in the PV.

The sales proceeds represent a flow of money, not affected by inflation, but this will now be discounted at a money rate, lowering the net present value of the project.

76 C

The true statement is 'the payback method is based on the project's cash flows'.

The payback method is based on cash flows whereas the ARR method is based on accounting profit.

77 B

Sensitivity analysis considers the effect of changing one variable at a time (A).

78 A

The tighter the distribution, the lower the standard deviation will be (B). The wider the dispersion, the more risky the situation (C). It is the expected value, not the standard deviation, that is the weighted average of all the possible outcomes (D).

BUSINESS FINANCE AND COST OF CAPITAL

79 9.2%

Return per CAPM = Rf + beta (Rm – Rf)

Return = 6% + (0.80 × 4%) = 9.2%

Note: market risk premium – (Rm – Rf)

80 B

81 C

The companies are identical except for their gearing and the beta factor of equity shares will increase with the gearing level. The beta of B plc (gearing 80%) is therefore higher than the beta for D plc (gearing 60%), i.e. over 1.22. The beta of C plc (gearing 35%) is higher than the beta for A plc (gearing 30%) and below the beta for D plc. It must therefore be in the range 0.89 to 1.22.

82 STATEMENTS 1 AND 3 ARE CORRECT

Statement 4: gross profit is calculated as gross profit divided by revenue.

83 9.1%

$$Kd = \frac{I\,(1-T)}{D} = \frac{12\times(1-0.30)}{92} = 9.1\%$$

84 C

$$k = \frac{0.18\times(24\times2.50)+(8/92)\times6\times0.92+0.125\times(1-0.30)\times8}{24\times2.50+6\times0.92+8} = 16.29$$

85 D

86 27.7%

$$\frac{25.6\times1.16}{280-25.6} + 0.16 = 27.7\%$$

87 D

Operating gearing = fixed costs divided by variable costs, so a decrease in the gearing ratio implies a lower proportion of fixed costs. Therefore C is wrong.

Consider the following example.

	Higher gearing $m	Lower gearing $m
Sales	100	100
Variable costs	(20)	(30)
Fixed costs	(30)	(20)
Profit	50	50
Operating gearing ratio	3/2	2/3

Suppose sales volume, and hence variable costs, fall by 20%

The profits will be affected as follows.

	$m	$m
Sales	80	80
Variable costs	(16)	(24)
Fixed costs	(30)	(20)
Profit	34	36

With the lower gearing ratio, profits are less affected by the change in volume. D is correct.

A is wrong – profitability is unconnected to gearing. B is wrong – profits are less risky, as the example shows above.

88 B

The traditional view is that, as an organisation introduces debt into its capital structure, the weighted average cost of capital will fall, because initially the benefit of cheap debt finance more than outweighs any increases in the cost of equity required to compensate equity holders for higher financial risk. As gearing continues to increase, equity holders will ask for progressively higher returns and eventually this increase will start to outweigh the benefit of cheap debt finance, and the weighted average cost of capital will rise.

89 A

It increases the number of shares without affecting the value of the company, so market price per share and earnings per share will fall.

90 Cost of equity: increases   WACC: decreases   Total MV: increases

In a perfect capital market the theories of Modigliani & Miller on gearing apply.

91 Financial risk: increases   operating risk: decreases

Financial risk is dependent on the debt/equity ratio: the lower its value the lower is the financial risk.

Operating risk is dependent on the ratio of variable costs to fixed costs: the lower its value the higher is the operating risk, due to the higher fluctuation of earnings as a percentage of sales.

92 Security X is overpriced.   Security Y is underpriced

If security Z is correctly priced, its actual return will be the return predicted by CAPM.

$13.2 = 6 + 1.2 (Rm - 6)$

$13.2 - 6 = 1.2 (Rm - 6)$

$7.2/1.2 + 6 = Rm = 12$

Security X has a beta value of 1.5 and should provide a return of $6 + 1.6 (12 - 6) = 15.6\%$

Security Y has a beta value of 0.8 and should provide a return of $6 + 0.9(12 - 6) = 11.4\%$

Security X does not give a high enough return, so is overpriced. Security Y gives too high a return, so is underpriced.

93 A

Gearing = $[(4,000 \times 1.05) + 6,200 + (2,000 \times 0.8)]/(8,000 \times 2 \times 5) = 12,000/80,000 = 15\%$

94 Systematic risk

Systematic risk cannot be diversified; it is linked to market factors which influence all shares in a similar way.

95 D

Under M&M (implied by the phrase 'perfect capital markets') with no tax, the WACC is unaffected by gearing, but the cost of equity starts to rise immediately gearing is introduced.

96 D

Intangible assets being a low proportion of assets. The quality of the asset base is more certain if few of the assets are intangible, and hence finance providers will be more willing to lend.

97 B

Because of the potential for making gains by conversion, investors are willing to accept a lower coupon rate on the debt

A The equity component is not a risk imposed on holders.

B Convertibles keep holders' options open.

C Additional payments are not required.

D They don't have to rank after ordinary debt and even if they did, this would increase their servicing cost.

98 D

A is a result of assuming that a perfect capital market exists; it is not a conclusion.

B is the Gordon growth model.

C contradicts the dividend valuation model, which is not disputed by M&M.

The correct answer is D.

99 A

$\beta e > \beta a$; WACC < Cost of equity calculated using βa; WACC < Cost of equity calculated using βe

$\beta e > \beta a$ because gearing increases equity risk.

Tax relief on debt finance always reduces WACC below the ungeared cost of equity and hence below the geared cost of equity.

100 B

If the company were to automate its production line, its level of fixed costs would increase and its variable costs (notably wage) decrease.

Therefore operating gearing would increase.

101 B

CAPM can be used to predict the cost of equity. Using an asset beta will predict the ungeared cost of equity. Using the equity beta (geared beta) will predict the geared cost of equity.

102 A

The formula for the required return is ke = risk free rate + beta × (market rate − risk free rate).

103 A

Interest cover measures a company's financial risk, gross profit margin measures operating profitability and return on capital employed measures how efficiently the company is using the funds available.

104 Increase current assets by 100 or decrease current liabilities by 50

For the current ratio to equal 2.0, current assets would need to move to $600 (or up by $100) or current liabilities would need to decrease to $250 (or down by $50). Remember that $CA - CL$ = working capital ($500 - 300 = 200$).

105 Preference shares are a form of <u>equity</u> capital which carry <u>lower</u> risk than ordinary shares.

Although they share many features in common with loan capital, preference shares give their holders certain ownership rights in the company, which means that their position is legally very different to that of lenders.

106 A

It is the interest yield which is the interest or coupon rate expressed as a percentage of the market price and this is a measure of return on investment for the debt holder (B). It is the total shareholder return ratio which measures the returns to the investor by taking account of dividend income and capital growth (C). It is the dividend per share ratio which helps individual shareholders see how much of the overall dividend payout they are entitled to (D).

107 A, B and D

The lessor does not retain the risks or rewards of ownership.

BUSINESS VALUATIONS

108 C

The preferred approach is a good spread of shares, as this minimises the risk in the portfolio and should ensure Mr Mays does achieve something approaching the average return for the market. Strong form efficiency means that Mr Mays cannot do anything to guarantee beating the market – even by insider trading, so options A and D are a waste of time.

109 $92.67

$MV = (7 \times 5.033) + (105 \times 0.547) = \$92.67$

110 $3.50

Monetary value of return = $3.10 \times 1.197 = \$3.71$

Current share price = $3.71 - \$0.21 = \$3.50$

111 A

The new ex-div market value per share = (4 × $4.10 + $2.50)/5 = $3.78

112 C

113 D

The period 20X1 to 20X5 covers four years of growth, and the average growth rate 'g' can be calculated as follows

$$1 + g = \frac{4,236}{2,200}$$

$1 + g = 1.178$

$g = 17.8\%$

Therefore, PO $= \frac{4,236 \times 1.178}{0.25 - 0.178} = \$69,306,000$

Price per share (50 million shares) = $1.39

114 A

$g = rb = 0.15 \times 0.7 = 0.105$

$$MV = \frac{D_0(1+g)}{K_e - g} = \frac{50,000,000 \times 1.105}{0.25 - 0.105} = \$381,000,000 \text{ rounded}$$

115 B

	$000
Value of Alpha and Beta combined (210 + 900 + 100) × 18	21,780
Value of Beta on its own 900 × 21	(18,900)
Maximum value of Alpha	2,880

116 A, B and D

A higher P/E ratio valuation may be justified when the target company has higher growth prospects, or when it is in an industry where the normal P/E ratio is higher than in the industry of the bidder. Better-quality assets might also be a reason for offering a price that values the target on a higher P/E. Higher gearing ratios are more likely to reduce the P/E ratio than increase it.

117 Weak form efficient

For the investor to make gains consistently from his policy, he must believe that he is 'one step ahead' of the market, i.e. that published information has not already been incorporated into the market price. Thus the market can be weak-form efficient at best.

118 B

$$P0 = d0 \; \frac{(1+g)}{(k_e - g)}$$

$G = rb = 0.4 \times 15\% = 6\%$

$$P0 = \frac{200{,}000 \times 1.06}{0.23 - 0.06} = \$1{,}247{,}000$$

119 Statement 1: false   Statement 2: true

EMH concerns share prices, not whether good projects exist, so statement 1 is false.

In a strong form market investors would know the reasons behind any change in dividends, so there would not be any new information content in them. Thus statement 2 is true.

120 B

Number of shares in issue = 400m + 30m = 430m

Earnings = $(120m + 35m + 4m)

= $159m

EPS = $159m/$430m = $0.370

Price per share = $3.00

P/E ratio = 3.0/0.370

= 8.11

121 C

The geometric average dividend growth rate is $(36.0/31.1)1/3 - 1 = 5\%$

The ex div share price = $(36.0 \times 1.05)/(0.16 - 0.05) = \$3.44$

122 B

When the company is being bought for the earnings/ cash flow that all of its assets can produce in the future, a price/ earnings ratio method or a discounted cash flow technique would be useful (A). Asset-based measures using net realisable values help to identify a minimum, not a maximum, price in a takeover (C). When the company has a highly-skilled workforce, this would not be reflected in the value of the assets within the statement of financial position (D). The correct answer is B – asset valuation models are useful in the situation that a company is going to be purchased to be broken up and its assets sold off.

123 A

Answer B = Value per share

Answer C = Earnings yield

Answer D = Price earnings ratio

124 $4.20

Dividend growth rate = 100 × ((33.6/32) − 1) = 5%

MV = 33.6/(0.13 − 0.05) = $4.20

125 D

Expected share price in three years' time = $3.50 × (1.04)3 = $3.94

Conversion value = $3.94 × 30 = $118.20

Compared with redemption at par value of $100, conversion will be preferred.

The current market value will be the present value of future interest payments, plus the present value of the conversion value, discounted at the cost of debt of 5% per year.

Market value of each convertible loan note = [($100 × 6%) × 3yr 5% AF] + ($118.20 × 3yr 5% DF)

= ($6 × 2.723) + ($118.20 × 0.864)

= $118.46

RISK MANAGEMENT

126 B

Matching refers to the balancing of receipts and payments in the same currency.

127 A

The hedge needs to create a peso liability to match the 500,000 peso future income.

6 month peso borrowing rate = 8/2 = 4%

6 month dollar deposit rate = 3/2 = 1.5%

Dollar value of money market hedge = 500,000 × 1.015/(1.04 × 15) = $32,532 or $32,500

128 C

Leading with the payment eliminates the foreign currency exposure by removing the liability. Borrowing short-term in euros to meet the payment obligation in three months' time matches assets and liabilities and provides cover against the exposure. A forward exchange contract is a popular method of hedging against exposure.

129 statement 1: true   statement 2: false

Matching receipts and payments is another method of hedging transaction exposure, not translation exposure.

130 UK exporter: gain   Swedish importer: no effect

The Swedish importer is unaffected as he is invoiced in local currency; the UK exporter will gain as more pounds will be received for the kroner.

131   2.0383 $/£

The company has to change £ to $ to buy the machine, and will be offered the lower rate for this conversion, 2.0383.

132   1.4379 $/£

Applying interest rate parity:

Invest £1,000 at 5.75% for three months (0.0575/4) = £1,014.375

Convert £1,000 to € at 1.4415 = €1,441.5

Invest that at 4.75% for three months (0.0475/4) = €1,458.62

Implied forward rate is therefore 1,458.62/1,014.375 = 1.4379

Incorrect answers – not converting the annual rate to the three monthly one

£1,000 becoming £1,057.50

€1,441.50 becoming €1,509.97

Forward rate = 1.4279

Applying wrong interest rates (£/€ mixed up)

1,000 × (1 + 0.0475/4) = 1,011.88

1,441.50 × (1 + 0.0575/4) = 1,462.22

Forward rate = 1.4451

1,000 × 1.0475 = 1,047.5

1,441.50 × 1.0575 = 1,524.39

Forward rate = 1.4553

133   the missing word is basis

134   B

135   A

(1)   The investor can buy £500,000 for US$950,000 compared to US$975,000 on the spot market.

(2)   The investor can sell the £400,000 for S$1,160,000 compared to S$1,180,000 on the spot market.

The call option should be exercised but the put option should not be exercised.

136 Eady plc: loss   Canadian supplier: no effect

The Canadian supplier is unaffected as it invoices in its local currency, the Canadian dollar. It will receive the same number of Canadian $ regardless of any movements of the C$ against the £. Eady plc will have to pay more £ to purchase the C$ payable, so will suffer a loss on the weakening of sterling.

137 C

Overseas customers will find the country's goods cheaper, thus boosting exports. On the other hand, imported raw materials will become more expensive resulting in inflationary pressure

138 A

A contract that gives one party the right to sell a stock at a certain price and the other party an obligation to buy the asset at that price, on or before a specific date in the future, is a put option. A contract that gives one party the right to buy a stock at a certain price and the other party an obligation to sell the asset at that price, on or before a specific date in the future, is a call option.

139 A BOTH STATEMENTS ARE TRUE

140 B

If you sell a futures contract you have a contract to borrow money (not lend). What you are selling is the contract to make interest payments.

141 C

142 B

143 B

A put option gives the holder the right to sell currency

144 B

145 D

Inflation rates are not relevant to Interest Rate Parity theory (they are relevant to Purchasing Power Parity Theory)

Section B

ANSWERS TO OBJECTIVE TEST CASE QUESTIONS

FINANCIAL MANAGEMENT FUNCTION AND ENVIRONMENT

1   COUNTRY A

(a)   **B and D**

A is false – MM suggested that the pattern of dividends was irrelevant

B is true – the fear that many shareholders will view the cut similarly is the clientele effect

C is false – residual theory suggests undertaking all investments before paying a dividend

D is true – the cut in dividend may signal to shareholders that the company is now higher risk.

(b)   **B**

PPPT suggests that exchange rates will move to compensate for differences in inflation rates.

(c)   **B and D**

A is false – profits have a poor correlation with shareholder value, so it is possible to boost short term profit at the expense of shareholder wealth

B is true.

C is false – the sackings may generate bad publicity that erodes investor confidence and hence reduces the share price

D is true.

(d)   **B**

Statement (i) is true – controlling the money supply has more impact on demand for goods, than, say, the oil price or wage demands

Statement (ii) is true – restricting the money supply will reduce the availability of funds and increase the cost of funds

Statement (iii) is false – restricting the money supply is part of monetary policy.

(e) C

A is true – this is known as economic inefficiency

B is true – the lack of competition means monopolies can make excessive profits without having to spend on new products or processes

C is false – monopolies are more likely to engage in price discrimination to boost profits

D is true – monopolies may charge high prices to deter entrants.

WORKING CAPITAL MANAGEMENT

2   GREEN CO

(a) B

Demand has to be constant so that average inventory is half of the order quantity. As long as the lead time is constant and known, this is sufficient for the EOQ formula to hold; it does not have to be zero.

(b) A

$C_o = \$10$; $D = 4,000$; $C_h = \$2 + 10\%$ of $\$480 = \$50$

$EOQ = \sqrt{(2 \times C_o \times D \div C_h)} = \sqrt{(2 \times 10 \times 4,000 \div 50)} = 40$ units

The alternative answers come from either ignoring the cost of capital tied up in inventory or including the irrelevant chief buyer's salary (or both).

(c) 77 UNITS

The company must be sure that there is sufficient inventory on hand when it places an order to last the weeks' lead time. It must therefore place an order when there is one weeks' worth of demand in inventory:

i.e. re-order level = 1 / 52 × 4,000 = **77 units** remaining in inventory.

(d) B

With deliveries being made on a daily (or more frequent) basis, ordering costs need to be low compared to the benefits of holding inventory. A two-bin system involves re-ordering when a main bin is empty and an inventory-holder needs to count on a second, reserve, bin which effectively constitutes the re-order level.

Periodic review means ordering inventory at a fixed and regular time interval. Inventory levels are reviewed at a fixed time. The inventory in hand is then made up to a predetermined level.

Statements (1) and (3) are correct.

(e) D

One of the earliest American firms to adopt JIT was Hewlett Packard who put forward all of these, based on a study of four of their divisions.

3 HALL CO

(a) **C**

Supplier's terms help determine credit policy in respect of accounts payable, rather than accounts receivable.

(b) **C**

Sales $1,600,000; business sales = 60% of $1.6m - $960,000

Receivables = (0.4 × 1/12 + 0.4 × 2/12 + 0.2 × 3/12) × $960,000 = $144,000

Interest costs = 10% of $144,000 = $14,400

Alternative answers come from taking costs of sales into account and reducing the time by which payment has been brought forward by a month.

(c) **A**

Monthly cost = [(100 ÷ 98.5) − 1] × 100 = 1.523%

Bringing payments forward 1 month has an annual cost of $(1.01523^{12} − 1) × 100 = 19.89\%$

Bringing payments forward 2 months has an annual cost of $(1.01523^{6} − 1) × 100 = 9.49\%$

Alternative answers come from confusing current receivables periods and reduction of receivables periods and reducing the time by which payment has been brought forward by a month.

Tutorial note

The IRR of a project that involves bringing forward the date of receipt of cash from a customer can be seen by looking at the comparative cash flows.

Time	0	month 1	month 2
No discount	–	–	*100*
With discount	–	*98.5*	*–*
Subtracting	–	*(98.5)*	*100*

An extra $1.50 is being made on an 'investment' of $98.50 by a customer, a return over the month of 1.523 per month, or 19.89 per annum.

(d) **B**

(e) **B**

The list (excluding B) has appeared in a model answer from the ACCA of roles of a credit control department. The second option would be part of the role of a purchase ledger department.

4   JEEPS CO

(a)   **A**

A saving of $2 is made for every $98 paid early, a return of $\{(2 \div 98) - 1\} \times 100 = 2.0408\%$

If early payment is made of amounts usually paid after 60 days, the return is made over 45 days. This represents an annual return of $(1.020408^{(365/45)} - 1) \times 100 = 17.8\%$

If early payment is made of amounts usually paid after 90 days, the return is made over 75 days. This represents an annual return of $(1.020408^{(365/75)} - 1) \times 100 = 10.3\%$

Since Jeeps Co's cost of capital is 12%, the prompt payment is worthwhile for 60 days, not for 90 days

Tutorial note

Marginally different annual returns are reached (17.8% and 10.2%) if the periods of the 'investment' are taken as 1½ months and 2½ months, but the conclusion is the same.

(b)   **B**

Total payables = $2m + $3m × 2 + $4m × 3 = $20m

Total credit purchases = ($2m + $3m + $4m) × 12 = $108m

Payables period = $20m × 365 ÷ $108m = $68m

Tutorial note

A weighted average of payables would give a figure of $67m (B is still closest).

(c)   **B**

Increasing shareholder funds suggests a business that is aware of an increasing need for extra capital as it expands and that shareholders understand that need.

(d)   **C**

Monthly rate = $(1.12^{(1/12)} - 1) \times 100 = 0.95\%$

Current PV of payment made in full after 3 months = $300,000 \div 1.0095^3 = \$291,620$

PV of instalments = $75 + \dfrac{45}{1.009^5} + \dfrac{45}{1.0095^2} + \dfrac{45}{1.0095^3} + \dfrac{45}{1.0095^4} + \dfrac{45}{1.0095^5} = \$293,734$

Paying by instalments will cost Jeeps Co $2,114

Alternative answers are arrived at by using 1% as the monthly rate and confusing costs and benefits.

Tutorial note

Using a 20 day rate gives a PV of $291,733 which still leaves C the closest answer.

(e)   B

5   KING CO

(a)   C

Baumol tranche size = √(2 × $500 × $1,000,000 ÷ 0.05) = $141,421

Alternative answers arise from not entering the interest rate as a decimal or using total demand for cash rather than annual demand.

(b)   D

Miller-Orr spread = 3 × (¾ × $50,000^2 × $500 ÷ 0.05)⅓ = $79,699

Alternative answers come from using standard deviation instead of variance or entering the interest rate as a decimal.

(c)   A

Month	3	4	5	6	7
Sales volume (000s)	10	11	13	16	20
Sales revenue ($000)	240	264	312	384	480
Cash sales (20%)	48.0	52.8	62.4	76.8	96
Receivables:					
1-month (25% of 80%)	–	48.0	52.8	62.4	76.8
2-month (50% of 80%)	–	–	96.0	105.6	124.8
3-month (25% of 80%)	–	–	–	48.0	52.8
			211.2		

The alternative answers come from not spotting that credit sales are only 80% of total sales and from getting the months muddled.

Tutorial note

The calculations for months other than Month 5 are not essential but tend to reduce the chance of making mistakes (although, without the need for calculations of payments, Months 6 and 7 could be ignored).

(d)   **Both statements are true.**

(e)   C

6   GRUMPY CO

(a)   **B**

Receivables period = $\dfrac{85,000}{480,000} \times 365 = 65$ days

(b)   **A**

Payables period = $\dfrac{30,000}{212,000} \times 365 = 52$ days

(c)   **B**

Inventory holding period = $\dfrac{52,000}{226,000} \times 365 = 84$ days

The cost of sales of £226,000 is equal to 45,000 + 233,000 − 52,000

(d)   The start of the cycle is the point at which the supplier is paid. This is on 25/2/15.

The end point of the cycle is the date on which Grumpy receives the case from the debtor. The goods were delivered 21 days after the order on 28/1/15. They were sold 62 days later on 28/3/15. The debtor then took 68 days to pay (the offered credit is irrelevant) and so Grumpy was paid on 4/6/15.

The number of days between 25/2/15 and 4/6/15 is the operating cycle for cycle X and this is 96 days.

(e)   **A**

A period of strong growth when a business has a long operating cycle is a classic example of over trading.

New business tend to struggle to get credit from suppliers and often have to give longer credit to customers for fear of breaking a new and fragile relationship with them.

INVESTMENT APPRAISAL

7   BELL CO

(a)   **A**

Money cost of capital = $(1.05 \times 1.02) - 1 = 7.1\%$

(b)   **CASH FLOW = $120,000 × 1.043 = $134,984**

Present value = $134,984 ÷ 1.08^4 = $99,217

Answer to the nearest thousand dollars is **$99,000**

(c) **D**

Time	0	1	2	3
	$000	$000	$000	$000
Inflow (in money terms)	–	2,040	3,121	2,122
Outflow (in money terms)	(1,000)	(1,854)	(2,652)	(1,639)
Net cash flow	(1,000)	186	469	483
Present value at 9%	(1,000)	171	395	373

NPV = $(61,000)

Answer A has discounted current cash flows at the rates of inflation rather than at the money cost of capital, answer B has ignored inflation and answer C has only used one year of inflation for the cash flows at times 2 and 3.

Tutorial note

This final mistake is easy to make; anyone who thought C was correct needs to check how the money cash flows in the model answer were calculated (the figures have been rounded to the nearest $'000 in the workings).

(d) **B**

A is incorrect. There is no decision rule with simulations. B is a clear advantage that simulations have over sensitivity analysis. C is incorrect. The input variables and distributions are estimates. D has some validity potentially, but is not necessarily the case.

(e) The **answer is yes** and the **reason is that it will happen if the rate of inflation exceeds the money cost of capital.**

This was a situation that was highlighted by Brian Carsberg and Tony Hope in the 1970s (a time of high inflation) in their book Business Investment Decisions under Inflation, ICAEW, 1976. With the current state of low interest rates, the situation may be just as relevant today.

Reason A is not correct, the only negative discount rate that makes calculating an NPV tricky is -100%. Tutorial note: You may wish use a spreadsheet to calculate the NPV of a simple project for a range of discount rates from -200% to +200%.

Reason B is not correct since there have been many instances of negative interest rates. The European Central Bank recently introduced negative rates which have also been seen in Sweden, Denmark and Switzerland.

Reason C is not correct since deflation (negative inflation) is likely to increase the chance of having a positive real discount rate (unless your money cost of capital is even more negative).

8 CARE CO

(a) D

Negative NPV ($000) = ($540 + $47 × 2.487 – ($120 ÷ 1.10^3) = $566.731

Equivalent annual cost = $566.731 ÷ 2.487 = $227.875, say $228,000

Answers A and C do not find an equivalent annual cost since they do not divide by an annuity factor, merely divide by 3 (or 4). Answers A and B assume the project lasts four years rather than three.

(b) Both statements are correct.

The EAC method assumes that the operating efficiency of the machines will be similar. The method also assumes that the assets will be replaced in perpetuity, or at least into the foreseeable future.

(c) C

Scrap Value	Probability		Expected value
$120,000	0.6 × 0.7	= 0.42	50,400
£108,000	0.4 × 0.7 + 0.6 × 0.3	= 0.46	49,680
$96,000	0.4 × 0.3	= 0.12	11,520
		1.00	$111,600

Answers B and D ignore joint probabilities; whereas answers A and B misinterpret the effects of a strong dollar (a strong dollar would make an overseas sale less attractive).

(d) Only statement 2 is true.

Simulation will not eliminate the effects of risk, it will merely help quantify the effects by producing a range of possible NPVs and an idea of the probability distribution of those NPVs.

(e) B

Using the 'lowest common multiple' approach (12 years) is an alternative to simple replacement decisions.

9   DEACON CO

(a)   B

Tax-allowable depreciation

	Balance $000	TA depreciation $000	Tax saved (20%) $000	Timing
Capital cost	1,280			
25%	320	320	64	Time 1
	960			
25%	240	240	48	Time 2
	720			
25%	180	180	36	Time 3 (20X3)
	540			
Sale proceeds	290			
Balancing all'nce	250	250	50	Time 4

PV of savings from tax-allowable depreciation in 20X3 = $\dfrac{36,000}{1.11^3}$ = $26,323

(b)   B

(c)   C

PV of Initial deposit   = $(300,000)

PV of tax savings from payment (2-year delay)   = $300,000 × 0.20 ÷ 1.11^2 = $48,697

(d)   C

It is not uncommon for finance leases to have a clause allowing the lessee to take the capital asset when its expected useful life is over either at a lower rent or for a small capital sum.

(e)   B

PV of three annual rental payments = $(375,000) × 2.444 × 1.11 = $(1,017,315)

PV of tax savings from rent = 20% with 2-year delay = $1,017,315 × 0.20 ÷ 1.112 = $165,135

NPV of operational lease = $165,135 - $1,017,315 = $(852,180)

Answer A indicates that the tax saving has only been delayed by one year; answer C misses out tax and has the lease payments a year later; answer D misses out tax, even though the correct timings for the lease payments has been used.

Tutorial note

Questions are sometimes written in a friendly way such that tax effects are always one year after the initial cash flows. Alternatively they can be written with company year ends and timings of cash flows (at the beginning or end of a financial year) in which case you need to read the question carefully and take care over the timings of tax effects.

10   EASTER CO

(a)   **C**

Hard rationing is the limit on the amount of finance imposed by the lending institutions. Soft rationing may arise as a means of controlling divisional managers.

(b)   **Projects A and E should be accepted.**

Project	NPV	Investment	NPV/$	Rank
	$000	$000	$	
A	4,900	3,200	1.53	2nd
B	7,400	9,320	0.80	5th
C	5,900	7,300	0.81	4th
D	7,500	5,200	1.44	3rd
E	9,000	5,600	1.61	1st

Total investment required is $34.7m, total available is $10m.

Possible combinations (assuming that will give a higher NPV than any single project):

Project A and D   NPV ($000) = 4,900 + 7,500 = 12,400

Projects A and E   NPV ($000) = 4,900 + 9,000 = 13,900

These are higher than the NPVs of any single project.

(c)   **A**

Based on the workings of the previous question, now the combination A and E is not possible (since they are mutually exclusive). This leaves the highest NPV as combination A and D.

(d)   **B**

Using the previous NPV/$ calculations and rankings, the combination accepted must be A plus E plus a portion of D.

Tutorial note

To reach the correct answer to this question, it doesn't matter what proportion of D is required, the answer to the correct option of the four is Option B. The next calculation is therefore unnecessary.

Projects A and E require a total investment of $8.8m, leaving $1.2m to invest in part of Project D. Since Project D requires a total investment of $5.2m, the proportion of that project undertaken can be:

1.2m ÷ 5.2m = 3/13 (as in Option B) or 23.1%

(e)   **B**

This project has two 'changes in sign' in the pattern of cash flows, therefore may have two positive IRRs

The NPV at a discount rate of zero (the net undiscounted cash flows) is $(30,000).

The NPV at an infinitely high discount rate (the initial investment) is $(4,000,000)

The NPV at 10% is - $4m + [$8.8m ÷ 1.10] – [$4.83m ÷ 1.10^2], i.e. $8,264

This indicates that there is likely to be an IRR between 0 and 10% and between 10% and infinity. Trial and error, or elementary algebra, can show that the two positive IRRs are 5% and 15%. These are shown on two graphs shown below, one for discount rates over a reasonable range and one for a much larger range of rates, some of which have little practical significance.

Graphs of NPV (in $00,000) against discount rate for a project.

Tutorial note

The second graph shows that strange things happen with a rate of –100%.

These graphs can be compared with those for a conventional project (investing $4m at time 0 and receiving $3m at time 1 and time 2).

11   ACE CO

(a)   **B**

NPV of project

Time	Description	CF	DF @ 12%	PV $
0	Loose tools	(6,000)	1	(6,000)
1-4	Contribution	25,000	3.037	75,925
1-4	Allocated overhead	0		0
2-5	Tax on contribution	(6,250)	2.712	(16,950)
	NPV			52,975

The allocated overhead is not a relevant cash flow.

(b)   **C**

The interest rates would have to more than double before the project would reach a breakeven NPV and so it is not very sensitive. The pattern of cash flows can affect this decision, for example, for projects where positive cash flows arise first with negative cash flows thereafter then the statement would be false.

(c)   **C**

The profits are not affected by tax-allowable depreciation.

(d)   **D**

The payback period is

In the first year the project spends 6,000 but receives 25,000. The tax flow does not arise until the following year. So the payback is (6000/25000) × 12 months = 2.9 months

(e)   **C**

One of payback's problems is the lack of a clear decision criterion

BUSINESS FINANCE AND COST OF CAPITAL

12   BRASH CO

(a)   **A**

Leasing companies sometimes pass the obligation for maintenance back to the lessee, as everything is negotiable.

(b)   **D**

To assess the cost of leasing against borrowing the post tax lease flows are discounted at the post tax cost of borrowing, this accounts for the interest cash flows concept. The savings on maintenance, payable if you buy an asset and the residual value receivable if you buy are relevant cash flows. Tax-allowable depreciation are taken by the lessee in either case and so are not relevant.

(c) **C**

Years 1 -5 maintenance of $20,000 discounted at 6% discount rate.

Annuity factor = 4.212

$20,000 × 4.212 = 84,240

(d) **D**

Years 2 -6 tax relief of $146,000 x 0.25 = $36,500 discounted at 6% discount rate.

Annuity factor = 3.974

$36,500 × 3.974 = $145,051

(e) **A**

The existence of an operating risk cannot affect traditional gearing ratios, but it does represent extra risk for shareholders that may be perceived.

13 KELVIN CO

(a) **B**

The TERP value is calculated as:

$$TERP = \frac{MV\ of\ existing\ shares + proceeds\ from\ issue}{Number\ of\ shares\ after\ issue}$$

$$TERP = \frac{(4m \times \$20) + (1m \times 20 \times 0.9)}{5m}$$

TERP = $19.60 per share

(b) **C**

Whilst the TERP would fall, it could not do so to the detriment of existing shareholders. In the formula above the top line would remain the same whilst the number of shares on the bottom line would increase.

(c) **A**

Both the statements are true. The discount makes the rights offer appear more attractive but the theory indicates it should make no difference to the accepting shareholder.

(d) **C**

As long as the shareholder takes some form of action they will be better off than doing nothing. The second worst action (by the way) is D as the shareholder will lose out on 50% of the offer.

(e) **A**

Dilution occurs if a shareholders % ownership reduces. This will not happen if a shareholder takes up 100% of the offer.

14 DOMINANCE CO

(a)   **D**

All the other options will involve at least the risk of new shareholders diluting ownership.

(b)   **D**

Option A has no new tax shield at all as preference dividend does not attract it. Option B does contain tax shield but presumably less than C and D given the lower value and interest rate. Option C has less interest on it and hence tax shield than D.

(c)   **B**

The cost of equity formula is:

$$Ke = \frac{D_1}{MV} + g$$

$$Ke = \frac{16(1.10)}{420-16} + 0.10$$

$$Ke = 14.4\%$$

(d)   **D**

The cost of debt formula is:

$$Kd = \frac{Interest\,(1-t)}{MV}$$

$$Kd = \frac{4(1-0.25)}{80}$$

$$Kd = 3.75\%$$

(e)   **D**

The tax shield is relevant but is minor when one considers the risk premium is approximately 10.4%.

The main driver for risk premium is systematic risk. All the specific risk will be ignored by the well diversified shareholder.

15 EMPIRE CO

(a)   **C**

(b)   **B**

(c)   **A**

(d)   **D**

(e)   **D**

A scrip issue gives more shares to shareholders but since the overall market value is not affected then the share price falls. The shareholder does not gain except for an increased marketability.

15   BANK

(a)   C

A bank is rather unusual in that many of the variables that would normally be counted as systematic risks for other businesses are in fact specific risks for the bank. Interest rates and defaults fall into this category. Equally the bank will compete for loans in the market and so that too is a specific risk.

(b)   C

(c)   D

The CAPM gives you the required return of equity shareholders for the level of risk indicated by the value of the beta used.

(d)   D

R = Rf + βj(Rm – Rf)

R = 5.2 + 1.52(12.8 – 5.2)

R = 16.75%

(e)   D

17   FREEDLING CO

(a)   B

Having fixed costs in a cost structure is risky since they have to be paid and are often unavoidable in the short run if the business starts to turn downwards. This has a magnifying effect on the businesses profit for a given volume change.

(b)   D

Cost structures can be changed. For example property can be rented on a needs only basis thus avoiding the heavy fixed cost of a lease for example. Equally it is often the case that a business will pay more for the flexibility of having variable costs rather than fixed costs.

(c)   D

Under M&M no tax the WACC would generally not change. M&M argued that the level of gearing was not relevant to a company WACC. With corporation tax introduced into their model a tax benefit tended to pull down the WACC as gearing increased.

Under the traditional theory of gearing modest amounts of debt often went unnoticed by shareholders and this lack of response (in the form of increased demands for higher return) meant the WACC fell.

(d)   D

It is a common error to think that M&M claimed 'it does not matter how a business raises its finance'. Finance can come with it a host of unpleasant conditions that are best avoided for example. The second statement is what they actually said and the first statement is a rather clumsy paraphrase.

(e)   A

All the statements are true.

BUSINESS VALUATIONS

18   KEVIN DUTTON

(a)   B

Consider a bond with a nominal value of $100

MV = PV of future receipts discounted at Kevin's required return of 30%

MV = (Interest of 4 × 5yr annuity factor @ 30%) + (redemption of 100 × 5yr DF @ 30%)

MV = (5 × 2.436) + (100 × 0.269) = 39.08

Thus total MV = $390,800 or $391,000 to the nearest $1,000

(b)   8.9%

An investment of 60 now will result in a cash receipt of 100 in 6 years

Solving $60 \times (1 + r)^6 = 100$, gives $1 + r = 1.0889$, so $r = 8.9\%$

(c)   C

Issue value $\times (1.10)^6 = 100$, giving an issue value of 56.447

Thus a discount of at least 43.55%, or 44% must be applied

(d)   C

Statement (i) is false, otherwise no companies would be able to issue deep discounted bonds in the first place. (Note: it is illegal for companies to issue **shares** at a discount)

Statement (ii) is true – the nature of forestry is that an initial investment is required (planting saplings), followed by no income until the trees are ready to be harvested. The repayment pattern with deep discounted bonds matches this. .

Statement (iii) is false – the price investors buy the bonds at reflects the risks and, hence, the required return. Thus the precise nature of the cash flows associated with a bond (e.g. coupon rate) are not important.

(e)   D

A: False: MV = PV of future receipts discounted at the investors' required return. A change in interest rates will affect investors' required returns and hence the bond price

B: False :MV = PV of future receipts discounted at investors' required return. A change in inflation rates will affect investors' required returns in money terms and hence the bond price.

C: False: the statement is the wrong way round – changes in the required return affect the bond value

D: True. As rates rise, investors require a higher return, hence the value of the receipts (interest and redemption) falls.

19 LOKI

(a) **C**

The break-up value of the assets normally represents the minimum price which should be accepted for the sale of a business as a going concern, since if the income based valuations give figures lower than the break-up value it is apparent that the owner would be better off by ceasing to trade and selling off all the assets piecemeal.

Replacement cost should provide a measure of the maximum amount that any purchaser should pay for the whole business, since it represents the total cost of forming the business from scratch.

Asset based measures typically ignore non statement of financial position intangible assets e.g. a highly skilled workforce, strong management team and competitive positioning of the company's products.

(b) **0.89**

Step 1: 'degear' Q's equity beta to give an asset beta

$$\beta_a = \beta_e \left[\frac{V_E}{V_E + V_D[1-t]} \right] = 1.2 \left[\frac{2}{2 + 1[1-0.3]} \right] = 0.8888... = 0.89$$

This can then be taken as Loki's asset beta as the two companies have similar business activities.

Given Loki is all equity financed, then this is also Loki's equity beta – no 'regearing' is required.

(c) **B**

Fair MV = PV of future dividends discounted at the K_e of 14%

Fair MV = 14/(0.14 – 0.04) = 140m or $0.70 per share

Note: the dividend of 14m is already a t=1 figure so does not need to be multiplied by a factor of 1.04.

However, the issue price will be at a 15% discount, giving 0.70 × 0.85 = 0.595 = $0.60

(d) **C**

Consider a bond with a nominal value of $100

MV = PV of future receipts discounted at investor's required return of 6%

MV = (Interest of 5 × 4yr annuity factor) + (redemption of 100 × 4yr DF)

MV = (5 × 3.630) + (100 × 0.792) = 97.35

(e) **B and C**

A is false – the secured bonds will have the lowest risk.

B is true – the option to convert acts as a sweetener, allowing Loki to pay lower dividends

C is true – the venture capital company is likely to have well diversified shareholders

D is false – the family are unlikely to want to lose control of their company

20   DAVID MCNABB

(a)   **C**

Company A is in a very capital intensive business and it is likely that the value of the housing stock is a very close estimate of the value of the company, particularly given recent losses.

Recent and even future losses make it difficult to use earnings (option A) and/or dividend (option B) approaches.

Given it is unquoted, there is no share price to use to estimate market capitalisation (option D).

(b)   **D**

MV = earnings × (1+g)/(earnings yield – g)

MV = 12.5 × 1.02/(0.12 – 0.02) = 12.75/0.10 = 127.5m

(c)   **B**

MV = PV of future dividends discounted at the K_e of 14%

MV = 5 × annuity factor for 3 years + value of growing perpetuity × 3yr simple discount factor

MV = 5 × 2.322 + [5 × 1.03/(0.14 – 0.03)] × 0.675

MV = 11.6 + 31.6 = 43.2m

(d)   **B**

A: Strong form implies all shares are fairly priced, even taking into account secret information.

B: In a semi strong market, secret information would enable an investor to outperform the market by identifying undervalued companies, so option B is true.

C: A semi-strong market will incorporate all publicly available information in the share price, so David will not unearth anything useful looking at such information.

D: Weak form efficiency is sufficient to imply that there are no trends in share prices and hence David will not find any useful by his 'chartism'.

(e)   **C**

Statement (i) is true. The shareholders of M Inc are likely to be well diversified (even M Inc is likely to be well diversified) so will not be interested in attempts to reduce unsystematic risk further.

Statement (ii) is false – David should be looking at risk **and** return and try to develop a portfolio where the anticipated return exceeds the CAPM required return.

Statement (iii) is false – only unsystematic risk can be diversified away, by definition.

21 PIKE

(a)   C

Minimum value to the seller is given by NRV (note: this would have already deducted the value of the loan)

(b) $50

MV = P/E × future sustainable earnings

To get an estimate of future earnings we need firstly to inflate the historic figure by 3% and then, secondly adjust for the post-tax salary

Sustainable earnings = (7,000,000 × 1.03) − (100,000 × 0.70) = 7,140,000

MV = 7 × 7,140,000 = 49,980,000, or $50m

(c)   A

PV of future CFs discounted at the WACC = 6/(0.12 − 0.04) = $75m

However, this gives the value of equity + debt, so the value of the debt must be deducted

MV equity = 75 − 2.5 = $72.5m

(d)   A and B

A is true. The decision by owner/managers how to take funds out of a company is usually made to reduce tax.

B is true. In a service business the goodwill may be tied up with the owner/manage rather than the company

C is false − in a strong form market the share price will react before information is made public

D is false − given Pike is listed and a conglomerate, then it is highly likely that its shareholders are well diversified and, hence, only concerned about **systematic** risk.

(e)   B

Statement (i) is true. Minnow operates in a service industry that is not capital intensive.

Statement (ii) is true − DCF approaches are generally seen as superior.

Statement (iii) is false for two reasons − firstly historic dividend shave been artificially high, a trend unlikely to continue and, secondly, DVM is less useful for valuing a majority stake

22 PREY CO

(a)   A

Value = (100 + 170) + (25 − 100) + (40 − 50) = $185,000

(b)   C

Value = (100 + 170) + (500 − 100) = $670,000

(c) **C**

Statement (i) is false. Despite operating in a capital intensive industry, without an estimate of the value of Prey Ltd's brand name, the asset valuation is likely to be far too low

Statement (ii) is true – Prey Ltd's value stems from the quality of its products and its reputation.

Statement (iii) is false – if the statement has said 'net realisable value' rather than 'net book value', then it would have been true.

(d) **B**

The P/E ratio of the quoted company will be based on historic eps but value is based on future earnings potential.

MV = 10 × 156 = $1,560,000

There are 200,000 shares, giving a share price of $7.080

(e) **9.5%**

The growth rate used in the DVM should be future growth

The best indicator of future growth can be calculated using years 20X4 to 20X6 (20X3 was a transition year and the impact of the boost in demand was only partially seen)

Solving $65(1 + g)^2 = 78$, gives g = 0.0954... or 9.5%

RISK MANAGEMENT

23 MALLETT CO

(a) **D**

Mallett Co will receive 850,000USD in 3 months' time

The company will (1) borrow the appropriate amount in US dollars now; (2) convert the US dollars to Australian dollars immediately; (3) invest the Australian dollars in an Australian dollar bank account knowing that it will grow over the next three months; (4) use the client's cash (US dollars) to pay off the US dollar borrowing (which will have grown with interest) and close the account; (5) take the Australian dollars out of its account, it will have increased by interest but will be a known amount that can be calculated now.

The amount to borrow now, as in (1), is 850,000 USD ÷ 1.00825 = 843,045 USD

This will be converted now, as in (2), to 843,045 ÷ 0.7233 AUD = 1,165,554 AUD

Placed on deposit, as in (3), it grows to 1,165,554 × 1.00725 AUD = 1,174,004 AUD

(The client's receipt will pay off the US dollar loan which has increased with interest.)

The alternative answers come from ignoring the need to allow for 3-month's interest on the Australian dollar account and from using annual rates instead of quarterly rates.

(b)   A

The expectation theory suggests that you would earn the same amount by investing in a one-year bond which is then rolled into a second one-year bond as you would by buying a two-year bond today.

(c)   C

The ACCA formula sheet tells you that interest rate parity says that: $F_0 = S_0 \times \dfrac{(1+i_c)}{(1+i_b)}$

Using more useful notation for this question: $F_0 = S_0 \times \dfrac{(1+US\,rate)}{(+Australian\,rate)}$

Three-month forward rate $= 0.7233 \times \dfrac{(1+0.033 \div 4)}{1+0.029 \div 4)} = 0.7240$ USD to the AUD

The alternative answers come from getting the formula the wrong way up and from using annual rates instead of quarterly ones.

(d)   D

Translation losses can, for example, result from restating the book-value of an overseas branch's assets at the exchange rate at the balance sheet date

(e)   D

The option provides you with the right, but not the obligation to exchange currencies.

24   NOON CO

(a)   B

Noon needs to pay 3 million Flyland Francs in three months

Using the 3-month forward rate, these will cost 3m ÷ 6.321 = 474,608 CC

Alternative answers are arrived at by using the spot rate or using the rate for selling Flyland Francs rather than buying them.

(b)   C

(c)   D

Noon needs to pay 3m Flyland Francs in three months

The company will (1) borrow the appropriate amount in Centreland Colons now; (2) convert the Colons into Flyland Francs immediately; (3) invest the Francs in a Flyland Franc bank account knowing that it will grow to 3 m Francs in three months' time; (4) pay the 3m Francs to the Flyland supplier and close the account; (5) repay the amount borrowed in (1) in Colons which will have increased by interest but will be a known amount that can be calculated now.

The amount to invest in step (3) in Francs at a rate of 13.5% per year or 3.375% over 3 months = 3m Francs ÷ 1.03375 = 2,902,056

The amount to convert to Francs now in step (2) = 2,902,056 ÷ 6.170 = 470,349 Colons

The amount that will have to be paid in three months' time to pay off this borrowing in Colons = 470,349 × 1.02025 = 479,874 Colons

The alternative answers come from using annual rates rather than 3-monthly ones and forgetting that we compare two payments made in three months' time, i.e. forgetting to increase the borrowing in Colons by 3 months' interest.

(d) **D**

(e) **A**

Purchasing power parity formula: $S1 = S0 \times \dfrac{1+h_c}{1+h_b}$

More usefully:

Spot rate in 3 months' time ≈ 3-month forward rate

$= \text{Spot rate} \times \dfrac{(1+\text{overseas inflation rate})}{(1+\text{domestic inflation rate})}$

Using lower of the two exchange rates (as recommended) and using quarterly inflation rates based on the annual rates given.

6.321 = 6.170 × (1 + [annual overseas inflation rate ÷ 4]) ÷ (1 + [0.038 ÷ 4])

1 + [annual overseas rate ÷ 4] = (6.321 ÷ 6.170) ×1.0095 = 1.0342

Annual overseas rate = 3.42 × 4 = 13.682, or 14%

Alternative answers come from getting the original purchasing power parity formula the wrong way up or from not spotting that you need to use quarterly inflation rates (since you have been given a three-month forward exchange rate).

Tutorial note

You get a similar result (13.684%) if you use the higher exchange rate, i.e. no difference when working to the nearest percentage point. Many pieces of information about money markets seem to take annual rates and divide them, by 4 to find quarterly rates or take quarterly rates and quadruple them when one would expect to use fourth roots of indexes or raise them to the power four. It only makes a small difference in this case. An annual inflation rate of 14.3% would be found by raising an index number based on a quarterly rate to the power 4, a perfectly understandable calculation in view of the way inflation operates. It was the reason for asking for an answer to the nearest percent.

25   PZK CO

(a)   **A**

The foreign exchange risk exposure relates to the value of the receipt for an individual transaction

(b)   **B**

The current dollar value of the future euro receipt = €1,200,000/4.2080 = $285,171

If a forward contract is taken out, PZK Co can lock into the six-month forward exchange rate of 4.2606 euros per dollar.

Future dollar value using the forward contract = €1,200,000/4.2606 = $281,651

Loss using the forward contract = 285,171 − 281,651 = $3,520

(c)   **D**

The implied interest rate in the foreign country can be calculated using interest rate parity.

From the formulae sheet, $F0 = S0 \times (1 + ic)/(1 + ib)$

Hence $4.3132 = 4.2080 \times (1 + ic)/1.04$

Rearranging, $(1 + ic) = 4.3132 \times 1.04/4.2080 = 1.066$

The implied annual interest rate in the foreign country is 6.6%.

(d)   **C**

The forward rates indicate that the dollar will buy more euros in the future.

Given the receipt is in euros, then PZK can expect the $ equivalent value of the receipt to fall as the dollar strengthens.

Thus PZK should consider 'leading' and trying to get the receipt sooner.

(e)   **C**

Statement (i) is false – PZK may still be exposed to transaction risk on purchases.

Statement (ii) is true – One of the simplest ways for PZK Co to avoiding exchange rate risk is to invoice in its home currency, which passes the exchange rate risk on to the foreign customer, who must effectively find the dollars with which to make the payment.

Statement (iii) is true - This strategy may not be commercially viable, however, since the company's foreign customers will not want to take on the exchange rate risk. They will instead transfer their business to those competitors of PZK Co who invoice in the foreign currency and who therefore shoulder the exchange rate risk.

26 H CO

(a) B and D

A is false- the factory doesn't exist yet so would not be good security on the loan.

B is true – MM with tax concluded that companies should gear up as much as possible.

C is false – some forms of equity, such as cutting a dividend, have very low issue costs

D is true – the cost of debt will (normally) be lower than the cost of equity, due mainly to lower investor risk and tax relief on interest.

(b) C

Market segmentation theory helps explain any 'wiggle' on the yield curve rather than why it might be normal instead of inverted.

(c) A

The interest payable on the actual loan will be linked to the spot rate of 7.6%

However, the FRA effectively locks into a reference rate of 7.8% (borrowing so use higher rate)

Thus F company will have to make a payment of 0.2%

This equates to 0.2% × 10m × 6/12 = $10,000

(d) A and C

A is correct – rounding the number of contracts may result in a mismatch

B is false – as long as the futures contract has not expired when the loan is needed, the hedge works

C is correct – the basis may not move as expected

D is false – unpredictability is why we hedge in the first place!

(e) C

Statements (i) and (iii) are true – the hedge is constructed by borrowing at the market rate and then the FRA/futures position will generate a gain or loss that can be offset against the loss or gain on the associated real world borrowing.

Statement (ii) is false – FRAs are OTC instruments arranged with a bank.

27   F CO

(a)   A and D

The main reason for an inverted curve is when interest rates are high but expected to fall. Historically, yield curves often invert before a major turning point in the business cycle and an economy heads into recession. A good example is when the U.S. Treasury yield curve inverted in 2000 just before the U.S. equity markets collapsed.

(b)   C

The interest receivable on the actual deposit will be linked to the spot rate of 5.5%

However, the FRA effectively locks into a reference rate of 5% (depositing so use the lower of the two quoted rates)

Thus F company will have to make a payment of 0.5%

This equates to 0.5% × 1m × 3/12 = $1,250

(c)   A

Interest rate options are the right to buy or sell interest rate futures. The option will only be exercised in order to make a profit on the futures which will help to mitigate any losses on a loan or deposit due to a rise in interest rates.

Interest rate options do not give entitlement to a loan or deposit. This is taken out independently of the options. An interest rate option does not give the right to an interest rate. It effectively increases deposit receipts when interest rates fall adversely by providing a profit on the futures that have been bought or sold.

(d)   C

An interest rate guarantee allows the company a period of time during which it has the option to buy an FRA at a set price (A). An interest rate future locks the company into an effective interest rate (B). An interest rate swap **does not** involve the exchange of the principal, only the exchange of a floating stream of interest payments for a fixed stream of interest payments and vice versa (D).

(e)   D

Statement (i) is true – lenders set rates primarily based on risk assessments

Statement (ii) is false – under swaps there is no exchange of principals.

Statement (iii) is false – F would only be liable for the loan it borrowed.

ANSWERS TO CONSTRUCTED RESPONSE PRACTICE QUESTIONS

FINANCIAL MANAGEMENT FUNCTION AND ENVIRONMENT

1   UUL CO

Key answer tips

This ratio combines a very examinable area (financial ratios) with the less frequently examined topic of stakeholder objectives and regulation.

Part (a) requires some calculations to be performed. Critically though, you must also comment on these calculations.

To answer parts (b) and (c) you will need to think practically and considering the real world position of water companies should help you generate ideas.

The highlighted words are key phrases that markers are looking for.

(a)   Equivalent annual growth in dividends – $(7.1/4.2)^{0.25} - 1 = 14.0\%$

Equivalent annual growth in earnings – $(41.3/31.6)^{0.25} - 1 = 6.9\%$

Share price – 20X2 – 31.6c × 17 = \$5.37

Share price – 20X6 – 41.3c × 22 = \$9.09

Equivalent annual growth in share price – $(9.09/5.37)^{0.25} - 1 = 14.1\%$

The chairman states that the company has delivered above average performance. However, whilst dividend growth has exceeded the water industry average, the growth in earnings and the growth in share price is significantly behind the water industry average. Hence, it is hard to justify the statement made by the chairman.

Indeed, the shareholders should be concerned that given the growth in earnings, the current dividend growth rate does not seem sustainable.

On the positive side, given the inflation rate during this period, the company has delivered real growth in earnings, dividends and share price. Additionally, the P/E ratio has grown, which indicates the market is increasingly confident about the future of the company.

(b)   Three other key stakeholders in UUL Co are the local community in the area that the company operates, the customers of the company and the government.

The local community will be interested in the financial success of the company, as this will potentially generate jobs and wealth in their region. Equally, they will be keen to ensure that the company adheres to best practice in the treatment and disposal of sewage and that the risk of pollution is minimised.

Customers of the company will be keen that their cost for water is minimised. At the same time, they will be keen to make sure that they have a constant, reliable and safe water supply.

The government will be keen to extract tax receipts and will be keen to see the company succeed so that those tax receipts grow. The government will also want to make sure that all the operations of the company comply with the relevant environmental legislation and that all developments by the company, such as the development of a new reservoir, comply with planning laws.

Tutorial note:

Sensible references to other stakeholders would have also been acceptable.

(d)   The government will be keen to minimise the impact that the likely monopoly position of UUL Co will have on its customers. The monopoly position may itself be tolerated as the water industry is a natural monopoly where it would be hard to introduce competition and where the economies of scale necessary to justify the infrastructure investment make a monopoly acceptable. Hence, the government is very likely to control price increases and limit the return that the company is able to make in order to make sure that UUL Co does not take advantage of its monopoly position. Equally the government is likely to impose minimum service standards that UUL Co must provide to its customers, as the customers do not have a choice of provider.

The government will also intervene to make sure that UUL Co is carrying out its operations in a way that will not cause unnecessary environmental damage.

As a public company UUL Co will suffer all the costs associated with making sure that they have, and are seen to have, good corporate governance.

Additionally, UUL Co will suffer interference from government, as water is a strategic commodity and the government have an obligation to make sure that the country's anticipated needs are forecast and planned for.

2   CCC

Key answer tips

Part (a) is a tricky question on objective setting that requires a reasonable depth of knowledge of NFPs to score well. Part (b) is more straightforward but needs good application to the two companies concerned. The highlighted words are key phrases that markers are looking for.

(a)   The key criteria that need to be considered when objective setting are as follows:

Stakeholder expectations

All organisations need to identify key stakeholders, examine their expectations and try to set objectives to meet them.

For CCC stakeholders include:

- Local residents want to see the provision of quality health and education services and value for money in response to paying local taxes.

- Local businesses who will be interested in local infrastructure when deciding whether to invest in the area. In particular, CCC may be keen to ensure that DDD does not close its local offices, with resulting job losses, and move to the capital city.

- Central Government committees who make funding decisions based on local population and deprivation.

For DDD stakeholders include:

- Shareholders want to see their wealth increased through a mixture of growing dividends and an increasing share price. DDD has reflected this in the objective to increase shareholder wealth by 10% per annum.

- Customers will expect a certain level of quality and value for money, depending on the nature of products sold.

- The local communities affected by DDD will expect them to be good citizens and operate at high levels of corporate social responsibility.

Stakeholder power

All organisations will find conflicts between stakeholders so they need to consider how to prioritise them.

For a company like DDD the expectations of shareholders come first for the following reasons:

- This is usually reflected in companies' legislation where directors have a duty in law to put shareholder interests first. Many governance recommendations focus on protecting shareholder interests.

- Failure to deliver shareholder expectations will result in a falling share price and difficulties raising finance. Ultimately, shareholders have the power to remove directors should they feel dissatisfied.

However, this does not mean that other stakeholders' needs are ignored. Clearly if customers are unhappy then sales will be lost with a resulting fall in profitability and shareholder wealth.

For CCC the problem is more complex:

- It is much more difficult to prioritise stakeholder expectations. For example, given limited funds, should community health care needs come before educational ones?

- Even individual stakeholder groups have multiple conflicting objectives. For example, residents want to pay less tax and have better provision of services. Thus even if some groups are satisfied, other may still vote for changes in CCC.

- With companies, customers pay directly for the products they receive, ensuring that customer needs are addressed. With CCC the bulk of its funding comes from central government, not the local community who benefit from CCC's actions. Thus the needs of the funding body may take priority over locals needs, otherwise funding may be cut (note: this is less likely here as funding is mainly driven by population size).

Measurement issues

For an organisation like DDD, once shareholders have been prioritised, all decisions can be evaluated by reference to financial measures such as profitability. While non-financial targets will be incorporated as well, the 'bottom line' will be seen as key. Thus financial targets can be set for most objectives.

For CCC it is much more difficult to measure whether it is achieving its stated aims and hence to set targets.

- For example, how do you assess whether somewhere is an 'attractive place to live and work' or whether health and education provision is 'excellent'?

Other issues

All organisations need to ensure that objectives set relate to controllable factors to ensure staff is motivated to meet them.

All organisations need to differentiate between cause and effect and have objectives for both. For example, DDD may have an objective of customer satisfaction, which will need to be translated into objectives for quality, cost, etc.

(b) As described above, companies make decisions with the primary objective of maximising shareholder wealth.

Investment decisions

Potential investments should thus be assessed using NPV or SVA, rather than ROCE to ensure that shareholder wealth is increased.

This should be the case for both MS and DDD, though the former will have more difficulty determining a suitable discount rate, being unquoted.

Dividend decisions

Once shareholder value has been created, the firm needs to decide how to return those gains to shareholders – either as dividends or reinvested to enhance the share price further.

Modigliani and Miller argued that, given certain assumptions, dividend policy was irrelevant to shareholder wealth. If a dividend was cut, for example, shareholders could manufacture dividends by selling shares without any overall loss of wealth. Central to their theory was the idea that shareholders had perfect information and would understand why a dividend policy was changed.

In the case of MS, shareholders are also employees so will have full information regarding any change in dividend policy and will not thus perceive any information content in the dividends themselves. However, should the dividend be cut, shareholders who require income will not be able to sell shares to generate cash as the company is unquoted. MS should thus try to continue the stable dividend policy it has adopted to date, even though historical dividend cover is lower than the 'rule of thumb' of two.

In the case of DDD, major institutional shareholders will have good information from the company but may have tax preferences regarding income and capital gains so DDD should adopt a consistent dividend policy to meet their requirements. DDD will probably have attracted a certain clientele of shareholder based on previous policies.

Financing decisions

Both firms need to raise finance in order to undertake new investments to increase shareholder wealth. The issue here is whether the finance used ultimately affects shareholder wealth as well.

From a theoretical point of view, Modigliani and Miller argued that in the absence of taxation, and certain other assumptions, the choice between debt or equity finance was irrelevant. With corporation tax they concluded that debt finance was preferable, due to the benefits of the tax shield. With personal taxes the conclusions depend on the specific circumstances of the company and its shareholders. Incorporating real world factors, many analysts argue that there is an optimal gearing level for each company.

DDD is already at the typical gearing ratio for its industry so it would reasonable to assume that this is their optimal gearing level. Future financing should involve a mixture of debt and equity to maintain this ratio.

MS is all-equity financed at present so it should seek to raise at least some of the $15 million required using debt finance to take advantage of the tax relief and low costs involved.

Interrelationships

All three types of decisions are inter-related, thus the financing decision will affect the cost of capital, and as a consequence, the net benefits obtainable from a particular project, thereby influencing the investment decision, while the financing decision concerning gearing will affect both the other decisions.

The dividend decision, in determining the level of retentions, will affect the cash available for investment, and the extent to which external sources of funds need to be sought in financing to optimise operations.

3   NEIGHBOURING COUNTRIES

Key answer tips

A careful read of the specifics of all parts of the question was needed to ensure you answered the requirement in full and didn't end up discussing areas that wouldn't earn marks. The highlighted words are key phrases that markers are looking for.

(a)   The objectives of the nationalised industry in Country A are likely to be influenced by the government, rather than by financial matters. The major objectives are likely to be the provision of a service to the public, and the provision of electricity for the economic development of the country. This may mean providing electricity at considerable cost to outlying areas, or to areas which the government wishes to develop. The financial objectives will be secondary, and will probably attempt to achieve a target rate of return, although the government may be prepared to accept a negative return in order to achieve its political objectives.

The primary objectives of the private sector companies in Country B will probably be the maximisation of shareholder wealth. The companies' managements will decide the objectives, which may be merely 'satisficing', with other non-financial objectives such as good working conditions for employees, market share and provision of a good service to customers. An important industry such as the provision of electricity will, however, be subject to strong government influences and constraints.

Investment planning and appraisal techniques will differ largely as a result of the differing objectives.

In the nationalised industry, strategic investment planning will be instigated by the government, with the tactical decisions left to the management of the industry. The amount of capital investment involved will be determined by the government, which is responsible for the supply of funds.

Appraisal techniques will be designed to ensure that the government targets are met, e.g. ROCE and budgetary control.

In the private sector, investment will be influenced by market forces, with managements attempting to maximise shareholder wealth, or at least satisfy their shareholders while meeting other objectives. Managements will be responsible for both strategic and tactical decisions.

Appraisal techniques will be introduced to ensure that the objectives are met, and will almost certainly include DCF and budgetary control. Failure to meet the objectives may have serious consequences on the share price, with the risk of take-over and possible job losses.

In conclusion, it may be that both the nationalised industry and the privately-controlled industry use the same evaluation techniques. It will be the objectives that are likely to be different, with the consequences of failure being more serious in the private sector.

(b)   (i)   Responding to various stakeholder groups

If a company has a single objective in terms of maximising profitability then it is only responding to one stakeholder group, namely shareholders. However, companies can no longer fail to respond to the interests and concerns of a wider range of groups, particularly with respect to those who may have a non-financial interest in the organisation. Stakeholder groups with a non-financial interest can therefore generate for companies non-financial objectives and place constraints on their operations to the extent that the company is prepared to respond to such groups.

Various stakeholder groupings can emerge. The following represents examples of likely groups, their non-financial objectives and/or the constraints they may place on a business:

Stakeholder	Objective	Constraints
Employees	Employee welfare	Maximum hours worked
Community	Responding to community concerns	Limits on activities
Customers	Product or service levels	Minimum quality standards
Suppliers	Good trading relationships	
Government	Protecting the consumer	Minimum standards on products or services
Trade bodies	Protecting professional reputation	Minimum standards on products or services

(ii)   The difficulties associated with managing organisations with multiple objectives

To the extent that an organisation faces a range of stakeholders, then they also face multiple objectives. This would not particularly be a problem if the multiple objectives were congruent, but they normally are not. There are a number of difficulties:

- Multiple stakeholders imply multiple objectives. To the extent that they conflict then compromises must be made. This will lead potentially to opportunity costs in that maximisation of profitability will potentially be reduced.

- Responding to stakeholders other than shareholders involves costs, either in management time or in directly responding to their needs.

- Some objectives are not clearly defined, for example what is actually meant by 'protecting the consumer'? It will therefore not always be clear to the organisation that they have met the needs of all of their stakeholders.

- Some of the objectives may actually be conflicting where compromise is not possible. Prioritisation and ranking will then have to take place. Questions then arise as to who is the most important stakeholder or what ranking should be assigned?

- New stakeholder groups often emerge. This can create a problem of longer-term strategic management in that plans can be diverted if new pressures arise. For example, environmental issues were not so important 20 years ago.

- Management of the organisation becomes complex when multiple objectives have to be satisfied. Each managerial decision is likely to face many constraints.

4 RZP CO

Key answer tips

Part (a) required a large volume of albeit, relatively straightforward calculations. You must be careful not to spend too much time on the numbers at the expense of the commentary. Parts (b) and (c) were more straightforward. The highlighted words are key phrases that markers are looking for.

(a) **Analysis of data provided**

Year	20X4	20X3	20X2	20X1	20X0
Dividend per share	2.8¢	2.3¢	2.2¢	2.2¢	1.7¢
Annual dividend growth	21.7%	4.5%	Nil	29.4%	
Earnings per share	19.04¢	14.95¢	11.22¢	15.84¢	13.43¢
Annual earnings growth	27.3%	33.2%	−29.2%	17.9%	

Year	20X4	20X3	20X2	20X1	20X0
Price/earnings ratio	22.0	33.5	25.5	17.2	15.2
Share price P/E×EPS	418.9¢	500.8¢	286.1¢	272.4¢	204.1¢
Annual share price growth	−16.3%	75.0%	5.0%	33.5%	
Dividend per share	2.8¢	2.3¢	2.2¢	2.2¢	1.7¢
General price index	117	113	110	105	100
Real dividend per share	2.4¢	2.0¢	2.0¢	2.1¢	1.7¢
Annual dividend growth	20.0%	Nil	−4.8%	23.5%	

Average dividend growth:

Arithmetic mean $= (21.7 + 4.5 + 0 + 29.4)/4 = 55.6/4 = 13.9\%$
Equivalent annual growth rate $= [(2.8/1.7)^{0.25} − 1] \times 100 = 13.3\%$

Average earnings per share growth:

Arithmetic mean $= (27.3 + 33.2 − 29.2 + 17.9)/4 = 49.2/4 = 12.3\%$
Equivalent annual growth rate $= [(19.04/13.43)^{0.25} − 1] \times 100 = 9.1\%$

Average share price growth:

Arithmetic mean $= (−16.3 + 75.0 + 5.0 + 33.5)/4 = 97.2/4 = 24.3\%$
Equivalent annual growth rate $= [(418.9/204.1)^{0.25} − 1] \times 100 = 19.7\%$

Average real dividend growth:

Arithmetic mean $= (20.0 + 0 − 4.8 + 23.5)/4 = 38.7/4 = 9.7\%$
Equivalent annual growth rate $= [(2.4/1.7)^{0.25} − 1] \times 100 = 9.0\%$

Discussion of analysis and views expressed by chairman

The chairman's statement claims that RZP Co has delivered growth in every year in dividends, earnings and ordinary share price, apart from 20X2. Analysis shows that the chairman is correct in excluding 20X2, when no growth occurred in dividends, earnings fell by 29.2%, and real dividends fell by 4.8%. Analysis also shows that no growth in real dividends occurred in 20X3 and that the company's share price fell by 16.3% in 20X4. It is possible the chairman may not have been referring to real dividend growth, in which case his statement could be amended. However, shareholders will be aware of the decline in share price in 20X4 or could calculate the decline from the information provided, so the chairman cannot claim that RZP Co has delivered share price growth in 20X4. In fact, the statement could explain the reasons for the decline in share price in order to reassure shareholders. It also possible for the five-year summary to be extended to include annual share price data, such as maximum, minimum and average share price, so that shareholders have this information readily available.

The chairman's statement claims that RZP Co has consistently delivered above-average performance. The company may have delivered above- or below-average performance in individual years but without further information in the form of sector averages for individual years, it is not possible to reach a conclusion on this point. The average growth rates for the sector cannot therefore be used to comment on the performance of RZP Co in individual years. If the company has consistently delivered above-average performance, however, the company's average annual growth rates should be greater than the sector averages.

The growth rates can be compared as follows:

	Arithmetic mean	Equivalent annual rate	Sector
Nominal dividends	13.9%	13.3%	10%
Real dividends	9.7%	9.0%	9%
Earnings per share	12.3%	9.1%	10%
Share price	24.3%	19.7%	20%

It can be seen that if the sector average growth rates are arithmetic mean growth rates, the chairman's statement is correct. If the sector average growth rates are equivalent annual growth rates, however, only the nominal dividend growth rate is greater than the sector average. The basis on which the sector average growth rates have been prepared should therefore be clarified in order to determine whether the chairman's statement is correct.

(b) The dividend yield and capital growth for 20X4 must be calculated with reference to the 20X3 end-of-year share price. The dividend yield is 0.56% (100 × 2.8/500.8) and the capital growth is −16.35% (100 × (418.9 − 500.8)/500.8), so the total shareholder return is −15.79% or −15.8% (0.56 − 16.35). A negative return of 15.8% looks even worse when it is noted that annual inflation for 20X4 was 3.5% (117/113).

While the negative total shareholder return is at odds with the chairman's claim to have delivered growth in dividends and share price in 20X4, a different view might have emerged if average share prices had been used, since the return calculation ignores share price volatility. The chairman should also be aware that share prices may be affected by other factors than corporate activity, so a good performance in share price terms may not be due to managerial excellence. It also possible that the negative return may represent a good performance when compared to the sector as a whole in 20X4: further information is needed to assess this.

Note that total shareholder return can also be found as (100 × (2.8 + 418.9 − 500.8)/500.8).

(c) The objectives of managers may conflict with the objectives of shareholders, particularly with the objective of maximisation of shareholder wealth. Management remuneration package are one way in which goal congruence between managers and shareholders may be increased. Such packages should motivate managers while supporting the achievement of shareholder wealth maximisation. The following factors should be considered when deciding on a remuneration package intended to encourage directors to act in ways that maximise shareholder wealth.

Clarity and transparency

The terms of the remuneration package should be clear and transparent so that directors and shareholders are in no doubt as to when rewards have been earned or the basis on which rewards have been calculated.

Appropriate performance measure

The managerial performance measure selected for use in the remuneration package should support the achievement of shareholder wealth maximisation. It is therefore likely that the performance measure could be linked to share price changes.

Quantitative performance measure

The managerial performance measure should be quantitative and the manner in which it is to be calculated should be specified. The managerial performance measure should ideally be linked to a benchmark comparing the company's performance with that of its peers. The managerial performance measure should not be open to manipulation by management.

Time horizon

The remuneration package should have a time horizon that is linked to that of shareholders. If shareholders desire long-term capital growth, for example, the remuneration package should discourage decisions whose objective is to maximise short-term profits at the expense of long-term growth.

Impartiality

In recent years there has been an increased emphasis on decisions about managerial remuneration packages being removed from the control of managers who benefit from them. The use of remuneration committees in listed companies is an example of this. The impartial decisions of non-executive directors, it is believed, will eliminate or reduce managerial self-interest and encourage remuneration packages that support the achievement of shareholder rather than managerial goals.

5   JJG CO

Key answer tips

This question may cause problems for some students, especially regarding the level of depth to go into on part (a).

Part (a) requires an evaluation of the performance of JJG. The provision of information on industry averages gives some clear indications of the ratios which any analysis should focus on.

Part (b) is a relatively straightforward calculation of the impact of a rights issue.

Part (c) gives plenty of opportunity to gain easy marks although the final words "for the expansion" means comments must be specific to the scenario presented.

The highlighted words are key phrases that markers are looking for.

(a)   **Financial Analysis**

	2008	2007	2006	2005
Turnover ($m)	28.0	24.0	19.1	16.8
Turnover growth	17%	26%	14%	
Geometric average growth: 18.6%				
Profit before interest and tax ($m)	9.8	8.5	7.5	6.8
PBIT growth	15%	13%	10%	
Geometric average growth: 13.0%				
Earnings ($m)	5.5	4.7	4.1	3.6
Earnings per share (cents)	100	85	75	66
EPS growth	18%	13%	14%	
Geometric average growth: 14.9%				

	2008	2007	2006	2005
Dividends ($m)	2.2	1.9	1.6	1.6
Dividends per share (cents)	40	35	29	29
DPS growth	14%	21%	nil	
Geometric average growth: 11.3%				
Ordinary shares ($m)	5.5	5.5	5.5	5.5
Reserves ($m)	13.7	10.4	7.6	5.1
Shareholders' funds ($)	19.2	15.9	13.1	10.6
8% Bonds, redeemable 2015 ($m)	20	20	20	20

Capital employed ($m)	39.2	35.9	33.1	30.6
Profit before interest and tax ($m)	9.8	8.5	7.5	6.8
Return on capital employed	25%	24%	23%	22%
Earnings ($m)	5.5	4.7	4.1	3.6
Return on shareholders' funds	29%	30%	31%	34%
8% Bonds, redeemable 2015 ($m)	20	20	20	20
Market value of equity ($m)	47.5	31.6	18.4	14.7
Debt/equity ratio (market value)	42%	63%	109%	136%
Share price (cents)	864	574	335	267
Dividends per share (cents)	40	35	29	29
Total shareholder return	58%	82%	36%	

Achievement of corporate objectives

JJG Co has shareholder wealth maximisation as an objective. The wealth of shareholders is increased by dividends received and capital gains on shares owned. Total shareholder return compares the sum of the dividend received and the capital gain with the opening share price. The shareholders of JJG Co had a return of 58% in 2008, compared with a return predicted by the capital asset pricing model of 14%. The lowest return shareholders have received was 21% and the highest return was 82%. On this basis, the shareholders of the company have experienced a significant increase in wealth. It is debatable whether this has been as a result of the actions of the company, however. Share prices may increase irrespective of the actions and decisions of managers, or even despite them. In fact, looking at the dividend per share history of the company, there was one year (2006) where dividends were constant, even though earnings per share increased. It is also difficult to know when wealth has been maximised.

Another objective of the company was to achieve a continuous increase in earnings per share. Analysis shows that earnings per share increased every year, with an average increase of 14.9%. This objective appears to have been achieved.

Comment on financial performance

Return on capital employed (ROCE) has been growing towards the sector average of 25% on a year-by-year basis from 22% in 2005. This steady growth in the primary accounting ratio can be contrasted with irregular growth in turnover, the reasons for which are unknown.

Return on shareholders' funds has been consistently higher than the average for the sector. This may be due more to the capital structure of JJG Co than to good performance by the company, however, in the sense that shareholders' funds are smaller on a book value basis than the long-term debt capital. In every previous year but 2008 the gearing of the company was higher than the sector average.

(b)   The current debt/equity ratio of JJG Co is 42% (20/47.5). Although this is less than the sector average value of 50%, it is more useful from a financial risk perspective to look at the extent to which interest payments are covered by profits.

	20X8	20X7	20X6	20X5
Profit before interest and tax ($m)	9.8	8.5	7.5	6.8
Bond interest ($m)	1.6	1.6	1.6	1.6
Interest coverage ratio (times)	6.1	5.3	4.7	4.3

The interest on the bond issue is $1.6 million (8% of $20m), giving an interest coverage ratio of 6.1 times. If JJG Co has overdraft finance, the interest coverage ratio will be lower than this, but there is insufficient information to determine if an overdraft exists. The interest coverage ratio is not only below the sector average, it is also low enough to be a cause for concern. While the ratio shows an upward trend over the period under consideration, it still indicates that an issue of further debt would be unwise.

A placing, or any issue of new shares such as a rights issue or a public offer, would decrease gearing. If the expansion of business results in an increase in profit before interest and tax, the interest coverage ratio will increase and financial risk will fall. Given the current financial position of JJG Co, a decrease in financial risk is certainly preferable to an increase.

A placing will dilute ownership and control, providing the new equity issue is taken up by new institutional shareholders, while a rights issue will not dilute ownership and control, providing existing shareholders take up their rights. A bond issue does not have ownership and control implications, although restrictive or negative covenants in bond issue documents can limit the actions of a company and its managers.

All three financing choices are long-term sources of finance and so are appropriate for a long-term investment such as the proposed expansion of existing business.

Equity issues such as a placing and a rights issue do not require security. No information is provided on the non-current assets of JJG Co, but it is likely that the existing bond issue is secured. If a new bond issue was being considered, JJG Co would need to consider whether it had sufficient non-current assets to offer as security, although it is likely that new non-current assets would be bought as part of the business expansion.

ACCA marking scheme		Marks
(a)	Relevant financial analysis	6 – 7
	Shareholder wealth discussion	2 – 3
	Earnings per share discussion	2 – 3
	Comment on financial performance	1 – 2
	Maximum	13
(b)	Financial analysis	1 – 2
	Discussion of rights issue and placing	2 – 3
	Discussion of bond issue	2 – 3
	Maximum	7
Total		20

Examiner's comments

This question provided historical information relating to a company and average values for its business sector.

In part (a), candidates were required to evaluate the financial performance of the company and to discuss the extent to which it had achieved its objectives of maximising shareholder wealth and continuous growth in earnings per share (EPS).

Many candidates had difficulty in calculating accounting ratios to compare with the sector averages provided. Accounting ratios have standard names and standard definitions and candidates should know these. Some candidates calculated profit after tax, even though the question gave annual earnings for each of four years. Some candidates averaged the four years of data provided, simply because the question provided average sector data. Some candidates calculated ratios for one year only and ignored the three other years.

Many candidates did not understand the significance of the inclusion in the question of an average sector value for the return predicted by the capital asset pricing model (CAPM). This value (14%) provided a way to assess whether the company had achieved its objective of maximising the wealth of shareholders. If the return that shareholders had received each year, in the form of capital gains and dividend, exceeded the return predicted by the CAPM, it could be argued that the objective had been achieved, since the company had outperformed the business sector as a whole. Since total shareholder return was 36%, 82% and 58%, this certainly seemed to be the case here. Some candidates argued that this objective had been achieved on the basis of inappropriate analysis, such as that the amount of reserves or the return on capital employed had increased each year.

It could be demonstrated that the objective of achieving continuous growth in EPS had been achieved by calculating the EPS figure for each year.

Part (b) asked for an analysis and discussion of the relative merits of a rights issue, a placing and an issue of bonds as ways of raising the $15 million of finance needed. Better answers started with analysis and used this as the basis for discussion. The effect of raising the $15 million of finance on gearing and interest cover, for example, had to be assessed before an informed answer could be offered.

Many answers had little or no analysis and compared the three financing methods in general terms, for example looking at ownership and control, increase or decrease in gearing and financial risk, issue costs, servicing costs and maturity.

6   NEWS FOR YOU

Key answer tips

To score well on part (a), you must ensure you apply your basic knowledge of economics to the specifics of News For You's situation. In part (b) the majority of marks are available for the justifications you provide as opposed to the conclusion you reach. The highlighted words are key phrases that markers are looking for.

(a)   Economic opinion on the effect of an **interest rate change** on News For You might vary. Keynesian economists argue that if base rate (and other interest rates) fall, this will lead to an increase in consumer demand (i.e. consumer spending). Unfortunately, however, even if the recent drop in the base rate increases consumer demand, it is unlikely to have any significant impact on the particular business of News For You. Sales are likely to remain unchanged, because newspapers and small confectionery items are low cost purchases, often bought on impulse. Interest rate movements will not make such items suddenly affordable where before they were not.

News For You needs to think about other ways in which the interest rate change might affect its business, and particularly its impact on business costs. If the company has an overdraft facility, its cost of borrowing will have been reduced. At the same time, the expansion plans require the business to raise $2 million, and changes in interest rates affect the cost of all types of capital, both loans and equity. Corporate borrowing rates are generally linked to the prevailing base rate or inter-bank lending rate, with companies paying a premium above base or interbank rate for their loans. The drop in interest rates will therefore affect the required return on the finance needed to fund the proposed expansion. If News For You uses Discounted Cash Flow analysis for investment appraisals, the fall in the cost of capital resulting from the drop in the base rate will mean that a lower discount rate can be applied to the investment evaluation. A lower rate of discount will result in a higher Net Present Value for any given proposal.

Keynesian economists, however, do not agree that changes in interest rates affect corporate investment decisions. They argue that investments are more dependent on the level of business confidence. It might be possible to suggest that News For You will see the fall in the base rate as stimulating general economic confidence. If so, it will be more confident about the future of its business, and so regardless of any changes in the cost of capital, it might be more willing to undertake the expansionary investment. (On the other hand, a fall in interest rates could be a response to a deterioration in the economy, and a loss of business confidence.)

The **inflation figures** are useful to News For You because they can directly affect profit and cash flow forecasts. The impact of inflation on cash flows and profit will be dependent to a large degree on the relative rates of increase in wages, the cost of wholesale supplies for the shop, and the prices that News For You can charge its customers. The quoted rate of inflation is very low at just over 1% per year and, although the rate is not expected to fall any further, its current level is unlikely to have a dramatic effect on the ability of the business to trade profitably. The greater risk for the business might come from the problem that, because inflation is so low, customers are not prepared to tolerate any price rises at all.

If so, News For You might become more vulnerable to loss of business to the large food stores which can draw away customers via price cutting campaigns.

Personal and corporation tax rates are relevant to the owners of News For You because they will affect the net gain to the business that may be generated by expansion. As with interest rates, tax rates can affect personal spending patterns and therefore affect the sales revenue of a particular business. News For You, however, is unlikely to have a business that is sensitive to tax rates, because its products are basic essentials and low cost items. Nonetheless, the information that tax rates will remain unchanged is useful because it allows the business to be certain of the amount of tax relief that may be available on loan finance, and the relief that equity investors may claim for investing in a small unquoted company. This information might be useful in deciding whether or not to go ahead with the expansion, because it may affect the relative cost and availability of capital.

The **changes in taxes on tobacco** might be expected to have had a significant effect on News For You because it is one of the relatively high value products sold by the stores. The question indicates that tobacco sales have been falling, but it is unclear whether this drop is linked to the 10% rise in tax over the last twelve months, or simply a result of the population becoming more health conscious and so buying fewer cigarettes. If customers are price-sensitive in their purchasing of tobacco, News For You might once again find itself vulnerable to competition from the food retailers that can exercise greater buying power and sell similar products at lower prices. The high cost of these items also means that inventory holding costs are high, and if inventory turnover is reduced because of tax increase, then the amount of working capital required by News For You will rise.

The **investigation into the food sector** might prove detrimental to News For You if it serves to initiate a price war amongst the retailers, all of whom will be anxious to prove that they look after their customers. The business grew very quickly between 20X2 and 20X6, but since then sales revenue has increased by just 2% per year, and the owners must be concerned that further growth potential is limited, at least within the existing outlets. Moving into the sale of basic foodstuffs has been used as a strategy to compensate for loss of sales in other products such as tobacco, but in many countries a large proportion of people do their food shopping in large retail outlets. By expanding their product range, News For You has also created for itself another set of competitors in the form of food retailers. The only way in which the business might gain from this investigation is if it also covers food wholesaling, and the result is a drop in the prices that News For You have to pay for their inventory.

(b)   **Arguments in favour of the expansion include the following:**

- The sales revenue figures suggest that there is only limited opportunity for the business to continue to grow organically. The business is seeking to replace sales of tobacco and newspapers with sales of foods, but as suggested in answer to (a), the potential of this side of the business may be limited. News For You may be advised to try to grow sales revenue by means of acquiring new outlets instead.

- If News For You is being forced into paying relatively high prices for supplies from a local wholesaler, then expansion may allow it to gain more bargaining power, and purchase at reduced rates from a national wholesale chain. Increased size will offer the opportunity to take advantage of possible economies of scale via bulk ordering. In this way, margins could be widened and the overall business made more profitable.

- With a larger number of stores covering a wider geographic area, News For You will be able to broaden the nature of their business base, so that it will be less vulnerable to regional economic trends.

Arguments against any expansion include the following:

- The potential to increase sales substantially via food sales is very limited. The majority of people purchase most of their food from larger stores, and will only use a local shop for small low cost items, for which it is not worthwhile making a special car journey to the supermarket. It is unlikely a profitable business can be created based on this type of sale.

- The widespread ownership of televisions and access to differing forms of mass media communications is likely to mean that fewer people will purchase newspapers on a daily basis. This is particularly true of those papers that are also published in electronic form. Many newsagents are dependent for the bulk of their sales on customers who come into the shop to buy a newspaper and then purchase additional items at the same time. If customers do not come in for a newspaper, then the associated sales income will also be lost. Expanding a business where there is such a risk of demand falling away may be regarded as very risky.

- The information in the question suggests that the competitive environment for News For You is becoming much tougher on a number of different fronts simultaneously, with rising excise duties, powerful food retailers and a reduction in tobacco and newspaper purchases. Expansion usually occurs because a business is very confident of the future, but in this case it is questionable whether News For You has much about which to be confident.

It would therefore seem advisable for News For You to postpone its expansion plans, and perhaps look at ways of using its existing outlets to sell very different products, thereby 're-inventing' their business, perhaps by moving completely away from confectionery and into, for example, video rental.

WORKING CAPITAL MANAGEMENT

7 GORWA CO

Key answer tips

In part (a) students may go into more depth about how to hedge interest rate risk and miss marks for analysing the effects of an increase in interest rates on the company concerned. Although the model answer presents a number of calculations that could be performed, there are only 1 – 2 marks available for the financial analysis. This is another reminder that the F9 paper is far from wholly numerical.

In part (b), again a huge range of calculations are possible. If students only manage a selection of those presented in the model answer, they should still be able to score highly. The weighting between calculations and discussion is 50:50 and the discussion provided in the model answer demonstrates the style the examiner is hoping for.

(a) **Financial analysis**

Fixed interest debt proportion (2006) = 100 × 2,425/(2,425 + 1,600) = 60%

Fixed interest debt proportion (2007) = 100 × 2,425/(2,425 + 3,225) = 43%

Fixed interest payments = 2,425 × 0.08 = $194,000

Variable interest payments (2006) = 274 − 194 = $80,000 or 29%

Variable interest payments (2007) = 355 − 194 = $161,000 or 45%

(Alternatively, considering the overdraft amounts and the average variable overdraft interest rate of 5% per year:

Variable interest payments (2006) = 1.6m × 0.05 = $80,000 or 29%

Variable interest payments (2007) = 3.225m × 0.05 = $161,250 or 45%)

Interest coverage ratio (2006) = 2,939/ 274 = 10.7 times

Interest coverage ratio (2007) = 2,992/ 355 = 8.4 times

Debt/equity ratio (2006) = 100 × 2,425/ 11,325 = 21%

Debt/equity ratio (2007) = 100 × 2,425/ 12,432 = 20%

Total debt/equity ratio (2006) = 100 × (2,425 + 1,600)/ 11,325 = 35%

Total debt/equity ratio (2007) = 100 × (2,425 + 3,225)/ 12,432 = 45%

Discussion

Gorwa Co has both fixed interest debt and variable interest rate debt amongst its sources of finance. The fixed interest bonds have ten years to go before they need to be redeemed and they therefore offer Gorwa Co long term protection against an increase in interest rates.

In 2006, 60% of the company's debt was fixed interest in nature, but in 2007 this had fallen to 43%. The floating-rate proportion of the company's debt therefore increased from 40% in 2006 to 57% in 2007. The interest coverage ratio fell from 10.7 times in 2006 to 8.4 times in 2007, a decrease which will be a cause for concern to the company if it were to continue. The debt/equity ratio (including the overdraft due to its size) increased over the same period from 35% to 45% (if the overdraft is excluded, the debt/equity ratio declines slightly from 21% to 20%). From the perspective of an increase in interest rates, the financial risk of Gorwa Co has increased and may continue to increase if the company does not take action to halt the growth of its variable interest rate overdraft. The proportion of interest payments linked to floating rate debt has increased from 29% in 2006 to 45% in 2007. An increase in interest rates will further reduce profit before taxation, which is lower in 2007 than in 2006, despite a 40% increase in turnover.

One way to hedge against an increase in interest rates is to exchange some or all of the variable-rate overdraft into long-term fixed-rate debt. There is likely to be an increase in interest payments because long-term debt is usually more expensive than short-term debt. Gorwa would also be unable to benefit from falling interest rates if most of its debt paid fixed rather than floating rate interest.

Interest rate options and interest rate futures may be of use in the short term, depending on the company's plans to deal with its increasing overdraft.

For the longer term, Gorwa Co could consider raising a variable-rate bank loan, linked to a variable rate-fixed interest rate swap.

(b) **Financial analysis**

		2007	2006
Inventory days	(365 × 2,400)/23,781		37 days
	(365 × 4,600)/34,408	49 days	
Receivables days	(365 × 2,200)/26,720		30 days
	(365 × 4,600)/37,400	45 days	
Payables days	(365 × 2,000)/23,781		31 days
	(365 × 4,750)/34,408	51 days	
Current ratio	4,600/3,600		1.3 times
	9,200/7,975	1.15 times	
Quick ratio	2,200/3,600		0.61 times
	4,600/7,975	0.58 times	
Sales/net working capital	26,720/1,000		26.7 times
	37,400/1,225	30.5 times	
Turnover increase	37,400/26,720	40%	
Non-current assets increase	13,632/12,750	7%	
Inventory increase	4,600/2,400	92%	
Receivables increase	4,600/2,200	109%	
Payables increase	4,750/2,000	138%	
Overdraft increase	3,225/1,600	102%	

Discussion

Overtrading or undercapitalisation arises when a company has too small a capital base to support its level of business activity. Difficulties with liquidity may arise as an overtrading company may have insufficient capital to meet its liabilities as they fall due. Overtrading is often associated with a rapid increase in turnover and Gorwa Co has experienced a 40% increase in turnover over the last year. Investment in working capital has not matched the increase in sales, however, since the sales/net working capital ratio has increased from 26.7 times to 30.5 times.

Overtrading could be indicated by a deterioration in inventory days. Here, inventory days have increased from 37 days to 49 days, while inventory has increased by 92% compared to the 40% increase in turnover. It is possible that inventory has been stockpiled in anticipation of a further increase in turnover, leading to an increase in operating costs.

Overtrading could also be indicated by deterioration in receivables days. In this case, receivables have increased by 109% compared to the 40% increase in turnover. The increase in turnover may have been fuelled in part by a relaxation of credit terms.

As the liquidity problem associated with overtrading deepens, the overtrading company increases its reliance on short-term sources of finance, including overdraft, trade payables and leasing. The overdraft of Gorwa Co has more than doubled in size to $3.225 million, while trade payables have increased by $2.74 million or 137%. Both increases are much greater than the 40% increase in turnover. There is evidence here of an increased reliance on short-term finance sources.

Overtrading can also be indicated by decreases in the current ratio and the quick ratio. The current ratio of Gorwa Co has fallen from 1.3 times to 1.15 times, while its quick ratio has fallen from 0.61 times to 0.58 times.

There are clear indications that Gorwa Co is experiencing the kinds of symptoms usually associated with overtrading. A more complete and meaningful analysis could be undertaken if appropriate benchmarks were available, such as key ratios from comparable companies in the same industry sector, or additional financial information from prior years so as to establish trends in key ratios.

ACCA marking scheme		
		Marks
(a) Discussion of effects of interest rate increase	3 – 4	
Relevant financial analysis	1 – 2	
Interest rate hedging	2 – 3	
	───	
		Max 9
(b) Financial analysis	5 – 6	
Discussion of overtrading	4 – 5	
Conclusion as to overtrading	1	
	───	
		Max 11
		──
Total		20
		──

8   FLG CO

Key answer tips

Parts (a) and (b) are both standard textbook material. In part (a), for six marks you should discuss at least three factors. Don't forget the requirement is to "discuss" not "state" so you must give some commentary: 'the length of the working capital cycle' will not get the full marks available.

In part (b) the requirement is again to "discuss". Given the emphasis is on how both factoring and invoice discounting can assist in the **management** of accounts receivable, there should be more discussion on factoring than invoice discounting (the latter being a tool for managing cash flow rather than managing accounts receivable). Don't forget to define each of the terms to collect some easy marks.

The calculation in part (c) requires some "out of the box" thinking in order to see how the brief information provided can be used to work out the size of the overdraft.

Not only does it involve re-arranging the usual working capital ratios we're used to seeing, it also requires a disaggregation of the operating cycle to reveal the inventory holding period.

In contrast, part (d) is a fairly straightforward application of the EOQ model which shouldn't pose many difficulties. The highlighted words are key phrases that markers are looking for.

(a) There are a number of factors that determine the level of investment in current assets and their relative importance varies from company to company.

Length of working capital cycle

The working capital cycle or operating cycle is the period of time between when a company settles its accounts payable and when it receives cash from its accounts receivable. Operating activities during this period need to be financed and as the operating period lengthens, the amount of finance needed increases. Companies with comparatively longer operating cycles than others in the same industry sector, will therefore require comparatively higher levels of investment in current assets.

Terms of trade

These determine the period of credit extended to customers, any discounts offered for early settlement or bulk purchases, and any penalties for late payment. A company whose terms of trade are more generous than another company in the same industry sector will therefore need a comparatively higher investment in current assets.

Policy on level of investment in current assets

Even within the same industry sector, companies will have different policies regarding the level of investment in current assets, depending on their attitude to risk. A company with a comparatively conservative approach to the level of investment in current assets would maintain higher levels of inventory, offer more generous credit terms and have higher levels of cash in reserve than a company with a comparatively aggressive approach. While the more aggressive approach would be more profitable because of the lower level of investment in current assets, it would also be more risky, for example in terms of running out of inventory in periods of fluctuating demand, of failing to have the particular goods required by a customer, of failing to retain customers who migrate to more generous credit terms elsewhere, and of being less able to meet unexpected demands for payment.

Industry in which organisation operates

Another factor that influences the level of investment in current assets is the industry within which an organisation operates. Some industries, such as aircraft construction, will have long operating cycles due to the length of time needed to manufacture finished goods and so will have comparatively higher levels of investment in current assets than industries such as supermarket chains, where goods are bought in for resale with minimal additional processing and where many goods have short shelf-lives.

(b) Factoring involves a company turning over administration of its sales ledger to a factor, which is a financial institution with expertise in this area. The factor will assess the creditworthiness of new customers, record sales, send out statements and reminders, collect payment, identify late payers and chase them for settlement, and take appropriate legal action to recover debts where necessary.

The factor will also offer finance to a company based on invoices raised for goods sold or services provided. This is usually up to 80% of the face value of invoices raised. The finance is repaid from the settled invoices, with the balance being passed to the issuing company after deduction of a fee equivalent to an interest charge on cash advanced.

If factoring is without recourse, the factor rather than the company will carry the cost of any bad debts that arise on overdue accounts. Factoring without recourse therefore offers credit protection to the selling company, although the factor's fee (a percentage of credit sales) will be comparatively higher than with non-recourse factoring to reflect the cost of the insurance offered.

(c) **Calculation of size of overdraft**

Inventory period = operating cycle + payables period − receivables period = 3 + 1 − 2 = 2 months

Inventory = 1.89m × 2/12 = $315,000

Accounts receivable = 4.2m × 2/12 = $700,000

Current assets = 315,000 + 700,000 = $1,015,000

Current liabilities = current assets/current ratio = 1,015,000/1.4 = $725,000

Accounts payable = 1.89m × 1/12 = $157,500

Overdraft = 725,000 − 157,500 = $567,500

Net working capital = current assets − current liabilities = 1,015,000 − 725,000 = $290,000

Short-term financing cost = 567,500 × 0.07 = $39,725

Long-term financing cost = 290,000 × 0.11 = $31,900

Total cost of financing current assets = 39,725 + 31,900 = $71,625

(d) (i) Economic order quantity = (2 × 6 × 60,000/0.5)0.5 = 1,200 units

Number of orders = 60,000/1,200 = 50 order per year

Annual ordering cost = 50 × 6 = $300 per year

Average inventory = 1,200/2 = 600 units

Annual holding cost = 600 × 0.5 = $300 per year

Inventory cost = 60,000 × 12 = $720,000

Total cost of inventory with EOQ policy = 720,000 + 300 + 300 = $720,600 per year

(ii)   Order size for bulk discounts = 10,000 units

Number of orders = 60,000/10,000 = 6 orders per year

Annual ordering cost = 6 × 6 = $36 per year

Average inventory = 10,000/2 =5,000 units

Annual holding cost = 5,000 × 2 = $10,000 per year

Discounted material cost =12 × 0.99 = $11.88 per unit

Inventory cost = 60,000 × 11.88 = $712,800

Total cost of inventory with discount = 712,800 + 36 + 10,000 = $722,836 per year

The EOQ approach results in a slightly lower total inventory cost

ACCA marking scheme			Marks
(a)	Discussion of key factors	Maximum	4
(b)	Discussion of factoring	Maximum	3
(c)	Value of inventory		1
	Accounts receivable and accounts payable		1
	Current liabilities		1
	Size of overdraft		1
	Net working capital		1
	Total cost of financing working capital		1
			6
(d)	(i) Economic order quantity		1
	Ordering cost and holding cost under EOQ		1
	Inventory cost under EOQ		1
	Total cost of inventory with EOQ policy		1
			4
	(ii) Ordering cost and holding cost with discount		1
	Inventory cost with discount		1
	Total cost of inventory with bulk purchase discount		1
	Conclusion		1
			3
	Maximum		
Total			20

Examiner's comments

Part (a) asked for a discussion of the factors which determine the level of investment in current assets. Although this topic is clearly identified in the F9 Study Guide (C3a), answers often referred incorrectly to working capital funding strategies (C3b). The suggested answer to this question refers to factors mentioned in the F9 Study Guide, such as length of working capital cycle, terms of trade, working capital policy and so on. Answers that discussed these or similar factors gained high marks.

Part (b) asked for a discussion of the ways in which factoring could help in managing accounts receivable. Many candidates discussed relevant points in relation to factoring and received credit accordingly.

In part (c), candidates were asked to calculate the size of an overdraft, the net working capital, and the total cost of financing current assets.

The variable quality of the answers indicates a need for candidates to ensure, not only that they are familiar with accounting ratios, but also that they are familiar with the accounting items to which the ratios relate, in this case sales, cost of sales, inventory, trade receivables, trade payables and so on. Many candidates were unable to calculate the inventory turnover period, given the operating cycle, the average collection period and the average payable period. Many candidates were also unable to work backwards from the provided ratios, for example to calculate the level of receivables given the average collection period and the amount of credit sales. Some candidates omitted the overdraft

when calculating net working capital, indicating unfamiliarity with the structure of the statement of financial position.

Part (d) asked candidates to calculate the total cost of inventory using the economic order quantity model (EOQ) and to evaluate a discount offered by a supplier. Many candidates gained high marks here by offering a comprehensive answer. Candidates who did not gain high marks appeared to be unsure of the meaning of the variables in the EOQ, even though the units of each were clearly specified in the question.

9   PKA CO   *Walk in the footsteps of a top tutor*

Key answer tips

This question combines elements from throughout the working capital management area of the syllabus with the foreign currency risk section. It is a good reflection of the examiner's style. The highlighted words are key phrases that markers are looking for.

Tutor's top tips:

Part (a) will require some thought. This is a fairly common exam question but the complexity of it can change depending on the information given. Your starting point should be to work out the economic order quantity (EOQ). We're given the formula in the exam so it's really just a case of finding the three pieces of information required, all of which are clearly stated in the scenario. Having calculated the EOQ, you are now equipped to work out the relative costs of the current policy compared to a potential new policy based on the EOQ. You will need to calculate:

— Total order costs (using annual demand, order size and cost per order)

— Total holding costs (using the cost of holding one unit and the average level of inventory)

Four of these five things are given to us in the scenario or have already been calculated. The tricky one is the average level of inventory as we need to consider not only the size of the order but also the level of buffer stocks held. You would be forgiven for thinking the buffer stock is 35,000 units, however you would be wrong. Some of these units would in fact be used in the two weeks it takes for the order to arrive. The information provided on annual demand will enable us to calculated how many units would be used in those two weeks, from which we can work out the level of inventory just prior to the order being delivered.

> *This is by far the trickiest part of this question and it's important to keep it in context. Had you not spotted this, you would only have lost 2 marks. Don't forget, the requirement asks for the saving – be sure that you specifically calculate this to get all the marks.*

(a)   **Cost of current ordering policy of PKA Co**

Ordering cost = €250 × (625,000/100,000) = €1,563 per year

Weekly demand = 625,000/50 = 12,500 units per week

Consumption during 2 weeks lead time = 12,500 × 2 = 25,000 units

Buffer stock = re-order level less usage during lead time = 35,000 – 25,000 = 10,000 units

Average stock held during the year = 10,000 + (100,000/2) = 60,000 units

Holding cost = 60,000 × €0.50 = €30,000 per year

Total cost = ordering cost plus holding cost = €1,563 + €30,000 = €31,563 per year

Economic order quantity = $((2 \times 250 \times 625{,}000)/0.5)_{1/2}$ = 25,000 units

Number of orders per year = 625,000/25,000 = 25 per year

Ordering cost = €250 × 25 = €6,250 per year

Holding cost (ignoring buffer stock) = €0.50 × (25,000/2) = €0.50 × 12,500 = €6,250 per year

Holding cost (including buffer stock) = €0.50 × (10,000 + 12,500) = €11,250 per year

Total cost of EOQ-based ordering policy = €6,250 + €11,250 = €17,500 per year

Saving for PKA Co by using EOQ-based ordering policy = €31,563 – €17,500 = €14,063 per year

---

Tutor's top tips:

A quick read of the scenario for accounts receivable management gives us some ideas for sub-headings to use to answer part (b); accounts receivable period and bad debts. For 5 marks you should be aiming for a couple of points under each heading.

(b)   The information gathered by the Financial Manager of PKA Co indicates that two areas of concern in the management of domestic accounts receivable are the increasing level of bad debts as a percentage of credit sales and the excessive credit period being taken by credit customers.

Reducing bad debts

The incidence of bad debts, which has increased from 5% to 8% of credit sales in the last year, can be reduced by assessing the creditworthiness of new customers before offering them credit and PKA Co needs to introduce a policy detailing how this should be done, or review its existing policy, if it has one, since it is clearly not working very well. In order to do this, information about the solvency, character and credit history of new clients is needed. This information can come from a variety of sources, such as bank references, trade references and credit reports from credit reference agencies. Whether credit is offered to the new customer and the terms of the credit offered can then be based on an explicit and informed assessment of default risk.

Reduction of average accounts receivable period

Customers have taken an average of 75 days credit over the last year rather than the 30 days offered by PKA Co, i.e. more than twice the agreed credit period.

As a result, PKA Co will be incurring a substantial opportunity cost, either from the additional interest cost on the short-term financing of accounts receivable or from the incremental profit lost by not investing the additional finance tied up by the longer average accounts receivable period. PKA Co needs to find ways to encourage accounts receivable to be settled closer to the agreed date.

Assuming that the credit period offered by PKA Co is in line with that of its competitors, the company should determine whether they too are suffering from similar difficulties with late payers. If they are not, PKA Co should determine in what way its own terms differ from those of its competitors and consider whether offering the same trade terms would have an impact on its accounts receivable. For example, its competitors may offer a discount for early settlement while PKA Co does not and introducing a discount may achieve the desired reduction in the average accounts receivable period. If its competitors are experiencing a similar accounts receivable problem, PKA Co could take the initiative by introducing more favourable early settlement terms and perhaps generate increased business as well as reducing the average accounts receivable period.

PKA Co should also investigate the efficiency with which accounts receivable are managed. Are statements sent regularly to customers? Is an aged accounts receivable analysis produced at the end of each month? Are outstanding accounts receivable contacted regularly to encourage payment? Is credit denied to any overdue accounts seeking further business? Is interest charged on overdue accounts? These are all matters that could be included by PKA Co in a revised policy on accounts receivable management.

Tutor's top tips:

Finally, in part (c), you must be very clear on the scenario before your start. PKA has a foreign supplier so to settle their debts, PKA will need to buy Dollars. If PKA is buying, the bank will be selling (remember the rhyme – the bank will always sell low (sounds like hello) and buy high (sounds like bye bye)!) We therefore know the appropriate spot rate is 1.998 – 0.002 = $1.996:€ and the appropriate forward rate is 1.979 – 0.004 = $1.975:€.

Once you're happy on which rates are to be used, you can calculate the Euros payable under the forward market hedge (don't let this term confuse you – it simply means a forward exchange contract) using the forward rate. You can also start the calculation for the lead payment using the spot rate. Finish this by thinking about the interest payable on the required loan. Since this is a Euro loan, you need half of the one year Euro borrowing rate.

Lastly, you can work on the money market hedge. Start by drawing out a diagram of the process, remembering the purpose is to eliminate the exchange risk by doing the translation now but then making sure that money continues to work for us by investing it in a Dollar bank account to earn interest.

(c)   **Money market hedge**

PKA Co should place sufficient dollars on deposit now so that, with accumulated interest, the six-month liability of $250,000 can be met. Since the company has no surplus cash at the present time, the cost of these dollars must be met by a short-term euro loan.

Six-month dollar deposit rate = 3.5/2 = 1.75%

Current spot selling rate = 1.998 – 0.002 = $1.996 per euro

Six-month euro borrowing rate = 6.1/2 = 3.05%

Dollars deposited now = 250,000/1.0175 = $245,700

Cost of these dollars at spot = 245,700/1.996 = 123,096 euros

Euro value of loan in six months' time = 123,096 × 1.0305 = 126,850 euros

Forward market hedge

Six months forward selling rate = 1.979 – 0.004 = $1.975 per euro

Euro cost using forward market hedge = 250,000/1.975 = 126,582 euros

Lead payment

Since the dollar is appreciating against the euro, a lead payment may be worthwhile.

Euro cost now = 250,000/1.996 = 125,251 euros

This cost must be met by a short-term loan at a six-month interest rate of 3.05%

Euro value of loan in six months' time = 125,251 × 1.0305 = 129,071 euros

Evaluation of hedges

The relative costs of the three hedges can be compared since they have been referenced to the same point in time, i.e. six months in the future. The most expensive hedge is the lead payment, while the cheapest is the forward market hedge. Using the forward market to hedge the account payable currency risk can therefore be recommended.

Tutor's top tips:

The key learning points from this question are the importance of doing the easy parts of the question first and making sure you maintain good time discipline to ensure you don't get bogged down in one part of the question at the expense of another part.

ACCA marking scheme		Marks
(a)	Cost of current ordering policy	2
	Cost of EOQ-based ordering policy	3
	Saving by using EOQ model	1
		———
		6
		———

(b)	Reduction of bad debts	2–3
	Reduction of average accounts receivable period	2–3
	Discussion of other improvements	1–2
		6
(c)	Money market hedge	3
	Forward market hedge	2
	Lead payment	2
	Evaluation	1
		8
Total		20

Examiner's comments

In part (a) candidates were asked to calculate the cost of a company's current ordering policy and to determine the saving that could be made by using the economic order quantity (EOQ) model. Many candidates gained high marks for their answers to this part of question 4, calculating correctly the ordering costs of both the current and the EOQ policies, and comparing the total costs of each policy to show the saving arising from adoption of the EOQ policy. Many of these comparisons, however, were based on incorrect calculations of the holding costs of each policy.

Some candidates failed to consider the buffer inventory in calculating holding costs. Others used the re-order inventory level as the buffer level, failing to reduce inventory by consumption during the lead time it took for orders to arrive after being placed. Others added the re-order level to order quantity before dividing by two to calculate average inventory level, when only the order quantity is averaged.

Part (b) required candidates to discuss the ways in which a company could improve the management of domestic accounts receivable and many gained full marks here. Candidates failing to gain high marks tended to offer a limited number of possible methods, for example by focussing at length on factoring to the exclusion of internal accounts receivables management methods. Despite the requirement to discuss domestic accounts receivable, some candidates discussed export factoring and exchange rate hedging.

In part (c) candidates were required to evaluate whether a money market hedge, a forward market hedge or a lead payment should be used to hedge a foreign account payable. Some candidates offered discursive answers, for which they gained little credit since the question asked for an evaluation of hedging methods.

Many candidates were unable to calculate correctly the spot and forward exchange rates from the information provided. Many candidates failed to compare all three hedges from a common time horizon perspective, i.e. either from the current time or from three months hence.

Since it was a foreign currency account payable that was being hedged (a liability), the money market hedge involved creating a foreign currency asset (a deposit). The hedging company therefore needed to borrow euros, exchange them into dollars and place these dollars on deposit. Some candidates offered the opposite hedge, i.e. borrowing dollars and exchanging them into euros.

10 KXP CO

Key answer tips

Part (a) draws heavily upon knowledge of financial ratios and how various figures in the financial statements relate to each other.

Part (b) is a fairly common requirement but does require students to work methodically through the information and lay out their working clearly in order for their thought process to be followed.

It is important to make sure the requirement in part (c) is read carefully to ensure students do not go off on a tangent. The words "working capital" and "policy" must not be ignored and discussion should not focus on investment and financing in detail.

The highlighted words are key phrases that markers are looking for.

(a) **Calculation of net cost/benefit**

Current receivables = $2,466,000

Receivables paying within 30 days = 15m × 0.5 × 30/365 = $616,438

Receivables paying within 45 days = 15m × 0.3 × 45/365 = $554,795

Receivables paying within 60 days = 15m × 0.2 × 60/365 = $493,151

Revised receivables = 616,438 + 554,795 + 493,151 = $1,664,384

Reduction in receivables = 2,466,000 – 1,664,384 = $801,616

Reduction in financing cost = 801,616 × 0.06 = $48,097

Cost of discount = 15m × 0.5 × 0.01 = $75,000

Net cost of proposed changes in receivables policy = 75,000 – 48,097 = $26,903

Alternative approach to calculation of net cost/benefit

Current receivables days = (2,466/15,000) × 365 = 60 days

Revised receivables days = (30 × 0.5) + (45 × 0.3) + (60 × 0.2) = 40.5 days

Decrease in receivables days = 60 – 40.5 = 19.5 days

Decrease in receivables = 15m × 19.5/365 = $801,370

(The slight difference compared to the earlier answer is due to rounding)

Decrease in financing cost = 801,370 × 0.06 = $48,082

Net cost of proposed changes in receivables policy = 75,000 – 48,082 = $26,918

Comment

The proposed changes in trade receivables policy are not financially acceptable. However, if the trade terms offered are comparable with those of its competitors, KXP Co needs to investigate the reasons for the (on average) late payment of current customers. This analysis also assumes constant sales and no bad debts, which is unlikely to be the case in reality.

(b) **Cost of current inventory policy**

Cost of materials = $540,000 per year

Annual ordering cost = 12 × 150 = $1,800 per year

Annual holding cost = 0.24 × (15,000/2) = $1,800 per year

Total cost of current inventory policy = 540,000 + 1,800 + 1,800 = $543,600 per year

Cost of inventory policy after bulk purchase discount

Cost of materials after bulk purchase discount = 540,000 × 0.98 = $529,200 per year

Annual demand = 12 × 15,000 = 180,000 units per year

KXP Co will need to increase its order size to 30,000 units to gain the bulk discount

Revised number of orders = 180,000/30,000 = 6 orders per year

Revised ordering cost = 6 × 150 = $900 per year

Revised holding cost = 0.24 × (30,000/2) = $3,600 per year

Revised total cost of inventory policy = 529,200 + 900 + 3,600 = $533,700 per year

Evaluation of offer of bulk purchase discount

Net benefit of taking bulk purchase discount = 543,600 − 533,700 = $9,900 per year

The bulk purchase discount looks to be financially acceptable. However, this evaluation is based on a number of unrealistic assumptions. For example, the ordering cost and the holding cost are assumed to be constant, which is unlikely to be true in reality. Annual demand is assumed to be constant, whereas in practice seasonal and other changes in demand are likely.

(c) Working capital investment policy is concerned with the level of investment in current assets, with one company being compared with another. Working capital financing policy is concerned with the relative proportions of short-term and long-term finance used by a company. While working capital investment policy is therefore assessed on an inter-company comparative basis, assessment of working capital financing policy involves analysis of financial information for one company alone.

Working capital financing policy uses an analysis of current assets into permanent current assets and fluctuating current assets. Working capital investment policy does not require this analysis. Permanent current assets represent the core level of investment in current assets that supports a given level of business activity. Fluctuating current assets represent the changes in the level of current assets that arise through, for example, the unpredictability of business operations, such as the level of trade receivables increasing due to some customers paying late or the level of inventory increasing due to demand being less than predicted.

Working capital financing policy relies on the matching principle, which is not used by working capital investment policy. The matching principle holds that long-term assets should be financed from a long-term source of finance. Non-current assets and permanent current assets should therefore be financed from a long-term source, such as equity finance or loan note finance, while fluctuating current assets should be financed from a short-term source, such as an overdraft or a short-term bank loan.

Both working capital investment policy and working capital financing policy use the terms conservative, moderate and aggressive. In investment policy, the terms are used to indicate the comparative level of investment in current assets on an inter-company basis. One company has a more aggressive approach compared to another company if it has a lower level of investment in current assets, and *vice versa* for a conservative approach to working capital investment policy. In working capital financing policy, the terms are used to indicate the way in which fluctuating current assets and permanent current assets are matched to short-term and long-term finance sources.

An aggressive financing policy means that fluctuating current assets and a portion of permanent current assets are financed from a short-term finance source. A conservative financing policy means that permanent current assets and a portion of fluctuating current assets are financed from a long-term source. An aggressive financing policy will be more profitable than a conservative financing policy because short-term finance is cheaper than long-term finance, as indicated for debt finance by the normal yield curve (term structure of interest rates).

However, an aggressive financing policy will be riskier than a conservative financing policy because short-term finance is riskier than long-term finance. For example, an overdraft is repayable on demand, while a short-term loan may be renewed on less favourable terms than an existing loan. Provided interest payments are made, however, long-term debt will not lead to any pressure on a company and equity finance is permanent capital.

Overall, therefore, it can be said that while working capital investment policy and working capital financing policy use similar terminology, the two policies are very different in terms of their meaning and application. It is even possible, for example, for a company to have a conservative working capital investment policy while following an aggressive working capital financing policy.

ACCA marking scheme		
		Marks
(a)	Revised trade receivables	1
	Reduction in trade receivables	1
	Reduction in financing cost	1
	Cost of early settlement discount	1
	Net cost of change in receivables policy	1
	Comment on findings	1
		———
	Maximum	6
		———
(b)	Current annual ordering cost	0.5
	Current holding cost	0.5
	Total cost of current inventory policy	1
	Revised cost of materials	0.5
	Revised number of orders	0.5
	Revised ordering cost	0.5
	Revised holding cost	0.5
	Net benefit of bulk purchase discount	1
	Comment on assumptions	1
		———
	Maximum	6
		———
(c)	Working capital investment policy	3–4
	Working capital financing policy	5–6
		———
	Maximum	8
		———
Total		20
		———

Examiner's comments

Part (a) asked students to calculate the net benefit or cost of proposed changes in receivables policy, commenting on findings. The cost of an early settlement discount had to be calculated, as well as the decrease in financing cost arising from a reduction in the trade receivables balance.

Candidates were expected to recognise that although current trade terms allowed credit customers to pay after 30 days, they were in fact paying on average after 60 days, as shown by a comparison between credit sales and the level of trade receivables. The average trade receivables period after introducing the proposed changes in receivables policy was 40.5 days, leading to a lower level of trade receivables and a lower financing cost.

Weaker answers showed a lack of understanding of how the receivables days' ratio links credit sales for a period with the trade receivables balance at the end of the period. Some answers, for example, tried to calculate the revised trade receivables balance by applying changed receivables days ratios to current receivables, instead of applying them to credit sales.

In part (b) candidates were asked here to calculate whether an offered bulk purchase discount was financially acceptable, commenting on assumptions made by the calculation.

Perhaps because information on holding cost and order cost was provided in the question, many candidates calculated the economic order quantity (EOQ). The question made no reference to the EOQ and an EOQ calculation was not necessary. In fact, what was needed was a comparison between the current ordering policy and the ordering policy employing the bulk discount. Candidates who wasted time calculating the EOQ found that the company was already using an EOQ approach to ordering inventory.

Some answers did not gain full credit because they did not comment on the assumptions made by their calculations. Credit was also lost by candidates who could not calculate order cost, or holding cost, or both.

The requirement in part (c) was to discuss the similarities and differences between working capital investment policy and working capital financing policy. Many answers struggled to gain good marks with this question, and yet the topics of working capital investment policy (the level of investment in current assets) and working capital financing policy (the balance between short-term and long-term funds in financing current assets) have been examined a number of times in recent years.

Some answers ignored the words "working capital" and "policy", and discussed investment and financing in some detail. These answers did not offer what was being looked for and, for example, discussed investment appraisal techniques (investment) and equity, bonds and leasing (financing). If you look at the question as a whole, you will see that it focuses on that part of the syllabus relating to working capital.

While many answers showed good understanding of working capital financing policy, fewer answers showed understanding of working capital investment policy, and fewer answers still could discuss the similarities and differences between the two policy areas. Both policies are characterised by an assessment of their risk (conservative, moderate or matching, and aggressive), but working capital investment policy is comparative (one company is conservative or aggressive compared to another), while working capital financing policy looks only at the long-term/short-term finance balance in a given company (for example, using mainly short-term financing for permanent current assets is an aggressive policy).

Many answers seemed to be unaware that it is possible for an aggressive working capital investment policy to occur in a given company at the same time as a conservative working capital financing policy, and vice versa. These answers assumed that a company was either aggressive in both kinds of policy, or not, for example.

11 ULNAD

Key answer tips

This question covers two of the key elements within the working capital management section of the syllabus. Part (a) requires a methodical approach, working though the impact of the proposed change. Part (b) is more straightforward given that the Miller Orr formula is provided in the exam; don't neglect to explain the relevance of the values though. Part (c) covers common discursive areas and should give an opportunity to just learn and churn. The highlighted words are key phrases that markers are looking for.

(a) **Evaluation of change in credit policy**

Current average collection period = 30 + 10 = 40 days

Current accounts receivable = 6m × 40/365 = $657,534

Average collection period under new policy = (0.3 × 15) + (0.7 × 60) = 46.5 days

New level of credit sales = $6.3 million

Accounts receivable after policy change = 6.3 × 46.5/ 365 = $802,603

Increase in financing cost = (802,603 – 657,534) × 0.07 = $10,155

	$
Increase in financing cost	10,155
Incremental costs = 6.3m × 0.005 =	31,500
Cost of discount = 6.3m × 0.015 × 0.3 =	28,350

Increase in costs	70,005
Contribution from increased sales = 6m × 0.05 × 0.6 =	180,000

Net benefit of policy change	109,995

The proposed policy change will increase the profitability of Ulnad Co

(b) Determination of spread:

Daily interest rate = 5.11/365 = 0.014% per day

Variance of cash flows = 1,000 × 1,000 = $1,000,000 per day

Transaction cost = $18 per transaction

Spread $\quad = 3 \times ((0.75 \times \text{transaction cost} \times \text{variance})/\text{interest rate})^{1/3}$

$\quad\quad\quad = 3 \times ((0.75 \times 18 \times 1,000,000)/0.00014)^{1/3} = 3 \times 4,585.7 = \$13,757$

Lower limit (set by Renpec Co) = $7,500

Upper limit = 7,500 + 13,757 =$21,257

Return point = 7,500 + (13,757/3) = $12,086

The Miller-Orr model takes account of uncertainty in relation to receipts and payment. The cash balance of Renpec Co is allowed to vary between the lower and upper limits calculated by the model. If the lower limit is reached, an amount of cash equal to the difference between the return point and the lower limit is raised by selling short-term investments. If the upper limit is reached an amount of cash equal to the difference between the upper limit and the return point is used to buy short-term investments. The model therefore helps Renpec Co to decrease the risk of running out of cash, while avoiding the loss of profit caused by having unnecessarily high cash balances.

(c) When considering how working capital is financed, it is useful to divide assets into non-current assets, permanent current assets and fluctuating current assets. Permanent current assets represent the core level of working capital investment needed to support a given level of sales. As sales increase, this core level of working capital also increases. Fluctuating current assets represent the changes in working capital that arise in the normal course of business operations, for example when some accounts receivable are settled later than expected, or when inventory moves more slowly than planned.

The matching principle suggests that long-term finance should be used for long-term assets. Under a matching working capital funding policy, therefore, long-term finance is used for both permanent current assets and non-current assets. Short-term finance is used to cover the short-term changes in current assets represented by fluctuating current assets.

Long-term debt has a higher cost than short-term debt in normal circumstances, for example because lenders require higher compensation for lending for longer periods, or because the risk of default increases with longer lending periods. However, long-term debt is more secure from a company point of view than short-term debt since, provided interest payments are made when due and the requirements of restrictive covenants are met, terms are fixed to maturity. Short-term debt is riskier than long-term debt because, for example, an overdraft is repayable on demand and short-term debt may be renewed on less favourable terms.

A conservative working capital funding policy will use a higher proportion of long-term finance than a matching policy, thereby financing some of the fluctuating current assets from a long-term source. This will be less risky and less profitable than a matching policy, and will give rise to occasional short-term cash surpluses.

An aggressive working capital funding policy will use a lower proportion of long-term finance than a matching policy, financing some of the permanent current assets from a short-term source such as an overdraft. This will be more risky and more profitable than a matching policy.

Other factors that influence a working capital funding policy include management attitudes to risk, previous funding decisions, and organisation size. Management attitudes to risk will determine whether there is a preference for a conservative, an aggressive or a matching approach. Previous funding decisions will determine the current position being considered in policy formulation. The size of the organisation will influence its ability to access different sources of finance. A small company, for example, may be forced to adopt an aggressive working capital funding policy because it is unable to raise additional long-term finance, whether equity of debt.

	ACCA marking scheme		Marks
(a)	Increase in financing cost	2 marks	
	Incremental costs	1 mark	
	Cost of discount	1 mark	
	Contribution from increased sales	1 mark	
	Conclusion	1 mark	
			6
(b)	Calculation of spread	2 marks	
	Calculation of upper limit	1 mark	
	Calculation of return point	1 mark	
	Explanation of findings	2 marks	
			6
(c)	Analysis of assets	1–2 marks	
	Short-term and long-term debt	2–3 marks	
	Discussion of policies	2–3 marks	
	Other factors	1–2 marks	
	Maximum		8
Total			20

12 APX CO

Key answer tips

This question approaches the topic of working capital management from a less frequently examined angle; providing a series of accounting ratios and asking students to work back to a forecast statement of profit or loss and statement of financial position. What makes this question tough is that parts (b) and (c) cannot be attempted without some stab at an answer to part (a). This means there are very few obvious "easy" marks on this question. The highlighted words are key phrases that markers are looking for.

(a) **Forecast statement of profit or loss**

	$m
Turnover = 16.00m × 1.084 =	17.344
Cost of sales = 17.344m – 5.203m =	12.141
Gross profit = 17.344m × 30% =	5.203
Other expenses = 5.203m – 3.469m =	1.734
Net profit = 17.344m × 20% =	3.469
Interest = (10m × 0.08) + 0.140m =	0.940
Profit before tax	2.529
Profit before tax	2.529
Tax = 2.529m × 0.3 =	0.759
Profit after tax	1.770
Dividends = 1.770m × 50% =	0.885
Retained profit	0.885

Tutor's top tips:

The best way to approach this part of the requirement is to work through the statement of profit or loss and statement of financial position line by line, recognising that the overdraft will be your balancing figure.

Forecast statement of financial position

	$m	$m
Non-current assets		22.00
Current assets		
Inventory	3.66	
Trade receivables	3.09	
	───	
		6.75
		───
Total assets		28.75
		───
Equity finance:		
Ordinary shares	5.00	
Reserves	8.39	
	───	
		13.39
Bank loan		10.00
		───
		23.39
Current liabilities		
Trade payables	2.49	
Overdraft	2.87	
	───	
		5.36
		───
Total liabilities		28.75
		───

Workings

Inventory = 12.141m × (110/365) = $3.66m

Trade receivables = 17.344m × (65/365) = $3.09m

Trade payables = 12.141m × (75/365) = $2.49m

Reserves = 7.5m + 0.885m = $8.39m

Overdraft = 28.75m − 23.39m − 2.49 = $2.87m (balancing figure)

(b) Working capital financing policies can be classified into conservative, moderate (or matching) and aggressive, depending on the extent to which fluctuating current assets and permanent current assets are financed by short-term sources of finance. Permanent current assets are the core level of investment in current assets needed to support a given level of business activity or turnover, while fluctuating current assets are the changes in the levels of current assets arising from the unpredictable nature of some aspects of business activity.

A conservative working capital financing policy uses long-term funds to finance non-current assets and permanent current assets, as well as a proportion of fluctuating current assets. This policy is less risky and less profitable than an aggressive working capital financing policy, which uses short-term funds to finance fluctuating current assets and a proportion of permanent current assets as well. Between these two extremes lies the moderate (or matching) policy, which uses long-term funds to finance long-term assets (non-current assets and permanent current assets) and short-term funds to finance short-term assets (fluctuating current assets).

The current statement of financial position shows that APX Co uses trade payables and an overdraft as sources of short-term finance. In terms of the balance between short- and long-term finance, 89% of current assets (100 × 4.1/4.6) are financed from short-term sources and only 11% are financed from long-term sources. Since a high proportion of current assets are permanent in nature, this appears to be a very aggressive working capital financing policy which carries significant risk. If the overdraft were called in, for example, APX Co might have to turn to more expensive short-term financing.

The forecast statement of financial position shows a lower reliance on short-term finance, since 79% of current assets (100 × 5.36/6.75) are financed from short-term sources and 21% are financed from long-term sources. This decreased reliance on an aggressive financing policy is sensible, although with a forecast interest coverage ratio of only 3.7 times (3.469/0.94), APX Co has little scope for taking on more long-term debt. An increase in equity funding to decrease reliance on short-term finance could be considered.

(c)   **Working capital management**

Financial analysis shows deterioration in key working capital ratios. The inventory turnover period is expected to increase from 81 days to 110 days, the trade receivables period is expected to increase from 50 days to 65 days and the trade payables period is expected to increase from 64 days to 75 days. It is also a cause for concern here that the values of these working capital ratios for the next year are forecast, i.e. APX Co appears to be anticipating a worsening in its working capital position. The current and forecast values could be compared to average or sector values in order to confirm whether this is in fact the case.

Because current assets are expected to increase by more than current liabilities, the current ratio and the quick ratio are both expected to increase in the next year, the current ratio from 1.12 times to 1.26 times and the quick ratio from 0.54 times to 0.58 times. Again, comparison with sector average values for these ratios would be useful in making an assessment of the working capital management of APX Co. The balance between trade payables and overdraft finance is approximately the same in both years (trade payables are 46% of current liabilities in the current statement of financial position and 47% of current liabilities in the forecast statement of financial position), although reliance on short-term finance is expected to fall slightly in the next year.

The deteriorating working capital position may be linked to an expected deterioration in the overall financial performance of APX Co. For example, the forecast gross profit margin (30%) and net profit margin (20%) are both less than the current values of these ratios (32% and 23% respectively), and despite the increase in turnover, return on capital employed (ROCE) is expected to fall from 16.35% to 14.83%.

Analysis

Extracts from current statement of profit or loss:

	$m
Turnover	16.00
Cost of sales	10.88
Gross profit	5.12
Other expenses	1.44
Net profit	3.68

	Current	Forecast
Gross profit margin (100 × 5.12/16.00)	32%	
		30%
Net profit margin (100 × 3.68/16.00)	23%	
		20%
ROCE (100 × 3.68/22.5)	16.35%	
(100 × 3.469/23.39)		14.83%
Inventory period (365 × 2.4/10.88)	81 days	
		110 days
Receivables period (365 × 2.2/16.00)	50 days	
		65 days
Payables period (365 × 1.9/10.88)	64 days	
		75 days
Current ratio (4.6/4.1)	1.12 times	
(6.75/5.36)		1.26 times
Quick ratio (2.2/4.1)	0.54 times	
(3.09/5.36)		0.58 times

ACCA marking scheme			
			Marks
(a)	Gross profit		1.0
	Net profit		1.0
	Profit before tax		1.0
	Retained profit		1.0
	Inventory		1.0
	Trade receivables		1.0
	Trade payables		1.0
	Reserves		1.0
	Overdraft		1.0
	Layout and format		1.0
		Maximum	9.0
(b)	Working capital financing policies		2–3
	Financial analysis		1–2
	Working capital financing policy of company		2–3
		Maximum	6.0

(c)	Discussion of working capital management		3–4
	Financial analysis		2–4
		Maximum	5.0
Total			20

Examiner's comments

Candidates often gained high marks in part (a) of this question, but answers to parts (b) and (c) lacked focus.

Part (a) required candidates to prepare a forecast statement of profit or loss and a forecast statement of financial position. Many answers were of a very good standard and gained full marks.

Some candidates ignored the forecast financial ratios and applied the expected turnover growth rate to cost of sales and other expenses. Other candidates showed a lack of knowledge of the structure of the statement of profit or loss by calculating the tax liability before subtracting the interest payments. Candidates should recognise that a good understanding of accounting ratios is needed if they expect to achieve a pass standard and they are advised to study the suggested answer carefully in comparison to the question set in the question paper.

Part (b) asked for an analysis and discussion of the working capital financing policy of the company in the question. Many students were not aware of the conservative, aggressive and matching approaches to working capital financing policy, and so were ill-prepared for this question.

Analysis of the statement of financial position shows that 89% of the current assets of the company are financed from a short-term source, while only 11% are financed from a long-term source. Noting this, good answers discussed the aggressive nature of the company's working capital financing policy and the risks to which it gave rise.

Weaker answers discussed conservative and aggressive approaches to the level of investment in working capital, or focused on the cash conversion cycle (operating cycle) of the company, or combined part (b) with part (c).

Part (c) asked for a discussion of the forecast financial performance of the company in terms of working capital management. Comparing the current position with the forecast position showed that a deterioration in financial performance was expected. Better answers recognised this and made appropriate comments. Weaker answers failed to focus on working capital ratios (for example by calculating and discussing ratios such as interest coverage, debt/equity ratio and dividend per share), or offered only general discussions of areas of working capital management (such as explaining ways in which inventory control or credit management could be improved).

13   HGR CO

Key answer tips

The generic requirement of part (a), to "discuss the working capital financing strategy of HGR" can result in a lack of direction and focus in your answer. This sort of question highlights the importance of good exam preparation that includes sitting as many past exam questions as possible as requirements such as this are not unusual.

Part (b) may overwhelm some students as the initial perception is that many calculations need to be made. However, this is not the case. Part (i) (for 2 marks) involves simply plugging in the numbers provided before doing a quick calculation of overdraft interest. In part (ii), (for 5 marks) you need to evaluate the impact of the finance director's proposals surrounding both accounts receivable and inventory management. Both calculations involve a manipulation of the standard working capital cycle formulae that students should be familiar, although this might not be obvious to some students. The model answer shows the most efficient way of laying out the answer. Of the 9 marks available for part (b), up to 3 are available for commenting on the forecast position and making suitable recommendations. This could easily be overlooked if you're not careful.

Finally, part (c) gives a good opportunity to pick up some easier marks. This part of the question should be attempted first. The highlighted words are key phrases that markers are looking for.

(a)   When considering the financing of working capital, it is useful to divide current assets into fluctuating current assets and permanent current assets. Fluctuating current assets represent changes in the level of current assets due to the unpredictability of business activity. Permanent current assets represent the core level of investment in current assets needed to support a given level of turnover or business activity. As turnover or level of business activity increases, the level of permanent current assets will also increase. This relationship can be measured by the ratio of turnover to net current assets.

The financing choice as far as working capital is concerned is between short-term and long-term finance. Short-term finance is more flexible than long-term finance: an overdraft, for example, is used by a business organisation as the need arises and variable interest is charged on the outstanding balance. Short-term finance is also more risky than long-term finance: an overdraft facility may be withdrawn, or a short-term loan may be renewed on less favourable terms. In terms of cost, the term structure of interest rates suggests that short-term debt finance has a lower cost than long-term debt finance.

The matching principle suggests that long-term finance should be used for long-term investment. Applying this principle to working capital financing, long-term finance should be matched with permanent current assets and non-current assets. A financing policy with this objective is called a 'matching policy'. HGR Co is not using this financing policy, since of the $16,935,000 of current assets, $14,000,000 or 83% is financed from short-term sources (overdraft and trade payables) and only $2,935,000 or 17% is financed from a long-term source, in this case equity finance (shareholders' funds) or traded bonds.

The financing policy or approach taken by HGR Co towards the financing of working capital, where short-term finance is preferred, is called an aggressive policy. Reliance on short-term finance makes this riskier than a matching approach, but also more profitable due to the lower cost of short-term finance. Following an aggressive approach to financing can lead to overtrading (undercapitalisation) and the possibility of liquidity problems.

(b)   Bank balance in three months' time if no action is taken:

Month	1	2	3
	$000	$000	$000
Receipts	4,220	4,350	3,808
Payments	(3,950)	(4,100)	(3,750)
Interest on bonds		(200)	
Overdraft interest	(19)	(18)	(18)
Capital investment			(2,000)
Net cash flow	251	32	(1,960)
Opening balance	(3,800)	(3,549)	(3,517)
Closing balance	(3,549)	(3,517)	(5,477)

Bank balance in three months' time if the finance director's proposals are implemented:

Month	1	2	3
	$000	$000	$000
Receipts	4,220	4,350	3,808
Payments	(3,950)	(4,100)	(3,750)
Interest on bonds		(200)	
Overdraft interest	(19)	(15)	(13)
Capital investment			(2,000)
Accounts receivable	270	270	270
Inventory	204	204	204
Net cash flow	725	509	(1,481)
Opening balance	(3,800)	(3,075)	(2,566)
Closing balance	(3,075)	(2,566)	(4,047)

Workings:

Reduction in accounts receivable days

Current accounts receivable days = (8,775/49,275) × 365 = 65 days

Reduction in days over six months = 65 – 53 = 12 days

Monthly reduction = 12/6 = 2 days

Each receivables day is equivalent to 8,775,000/65 =$135,000 (Alternatively, each receivables day is equivalent to 49,275,000/365 =$135,000)

Monthly reduction in accounts receivable = 2 × 135,000 = $270,000

Reduction in inventory days

Current inventory days = (8,160/37,230) × 365 = 80 days

Each inventory day is equivalent to 8,160,000/80 = $102,000 (Alternatively, each inventory day = 37,230,000/365 = $102,000)

Monthly reduction in inventory = 102,000 × 2 = $204,000

Overdraft interest calculations

Monthly overdraft interest rate = 1.06171/12 = 1.005 or 0.5%

If no action is taken:

Period 1 interest = 3,800,000 × 0.005 = $19,000

Period 2 interest = 3,549,000 × 0.005 = $17,745 or $18,000

Period 3 interest = 3,517,000 × 0.005 = $17,585 or $18,000

If action is taken:

Period 1 interest = 3,800,000 × 0.005 = $19,000

Period 2 interest = 3,075,000 × 0.005 = $15,375 or $15,000

Period 3 interest = 2,566,000 × 0.005 = $12,830 or $13,000

Discussion

If no action is taken, the cash flow forecast shows that HGR Co will exceed its overdraft limit of $4 million by $1.48 million in three months' time. If the finance director's proposals are implemented, there is a positive effect on the bank balance, but the overdraft limit is still exceeded in three months' time, although only by $47,000 rather than by $1.47 million.

In each of the three months following that, the continuing reduction in accounts receivable days will improve the bank balance by $270,000 per month. Without further information on operating receipts and payments, it cannot be forecast whether the bank balance will return to less than the limit, or even continue to improve.

The main reason for the problem with the bank balance is the $2 million capital expenditure. Purchase of non-current assets should not be financed by an overdraft, but a long-term source of finance such as equity or bonds. If the capital expenditure were removed from the area of working capital management, the overdraft balance at the end of three months would be $3.48 million if no action were taken and $2.05 million if the finance director's proposals were implemented. Given that HGR Co has almost $50 million of non-current assets that could possibly be used as security, raising long-term debt through either a bank loan or a bond issue appears to be sensible. Assuming a bond interest rate of 10% per year, current long-term debt in the form of traded bonds is approximately ($200m × 2)/0.1 = $4m, which is much less than the amount of noncurrent assets.

A suitable course of action for HGR Co to follow would therefore be, firstly, to implement the finance director's proposals and, secondly, to finance the capital expenditure from a long-term source. Consideration could also be given to using some long-term debt finance to reduce the overdraft and to reduce the level of accounts payable, currently standing at 100 days.

(c)   When credit is granted to foreign customers, two problems may become especially significant. First, the longer distances over which trade takes place and the more complex nature of trade transactions and their elements means foreign accounts receivable need more investment than their domestic counterparts. Longer transaction times increase accounts receivable balances and hence the level of financing and financing costs. Second, the risk of bad debts is higher with foreign accounts receivable than with their domestic counterparts. In order to manage and reduce credit risks, therefore, exporters seek to reduce the risk of bad debt and to reduce the level of investment in foreign accounts receivable.

Many foreign transactions are on 'open account', which is an agreement to settle the amount outstanding on a predetermined date. Open account reflects a good business relationship between importer and exporter. It also carries the highest risk of non-payment.

One way to reduce investment in foreign accounts receivable is to agree early payment with an importer, for example by payment in advance, payment on shipment, or cash on delivery. These terms of trade are unlikely to be competitive, however, and it is more likely that an exporter will seek to receive cash in advance of payment being made by the customer.

One way to accelerate cash receipts is to use bill finance. Bills of exchange with a signed agreement to pay the exporter on an agreed future date, supported by a documentary letter of credit, can be discounted by a bank to give immediate funds. This discounting is without recourse if bills of exchange have been countersigned by the importer's bank.

Documentary letters of credit are a payment guarantee backed by one or more banks. They carry almost no risk, provided the exporter complies with the terms and conditions contained in the letter of credit. The exporter must present the documents stated in the letter, such as bills of lading, shipping documents, bills of exchange, and so on, when seeking payment. As each supporting document relates to a key aspect of the overall transaction, letters of credit give security to the importer as well as the exporter.

Companies can also manage and reduce risk by gathering appropriate information with which to assess the creditworthiness of new customers, such as bank references and credit reports.

Insurance can also be used to cover some of the risks associated with giving credit to foreign customers. This would avoid the cost of seeking to recover cash due from foreign accounts receivable through a foreign legal system, where the exporter could be at a disadvantage due to a lack of local or specialist knowledge.

Export factoring can also be considered, where the exporter pays for the specialist expertise of the factor as a way of reducing investment in foreign accounts receivable and reducing the incidence of bad debts.

ACCA marking scheme			
			Marks
(a)	Analysis of current assets	1 – 2	
	Short-term and long-term finance	2 – 3	
	Matching principle	1 – 2	
	Financing approach used by company	1 – 2	
		Maximum	6
(b)	Bank balance if no action is taken	2	
	Bank balance if action is taken	5	
	Working capital management implications	1 – 2	
	Advice on course of action	1 – 2	
		Maximum	9
(c)	Relevant discussion	5	
Total			25

Examiner's comments

Part (a) required candidates to discuss the working capital financing strategy of a company. Some candidates ignored the word 'financing' and discussed working capital strategy in general. Other candidates took 'working capital financing strategy' to mean the proposals in the question to reduce the level of account receivables and inventory by operational improvements.

The question gave extracts from a statement of financial position which showed that the company was financing 83% of its current assets from short-term sources, namely a bank overdraft and trade receivables. This is an aggressive rather than a conservative financing strategy and better answers recognised this, discussing how current assets could be divided into fluctuating and permanent current assets, and linking this analysis of current assets via the matching principle to the use of short-term and long-term finance.

Part (b) asked candidates to calculate the bank balance in three months' time if no action were taken, and if the proposals were implemented. Many candidates had great difficulty in rolling forward the current cash balance (the overdraft of $3.8 million) using the receipts and payments given in the question, while allowing for one month's interest on the balance of the account at the start of each month. Common errors included failing to recognise that the opening balance was the overdraft and therefore having no opening balance: calculating annual interest rather than monthly interest; and including cash flows other

than those given in the question (for example from the credit sales and cost of sales figures given in the question). All candidates are expected to be able to prepare cash flow forecasts and the general standard of answers to this question showed that many candidates need further preparation in this important area.

Part (c) required candidates to discuss how risks arising from granting credit to foreign customers could be managed and reduced. Many candidates gave answers of a good standard, although some answers were one-sided, concentrating on exchange rate risk rather than on credit risk. Since the question referred to foreign customers, it was inappropriate to limit answers to a discussion of domestic receivables management.

14   ANJO

Key answer tips

This is a fairly straightforward question. The highlighted words are key phrases that markers are looking for.

(a)   **Calculation of ratios**

Inventory days	20X6:	(3,000/9,300) × 365	= 118 days
	20X5:	(1,300/6,600) × 365	= 72 days
		Sector average: 90 days	
Receivables days	20X6:	(3,800/15,600) × 365	= 89 days
	20X5:	(1,850/11,100) × 365	= 61 days
		Sector average: 60 days	
Payables days	20X6:	(2,870/9,300 × 0.95) × 365	= 119 days
	20X5:	(1,600/6,600 × 0.95) × 365	= 93 days
		Sector average: 80 days	

In each case, the ratio in 20X6 is higher than the ratio in 20X5, indicating that deterioration has occurred in the management of inventories, receivables and payables in 20X6.

Inventory days have increased by 46 days or 64%, moving from below the sector average to 28 days – one month – more than it. Given the rapid increase in sales revenue (40%) in 20X6, Anjo Inc may be expecting a continuing increase in the future and may have built up inventories in preparation for this, i.e. inventory levels reflect future sales rather than past sales. Accounting statements from several previous years and sales forecasts for the next period would help to clarify this point.

Receivables days have increased by 28 days or 46% in 20X6 and are now 29 days above the sector average. It is possible that more generous credit terms have been offered in order to stimulate sales. The increased sales revenue does not appear to be due to offering lower prices, since both gross profit margin (40%) and net profit margin (34%) are unchanged.

In 20X5, only management of payables was a cause for concern, with Anjo Inc taking 13 more days on average to settle liabilities with trade payables than the sector. This has increased to 39 days more than the sector in 20X6. This could lead to difficulties between the company and its suppliers if it is exceeding the credit periods they have specified. Anjo Inc has no long-term debt and the statement of financial position indicates an increased reliance on short-term finance, since cash has reduced by $780,000 or 87% and the overdraft has increased by $850,000 to $1 million.

Perhaps the company should investigate whether it is undercapitalised (overtrading). It is unusual for a company of this size to have no long-term debt.

(b)   Cash operating cycle (20X5) = 72 + 61 – 93 = 40 days

Cash operating cycle (20X6) = 118 + 89 – 119 = 88 days

The cash operating cycle or working capital cycle gives the average time it takes for the company to receive payment from receivables after it has paid its trade payables. This represents the period of time for which payables require financing. The cash operating cycle of Anjo Inc has lengthened by 48 days in 20X6 compared with 20X5. This represents an increase in working capital requirement of approximately $15,600,000 × 48/365 = $2.05 million.

(c)

	$000
Current receivables =	3,800
Receivables under factor = 3,800 × 0.7 =	2,660
Reduction in receivables =	1,140

	$000
Finance cost saving = 1,140 × 0.08 =	91.2
Administration cost saving = 1,000 × 0.02 =	20.0
Interest on advance = 2,660 × 0.8 × 0.01 =	(21.3)
Factor's annual fee = 15,600 × 0.005 =	(78.0)
Net benefit of accepting factor's offer	11.9

Although the terms of the factor's offer are financially acceptable, suggesting a net financial benefit of $11,900, this benefit is small compared with annual sales revenue of $15.6 million. Other benefits, such as the application of the factor's expertise to the receivables management of Anjo Inc, might also be influential in the decision on whether to accept the offer.

15   ZSE CO

Key answer tips

This question combines the key area of working capital management with the slightly less examined area of probability analysis and expected values. The calculations required in part (a) are fairly straightforward. However, the unusual combination of these two syllabus areas may confuse some students. Parts (b) and (c) require a 'learn and churn' type discussion so students should feel more comfortable with this. The highlighted words are key phrases that markers are looking for.

(a)　(i)　**Period 1 closing balance**

Opening balance	Cash flow	Closing balance	Probability	Expected value
$000	$000	$000	$000	$000
(500)	8,000	7,500	0.1	750
(500)	4,000	3,500	0.6	2,100
(500)	(2,000)	(2,500)	0.3	(750)
				2,100

The expected value of the period 1 closing balance is $2,100,000

Tutorial note:

An alternative approach to this part of the question is to calculate the expected value of the cash flow in period 1, and then add this to the opening balance. This could be achieved as follows:

(8,000 × 0.1) + (4,000 × 0.6) – (2,000 × 0.3) = 2,600

(500) + 2,600 = $2,100k

(ii)　**Period 2 closing balance**

Period 1 closing balance	Probability	Period 2 cash flow	Probability	Period 2 closing balance	Joint probability	Expected value
$000		$000		$000		$000
7,500	0.1	7,000	0.3	14,500	0.03	435
		3,000	0.5	10,500	0.05	525
		(9,000)	0.2	(1,500)	0.02	(30)
3,500	0·6	7,000	0.3	10,500	0.18	1,890
		3,000	0.5	6,500	0.30	1,950
		(9,000)	0.2	(5,500)	0.12	(660)
(2,500)	0·3	7,000	0.3	4,500	0.09	405
		3,000	0.5	500	0.15	75
		(9,000)	0.2	(11,500)	0.06	(690)
						3,900

The expected value of the period 2 closing balance is $3,900,000

(iii)

Tutorial note:

The key to answering parts (iii) and (iv) is to consider the net effect of the flows. For part (iii), if the period 2 cash flow was ($9,000,000) then it wouldn't matter what the period 1 cash flow was, the balance would be negative at the end of period 2. With any of the other two possibilities, the balance would be positive, regardless of what cash flow arose in period 1. The answer is therefore the probability of the $9,000,000 cash outflow in period 2 which is 20%.

For part (iv), the same thought process can be used, except this time you're not looking at whether the balance is above or below zero; your benchmark changes to the overdraft limit of $2m.

The probability of a negative cash balance at the end of period 2 = 0.02 + 0.12 + 0.06 = 20%

(iv)   The probability of exceeding the overdraft limit in period 2 is 0.12 + 0.06 = 18%

Tutor's top tips:

Ensure you cover off all parts of the requirement. In part (a) it is easy to drop marks by failing to discuss whether your analysis can assist the company in managing its cash flows.

Discussion

The expected value analysis has shown that, on an average basis, ZSE Co will have a positive cash balance at the end of period 1 of $2.1 million and a positive cash balance at the end of period 2 of $3.9 million. However, the cash balances that are expected to occur are the specific balances that have been averaged, rather than the average values themselves.

There could be serious consequences for ZSE Co if it exceeds its overdraft limit. For example, the overdraft facility could be withdrawn. There is a 30% chance that the overdraft limit will be exceeded in period 1 and a lower probability, 18%, that the overdraft limit will be exceeded in period 2. To guard against exceeding its overdraft limit in period 1, ZSE Co must find additional finance of $0.5 million ($2.5m – $2.0m). However, to guard against exceeding its overdraft limit in period 2, the company could need up to $9.5 million ($11.5m – $2.0m). Renegotiating the overdraft limit in period 1 would therefore be only a short-term solution.

One strategy is to find now additional finance of $0.5 million and then to re-evaluate the cash flow forecasts at the end of period 1. If the most likely outcome occurs in period 1, the need for additional finance in period 2 to guard against exceeding the overdraft limit is much lower.

The expected value analysis has been useful in illustrating the cash flow risks faced by ZSE Co. Although the cash flow forecasting model has been built with the aid of a firm of financial consultants, the assumptions used in the model must be reviewed before decisions are made based on the forecast cash flows and their associated probabilities.

Expected values are more useful for repeat decisions rather than one-off activities, as they are based on averages. They illustrate what the average outcome would be if an activity was repeated a large number of times. In fact, each period and its cash flows will occur only once and the expected values of the closing balances are not closing balances that are forecast to arise in practice. In period 1, for example, the expected value closing balance of $2.1 million is not forecast to occur, while a closing balance of $3.5 million is likely to occur.

(b)   The factors to be considered in formulating a policy to manage the trade receivables of ZSE Co will relate to the key areas of credit assessment or analysis, credit control and collection procedures. A key factor is the turbulence in the company's business environment and the way it affects the company's customers.

Credit analysis

The main objective of credit analysis is to ensure that credit is granted to customers who will settle their account at regular intervals in accordance with the agreed terms of sale. The risk of bad debts must be minimised as much as possible.

Key factors to consider here are the source and quality of the information used by ZSE Co to assess customer creditworthiness. The information sources could include bank references, trade references, public information such as published accounts, credit reference agencies and personal experience. The quality of the information needs to be confirmed as part of the credit analysis process. Some organisations have developed credit scoring systems to assist in the assessment of creditworthiness.

Credit control

Once credit has been granted, it is essential to ensure that agreed terms and conditions are adhered to while the credit is outstanding. This can be achieved by careful monitoring of customer accounts and the periodic preparation of aged debtor analyses. A key factor here is the quality of the staff involved with credit control and the systems and procedures they use to maintain regular contact with customers, for example invoices, statements, reminders, letters and telephone contacts.

ZSE Co has been experiencing difficulties in collecting amounts due because its customers have been experiencing difficult trading conditions. Close contact with customers is essential here in order to determine where revised terms can be negotiated when payment is proving hard, and perhaps to provide advance warning of serious customer liquidity or going concern problems.

Collection procedures

The objective here is to ensure timely and secure transfer of funds when they are due, whether by physical means or by electronic means. A key factor here is the need to ensure that the terms of trade are clearly understood by the customer from the point at which credit is granted. Offering credit represents a cost to the seller and ensuring that payment occurs as agreed prevents this cost from exceeding budgeted expectations.

Procedures for chasing late payers should be clearly formulated and trained personnel must be made responsible for ensuring that these procedures are followed. Legal action should only be considered as a last resort, since it often represents the termination of the business relationship with a customer.

(c) Profitability and liquidity are usually cited as the twin objectives of working capital management. The profitability objective reflects the primary financial management objective of maximising shareholder wealth, while liquidity is needed in order to ensure that financial claims on an organisation can be settled as they become liable for payment.

The two objectives are in conflict because liquid assets such as bank accounts earn very little return or no return, so liquid assets decrease profitability. Liquid assets in fact incur an opportunity cost equivalent either to the cost of short-term finance or to the profit lost by not investing in profitable projects.

Whether profitability is a more important objective than liquidity depends in part on the particular circumstances of an organisation. Liquidity may be the more important objective when short-term finance is hard to find, while profitability may become a more important objective when cash management has become too conservative. In short, both objectives are important and neither can be neglected.

ACCA marking scheme		
		Marks
(a) Expected value of period 1 closing balance		2
Expected value of period 2 closing balance		5
Probability of negative cash balance		1
Probability of exceeding overdraft limit		2
Discussion of expected value analysis		3
	Maximum	12
(b) Credit analysis		2–3
Credit control		2–3
Collection procedures		2–3
	Maximum	5
(c) Relevant discussion		3
Total		20

Examiner's comments

This part (a) required candidates to calculate expected values and probabilities from data given in the question, and to discuss the usefulness of expected value analysis.

A number of candidates lost marks by calculating the expected values of the cash flows for period 1 and period 2, but not calculating the closing balances for period 1 and period 2, which is what the question had asked for. There is clearly a difference between cash flow and closing balance.

Candidates were expected to calculate the closing balances using a probability table approach, but many candidates calculated the closing balances using an average cash flow approach. While this provided correct values for the closing balances and hence was given full credit, it did not help with calculating the probability of a negative closing balance in period 2, and it did not help with calculating the probability of exceeding the overdraft limit at the end of period 2. Many candidates were unable to calculate these probabilities because they did appreciate the importance of the joint probabilities used in a probability table.

Candidates were then asked to discuss whether the expected value analysis could assist the company to manage its cash flows. Many candidates tended to discuss ways in which the company could manage cash flows in general, even in some cases discussing cash management models, rather than discussing the usefulness of an expected value analysis. Better answers discussed the benefits and limitations of the analysis that had been undertaken.

In part (b), candidates were asked to identify and discuss factors relevant to formulating a trade receivables management policy. While many candidates gained good marks here, there was a very strong tendency for answers to be framed around lists of ways of improving trade receivables management (a question that has been asked in the past), rather than around factors influencing trade receivables policy. Fortunately, a strong relationship exists between the two areas, and it was possible to give credit for knowledge about the management of trade receivables.

Part (c) asked candidates to discuss whether profitability or liquidity was the primary objective of working capital management. Many candidates answered appropriately that both profitability and liquidity were important: profitability because it related to the overall objective of wealth maximisation and liquidity because of the need to meet liabilities as they became due for settlement.

16   PNP PLC

Key answer tips

Part (a) requires the usual comparison of the costs and benefits of implementing a discount. The complexity of the question means there are a large number of elements to consider and key to tackling the calculations is to recognise that the average payment period per class of receivable will equal the receivables days. Remember, each individual calculation will earn marks so you don't need to have identified all of them to score well. Both parts (a) and (b) of this question require a significant amount of workings. Laying your workings out neatly and clearly cross referencing them to your answer will ensure you have the best chance of scoring well. When laying out your answer to part (c), use plenty of sub-headings to clearly indicate to your marker the points you are making. The highlighted words are key phrases that markers are looking for.

(a)   **Effect on profitability of implementing the proposal**

	£	£
Benefits:		
Increased contribution (W1)	200,000	
Decrease in irrecoverable debts (W2)	6,300	
		206,300
Costs		
Increase in current Class 1 discount (W3)	12,167	
Discount from transferring Class 2 receivables (W4)	11,498	
Discount from new Class 1 receivables (W5)	3,750	
Increase in irrecoverable debts, new Class 2 receivables (W6)	2,055	
Increase in financing cost from new receivables (W7)	4,932	34,402
Net benefit of implementing the proposal		171,898

The proposed change appears to be financially acceptable and so may be recommended. Uncertainty with respect to some of the assumptions underlying the financial evaluation would be unlikely to change the favourable recommendation.

Workings

Contribution/sales ratio = 100 × (5,242 − 3,145)/5,242 = 40%

Irrecoverable debts ratio for Class 2 receivables = 100 × (12,600/252,000) = 5%

Increase in Class 1 receivables from new business = 250,000 × 30/365 = £20,548

Increase in Class 2 receivables from new business = 250,000 × 60/365 = £41,096

(W1) Contribution from increased business = 500,000 × 40% = £200,000

(W2) Decrease in irrecoverable debts for transferring current Class 2 receivables = 12,600 × 0.5 = £6,300

   (Note that other assumptions regarding irrecoverable debts are possible here)

(W3) Current sales of Class 1 receivables = 200,000 × (365/30) = £2,433,333

   Rise in discount cost for current Class 1 receivables = 2,433,333 × 0.005 = £12,167

(W4) Current sales of Class 2 receivables = 252,000 × (365/60) = £1,533,000

   Discount cost of transferring Class 2 receivables = 1,533,000 × 0.5 × 0.015 = £11,498

(W5) Discount cost for new Class 1 receivables = 250,000 × 0.015 = £3,750

(W6) Irrecoverable debts arising from new Class 2 receivables = 41,096 × 0.05 = £2,055

   (Note that other assumptions regarding irrecoverable debts are possible here)

(W7) Increase in financing cost from new receivables = (20,548 + 41,096) × 0.08 = £4,932

(**Note** that it could be assumed that transferring receivables pay after 30 days rather than 60 days)

Examiner's Note: because of the various assumptions that could be made regarding irrecoverable debts and payment period, other approaches to a solution are also acceptable.

Tutorial note:

An alternative approach to this part of the question is to lay out all of the calculations regarding the current and revised position before getting into the detail. This can often allow a clearer thought process and a more time efficient approach to the question.

You know from your studies that the main costs and benefits to consider when deciding on a level of discount to offer are:

— *The cost of the discount itself (for this you will need to know the value of sales for each class)*

— *The benefit of reduced financing costs (for this you will need to know the level of receivables under the current strategy and the proposed strategy*

— *The benefit of reduced irrecoverable debts (for this you will need to know the new level of receivables by class together with the typical ratio of bad debts)*

In this particular case, we will also need to consider the contribution that will be earned on the additional sales resulting from the revised policy.

Now we know the information we will require, we can set about obtaining it

	Current level of discount		Revised level of discount	
		£000		£000
Class 1 sales	£200k × 365/30	2,433.3	£2,433.3k + £250k (being half of the new sales) + £766.5k (being half of the previous class 2 receivables)	3,449.8
Class 1 receivables	Per question	200	£3,449.8k × 30/365	283.5
Cost of financing class 1 receivables	£200k × 8%	16	£283.5k × 8%	22.7
Class 2 sales	£252k × 365/60	1,533	£1,533k / 2 + £250k	1,016.5
Class 2 receivables	Per question	252	£1,016.5k × 60/365	167
Cost of financing class 2 receivables	£252k × 8%	20.2	£167k × 8%	13.4

The other pieces of information required were shown at the beginning of this answer; the contribution/sales ratio of 40% and the irrecoverable debts ratio for class 2 receivables of 5%.

Having gathered all of the information, it is quite a simple job to detail out the costs and benefits.

> *Costs*
>
> *Additional discount*
>
> *Remember this will need to reflect both the additional 0.5% payable on existing class 1 sales as well as the full 1.5% payable on all new sales and the previous class 2 sales that will now pay promptly.*
>
> | | |
> |---|---:|
> | *£2,433.3k × 0.5%* | *= £12.2k* |
> | *(£3,449.8k – £2,433.3k) × 1.5%* | *= £15.2k* |
> | ***Total cost*** | ***= £27.4k*** |
> | ***Benefits*** | |
> | *Additional contribution* | |
> | *£500k × 40%* | *= £200k* |
> | *Reduction in irrecoverable debts* | |
> | *(£167k – £252k) × 5%* | *= £4.2k* |
> | *Reduction in financing costs* | |
> | *(£16k + £20.2k) – (£22.7k + £13.4k)* | *= £0.1k* |
> | ***Total benefit*** | ***= £204.3k*** |
> | ***Net benefit*** | ***= £176.9k*** |
>
> ***Note:*** *this answer differs from that presented above due to the approach taken. It would however, score in full.*

(b)   Current cash operating cycle:

Inventory days = (603/3,145) × 365 = 70 days

Payables days = (574.5/3,145) × 365 = 67 days

Average receivables days = (744.5/5,242) × 365 = 52 days

Cash operating cycle = 70 + 52 – 67 = 55 days

After implementation of the proposal, it is reasonable to assume that inventory days and payables days remain unchanged. Total receivables have increased by £61,644 to £806,144 and sales revenue has increased to £5.742m. Average receivables days are now 365 × (806/5,742) = 51 days. The cash operating cycle has marginally decreased by one day to 54 days (70 + 51 – 67).

(c)   The key elements of a receivables management system may be described as establishing a credit policy, credit assessment, credit control and collection of amounts due.

Establishing credit policy

The credit policy provides the overall framework within which the receivables management system of PNP plc operates and will cover key issues such as the procedures to be followed when granting credit, the usual credit period offered, the maximum credit period that may be granted, any discounts for early settlement, whether interest is charged on overdue balances, and actions to be taken with accounts that have not been settled in the agreed credit period. These terms of trade will depend to a considerable extent on the terms offered by competitors to PNP plc, but they will also depend on the ability of the company to finance its receivables (financing costs), the need to meet the costs of administering the system (administrative costs) and the risk of irrecoverable debts.

Credit assessment

In order to minimise the risk of irrecoverable debts, PNP plc should assess potential customers as to their creditworthiness before offering them credit. The depth of the credit check depends on the amount of business being considered, the size of the client and the potential for repeat business. The credit assessment requires information about the customer, whether from a third party as in a trade reference, a bank reference or a credit report, or from PNP itself through, for example, its analysis of a client's published accounts. The benefits of granting credit must always be greater than the cost involved. There is no point, therefore, in PNP plc paying for a detailed credit report from a credit reference agency for a small credit sale.

Credit control

Once PNP plc has granted credit to a customer, it should monitor the account at regular intervals to make sure that the agreed terms are being followed. An aged receivables analysis is useful in this respect since it helps the company focus on those clients who are the most cause for concern. Customers should be reminded of their debts by prompt despatch of invoices and regular statements of account. Customers in arrears should not be allowed to take further goods on credit.

Collection of amounts due

The customers of PNP plc should ideally settle their accounts within the agreed credit period. There is no indication as to what this might be, but the company clearly feels that a segmental analysis of its clients is possible given their payment histories, their potential for irrecoverable debts and their geographical origin. Clear guidelines are needed over the action to take when customers are late in settling their accounts or become irrecoverable debts, for example indicating at what stage legal action should be initiated.

17   PLOT CO

Key answer tips

Care must be taken in parts (a) and (b) due to the number of calculations necessary to fulfil the various requirements. A clear and methodical approach to the **Workings** is vital.

Part (c) should be a straight forward repetition of knowledge in this small syllabus area.

The highlighted words are key phrases that markers are looking for.

(a)   (i)   **Cost of current ordering policy**

Ordering cost = 12 × 267 = $3,204 per year

Monthly order = monthly demand = 300,000/12 = 25,000 units

Buffer inventory = 25,000 × 0.4 = 10,000 units

Average inventory excluding buffer inventory = 25,000/2 = 12,500 units

Average inventory including buffer inventory = 12,500 + 10,000 = 22,500 units

Holding cost = 22,500 × 0.1 = $2,250 per year

Total cost = 3,204 + 2,250 = $5,454 per year

    (ii)   **Cost of ordering policy using economic order quantity (EOQ)**

EOQ = ((2 × 267 × 300,000)/0.10)0.5 = 40,025 or 40,000 units per order

Number of orders per year = 300,000/40,000 = 7.5 orders per year

Order cost = 7.5 × 267 = $2,003

Average inventory excluding buffer inventory = 40,000/2 = 20,000 units

Average inventory including buffer inventory = 20,000 + 10,000 = 30,000 units

Holding cost = 30,000 × 0.1 = $3,000 per year

Total cost = $2,003 + $3,000 = $5,003 per year

    (iii)   Saving from introducing EOQ ordering policy = 5,454 − 5,003 = $451 per year

(b)   Product Q trade payables at end of year = 456,000 × 1 × 60/365 = $74,959

Product Q trade payables after discount = 456,000 × 1 × 0.99 × 30/365 = $37,105

Decrease in Product Q trade payables = 74,959 − 37,105 = $37,854

Increase in financing cost = 37,854 × 0.05 = $1,893

Value of discount = 456,000 × 0.01 = $4,560

Net value of offer of discount = 4,560 − 1,893 = $2,667

(c)   The objectives of working capital management are usually taken to be profitability and liquidity. Profitability is allied to the financial objective of maximising shareholder wealth, while liquidity is needed in order to settle liabilities as they fall due. A company must have sufficient cash to meet its liabilities, since otherwise it may fail.

However, these two objectives are in conflict, since liquid resources have no return or low levels of return and hence decrease profitability. A conservative approach to working capital management will decrease the risk of running out of cash, favouring liquidity over profitability and decreasing risk. Conversely, an aggressive approach to working capital management will emphasise profitability over liquidity, increasing the risk of running out of cash while increasing profitability.

Working capital management is central to financial management for several reasons.

First, cash is the life-blood of a company's business activities and without enough cash to meet short-term liabilities, a company would fail.

Second, current assets can account for more than half of a company's assets, and so must be carefully managed. Poor management of current assets can lead to loss of profitability and decreased returns to shareholders.

Third, for SMEs current liabilities are a major source of finance and must be carefully managed in order to ensure continuing availability of such finance.

				Marks
ACCA marking scheme				
(a)	(i)	Current ordering cost		
		Buffer inventory		0.5
		Average inventory		0.5
		Holding cost		0.5
		Total cost		0.5
			Maximum	3
	(ii)	Economic order quantity		1
		EOQ order cost		1
		Holding cost		0.5
		Total cost		0.5
			Maximum	3
	(iii)	Saving from EOQ ordering policy		1
(b)		Current trade payables		1
		Trade payables after discount		1
		Increase in finance costs		1
		Value of discount		1
		Net value of discount offer		1
			Maximum	5
(d)		Objectives of working capital management		3–4
		Role of working capital management		3–4
			Maximum	8
Total				**20**

Examiner's comments

Part (a) asked candidates to calculate the total cost of the current ordering policy, the total cost of an ordering policy using the economic order quantity (EOQ), and the net cost or saving of introducing an ordering policy using the EOQ. Many answers gained good marks here. Where candidates made calculation errors, these showed a lack of understanding of the calculation process, for example including only half of buffer inventory in average inventory, or using annual demand as average inventory, or omitting holding cost completely.

Almost all candidates who calculated the two total costs also calculated the net cost or saving of introducing an ordering policy using the EOQ.

In part (b) candidates had to calculate the purchase cost saving if the early settlement discount were accepted and the increase in finance cost due to paying the supplier 30 days earlier. Some candidates ran into difficulties because they included total purchase costs in a comparison of current and revised costs, but only incremental costs and benefits are relevant here, so there was no need to include total purchase costs.

Errors that were made included:

- Treating the reduction in trade payables as a benefit
- Comparing annual benefit with monthly cost, and vice versa
- Including only a benefit, or including only a cost
- Calculating an annual percentage cost, when the question asked for net value in dollars.

Some candidates, having calculated net value of the early settlement discount, went on to discuss whether it should be accepted. No credit was given to such a discussion, however, as the question asked only for calculation.

In part (c) better answers identified profitability and liquidity as the main objectives of working capital management, perhaps briefly explaining the conflict between the two, before focusing on a discussion of the central role of working capital management in financial management, referring perhaps to the importance of cash and cash management, the importance of currents assets to a company, the importance of current liabilities as a source of finance, especially for SMEs, the need to have policies relating to the elements of working capital such as trade receivables and inventory, and so on

18 WQZ

Key answer tips

This question covers two popular areas of working capital management: inventory and accounts receivable management. The calculations in part (a) give some early chances to pick up some relatively easy marks. Part (b) and (d) are both discursive requirements that should also prove relatively straightforward. The trickiest element is part (c) although the requirement to calculate the maximum early settlement discount that could be offered is only worth one mark: don't let this put you off gathering the marks for the earlier parts of the process. The highlighted words are key phrases that markers are looking for.

(a)   **Cost of the current ordering policy**

Order size = 10% of 160,000 = 16,000 units per order

Number of orders per year = 160,000/16,000 = 10 orders per year

Annual ordering cost = 10 × 400 = $4,000 per year

Holding cost ignoring buffer stock = 5.12 × (16,000/2) = $40,960 per year

Holding cost of buffer inventory = 5.12 × 5,000 = $25,600 per year

Total cost of current policy = 4,000 + 40,960 + 25,600 = $70,560 per year

Cost of the ordering policy using the EOQ model

Order size = $(2 \times 400 \times 160,000/5.12)^{0.5}$ = 5,000 units per order

Number of orders per year = 160,000/5,000 = 32 orders per year

Annual ordering cost = 32 × 400 = $12,800 per year

Holding cost ignoring buffer stock = 5.12 × (5,000/2) = $12,800 per year

Holding cost of buffer inventory = 5.12 × 5,000 = $25,600 per year

Total cost of current policy = 12,800 + 12,800 + 25,600 = $51,200 per year

Change in costs of inventory management by using EOQ model

Decrease in costs = 70,560 – 51,200 = $19,360

Tutorial note:

Since the buffer inventory is the same in both scenarios, its holding costs do not need to be included in calculating the change in inventory management costs.

(b) Holding costs can be reduced by reducing the level of inventory held by a company. Holding costs can be reduced to a minimum if a company orders supplies only when it needs them, avoiding the need to have any inventory at all of inputs to the production process. This approach to inventory management is called just-in-time (JIT) procurement.

The benefits of a JIT procurement policy include a lower level of investment in working capital, since inventory levels have been minimised: a reduction in inventory holding costs; a reduction in materials handling costs, due to improved materials flow through the production process; an improved relationship with suppliers, since supplier and customer need to work closely together in order to make JIT procurement a success; improved operating efficiency, due to the need to streamline production methods in order to eliminate inventory between different stages of the production process; and lower reworking costs due to the increased emphasis on the quality of supplies, since hold-ups in production must be avoided when inventory between production stages has been eliminated.

(c) **Evaluation of changes in receivables management**

Tutor's top tips:

When asked to evaluate a proposed change in policy you should always focus on quantifying the additional costs and benefits. Start by listing them out, and then begin with the easier calculations first. You don't need to complete the evaluation in order to score reasonable marks.

The current level of receivables days = (18/87.6) × 365 = 75 days

Since 25% of credit customers will take the discount, 75% will not be doing so.

The revised level of receivables days = (0.25 × 30) + (0.75 × 60) = 52.5 days

Current level of trade receivables = $18m

Revised level of trade receivables = 87.6 × (52.5/365) = $12.6m

Reduction level of trade receivables = 18 – 12.6 = $5.4m

Cost of short-term finance = 5.5%

Reduction in financing cost = 5.4m × 0.055 = $297,000

Administration and operating cost savings = $753,000

Total benefits = 297,000 + 753,000 = $1,050,000

Cost of early settlement discount = 87.6m × 0.25 × 0.01 = $219,000

Net benefit of early settlement discount = 1,050,000 − 219,000 = $831,000

The proposed changes in receivables management are therefore financially acceptable, although they depend heavily on the forecast savings in administration and operating costs.

Maximum early settlement discount

Tutor's top tips:

To calculate this you must start with the awareness that the maximum discount that could be offered is one where the cost equals the benefit. Anything above this, and it wouldn't be worth offering the discount.

You've already calculated the value of the benefit, so all that remains is to convert this figure into a percentage of sales revenue, remembering that only 25% of customers are expected to take up the offer.

Comparing the total benefits of $1,050,000 with 25% of annual credit sales of $87,600,000, which is $21,900,000, the maximum early settlement discount that could be offered is 4.8% (100 × (1.050k/21.9m)).

(d) Factors that should be considered when formulating working capital policy on the management of trade receivables include the following:

The level of investment in trade receivables

If the amount of finance tied up in trade receivables is substantial, receivables management policy may be formulated with the intention of reducing the level of investment by tighter control over the way in which credit is granted and improved methods of assessing client creditworthiness.

The cost of financing trade credit

If the cost of financing trade credit is high, there will be pressure to reduce the amount of credit offered and to reduce the period for which credit is offered.

The terms of trade offered by competitors

In order to compete effectively, a company will need to match the terms offered by its competitors, otherwise customers will migrate to competitors, unless there are other factors that will encourage them to be loyal, such as better quality products or a more valuable after-sales service.

The level of risk acceptable to the company

Some companies may feel that more relaxed trade credit terms will increase the volume of business to an extent that compensates for a higher risk of bad debts. The level of risk of bad debts that is acceptable will vary from company to company. Some companies may seek to reduce this risk through a policy of insuring against non-payment by clients.

The need for liquidity

Where the need for liquidity is relatively high, a company may choose to accelerate cash inflow from credit customers by using invoice discounting or by factoring.

The expertise available within the company

Where expertise in the assessment of creditworthiness and the monitoring of customer accounts is not to a sufficiently high standard, a company may choose to outsource its receivables management to a third party, i.e. a factor.

	ACCA marking scheme		Marks
(a)	Current policy:		
	Annual ordering cost		1
	Annual holding cost		1
	Total annual cost		1
	EOQ policy:		
	Annual order size		1
	Annual ordering cost and holding cost		1
	Change in inventory management cost		1
			————
		Maximum	6
(b)	Benefits of JIT procurement policy		3
(c)	Reduction in trade receivables		2
	Financing cost saving		1
	Cost of early settlement discount		1
	Comment on net benefit		1
	Maximum early settlement discount		1
			————
		Maximum	6
(d)	Relevant discussion		5
			————
Total			25
			————

Examiner's comments

Many candidates gained full marks in answering part (a), picked up reasonable marks on parts (b) and (d), but in many cases gave poor answers to part (c).

Part (a) required candidates to calculate the cost of a current inventory ordering policy, and the change in inventory management costs when the economic ordering quantity (EOQ) model was used to find the optimum order size.

A number of answers failed to gain full marks because they did not calculate the change in inventory management costs, even after correctly calculating these costs under the current ordering policy and after applying the EOQ model.

Poorer answers showed a lack of understanding of the relationship between ordering costs and holding costs, and an inability to calculate these costs.

In part (b), candidates were required to describe briefly the benefits of a just-in-time (JIT) procurement policy. No credit was given for discussing the disadvantages of such a policy, as these were not required. Many answers gave a short list of benefits, rather than a description of the benefits, and so were not able to gain full marks.

Part (c) asked candidates to calculate and comment on whether a proposed change in receivables management (offering an early settlement discount) was acceptable, and to calculate the maximum discount that could be offered.

Some candidates gained full marks for calculating correctly the reduction in financing cost, the cost of the discount and the net benefit of offering the discount. The reduction in financing cost and the cost of the discount were both based on credit sales for the year of $87.6 million.

Poorer answers based their calculations on current trade receivables of $18 million, even though the question stated that the early settlement discount would be offered to 25% of credit customers. Comparing current trade receivables and current credit sales showed that current receivables paid on average after 75 days, a credit period that would be reduced to 60 days through improved operational procedures. Some candidates assumed incorrectly that the current trade receivables period was 60 days and made incorrect calculations as a result.

The maximum discount that could be offered would be equal to the benefit gained from the discount, i.e. the saving in administration and operating costs added to the reduction in financing cost

Feedback from markers indicated that some answers to this part of question 3 were disorganised, with unlabelled calculations and a lack of explanation. It is important to help the marking process by labelling calculations, explaining workings and using correct notation, e.g. '$ per year', '$m', 'days' and so on.

Part (d) required candidates to discuss the factors that should be considered in formulating working capital policy on the management of trade receivables.

Poorer answers offered a list of actions that could be met in trade receivables management, such as "send out letters to trade receivables", "call customers on the telephone", "produce an aged receivables analysis regularly". Working capital policy on trade receivables management should consider what period of credit to offer, how to determine the amount of credit offered, when creditworthiness needs to be assessed and to what extent, and so on, and it is often informed by the trade receivables management policies of competitors. The policy should provide the framework within which the actions referred to above would be undertaken.

INVESTMENT APPRAISAL

19 ARMCLIFF CO

Key answer tips

In part (a) the first part of the data in the question relates to current operations – try to think why the examiner has given you this. The requirement is to determine whether the proposed project is attractive to *Armcliff* – not the parent company. Presumably what will make a project attractive to a division's management is one that will improve their current performance measure. Thus it is useful to know what the current level of ARR being achieved. This can then be compared with the project ARR.

Remember that the ARR is a financial accounting based measure – returns are in terms of accounting profits, and investments valued at statement of financial position amounts – you must try to put all 'relevant cost' principles to the back of your mind. Whilst there are various possible definitions of the ARR (a point that can be raised in (b)) here you are given precise directions, so make sure you follow them. Both average profits and average investment need to be ascertained.

> Don't forget to conclude by comparison with both current and required rates of return.
>
> In part (b) the question requires you to show both theoretical and practical knowledge about investment appraisal methods.
>
> In part (c), even though this is a examining a general area of credit management, try wherever you can to relate your points to the business in the question – it is stated that Armcliff intends to extend its credit to improve sales. Again make sure that you explain points enough to get the marks available, whilst still offering sufficient variety. Note that it is not enough simply to say that the advantage of ARR is its simplicity. With spreadsheets, this is hardly going to be a consideration. Show instead that you appreciate that mangers are influenced by the methods used for their performance measurement – both internally and externally. The highlighted words are key phrases that markers are looking for.

(a) **Current return on capital employed**

= Operating profit/capital employed

= $20m/($75m + $25m) = $20m/$100m = 20%.

Analysis of the project

Project capital requirements are $14 million fixed capital plus $0.5 million inventory. The annual depreciation charge (straight line) is:

($14m − expected residual value of $2m)/4 = $3 million per annum.

Profit profile ($m)

Year	1	2	3	4
Sales revenue	(5.00 × 2m) = 10.00	(4.50 × 1.8m) = 8.10	(4.00 × 1.6m) = 6.40	(3.50 × 1.6m) = 5.60
Operating costs	(2.00)	(1.80)	(1.60)	(1.60)
Fixed costs	(1.50)	(1.35)	(1.20)	(1.20)
Depreciation	(3.00)	(3.00)	(3.00)	(3.00)
Profit	3.50	1.95	0.60	(0.20)

Total profit over four years = $5.85 million.

Capital employed (start-of-year):

	1	2	3	4
Non-current assets	14.00	11.00	8.00	5.00
Inventories	0.50	0.50	0.50	0.50
Profit	14.50	11.50	8.50	5.50

Average capital employed = (14.50 + 11.50 + 8.50 + 5.50)/4 = $10 million.

Average rate of return = $\dfrac{\text{Average profit}}{\text{Average capital employed}} = \dfrac{\$5.85m/4}{\$10.0m} = \dfrac{\$1.46m}{\$10.0m}$

= 14.6%

Note: If receivables were to be included in the definition of capital employed, this would reduce the calculated rate of return, while the inclusion of payables would have an offsetting effect. However, using the ARR criterion as defined, the proposal has an expected return above the minimum stipulated by Shevin Inc. It is unlikely that the managers of Armcliff will propose projects which offer a rate of return below the present 20% even where the expected return exceeds the minimum of 10%. To undertake projects with returns in this range will depress the overall divisional return and cast managerial performance in a weaker light.

However, it is unlikely that the senior managers of the Armcliff subsidiary would want to undertake the project.

(b) (i) The **ARR can be expressed in a variety of ways**, and is therefore susceptible to manipulation. Although the question specifies average profit to average capital employed, many other variants are possible, such as average profit to initial capital, which would raise the computed rate of return.

It is also **susceptible to variation in accounting policy** by the same firm over time, or as between different firms at a point in time. For example, different methods of depreciation produce different profit figures and hence different rates of return.

Perhaps, most fundamentally, it is **based on accounting profits expressed net of deduction for depreciation provisions, rather than cash flows**. This effectively results in double-counting for the initial outlay i.e. the capital cost is allowed for twice over, both in the numerator of the ARR calculation and also in the denominator. This is likely to depress the measured profitability of a project and result in rejection of some worthwhile investment.

Finally, because it simply averages the profits, it **makes no allowance for the timing of the returns** from the project.

(ii) The continuing use of the ARR method can by explained largely by its utilisation of statement of financial position and statement of profit or loss magnitudes familiar to managers, namely 'profit' and 'capital employed'. In addition, the impact of the project on a company's financial statements can also be specified. Return on capital employed is still the commonest way in which business unit performance is measured and evaluated, and is certainly the most visible to shareholders. It is thus not surprising that some managers may be happiest in expressing project attractiveness in the same terms in which their performance will be reported to shareholders, and according to which they will be evaluated and rewarded.

(c) Armcliff intends to achieve a sales increase by extending its receivables collection period. This policy carries several dangers. It implies that credit will be extended to customers for whom credit is an important determinant of supplier selection, hinting at financial instability on their part. Consequently, the risk of later than expected, or even no payment, is likely to increase. Although losses due to default are limited to the incremental costs of making these sales rather than the invoiced value, Armcliff should recognise that there is an opportunity cost involved in tying up capital for lengthy periods. In addition, companies which are slow payers often attempt to claim discounts to which they are not entitled. Armcliff may then face the difficult choice between acquiescence to such demands versus rejection, in which case, it may lose repeat sales.

20 WARDEN CO

Key answer tips

Tackling this question requires a methodical and logical approach. The requirements must be attempted in the order given. It is an excellent test of your understanding on the key investment appraisal topic.

The highlighted words are key phrases that markers are looking for.

(a) **Calculation of net present value (NPV)**

Year	1	2	3	4	5	6
	$000	$000	$000	$000	$000	$000
Sales revenue	1,600	1,600	1,600	1,600	1,600	
Variable costs	(1,100)	(1,100)	(1,100)	(1,100)	(1,100)	
Contribution	500	500	500	500	500	
Fixed costs	(160)	(160)	(160)	(160)	(160)	
Taxable cash flow	340	340	340	340	340	
Tax liabilities		(102)	(102)	(102)	(102)	(102)
After-tax cash flow	340	238	238	238	238	(102)
Working capital					90	
Scrap value					40	
Net cash flow	340	238	238	238	368	(102)
Discount factors	0.901	0.812	0.731	0.659	0.593	0.535
Present values	306	193	174	157	218	(55)

	$000
Present value of cash inflows	993
Working capital investment	(90)
Cost of machine	(800)
NPV	103

Since the investment has a positive NPV, it is financially acceptable.

Alternative layout of NPV calculation

	$000
PV of sales revenue = 100,000 × 16 × 3.696 =	5,914
PV of variable costs = 100,000 × 11 × 3.696 =	(4,066)
PV of contribution	1,848
PV of fixed costs = 160,000 × 3.696 =	(591)
PV of taxable cash flow	1,257
PV of tax liabilities = (340,000 × 0.3 × 3.696) × 0.901 =	(340)
	917
PV of working capital recovered = 90,000 × 0.593 =	53
PV of scrap value = 800,000 × 0.05 × 0.593 =	24
PV of cash inflows	994
Initial working capital investment	(90)
Initial purchase cost of new machine	(800)
Net present value	104

(b) **Calculation of internal rate of return (IRR)**

NPV at 11% was found to be $103,000

NPV at 17%:

Net cash flow	340	238	238	238	368	(102)
Discount factors	0.855	0.731	0.624	0.534	0.456	0.390
Present values	291	174	149	127	168	(40)

	$000
Present value of cash inflows	869
Working capital investment	(90)
Cost of machine	(800)
NPV	(21)

IRR = 11 + (((17 − 11) × 103,000)/(103,000 + 21,000)) = 11 + 5.0 = 16.0%

Since the internal rate of return of the investment (16%) is greater than the cost of capital of Warden Co, the investment is financially acceptable.

Examiner's note: *although the value of the calculated IRR will depend on the two discount rates used in linear interpolation, other discount rate choices should produce values close to 16%.*

(c)   **(i) Sensitivity**

Sensitivity analysis indicates which project variable is the key or critical variable, i.e. the variable where the smallest relative change makes the net present value (NPV) zero. Sensitivity analysis can show where management should focus attention in order to make an investment project successful, or where underlying assumptions should be checked for robustness.

The sensitivity of an investment project to a change in a given project variable can be calculated as the ratio of the NPV to the present value (PV) of the project variable. This gives directly the relative change in the variable needed to make the NPV of the project zero.

(ii) Selling price sensitivity

The PV of sales revenue = 100,000 × 16 × 3.696 = $5,913,600

The tax liability associated with sales revenue needs be considered, as the NPV is on an after-tax basis.

Tax liability arising from sales revenue = 100,000 × 16 × 0.3 = $480,000 per year

The PV of the tax liability without lagging = 480,000 × 3.696 = $1,774,080

(Alternatively, PV of tax liability without lagging = 5,913,600 × 0.3 = $1,774,080)

Lagging by one year, PV of tax liability = 1,774,080 × 0.901 = $1,598,446 After-tax PV of sales revenue = 5,913,600 – 1,598,446 = $4,315,154

Sensitivity = 100 × 103,000/4,315,154 = 2.4%

Discount rate sensitivity

The breakeven discount rate is the IRR calculated in part (b).

Increase in discount rate needed to make NPV zero = 16 – 11 = 5%

Relative change in discount rate needed to make NPV zero = 100 × 5/11 = 45%

Conclusion

Of the two variables, the key or critical variable is selling price, since the investment is more sensitive to a change in this variable (2.4%) than it is to a change in discount rate (45%).

ACCA marking scheme		
		Marks
(a)	Sales income	0.5
	Variable costs	0.5
	Fixed costs	0.5
	Tax liabilities	1
	Working capital recovered	0.5
	Scrap value	0.5
	Initial working capital investment	0.5
	Initial investment	0.5
	Discount factors	0.5
	Net present value	1
	Comment on financial acceptability	1
	Maximum	7
(b)	Calculation of revised NPV	1
	Calculation of IRR	2
	Comment on financial acceptability	1
	Maximum	4

(c)	(i)	Explanation of sensitivity analysis	2
	(ii)	After-tax present value of sales revenue	2
		Selling price sensitivity	2
		Discount rate sensitivity	1
		Comment on findings	2
		Maximum	7
Total			**20**

Examiner's comments

Part (a) asked for a calculation of (NPV. Many answers scored full marks here. Some answers lost marks because they left something out (error of omission). These answers, for example, did not include incremental fixed costs, or working capital investment, or working capital recovery, or scrap value, or even in some cases one whole year of income and costs (the evaluation was over five years). Other answers lost marks because there was a mistake in the way that NPV was calculated (error of principle). Such mistakes included treating working capital recovery or scrap value as tax-allowable deductions, and calculated tax liability on sales or on contribution, rather than on net taxable cash flow.

Part (b) asked students to calculate the internal rate of return (IRR) of an investment and many answers gained full marks. Some answers lost marks due to calculation errors, while as in previous examinations, there were a small number of answers that calculated ARR (accounting rate of return or return on capital employed) instead of IRR. Some candidates did not understand the IRR decision rule, claiming wrongly that the investment was not acceptable because the IRR was greater than the cost of capital of the investing company.

Part (c)(i) asked for an explanation of sensitivity analysis. Weaker answers did not refer to investment appraisal, or suggested that project variables were sensitive to NPV, rather than NPV being sensitive to project variables.

In part (c) (ii) candidates were asked here to calculate the sensitivity to a change in selling price and discount rate, and comment on the findings. Many candidates had difficulty with the brief calculations required here. Looking first at selling price, many answers noted correctly that sensitivity could be found by dividing NPV by the present value (PV) of the relevant project variable. Many answers calculated correctly the PV of sales income, but did not adjust this for tax liability. Weaker answers used the PV of selling price, or the PV of total sales income, or did not use a present value at all.

Some answers used an algebraic version of the NPV calculation, with selling price as the unknown variable. While this is an acceptable alternative to the simpler method of dividing NPV by PV of relevant project variable, answers often contained calculation errors, or incorrect adjustments for tax liability, or omitted some of the one-off project cash flows.

Turning to the discount rate sensitivity, what was needed was a simple comparison of the IRR with the company's discount rate. Many candidates seemed unaware of this and wasted valuable time with calculations that had no merit at all.

Sensitivity analysis can also be undertaken by changing a project variable by a set amount and calculating the change in the NPV. Some answers used this method correctly and gained credit. Since only one variable at a time is changed in sensitivity analysis, answers that changed simultaneously both selling price and discount showed a lack of understanding and gained little credit.

21   DAIRY CO

Key answer tips

Tackling this question requires a methodical and logical approach. The requirements must be attempted in the order given. The highlighted words are key phrases that markers are looking for.

(a)

Tutor's top tips:

A careful read of the question is essential. For example, the increases in maintenance payments only occur after the first payment (which will be made at the end of the first year of the project i.e. T_1). This could easily have been mis-interpreted. Writing down the timescales is a good way of ensuring you have everything clear in your mind. With so many calculations, be careful to layout your workings neatly and cross reference fully where applicable.

Option 1 – Replace the machine:

Year	Capital cost and maintenance		Contribution $	Net cash flow $	Discount factors	Present value $
0	450,000			(450,000)	1.000	(450,000)
1	25,000		150,000	125,000	0.893	111,625
2	$25,000 \times 1.075$	= 26,875	170,000	143,125	0.797	114,071
3	$25,000 \times 1.075^2$	= 28,891	190,000	161,109	0.712	114,710
4	$25,000 \times 1.075^3$	= 31,057	210,000	178,943	0.636	113,808
5	$25,000 \times 1.075^4$	= 33,387	220,000	186,613	0.567	105,810
				Net present value		110,024

Option 2 – Overhaul the machine:

Year	Capital cost and maintenance		Contribution $	Net cash flow $	Discount factors	Present value $
0	275,000			(275,000)	1.000	(275,000)
1	40,000		130,000	90,000	0.893	80,370
2	$40,000 \times 1.105$	= 44,200	145,000	100,800	0.797	80,338
3	$40,000 \times 1.105^2$	= 48,841	155,000	106,159	0.712	75,585
4	$40,000 \times 1.105^3$	= 53,969	160,000	106,031	0.636	67,436
5	$40,000 \times 1.105^4$	= 59,636	160,000	100,364	0.567	56,906
				Net present value		85,635

(b)

Year	Discount factor (20%)	Replace the machine		Overhaul the machine	
		Net cash flow	Present value	Net cash flow	Present value
		$	$	$	$
0	1.000	(450,000)	(450,000)	(275,000)	(275,000)
1	0.833	125,000	104,125	90,000	74,970
2	0.694	143,125	99,329	100,800	69,955
3	0.579	161,109	93,282	106,159	61,466
4	0.482	178,943	86,251	106,031	51,107
5	0.402	186,613	75,018	100,364	40,346
			8,005		**22,844**

$$\text{IRR of replacement} = 12\% + \frac{110,024}{110,024 \quad 8,005} \times (20\% - 12\%) = 12 + 8.6 = 20.6\%$$

$$\text{IRR of overhaul} = 12\% + \frac{85,635}{85,635 \quad 22,844} \times (20\% - 12\%) = 12 + 10.9 = 22.9\%$$

Tutor's top tips:

Don't forget, the IRR formula is not supplied in the exam so you will need to memorise it.

Tutorial note:

20% is not the only possible discount factor to use here; any value over 12% is acceptable. The IRR may differ slightly, but should not be significantly different if alternative values are used.

(c)

Tutor's top tips:

This part of the question is just about clearly stating what all of your calculations mean and why.

Both methods of investment appraisal use relevant cash flows to appraise the alternative investments and take account of the time value of money.

The net present value is the profit in present value terms. If the cost of capital is 12%, the machine should be replaced, since this option has the higher NPV.

The internal rate of return is the percentage return on the investment, taking into account the time value of money. The higher the return, the better. Overhauling the current machine has a higher IRR and so should be chosen using this appraisal technique.

Overall, to maximise shareholder wealth, the project with the highest NPV should be chosen which means that, provided the outcomes are not risky and 12% is the appropriate cost of capital, the machine should be replaced.

(d)   **Finance department**

When considering a new investment, the finance department will perform the investment appraisal calculations. This will involve identifying and forecasting costs and revenues, and deciding which method(s) of investment appraisal should be used (e.g. NPV, payback period, or other alternative methods).

If the directors decide to go ahead with a project, the finance department will then negotiate the terms of contracts, and will oversee the implementation of the project, investigating any variances as they arise.

Treasury department

The treasury department will calculate the necessary cost of capital for the project appraisal. If new finance is required, the treasury department will decide whether equity or debt finance should be used, and will liaise with finance providers to ensure that financing costs are kept to a minimum.

The treasury department will also identify any risks which might arise on the project (e.g. currency risks, credit risks) and will manage these risks by setting up hedging strategies.

Need for liaison

Before the finance department can perform an investment appraisal calculation, the treasury department will need to calculate a suitable cost of capital. There will need to be close liaison here, to ensure that the calculated cost of capital reflects the business risk of the new project and also the likely financing position of the business.

The finance department will need to keep the treasury department fully informed about the financing requirement for the new project, so that the treasury department can arrange any extra financing as required.

22   INVESTMENT APPRAISAL

Key answer tips

Parts (a) & (b)(i) should present an opportunity to gain some easy marks by outlining some basic areas of the syllabus. The calculations in part (b) (ii) were relatively straightforward. Make sure you don't neglect the final part of the requirement – to identify other factors that the company should take into account when deciding of the optimal cycle.   The highlighted words are key phrases that markers are looking for.

(a)   Accounting rate of return (ARR) is a measure of the return on an investment where the annual profit before interest and tax is expressed as a percentage of the capital sum invested.

There are a number of alternative formulae which can be used to calculate ARR, which differ in the way in which they define capital cost. The more common alternative measures available are:

- average annual profit to initial capital invested, and

- average annual profit to average capital invested.

The method selected will affect the resulting ARR figure, and for this reason it is important to recognise that the measure might be subject to manipulation by managers seeking approval for their investment proposals. The value for average annual profit is calculated after allowances for depreciation, as shown in the example below:

Suppose ARR is defined as: $\dfrac{\text{Average profit (after depreciation)}}{\text{Initial capital invested}} \times 100\%$

A project costing $5 million, and yielding average profits of $1,250,000 per year after depreciation charges of $500,000 per year, would give an ARR of:

1,250,000/5,000,000 × 100% = 25%

If the depreciation charged were to be increased to $750,000 per year, for example as a result of technological changes reducing the expected life of an asset, the ARR becomes:

1,000,000/5,000,000 × 100% = 20%

The attraction of using ARR as a method of investment appraisal lies in its simplicity and the ease with which it can be used to specify the impact of a project on a company's statement of profit or loss. The measure is easily understood and can be directly linked to the use of ROCE as a performance measure. Nonetheless, ARR has been criticised for a number of major drawbacks, perhaps the most important of which is that it uses accounting profits after depreciation rather than cash flows in order to measure return. This means that the capital cost is over-stated in the calculation, via both the numerator and the denominator. In the numerator, the capital cost is taken into account via the depreciation charges used to derive accounting profit, but capital cost is also the denominator. The practical effect of this is to reduce the ARR and thus make projects appear less profitable. This might in turn result in some worthwhile projects being rejected. Note, however, that this problem does not arise where ARR is calculated as average annual profit as a percentage of average capital invested.

The most important criticism of ARR is that it takes no account of the time value of money. A second limitation of ARR, already suggested, is that its value is dependent on accounting policies and this can make comparison of ARR figures across different investments very difficult. A further difficulty with the use of ARR is that it does not give a clear decision rule. The ARR on any particular investment needs to be compared with the current returns being earned within a business, and so unlike NPV for example, it is impossible to say 'all investments with an ARR of x or below will always be rejected.

The payback method of investment appraisal is used widely in industry – generally in addition to other measures. Like ARR, it is easily calculated and understood. The payback approach simply measures the time required for cumulative cash flows from an investment to sum to the original capital invested.

Example

Original investment $100,000

Cash flow profile: Years 1–3 $25,000 p.a.

Years 4 – 5 $50,000 p.a.

Year 6 $5,000

The cumulative cash flows are therefore:

End Year 1	$25,000
End Year 2	$50,000
End Year 3	$75,000
End Year 4	$125,000
End Year 5	$175,000
End Year 6	$180,000

The original sum invested is returned via cash flows some time during the course of Year 4. If cash flows are assumed to be even throughout the year, the cumulative cash flow of $100,000 will have been earned halfway through year 4. The payback period for the investment is thus 3 years and 6 months.

The payback approach to investment appraisal is useful for companies which are seeking to claw back cash from investments as quickly as possible. At the same time, the concept is intuitively appealing as many businessmen will be concerned about how long they may have to wait to get their money back, because they believe that rapid repayment reduces risks. This means that the payback approach is commonly used for initial screening of investment alternatives.

The disadvantages of the payback approach are as follows:

(i)   Payback ignores the overall profitability of a project by ignoring cash flows after payback is reached. In the example above, the cash flows between 3–4 years and the end of the project total $80,000. To ignore such substantial cash flows would be naïve. As a consequence, the payback method is biased in favour of fast-return investments. This can result in rejecting investments that generate cash flows more slowly in the early years, but which are overall more profitable.

(ii)   As with ARR, the payback method ignores the time value of money.

(iii) The payback method, in the same way as ARR, offers no objective measure of what is the desirable return, as measured by the length of the payback period.

(b)   (i)   Discounted cash flow analysis is a technique whereby the value of future cash flows is discounted back to a present value, so that the monetary values of all cash flows are equivalent, regardless of their timing. The logic for discounting is that the value of money declines over time because of individual time preferences and the impact of inflation in eroding spending power. People value money received sooner rather than later because as soon as cash is received they can increase consumption, or re-invest the capital.

NPV uses discounting to calculate the present value of all cash flows associated with a project. The present value of cash outflows is then compared with the present value of cash inflows, to obtain a net present value (NPV). If the present value (PV) of cash outflows exceeds the PV of cash inflows, then the NPV will be negative. If the present value (PV) of cash inflows exceeds the PV of cash outflows, then the NPV will be positive. The size of the NPV is dependent on the cash flow pattern and the rate of discount that is applied. The general rule is that a company will discount the forecast cash flows at a rate equal to its cost of capital. The reason for this is that if a company has an overall cost of capital of, for example, 12%, it is essential that the rate of return exceeds 12% or the funding costs will not be covered. Hence if the cash flows are discounted at the cost of capital and the project yields a positive NPV, this implies that the return exceeds the cost of capital. When using NPV for investment appraisal then a simple rule is applied: invest if NPV is positive, and do not invest if it is negative.

IRR uses discounting in a slightly different way to determine the profitability of an investment. The Internal Rate of Return is defined as the discount rate at which the net present value equals zero. For example, an investment may yield a forecast NPV of $15,000 when the cash flows are discounted at 10%. If the rate of discount is increased, the net present value will fall, and the IRR represents the effective, break-even discount rate for the investment. Suppose, for example, that the IRR is 15%, this figure can then be used to establish a decision rule for investments. An IRR of 15% means that if the cost of capital exceeds 15% then the investment would generate a negative NPV. If the company is currently having to pay 12% on its investment funds, then it knows that it can afford to see its cost of capital rise by 3% before the investment will become financially non-viable. As long as the IRR exceeds the cost of capital, then the company should invest and so, as a general rule, the higher the IRR the better.

NPV and IRR measures may sometimes contradict one another when used in relation to mutually exclusive investments. An example of the ambiguity which can occur when choosing between mutually exclusive decisions is when one of the investments has a higher NPV than the other, and so is preferable on that basis, but at the same time it has a lower IRR. When IRR and NPV give conflicting results, the preferred alternative is the project with the highest NPV.

In conclusion, although both NPV and IRR use discounted cash flows as a method of arriving at an investment decision, the results that they generate need to be interpreted with care, and they do not always yield the same investment decisions. NPV is the preferred criterion for selecting between two or more mutually exclusive investments, where the two approaches give differing recommendations.

(ii)   If the laptops are replaced every year:

NPV of one year replacement cycle

Year	Cash flow $	DF at 14%	PV $
0	(2,400)	1.000	(2,400.0)
1	1,200	0.877	1,052.4
			(1,347.6)

Equivalent annual cost = PV of cost of one replacement cycle/Cumulative discount factor

= $1,347.6/0.877 = $1,536.6

NPV of two-year replacement cycle

Year	Cash flow	DF at 14%	PV
	$		$
0	(2,400)	1.000	(2,400.0)
1	(75)	0.877	(65.8)
2	800	0.769	615.2
			(1,850.6)

EAC = $1,850.6/1.647 = $1,123.6

NPV of three-year replacement cycle

Year	Cash flow	DF at 14%	PV
	$		$
0	(2,400)	1.000	(2,400.0)
1	(75)	0.877	(65.8)
2	(150)	0.769	(115.4)
3	300	0.675	202.5
			(2,378.7)

EAC = $2,378.7/2.322 = $1,024.4

Conclusion

The optimal cycle for replacement is every three years, because this has the lowest equivalent annual cost. Other factors which need to be taken into account are the non-financial aspects of the alternative cycle choices. For example, computer technology and the associated software is changing very rapidly and this could mean that failure to replace annually would leave the salesmen unable to utilise the most up to date systems for recording, monitoring and implementing their sales. This could have an impact on the company's competitive position. The company needs to consider also the compatibility of the software used by the laptops with that used by the in-house computers and mainframe. If system upgrades are made within the main business that render the two computers incompatible, then rapid replacement of the laptops to regain compatibility is essential.

23   DARN CO

(a)   Calculating the net present value of the investment project using a nominal terms approach requires the discounting of nominal (money terms) cash flows using a nominal discount rate, which is given as 12%.

Year	1	2	3	4	5
	$000	$000	$000	$000	$000
Sales revenue	1,308.75	2,817.26	7,907.87	5,443.58	
Costs	(523.50)	(1,096.21)	(2,869.33)	(2,102.93)	
Net revenue	785.25	1,721.05	5,038.54	3,340.65	
Tax payable		(235.58)	(516.32)	(1,511.56)	(1,002.20)
CA tax benefits		150.00	112.50	84.38	253.13
After-tax cash flow	785.25	1,635.47	4,634.72	1,913.47	(749.07)
Working capital	(150.86)	(509.06)	246.43	544.36	
Project cash flow	634.39	1,126.41	4,881.15	2,457.83	(749.07)
Discount at 12%	0.893	0.797	0.712	0.636	0.567
Present values	566.51	897.75	3,475.38	1,563.18	(424.72)

	$000
PV of future cash flows	6,078.10
Initial investment	(2,000.00)
Working capital	(130.88)
NPV	3,947.22

The net present value is $3,947,220 and so the investment project is financially acceptable.

Workings

Year	1	2	3	4
Sales revenue ($000)	1,250	2,570	6,890	4,530
Inflated sales revenue ($000)	1,308.75	2,817.26	7,907.87	5,443.58

Year	1	2	3	4
Costs ($000)	500	1,000	2,500	1,750
Inflated costs ($000)	523.50	1,096.21	2,869.33	2,102.93

Year	1	2	3	4
Inflated sales revenue ($000)	1,308.75	2,817.26	7,907.87	5,443.58
Working capital ($000)	130.88	281.73	790.79	544.36
Incremental ($000)	(130.88)	(150.86)	(509.06)	246.43

Year	1	2	3	4
Taxa allowable dep'n ($000)	500.00	375.00	281.25	843.75
Tax benefit ($000)	150.00	112.50	84.38	253.13

(b) The directors of Darn Co can be encouraged to achieve the objective of maximising shareholder wealth through managerial reward schemes and through regulatory requirements.

Managerial reward schemes

As agents of the company's shareholders, the directors of Darn Co may not always act in ways which increase the wealth of shareholders, a phenomenon called the agency problem. They can be encouraged to increase or maximise shareholder wealth by managerial reward schemes such as performance-related pay and share option schemes. Through these methods, the goals of shareholders and directors may increase in congruence.

Performance-related pay links part of the remuneration of directors to some aspect of corporate performance, such as levels of profit or earnings per share. One problem here is that it is difficult to choose an aspect of corporate performance which is not influenced by the actions of the directors, leading to the possibility of managers influencing corporate affairs for their own benefit rather than the benefit of shareholders, for example, focusing on short-term performance while neglecting the longer term.

Share option schemes bring the goals of shareholders and directors closer together to the extent that directors become shareholders themselves. Share options allow directors to purchase shares at a specified price on a specified future date, encouraging them to make decisions which exert an upward pressure on share prices. Unfortunately, a general increase in share prices can lead to directors being rewarded for poor performance, while a general decrease in share prices can lead to managers not being rewarded for good performance. However, share option schemes can lead to a culture of performance improvement and so can bring continuing benefit to stakeholders.

Regulatory requirements

Regulatory requirements can be imposed through corporate governance codes of best practice and stock market listing regulations.

Corporate governance codes of best practice, such as the UK Corporate Governance Code, seek to reduce corporate risk and increase corporate accountability.

Responsibility is placed on directors to identify, assess and manage risk within an organisation. An independent perspective is brought to directors' decisions by appointing non-executive directors to create a balanced board of directors, and by appointing non-executive directors to remuneration committees and audit committees.

Stock exchange listing regulations can place obligations on directors to manage companies in ways which support the achievement of objectives such as the maximisation of shareholder wealth. For example, listing regulations may require companies to publish regular financial reports, to provide detailed information on directorial rewards and to publish detailed reports on corporate governance and corporate social responsibility.

ACCA marking scheme		Marks
(a)	Inflated sales revenue	1
	Inflated costs	1
	Tax liability	1
	TA depreciation, years 1 to 3	1
	Balancing allowance, year 4	1
	TA depreciation tax benefits	1
	Timing of tax liabilities and benefits	1
	Incremental working capital investment	1
	Recovery of working capital	1
	Market research omitted as sunk cost	1
	Calculation of nominal terms NPV	1
	Comment on financial acceptability	1
	Maximum	12
(b)	Managerial reward schemes	3–5
	Regulatory requirements	3–4
	Other relevant discussion	1–2
	Maximum	8
Total		**20**

24   CHARM INC

Key answer tips

In part (a) the NPV calculation is reasonably straightforward provided you read the information carefully. The calculation of fixed costs is an easy number to get wrong if you didn't carefully read that the financial information presented on 'Fingo' was for the first year of production.

In part (b) ensure you compare with NPV with other appraisal methods rather than just stating the benefits of NPV. The highlighted words are key phrases that markers are looking for.

(a)   **Calculation of NPV of 'Fingo' investment project**

Year	1	2	3	4
	$000	$000	$000	$000
Sales revenue	3,750	1,680	1,380	1,320
Direct materials	(810)	(378)	(324)	(324)
Variable production	(900)	(420)	(360)	(360)
Advertising	(650)	(100)		
Fixed costs (W1)	(600)	(600)	(600)	(600)
Taxable cash flow	790	182	96	36
Taxation	(237)	(55)	(29)	(11)
	553	127	67	25
CA tax benefits (W2)	60	45	34	101
Net cash flow	613	172	101	126
Discount at 10%	0.909	0.826	0.751	0.683
Present values	557.2	142.1	75.9	86.1

	$000
Present value of future benefits	861.3
Initial investment	800.0
Net present value	61.3

Workings

(W1) Fixed costs in year 1 = $150,000 × 4 = $600,000 and since these represent a one-off increase in fixed production overheads, these are the fixed costs in subsequent years as well.

(W2) **Tax allowable depreciation tax benefits**

Year	TA depreciation ($)		Tax benefit ($)	
1	200,000	(800,000 × 0.25)	60,000	(0.3 × 200,000)
2	150,000	(600,000 × 0.25)	45,000	(0.3 × 150,000)
3	112,500	(450,000 × 0.25)	33,750	(0.3 × 112,500)
	462,500			
	nil	(scrap value)		
	462,500			
4	337,500	(by difference)	101,250	(0.3 × 337,500)
	800,000			

Comment

The net present value of $61,300 is positive and the investment can therefore be recommended on financial grounds. However, it should be noted that the positive net present value depends heavily on sales in the first year. In fact, sensitivity analysis shows that a decrease of 5% in first year sales will result in a zero net present value. (Note: you are not expected to conduct a sensitivity analysis)

(b) There are many reasons that could be discussed in support of the view that net present value (NPV) is superior to other investment appraisal methods.

NPV considers cash flows

This is the reason why NPV is preferred to return on capital employed (ROCE), since ROCE compares average annual accounting profit with initial or average capital invested. Financial management always prefers cash flows to accounting profit, since profit is seen as being open to manipulation. Furthermore, only cash flows are capable of adding to the wealth of shareholders in the form of increased dividends. Both internal rate of return (IRR) and Payback also consider cash flows.

NPV considers the whole of an investment project

In this respect NPV is superior to Payback, which measures the time it takes for an investment project to repay the initial capital invested. Payback therefore considers cash flows within the payback period and ignores cash flows outside of the payback period. If Payback is used as an investment appraisal method, projects yielding high returns outside of the payback period will be wrongly rejected. In practice, however, it is unlikely that Payback will be used alone as an investment appraisal method.

NPV considers the time value of money

NPV and IRR are both discounted cash flow (DCF) models which consider the time value of money, whereas ROCE and Payback do not. Although Discounted Payback can be used to appraise investment projects, this method still suffers from the criticism that it ignores cash flows outside of the payback period. Considering the time value of money is essential, since otherwise cash flows occurring at different times cannot be distinguished from each other in terms of value from the perspective of the present time.

NPV is an absolute measure of return

NPV is seen as being superior to investment appraisal methods that offer a relative measure of return, such as IRR and ROCE, and which therefore fail to reflect the amount of the initial investment or the absolute increase in corporate value. Defenders of IRR and ROCE respond that these methods offer a measure of return that is understandable by managers and which can be intuitively compared with economic variables such as interest rates and inflation rates.

NPV links directly to the objective of maximising shareholders' wealth

The NPV of an investment project represents the change in total market value that will occur if the investment project is accepted. The increase in wealth of each shareholder can therefore be measured by the increase in the value of their shareholding as a percentage of the overall issued share capital of the company. Other investment appraisal methods do not have this direct link with the primary financial management objective of the company.

NPV always offers the correct investment advice

With respect to mutually exclusive projects, NPV always indicates which project should be selected in order to achieve the maximum increase on corporate value. This is not true of IRR, which offers incorrect advice at discount rates which are less than the internal rate of return of the incremental cash flows. This problem can be overcome by using the incremental yield approach.

NPV can accommodate changes in the discount rate

While NPV can easily accommodate changes in the discount rate, IRR simply ignores them, since the calculated internal rate of return is independent of the cost of capital in all time periods.

NPV has a sensible re-investment assumption

NPV assumes that intermediate cash flows are re-invested at the company's cost of capital, which is a reasonable assumption as the company's cost of capital represents the average opportunity cost of the company's providers of finance, i.e. it represents a rate of return which exists in the real world. By contrast, IRR assumes that intermediate cash flows are reinvested at the internal rate of return, which is not an investment rate available in practice,

NPV can accommodate non-conventional cash flows

Non-conventional cash flows exist when negative cash flows arise during the life of the project. For each change in sign there is potentially one additional internal rate of return. With non-conventional cash flows, therefore, IRR can suffer from the technical problem of giving multiple internal rates of return.

25 PLAY CO

Key answer tips

This is a fairly typical NPV with tax and inflation question. The key to picking up the easy marks in the calculative part (a) is to take a methodical approach that you show clearly in a series of workings.

Parts (b) & (c) are more discursive and require you to demonstrate your knowledge in the context of this scenario. Try to think broadly and ensure you go into sufficient depth in your answer to score highly.

The highlighted words in the written sections are key phrases that markers are looking for.

(a)

Year	1	2	3	4	5
	$000	$000	$000	$000	$000
Costs saved (W1)	350	385	455	560	
Variable costs (W2)	(82)	(94)	(113)	(144)	
Maintenance costs	(42)	(44)	(46)	(49)	
Fixed costs (W3)	(66)	(68)	(69)	(70)	
	___	___	___	___	
Taxable cash flow	160	180	227	297	
Taxation		(48)	(54)	(68)	(89)
CA tax benefits (W4)		30	23	17	36
Scrap value				50	
	___	___	___	___	___
After-tax cash flows	160	162	196	296	(53)
Discount at 15%	0.870	0.756	0.658	0.572	0.497
	___	___	___	___	___
Present values	139	122	129	169	(26)
	___	___	___	___	___

	$000
Present value of benefits	533
Initial investment	400
Early termination fine	150
	___
Net present value	(18)
	___

The net present value is negative and so the investment is not financially acceptable.

Workings

(W1) **Costs saved**

Year	1	2	3	4
Demand (tonnes/yr)	100,000	110,000	130,000	160,000
Cost ($/tonne)	3.50	3.50	3.50	3.50
	___	___	___	___
Contribution ($/yr)	350,000	385,000	455,000	560,000
	___	___	___	___

(W2) Variable costs incurred

Year	1	2	3	4
Demand (tonnes/yr)	100,000	110,000	130,000	160,000
Cost ($/tonne) – 3% inflation	0.82	0.85	0.87	0.90
Contribution ($/yr)	82,000	93,500	113,100	144,000

(W3) Fixed costs incurred

Annual depreciation = ($400,000 – $50,000) ÷ 4 = $87,500

Other fixed costs = $192,500 – $87,500 – $40,000 = $65,000

Inflating at 2% per annum

(W4) Tax allowable depreciation tax benefits

Year	TA depreciation ($)		Tax benefit ($)	
1	100,000	(400,000 × 0.25)	30,000	(0.3 × 100,000)
2	75,000	(300,000 × 0.25)	22,500	(0.3 × 75,000)
3	56,250	(225,000 × 0.25)	16,875	(0.3 × 56,250)
	231,250			
	50,000	(scrap value)		
	281,250			
4	118,750	(by difference)	35,625	(0.3 × 118,750)
	400,000			

(b)

> *Tutorial note:*
>
> *There are more points noted below than would be needed to earn full marks, however, they do reflect the full range of limitations that could be discussed.*

NPV is a commonly used technique employed in investment appraisal, but it is subject to a number of restrictive assumptions and limitations which call into question its general relevance. Nonetheless, if the assumptions and limitations are understood then its application is less likely to be undertaken in error.

Some of the difficulties with NPV are listed below:

(i)   NPV assumes that firms pursue an objective of maximising the wealth of their shareholders. This is questionable given the wider range of stakeholders who might have conflicting interests to those of the shareholders. NPV is largely redundant if organisations are not wealth maximising. For example, public sector organisations may wish to invest in capital assets but will use non-profit objectives as part of their assessment.

(ii) NPV is potentially a difficult method to apply in the context of having to estimate what is the correct discount rate to use. This is particularly so when questions arise as to the incorporation of risk premia in the discount rate, since an evaluation of the riskiness of the business, or of the project in particular, will have to be made but may be difficult to discern. In this instance, the additional fixed costs will increase the risk profile of the business and this will need to be factored in.

(iii) NPV can most easily cope with cash flows arising at period ends and is not a technique that is used easily when complicated, mid-period cash flows are present.

(iv) NPV is not universally employed, especially in a small business environment. The available evidence suggests that businesses assess projects in a variety of ways (payback, IRR, accounting rate of return). The fact that such methods are used which are theoretically inferior to NPV calls into question the practical benefits of NPV, and therefore hints at certain practical limitations.

(v) The conclusion from NPV analysis is the present value of the surplus cash generated from a project. If reported profits are important to businesses, then it is possible that there may be a conflict between undertaking a positive NPV project and potentially adverse consequences on reported profits. This will particularly be the case for projects with long time horizons, large initial investment and very delayed cash inflows. In such circumstances, businesses may prefer to use accounting measures of investment appraisal.

(vi) Managerial incentive schemes may not be consistent with NPV, particularly when long time horizons are involved. Thus managers may be rewarded on the basis of accounting profits in the short term and may be incentivised to act in accordance with these objectives, and thus ignore positive NPV projects. This may be a problem of the incentive schemes and not of NPV; nonetheless, a potential conflict exists and represents a difficulty for NPV.

(vii) NPV treats all time periods equally, with the exception of discounting far cash flows more than near cash flows. In other words, NPV only accounts for the time value of money. To many businesses, distant horizons are less important than near horizons, if only because that is the environment in which they work. Other factors besides applying higher discount rates may work to reduce the impact of distant years. For example, in the long term, nearly all aspects of the business may change and hence a too-narrow focus on discounting means that NPV is of limited value and more so the further the time horizon considered.

(viii) NPV is of limited use in the face of non-quantifiable benefits or costs. NPV does not take account of non-financial information which may even be relevant to shareholders who want their wealth maximised. For example, issues of strategic or environmental benefit may arise against which it is difficult to immediately quantify the benefits but for which there are immediate costs. NPV would treat such a situation as an additional cost since it could not incorporate the indiscernible benefit.

(c)

Tutor's top tips:

Start by identifying the range of stakeholders affected before considering the impact this proposal will have on them. Make sure you include the details given in the scenario to ensure you give a tailored answer.

The project should affect the different stakeholders of Play Co as follows:

Stakeholder	Impact
Shareholders	• Wealth would decrease by the negative NPV of the project – i.e. $18,000 • Risks will increase due the higher fixed costs (increased operational gearing)
Society	• More tyres will be recycled, protecting the environment
Customers	• Customers may perceive the quality of the product to increase because it is more environmentally friendly
Suppliers	• Existing suppliers of particles will lose business (although they will receive the $150,000 early termination fine)
Potential investors	• Play Co will become more attractive to "green chip" investors, possibly making future financing easier.

26 DUO CO *Walk in the footsteps of a top tutor*

Key answer tips

Given the generic nature of part (b) and the significant number of marks available, it would be sensible to tackle this part of the requirement first. You can then follow on with the calculations in part (a)

The key learning point from this question is the importance of being efficient when reading the scenario to cut down on the amount of time wasted trying to locate information. By forming an expectation of what you'll be given and considering the significance of information that you read, you can easily complete the question in the time allocated. The highlighted words are key phrases that markers are looking for.

(a)   **Net present value evaluation of investment**

Tutor's top tips:

An NPV calculation in part (a) followed by an IRR calculation in part (b) is a fairly common exam question. Clearly it is more logical to tackle part (a) first. One important aspect to note from the requirement is to work to the nearest $1,000. This can help to save a significant amount of time when performing the calculations and noting your workings.

Knowing that you must calculate an NPV, you should carefully read the scenario, looking for details on:

- *Relevant cash flows*
- *Tax payments (1 year time lag or not)*
- *Capital expenditure and scrap values*
- *Timescales and length of the project*
- *Working capital*
- *Inflation*
- *Discount rate*

Whenever you read any details, make a note in the margin on what that section provides you information on. This will help prevent you having to re-read the scenario several times to find the bit of information you require.

From reading this scenario, you should have noted that:

- *Relevant cash flows will be the incremental contribution and fixed costs only*
- *Incremental contribution will be calculated based on the excess of demand over current production capacity (one million kilograms)*
- *The maximum output of the new machine is 600,000 kg meaning that even with the new machine, Duo will be unable to produce more that 1.6 million kg.*
- *The tax rate is 30% and there is a one year time lag*
- *The cost of the machine is $800,000 and it will be scrapped in four years time for $30,000*
- *The length of the project is four years*
- *You are not given any information on working capital requirements or inflation. These can therefore be ignored.*
- *You have not been told what discount rate to use. Instead you've been given information on the cost of equity and the cost of debt, together with the capital structure (ratio of equity to debt) in the company*

Having gleaned this information, you should start by setting up your proforma NPV calculation based on 5 periods (4 years of the project + 1 year time lag for tax). Next you should enter in any easy numbers that require little or no calculation. This would include the asset purchase and scrap and the incremental fixed costs.

Now you can move on to calculating some of the more complex numbers. All of these calculations should be performed using workings that should be clearly cross referenced to your main NPV calculation. You should end up with workings for contribution (make sure you clearly show how many extra units will be sold), the tax effect of tax allowable depreciation and the weighted average cost of capital / discount factors. As you complete each working, transfer the numbers into your main calculation and add anything extra that you can now complete (for example, once you have calculated contribution, you can enter the tax charge at 30%). When all of your workings are complete, discount the cash flow in each year and work out the net present value. Don't forget that the requirement is to calculate and advise. There will always be marks available for reaching a conclusion and stating whether the project should be accepted or not. Note the examiner's comment (below) about explaining your decision.

After-tax weighted average cost of capital = $(11 \times 0.8) + (8.6 \times (1 - 0.3) \times 0.2) = 10\%$

Year	1	2	3	4	5
	$000	$000	$000	$000	$000
Contribution	440	550	660	660	
Fixed costs	(240)	(260)	(280)	(300)	
Taxable cash flow	200	290	380	360	
Taxation		(60)	(87)	(114)	(108)
CA tax benefits		60	45	34	92
Scrap value				30	
After-tax cash flows	200	290	338	310	(16)
Discount at 10%	0.909	0.826	0.751	0.683	0.621
Present values	182	240	254	212	(10)

	$000
Present value of benefits	878
Initial investment	800
Net present value	78

The net present value is positive and so the investment is financially acceptable. However, demand becomes greater than production capacity in the fourth year of operation and so further investment in new machinery may be needed after three years. The new machine will itself need replacing after four years if production capacity is to be maintained at an increased level. It may be necessary to include these expansion and replacement considerations for a more complete appraisal of the proposed investment.

A more complete appraisal of the investment could address issues such as the assumption of constant selling price and variable cost per kilogram and the absence of any consideration of inflation, the linear increase in fixed costs of production over time and the linear increase in demand over time. If these issues are not addressed, the appraisal of investing in the new machine is likely to possess a significant degree of uncertainty.

Workings

Annual contribution

Year	1	2	3	4
Excess demand (kg/yr)	400,000	500,000	600,000	700,000
New machine output (kg/yr)	400,000	500,000	600,000	600,000
Contribution ($/kg)	1.1	1.1	1.1	1.1
Contribution ($/yr)	440,000	550,000	660,000	660,000

Tax allowable depreciation tax benefits

Year	TA depreciation ($)		Tax benefit ($)	
1	200,000	(800,000 × 0.25)	60,000	(0.3 × 200,000)
2	150,000	(600,000 × 0.25)	45,000	(0.3 × 150,000)
3	112,500	(450,000 × 0.25)	33,750	(0.3 × 112,500)
	462,500			
	30,000	(scrap value)		
	492,500			
4	307,500	(by difference)	92,250	(0.3 × 307,500)
	800,000			

Tutor's top tips:

A careful read of the requirement shows that part (b) is essentially three requirements rolled into one:

(i)   Explain the difference between risk and uncertainty

(ii)   Describe how sensitivity analysis can be used to incorporate risk into investment appraisal

(iii)   Describe how probability analysis can be used to incorporate risk into investment appraisal

Given the verbs being used (both 'explain' and 'describe' imply much more that merely 'stating') we can expect between 2 & 3 marks for each section, with 2 or 3 relevant comments picking up those marks.

Don't forget, there are often marks available for defining terms. So in part (i), a definition should be given of both risk and uncertainty before the differences between the two are explained. Similarly, in parts (ii) & (iii), you could define both sensitivity analysis and probability analysis before describing how they incorporate risk into the appraisal process.

Finally, you could touch on the common problems with the two techniques although be careful not to spend too much time on this as it wasn't specifically mentioned in the requirement. Now you can move on to the numerical aspects of the question.

(b)   Risk refers to the situation where probabilities can be assigned to a range of expected outcomes arising from an investment project and the likelihood of each outcome occurring can therefore be quantified. Uncertainty refers to the situation where probabilities cannot be assigned to expected outcomes. Investment project risk therefore increases with increasing variability of returns, while uncertainty increases with increasing project life. The two terms are often used interchangeably in financial management, but the distinction between them is a useful one.

Sensitivity analysis assesses how the net present value of an investment project is affected by changes in project variables. Considering each project variable in turn, the change in the variable required to make the net present value zero is determined, or alternatively the change in net present value arising from a fixed change in the given project variable. In this way the key or critical project variables are determined. However, sensitivity analysis does not assess the probability of changes in project variables and so is often dismissed as a way of incorporating risk into the investment appraisal process.

Probability analysis refers to the assessment of the separate probabilities of a number of specified outcomes of an investment project. For example, a range of expected market conditions could be formulated and the probability of each market condition arising in each of several future years could be assessed. The net present values arising from combinations of future economic conditions could then be assessed and linked to the joint probabilities of those combinations. The expected net present value (ENPV) could be calculated, together with the probability of the worst-case scenario and the probability of a negative net present value. In this way, the downside risk of the investment could be determined and incorporated into the investment decision.

ACCA marking scheme		
		Marks
(a)	After-tax weighted average cost of capital	2
	Annual contribution	2
	Fixed costs	1
	Taxation	1
	TAX depreciation tax benefits	3
	Scrap value	1
	Discount factors	1
	Net present value	1
	Comment	1–2
		13
(b)	Risk and uncertainty	2–3
	Discussion of sensitivity analysis	2–3
	Discussion of probability analysis	2–3
		7
Total		20

Examiner's comments

Part (a) of this question asked candidates to calculate the net present value (NPV) of buying a new machine and to advise on its acceptability. Many candidates gained very high marks here.

Common errors (where there were errors) included failing to calculate correctly the weighted average cost of capital of the investing company (for example using the before-tax rather than the after-tax cost of debt in the calculation): failing to use incremental demand as the production volume of the new machine; failing to recognise the cap on production in Year 4 compared to demand; failing to lag tax liability by one year; including scrap value or tax benefits of tax allowable depreciation with taxable income; incorrect calculation of balancing allowance; treating initial investment as a Year 1 rather than a Year 0 cash flow; and using annuity factors rather than discount factors in calculating NPV.

A number of candidates lost straightforward marks by failing to comment on the calculated NPV, or by simply saying 'accept' without referring to the NPV decision rule. The reason for accepting an investment project must be clearly explained.

Candidates were asked in part (b) to explain the difference between risk and uncertainty in the context of investment appraisal, and to describe how sensitivity analysis and probability analysis could be used to incorporate risk and uncertainty into investment appraisal. Answers here tended to be weaker than answers to parts (a).

Many candidates were not able to explain the difference between risk and uncertainty in investment appraisal, offering answers that were founded on interpretations of the words 'risk' and 'uncertainty', or which discussed the various kinds of risk to be found in financial management. The key point is to recognise that risk can be quantified (probabilities can be assigned and outcomes can be predicted) while uncertainty cannot be quantified. Answers that offered numerical examples of sensitivity analysis or probability analysis gained credit, although candidates should note that sensitivity analysis is not a method of measuring or predicting risk.

27 OKM CO

Key answer tips

The style of this question is not something we've seen regularly from the examiner. Based on the core topic of investment appraisal, students should easily be able to spot the mistakes in the appraisal presented and, having done that, should not encountered many problems preparing a revised calculation. The highlighted words are key phrases that markers are looking for.

(a) **Errors in the original investment appraisal**

Inflation was incorrectly applied to selling prices and variable costs in calculating contribution, since only one year's inflation was allowed for in each year of operation.

The fixed costs were correctly inflated, but included $200,000 per year before inflation that was not a relevant cost. Only relevant costs should be included in investment appraisal.

Straight-line accounting depreciation had been used in the calculation, but this depreciation method is not acceptable to the tax authorities. The approved method using 25% reducing balance tax allowable depreciation should be used.

Interest payments have been included in the investment appraisal, but these are allowed for by the discount rate used in calculating the net present value.

The interest rate on the debt finance has been used as the discount rate, when the nominal weighted average cost of capital should have been used to discount the calculated nominal after-tax cash flows.

(b)   Nominal weighted average cost of capital = 1.07 × 1.047 = 1.12, i.e. 12% per year

Year	1	2	3	4	5
	$000	$000	$000	$000	$000
Contribution	1,330	2,264	3,010	1,600	
Fixed costs	(318)	(337)	(357)	(379)	
Taxable cash flow	1,012	1,927	2,653	1,221	
Taxation		(304)	(578)	(796)	(366)
CA tax benefits		150	112	84	178
After-tax cash flow	1,012	1,773	2,187	509	(188)
Scrap value				250	
After-tax cash flows	1,012	1,773	2,187	759	(188)
Discount at 12%	0.893	0.797	0.712	0.635	0.567
Present values	904	1,413	1,557	482	(107)

	$000
Present value of future cash flows	4,249
Initial investment	2,000
Net present value	2,249

The net present value is positive and so the investment is financially acceptable.

Alternative NPV calculation using taxable profit calculation

Year	1	2	3	4	5
	$000	$000	$000	$000	$000
Contribution	1,330	2,264	3,010	1,600	
Fixed costs	(318)	(337)	(357)	(379)	
Taxable cash flow	1,012	1,927	2,653	1,221	
TA depreciation	(500)	(375)	(281)	(594)	
Taxable profit	512	1,552	2,372	627	
Taxation	(154)	(466)	(712)	(188)	
Profit after tax	512	1,398	1,906	(85)	(188)
TA depreciation	500	375	281	594	
After-tax cash flow	1,012	1,773	2,187	509	(188)
Scrap value		250			
After-tax cash flows	1,012	1,773	2,187	759	(188)
Discount at 12%	0.893	0.797	0.712	0.635	0.567
Present values	904	1,413	1,557	482	(107)

	$000
Present value of future cash flows	4,249
Initial investment	2,000
Net present value	2,249

Workings

Annual contribution

Year	1	2	3	4
Sales volume (units/yr)	250,000	400,000	500,000	250,000
Selling price ($/unit)	12.60	13.23	13.89	14.59
Variable cost ($/unit)	7.28	7.57	7.87	8.19
Contribution ($/unit)	5.32	5.66	6.02	6.40
Contribution ($/yr)	1,330,000	2,264,000	3,010,000	1,600,000

Tax allowable depreciation tax benefits

Year	TA depreciation ($)	Tax benefit ($)
1	500,000	150,000
2	375,000	112,500
3	281,250	84,375
4	593,750	178,125
Scrap value	250,000	
	————	
	2,000,000	
	————	

(c) (i) **Multiple internal rates of return**

An investment project may have multiple internal rates of return if it has unconventional cash flows, that is, cash flows that change sign over the life of the project. A mining operation, for example, may have initial investment (cash outflow) followed by many years of successful operation (cash inflow) before decommissioning and environmental repair (cash outflow). This technical difficulty makes it difficult to use the internal rate of return (IRR) investment appraisal method to offer investment advice.

One solution is to use the net present value (NPV) investment appraisal method instead of IRR, since the non-conventional cash flows are easily accommodated by NPV. This is one area where NPV is considered to be superior to IRR.

(ii) **Projects with significantly different business risk to current operations**

Where a proposed investment project has business risk that is significantly different from current operations, it is no longer appropriate to use the weighted average cost of capital (WACC) as the discount rate in calculating the net present value of the project. WACC can only be used as a discount rate where business risk and financial risk are not significantly affected by undertaking an investment project.

Where business risk changes significantly, the capital asset pricing model should be used to calculate a project-specific discount rate which takes account of the systematic risk of a proposed investment project.

ACCA marking scheme			Marks
(a)	Identification of errors in the evaluation		
		Maximum	5
(b)	Nominal weighted average cost of capital		1
	Inflated selling prices		1
	Inflated variable costs		1
	Inflated contribution		1
	Inflated fixed costs		1
	TA depreciation and/or related tax benefits		3
	Scrap value		1
	Discount factors		1
	Net present value		1
	Comment		1–2
			———
		Maximum	12

	(c)	Discussion of projects with several IRR		2
		Discussion of projects with different business risk		3

			Maximum	5
	Total			20

Examiner's comments

Many students did well on parts (a) and (b) of this question, while finding part (c) to be more challenging.

In part (a), candidates were asked to identify and comment on any errors in an investment appraisal prepared by a trainee accountant. Candidates who did not gain full marks failed to identify clearly the errors they had identified, or did not comment on these errors, or identified errors that did not exist.

Part (b) required candidates to prepare a revised calculation of the NPV of an investment project and to comment on its acceptability.

Many candidates did well here, using the template of the NPV calculation provided in the question to prepare a corrected calculation. The contribution had to be inflated correctly, the fixed costs had to be calculated correctly, the depreciation and interest payments had to be stripped out, the tax effect of tax allowable depreciation needed to be calculated and included, and the correct discount rate had to be used.

Candidates who did not amend the provided contribution figures were not aware that inflation must be applied every year and not just in the first year. The development costs had to be excluded from the fixed costs in the investment appraisal because they had already been incurred, i.e. they were not relevant costs. Depreciation had to be stripped out because it is not a cash flow, and NPV is an investment appraisal method that uses cash flows. Interest payments had to be excluded because they would be taken account of by the discount rate.

The tax effect of tax allowable depreciation could be included by any one of three methods: by using the correctly timed tax benefits of each tax allowable depreciation; by subtracting the tax allowable depreciation from taxable cash flow to give taxable profit and then adding them back after calculating the tax liability; and by carrying out a separate tax calculation.

Within the investment appraisal, cash flows had been inflated by specific inflation rates and so the evaluation was a nominal terms (or money terms) evaluation, requiring a nominal discount rate. The real discount rate was provided in the question, together with the general rate of inflation, and the nominal discount rate could be calculated from these two pieces of information using the Fisher equation.

Part (c) tested candidates' understanding of different aspects of investment appraisal by asking what problems were faced, and how these problems could be overcome, in three different investment appraisal areas.

The first investment appraisal area related to multiple internal rates of return, a technical problem associated with non-conventional cash flows that is not experienced by NPV.

The second investment appraisal area related to investments with a different level of business risk than the investing company. Many candidates identified correctly here that the capital asset pricing model could be used to calculate a project-specific discount rate that reflected project risk.

28 BRT CO

Key answer tips

It is reasonable to expect a good mark to be achieved for part (a) as this is a commonly tested area with nothing out of the ordinary. It is important not to ignore the stated requirement to use a nominal terms approach.

Part (b) should also have been straightforward, being essentially bookwork.

The highlighted words are key phrases that markers are looking for.

(a) **Net present value evaluation of new confectionery investment**

Year	1	2	3	4	5
	$000	$000	$000	$000	$000
Sales	3,605	8,488	11,474	16,884	
Variable cost	(2,019)	(5,093)	(6,884)	(10,299)	
Fixed costs	(1,030)	(1,910)	(3,060)	(4,277)	
Taxable cash flow	556	1,485	1,530	2,308	
Taxation		(167)	(446)	(459)	(692)
CA tax benefits		150	113	84	253
After-tax cash flows	556	1,468	1,197	1,933	(439)
Discount at 12%	0.893	0.797	0.712	0.636	0.567
Present values	497	1,170	852	1,229	(249)

	$000
Sum of present values	3,499
Initial investment	(2,000)
Net present value	1,499

Comment:

The proposed investment in the new product is financially acceptable, as the NPV is positive.

Examiner's note:

Including tax-allowable depreciation tax benefits by subtracting tax-allowable depreciation, calculating tax liability and then adding back the tax-allowable depreciation is also acceptable.

Workings

Year	1	2	3	4
Sales volume (boxes)	700,000	1,600,000	2,100,000	3,000,000
Inflated selling price ($/box)	5.150	5.305	5.464	5.628
Sales ($000/yr)	3,605	8,488	11,474	16,884

Year	1	2	3	4
Sales volume (boxes)	700,000	1,600,000	2,100,000	3,000,000
Variable cost ($/box)	2.80	3.00	3.00	3.05
Inflated variable cost ($/box)	2.884	3.183	3.278	3.433
Variable cost ($000/yr)	2,019	5,093	6,884	10,299

Year	1	2	3	4
Sales volume (boxes)	700,000	1,600,000	2,100,000	3,000,000
Fixed costs ($000)	1,000	1,800	2,800	3,800
Inflated fixed costs ($000)	1,030	1,910	3,060	4,277

Year	1	2	3	4
	$	$	$	$
Tax-allowable depreciation	500,000	375,000	281,250	843,750
Tax benefit (30%)	150,000	112,500	84,375	253,125

(b)   **Examiner note: only THREE ways of incorporating risk into investment appraisal were required to be discussed.**

Risk and uncertainty

Risk in investment appraisal refers to the attachment of probabilities to the possible outcomes from an investment project and therefore represents a quantified assessment of the variability of expected returns.

Uncertainty cannot be quantified by attaching probabilities and although the terms are often used interchangeably, the difference is important in investment appraisal.

Sensitivity analysis

This assesses the sensitivity of project NPV to changes in project variables. It calculates the relative change in a project variable required to make the NPV zero, or the relative change in NPV for a fixed change in a project variable. Only one variable is considered at a time. When the sensitivities for each variable have been calculated, the key or critical variables can be identified. These show where assumptions may need to be checked and where managers could focus their attention in order to increase the likelihood that the project will deliver its calculated benefits. However, since sensitivity analysis does not incorporate probabilities, it cannot be described as a way of incorporating risk into investment appraisal, although it is often described as such.

Probability analysis

This approach involves assigning probabilities to each outcome of an investment project, or assigning probabilities to different values of project variables. The range of net present values that can result from an investment project is then calculated, together with the joint probability of each outcome. The net present values and their joint probabilities can be used to calculate the mean or average NPV (the expected NPV or ENPV) which would arise if the investment project could be repeated a large number of times. Other useful information that could be provided by the probability analysis includes the worst outcome and its probability, the probability of a negative NPV, the best outcome and its probability, and the most likely outcome. Managers could then make a decision on the investment that took account more explicitly of its risk profile.

Risk-adjusted discount rate

It appears to be intuitively correct to add a risk premium to the 'normal' discount rate to assess a project with greater than normal risk. The theoretical approach here would be to use the capital asset pricing model (CAPM) to determine a project-specific discount rate that reflected the systematic risk of an investment project. This can be achieved by selecting proxy companies whose business activities are the same as the proposed investment project: removing the effect of their financial risk by ungearing their equity betas to give an average asset beta; regearing the asset beta to give an equity beta reflecting the financial risk of the investing company; and using the CAPM to calculate a project-specific cost of equity for the investment project.

Adjusted payback

Payback can be adjusted for risk, if uncertainty is considered to be the same as risk, by shortening the payback period. The logic here is that as uncertainty (risk) increases with the life of the investment project, shortening the payback period for a project that is relatively risky will require it to pay back sooner, putting the focus on cash flows that are more certain (less risky) because they are nearer in time.

Payback can also be adjusted for risk by discounting future cash flows with a risk-adjusted discount rate, i.e. by using the discounted payback method. The normal payback period target can be applied to the discounted cash flows, which will have decreased in value due to discounting, so that the overall effect is similar to reducing the payback period with undiscounted cash flows.

ACCA marking scheme		Marks
(a)	Inflated selling price per box	1
	Sales	1
	Inflated variable cost per box	1
	Variable cost	1
	Inflated fixed costs	1
	Tax payable	1
	TA depreciation tax benefits	1
	Balancing allowance	1
	Timing of tax payments or benefits	1
	Initial working capital investment	1
	Incremental working capital investment	1
	Working capital recovery	1
	Discount factors	1
	Net present value	1
	Comment on acceptability	1
	Maximum	13

(d)	Discussion of three methods, 2–3 marks per method	7
	Maximum	7
Total		20

Examiner's comments

Part (a) asked candidates to calculate the net present value (NPV) of a new confectionary line using a nominal terms approach, allowing for inflation and taxation.

Some candidates said that, because the same rate of inflation was applied to selling price, variable cost and fixed cost, inflation could be ignored and their answers used a real terms approach. This ignores the stated requirement to use a nominal terms approach and is also not correct in this case, as profit tax was payable in arrears. A nominal terms approach discounts nominal (inflated) cash flows with a nominal cost of capital, which was given in the question. Some answers made the mistake of either inflating or deflating the provided nominal cost of capital.

Some answers did not defer the tax liabilities, or the tax benefits on the tax-allowable depreciation available on the cost of equipment, or both, although the question required this. Although the question said that a balancing allowance would be claimed in the fourth year of production, some candidates did not calculate this.

Almost all answers correctly located the discount factors from the tables provided in the examination paper, although as mentioned earlier a few answers used a discount rate that was different from the one provided in the question. In a very small number of answers, annuity factors were used instead of discount factors.

Almost all answers calculated a net present value. Although the question required that the candidate advise on the financial acceptability of the proposed investment, some answers did not do this, or made a casual comment that did not gain full marks.

In part (c), candidates were required to discuss three ways of incorporating risk into the investment appraisal process. Many candidates lost marks by not reading the question correctly and discussing the nature of different kinds of risk, rather than how risk could be incorporated in the investment appraisal process. Better answers discussed ways of incorporating risk into investment appraisal that were covered in the syllabus, such as sensitivity analysis, probability analysis, and the capital asset pricing model.

29 UMUNAT INC

Key answer tips

The calculations in this question are quite straightforward although you would not be able to pass the question if you focussed on the numbers alone. Don't neglect the discussional element of parts of the requirement that might at first appear to be numerical. Virtually half of the marks available in parts (b) & (c), will be for the commentary that accompanies your calculations. The highlighted words are key phrases that markers are looking for.

(a) The investment appraisal process is concerned with assessing the value of future cash flows compared to the cost of investment.

Since future cash flows cannot be predicted with certainty, managers must consider how much confidence can be placed in the results of the investment appraisal process. They must therefore be concerned with the risk and uncertainty of a project. Uncertainty refers to the situation where probabilities cannot be assigned to future cash flows. Uncertainty cannot therefore be quantified and increases with project life: it is usually true to say that the more distant is a cash flow, the more uncertain is its value. Risk refers to the situation where probabilities can be assigned to future cash flows, for example as a result of managerial experience and judgement or scenario analysis. Where such probabilities can be assigned, it is possible to quantify the risk associated with project variables and hence of the project as a whole.

If risk and uncertainty were not considered in the investment appraisal process, managers might make the mistake of placing too much confidence in the results of investment appraisal, or they may fail to monitor investment projects in order to ensure that expected results are in fact being achieved. Assessment of project risk can also indicate projects that might be rejected as being too risky compared with existing business operations, or projects that might be worthy of reconsideration if ways of reducing project risk could be found in order to make project outcomes more acceptable.

(b) **Calculation of project net present value**

Annual cash flow = ((20,000 × (3 – 1.65)) – 10,000 = $17,000 per year

Net present value = (17,000 × 3.605) – 50,000 = 61,285 – 50,000 = $11,285

	PV ($)
Alternatively:	
Sales revenue: 20,000 × 3.00 × 3.605 =	216,300
Variable costs: 20,000 × 1.65 × 3.605 =	(118,965)
Contribution	97,335
Initial investment	(50,000)
Fixed costs: 10,000 × 3.605 =	(36,050)
Net present value:	11,285

Sensitivity of NPV to sales volume

Sales volume giving zero NPV = ((50,000/3.605) + 10,000)/1.35 = 17,681 units.

This is a decrease of 2,319 units or 11.6%.

Alternatively, sales volume decrease = 100 × 11,285/97,335= 11.6%.

Tutorial note:

The second method presented above is probably the method most people will feel comfortable with. This uses the generic formula of:

$$\frac{NPV}{PV\ of\ affected\ cashflow} \times 100\%$$

Sensitivity of NPV to sales price

Sales price for zero NPV = (((50,000/3.605) + 10,000)/20,000) + 1.65 = $2.843.

This is a decrease of 15.7¢ or 5.2%.

Alternatively, sales price decrease = 100 × 11,285/216,300 = 5.2%.

Sensitivity of NPV to variable cost

Variable cost must increase by 15.7¢ or 9.5% to make the NPV zero.

Alternatively, variable cost increase = 100 × 11,285/118,965 = 9.5%.

Sensitivity analysis evaluates the effect on project net present value of changes in project variables. The objective is to determine the key or critical project variables, which are those where the smallest change produces the biggest change in project NPV. It is limited in that only one project variable at a time may be changed, whereas in reality several project variables may change simultaneously. For example, an increase in inflation could result in increases in sales price, variable costs and fixed costs. Sensitivity analysis is not a way of evaluating project risk, since although it may identify the key or critical variables, it cannot assess the likelihood of a change in these variables. In other words, sensitivity analysis does not assign probabilities to project variables. Where sensitivity analysis is useful is in drawing the attention of management to project variables that need careful monitoring if a particular investment project is to meet expectations. Sensitivity analysis can also highlight the need to check the assumptions underlying the key or critical variables.

(c) **Expected value of sales volume**

(17,500 × 0.3) + (20,000 × 0.6) + (22,500 × 0.1) = 19,500 units

Expected NPV = (((19,500 × 1.35) − 10,000) × 3.605) − 50,000 = $8,852

Since the expected net present value is positive, the project appears to be acceptable. From earlier analysis we know that the NPV is positive at 20,000 per year, and the NPV will therefore also be positive at 22,500 units per year. The NPV of the worst case is:

(((17,500 × 1.35) − 10,000) × 3.605) − 50,000 = ($882)

The NPV of the best case is:

(((22,500 × 1.35) − 10,000) × 3.605) − 50,000 = $23,452

There is thus a 30% chance that the project will produce a negative NPV, a fact not revealed by considering the expected net present value alone.

The expected net present value is not a value that is likely to occur in practice: it is perhaps more useful to know that there is a 30% chance that the project will produce a negative NPV (or a 70% chance of a positive NPV), since this may represent an unacceptable level of risk as far as the managers of Umunat Inc are concerned. It can therefore be argued that assigning probabilities to expected economic states or sales volumes has produced useful information that can help the managers of Umunat Inc to make better investment decisions. The difficulty with this approach is that probability estimates of project variables or future economic states are likely to carry a high degree of uncertainty and subjectivity.

30 VICTORY

Key answer tips

Parts (a) and (c) offer some good opportunities to pick up some relatively easy marks. Both require you to apply a sound knowledge base to the scenario given. Part (c) should be attempted first in order to manage time more effectively for the required calculations.

Part (b) is slightly more challenging although those who keep going and apply some of the basic principles should be able to comfortably achieve a pass mark.

(a) **NPV**

$000	T0	T1	T2	T3
Sales (60,000 × $40)		2,400	2,400	2,400
Variable costs (60,000 × $25)		(1,500)	(1,500)	(1,500)
Fixed costs (W1)		(355)	(355)	(355)
Rent	(80)	(80)	(80)	
Net operating cash flows	(80)	465	465	545
Tax	24	(140)	(140)	(164)
Initial cost	(1,200)			
TA depreciation (W2)		90	68	22
Residual value				600
WC	(340)	(60)	(50)	450
Totals	**(1,596)**	**355**	**343**	**1,453**
10% DF	1	0.909	0.826	0.751
PV	**(1,596)**	**323**	**283**	**1,091**

Hence the NPV is about $101,000, which would suggest that the equipment is purchased.

Tutorial note:

Remember, relevant cash flows are those which are in the future, incremental to the project and that correspond to actual cash flows and not notional charges. You must also remember that any cash flows relating to the financing of a project should be excluded from your NPV calculation. The discounting process takes account of these so, if you included them, you would effectively be double counting them.

Workings

(W1) **Relevant fixed costs**

	$000
Amount charged to project	715
Bank interest (not relevant – covered by discount rate)	(86)
Head office overheads (not incremental)	(74)
Depreciation (non-cash – $1.2m – £600k ÷ 3)	(200)
Relevant fixed costs	355

(W2) **Tax allowable depreciation**

Year	TWDV – $000	Tax saving at 30%	Timing
1	1,200		
TA depreciation	(300)	90	T1
2	900		
TA depreciation	(225)	68	T2
3	675		
Balancing allowance	(75)	22	T3
RV	600		

It has been assumed that the asset is bought on the first day of an accounting period and that the first tax allowable depreciation will be received 12 months later.

(b)

Tutorial note:

When calculating sensitivity you must remember to include the tax effects relating to each of the cash flows.

Sensitivity of annual sales volume

Total current annual contribution	
([$40 – $25] × 60,000	$900,000
Less tax @ 30%	($270,000)
	$630,000
Annuity factors (years 1 – 3)	× 2.487
	$1,566,810
Net present value of scheme	$101,000
Sensitivity of annual sales	
($101,000 ÷ $1,566,810)	6.45%
(6.45% × 60,000 units)	3,870 units
Break-even level of annual sales	
(60,000 – 3,870)	56,130 units

Annual sales volume is fairly sensitive – a 6.45% overestimation of the expected volume increase would mean that the investment is no longer worthwhile. This would therefore be of concern to the management of Victory. Further research to ensure the validity of these estimates should be performed before the equipment is purchased.

(c) Risk refers to the situation where probabilities can be assigned to a range of expected outcomes arising from an investment project and the likelihood of each outcome occurring can therefore be quantified. Uncertainty refers to the situation where probabilities cannot be assigned to expected outcomes. Investment project risk therefore increases with increasing variability of returns, while uncertainty increases with increasing project life. The two terms are often used interchangeably in financial management, but the distinction between them is a useful one.

One way of incorporating risk into investment decision making is using probability analysis. A probability distribution of expected cash flows may be determined and the expected net present value (ENPV) could be calculated, together with the probability of the worst-case scenario and the probability of a negative net present value. In this way, the downside risk of the investment could be determined and incorporated into the investment decision.

A second way of incorporating risk into the decision is to add an additional premium to the discount rate. This will provide a safety margin meaning that marginally profitable projects (perhaps the riskiest) are less likely to have a positive NPV. The premium applied can vary from project to project to reflect the different levels of risk.

31   CJ CO

Key answer tips

Part (a) is a fairly typical exam requirement on the frequently visited topic of investment appraisal with inflation and tax.

To score well on the discursive element in part (b), you need to go beyond a simple critique of payback v ROCE. There are a number of different factors presented within the section containing the directors' views, and all must be commented on in order to pick up the full range of marks on offer.

Part (c) covers the more difficult topic of calculating a risk-adjusted cost of equity by de-gearing and re-gearing betas. This is an area that typically students tend not to like. However, the formulas are provided in the exam so, once you've practised the calculation a few times, this should represent some fairly easy marks. The highlighted words are key phrases that markers are looking for.

(a) **Net present value evaluation**

Year	1	2	3	4	5
	$000	$000	$000	$000	$000
Sales revenue (W)	1,575	1,654	1,736	1,823	
Selling costs (W)	(32)	(33)	(35)	(37)	
Variable costs (W)	(624)	(649)	(675)	(702)	
Before-tax cash flows	919	972	1,026	1,084	
Taxation at 30%		(276)	(292)	(308)	(325)
Tax benefits		263	197	148	443
After-tax cash flows	919	959	931	924	118
Working capital	(11)	(12)	(12)	(13)	
Project cash flows	908	947	919	911	118
Discount at 10%	0.909	0.826	0.751	0.683	0.621
Present values	825	782	690	622	73

	$000
PV of cash flows:	2,992
Working capital:	(250)
Initial investment:	(3,500)
Net present value:	(758)

The NPV is negative, with a value of minus $758,000, and Project A is therefore not financially acceptable.

Tutor's top tips:

The term 'nominal' weighted average cost of capital means this already includes the effects of inflation.

Workings

Year	1	2	3	4
Selling price ($/unit)	2.100	2.205	2.315	2.431
Sales volume (units/year)	750,000	750,000	750,000	750,000
Sales revenue ($/years)	1,575,000	1,653,750	1,736,250	1,823,250

Year	1	2	3	4
Selling cost ($/unit)	0.042	0.044	0.046	0.049
Sales volume (units/year)	750,000	750,000	750,000	750,000
Selling cost ($/years)	31,500	33,000	34,500	36,750

Year	1	2	3	4
Variable cost ($/unit)	0.832	0.865	0.900	0.936
Sales volume (units/year)	750,000	750,000	750,000	750,000
Variable cost ($/years)	624,000	648,750	675,000	702,000

Year	TA depreciation ($)	30% Tax benefit ($)	Year taken
1	875,000	262,500	2
2	656,250	196,875	3
3	492,188	147,656	4
4	1,476,562*	442,969	5

*This figure includes the balancing allowance

Tutorial note:
Even though the volume of business remains constant, the presence of inflation will mean the investment in working capital will increase over time. This is therefore a relevant cash flow that must be included.

Year	Working capital ($)	Incremental investment ($)
0	250,000	
1	261,250	11,250
2	273,006	11,756
3	285,292	12,286
4	298,130	12,838

Alternative NPV evaluation

An alternative approach to evaluating the NPV of Project A is to subtract and add back the ta allowable depreciation, which are not cash flows.

Year	1	2	3	4	5
	$000	$000	$000	$000	$000
Before-tax cash flows	919	972	1,026	1,084	
TA depreciation	(875)	(656)	(492)	(1,477)	
Taxable profit	44	316	534	(393)	
Taxation		(13)	(95)	(160)	118
After-tax profit	44	303	439	(553)	118
Add TA depreciation	875	656	492	1,477	
After-tax cash flows	919	959	931	924	118

The evaluation will then proceed as earlier.

(b)

Tutor's top tips:

Always make sure you read the requirement and the relevant part of the scenario carefully before answering the question.

The directors' views on investment appraisal are discussed in turn.

Evaluation using either payback or return on capital employed

Both payback period and return on capital employed (ROCE) are inferior to discounted cash flow (DCF) methods such as net present value (NPV) and internal rate of return (IRR). Payback ignores the time value of money and cash flows outside of the payback period. ROCE uses profit instead of cash flow. Both payback and ROCE have difficulty in justifying the target value used to determine acceptability. Why, for example, use a maximum payback period of two years? DCF methods use the weighted average cost of capital of an investing company as the basis of evaluation, or a project-specific cost of capital, and both can be justified on academic grounds.

The company should also clarify why either method can be used, since they assess different aspects of an investment project.

Evaluation over a four-year planning period

Using a planning period or a specified investment appraisal time horizon is a way of reducing the uncertainty associated with investment appraisal, since this increases with project life. However, it is important to determine the expected life of an investment project if at all possible, since evaluation over the whole life of a project may help a company avoid sub-optimal investment decisions. In the case of CJ Co, for example, a further year of operation may lead to Project A generating a positive NPV.

Scrap value is ignored

Scrap value, salvage value or terminal value must be included in the evaluation of a project since it is a cash inflow. Ignoring scrap value will reduce the NPV and may lead to rejection of an otherwise acceptable investment project.

Working capital recovery is ignored

If an investment project ends, then working capital can be recovered and it must be included in the evaluation of an investment project, since it is a cash inflow. In the case of CJ Co, the directors' decision to ignore working capital recovery means ignoring a fourth year cash inflow of $298,130.

A balancing allowance is claimed at the end of the fourth year of operation

Introducing a balancing allowance which can only be claimed when allowed by the taxation authorities will distort the taxation aspects of the investment appraisal. If it is anticipated that a project will continue beyond the fourth year, including a balancing allowance in the evaluation will overstate cash inflows and hence the NPV, potentially leading to incorrect investment decisions being made.

ACCA marking scheme		Marks
(a)	Sales revenue	1
	Selling costs	1
	Variable costs	1
	TA depreciation, years 1 to 3	1
	TA depreciation/balancing allowance, year 4	1
	Tax liabilities	1
	Timing of taxation	1
	Incremental working capital	2
	Discount factors	1
	NPV calculation	1
	Decision as to financial acceptability	1
	Maximum	12
(b)	Discussion of payback and ROCE	2–3
	Discussion of planning period	1–2
	Discussion of scrap value	1–2
	Discussion of working capital recovery	1–2
	Discussion of balancing allowance	1–2
	Maximum	8
Total		**20**

Examiner's comments

Most candidates gained good marks in parts (a), while part (b) was rarely answered well.

Part (a) asked candidates to calculate the net present value (NPV) of Project A, allowing for inflation and taxation.

Most candidates inflated correctly selling price, selling cost and variable cost in order to find the before-tax cash flows over the four year appraisal period required by the directors of the company. Some candidates did not defer tax liability by one year, although the question required this. Some candidates calculated correctly the tax benefit arising from tax allowable depreciation, but did not provide a balancing allowance in the final year, as the directors required. The directors also required that scrap value be excluded from the evaluation.

The treatment of working capital was a problem for some candidates. Three elements of working capital can be relevant in investment appraisal, namely initial investment, incremental investment and recovery at the end of the investment project. The first two elements were needed here, with incremental investment arising from general inflation. Working capital recovery was excluded by the directors' views on investment appraisal. Even though working capital investment was specified in the question as an initial investment, some candidates inflated the initial investment and placed it at the end of year one.

The inflated after-tax cash flows were nominal (money terms) cash flows and the question provided a nominal weighted average after-tax cost of capital. This was the discount rate needed for Project A, although some candidates calculated another incorrect discount rate by either inflating or deflating the discount rate provided.

The calculated NPV of Project A was negative and so the investment project was not financially acceptable.

In part (b), candidates were asked to critically discuss the directors' views on investment appraisal. These views were requirements to use either payback period or return on capital employed (ROCE), to evaluate over a four year planning period, to ignore any scrap value or working capital recovery, and to claim a balancing allowance at the end of the four-year evaluation period.

Although part (b) asked for a critical discussion, a significant number of candidates calculated and commented on the payback period and the ROCE of Project A. This was not what the question asked for and gained no credit. Many candidates limited their discussion to payback and ROCE, and therefore lost marks because they did not discuss the four-year planning period, ignoring any scrap value or working capital recovery, and claiming a balancing allowance at the end of four years.

The directors' views were not consistent with a theoretically sound evaluation of Project A using relevant cash flows, A critical discussion should have focused on this.

32 BASRIL

Key answer tips

Students who score badly on this question do so because they get bogged down in the numerical calculations in part (a). The best way to avoid this trap is to tackle the wordy parts of the requirement first. The highlighted words are key phrases that markers are looking for.

(a) (i)   **Analysis of projects assuming they are divisible**

	Discount factor at 12%	Project 1 Cash flow	PV	Project 3 Cash flow	PV
		$	$	$	$
Initial investment	1.000	(300,000)	(300,000)	(400,000)	(400,000)
Year 1	0.893	85,000	75,905	124,320	111,018
Year 2	0.797	90,000	71,730	128,795	102,650
Year 3	0.712	95,000	67,640	133,432	95,004
Year 4	0.636	100,000	63,600	138,236	87,918
Year 5	0.567	95,000	53,865	143,212	81,201
PV of savings			332,740		477,791
NPV			32,740		77,791
Profitability index			332,740/300,000 = 1.11		477,791/400,000 = 1.19

	Discount factor at 12%	Project 2 Cash flow	PV
		$	$
Initial investment	1.000	(450,000)	(450,000)
Annual cash flows, years 1 – 5	3.605	140,800	507,584
Net present value			57,584

Profitability index	507,584/450,000		= 1.13

Order of preference (in order of profitability index) = Project 3 then Project 2 then Project 1.

Project	Profitability index	Ranking	Investment	NPV	
			$	$	
3	1.19	1st	400,000	77,791	
2	1.13	2nd	400,000	51,186	(= 57,584 × 400/450)
			800,000	128,977	

(ii) **Analysis of projects assuming they are indivisible**

If the projects are assumed to be indivisible, the total NPV of combinations of projects must be considered.

Projects	Investment	NPV	
	$	$	
1 and 2	750,000	90,324	£(32,740 + 57,584)
1 and 3	700,000	110,531	£(32,740 + 77,791)
2 and 3	850,000	not feasible, too much investment	

The optimum combination is now projects 1 and 3.

(b) The NPV decision rule requires that a company invest in all projects that have a positive net present value. This assumes that sufficient funds are available for all incremental projects, which is only true in a perfect capital market. When insufficient funds are available, that is when capital is rationed, projects cannot be selected by ranking by absolute NPV. Choosing a project with a large NPV may mean not choosing smaller projects that, in combination, give a higher NPV. Instead, if projects are divisible, they can be ranked using the profitability index in order make the optimum selection. If projects are not divisible, different combinations of available projects must be evaluated to select the combination with the highest NPV.

(c) The NPV decision rule, to accept all projects with a positive net present value, requires the existence of a perfect capital market where access to funds for capital investment is not restricted. In practice, companies are likely to find that funds available for capital investment are restricted or rationed.

Hard capital rationing is the term applied when the restrictions on raising funds are due to causes external to the company. For example, potential providers of debt finance may refuse to provide further funding because they regard a company as too risky. This may be in terms of financial risk, for example if the company's gearing is too high or its interest cover is too low, or in terms of business risk if they see the company's business prospects as poor or its operating cash flows as too variable. In practice, large established companies seeking long-term finance for capital investment are usually able to find it, but small and medium-sized enterprises will find raising such funds more difficult.

Soft capital rationing refers to restrictions on the availability of funds that arise within a company and are imposed by managers. There are several reasons why managers might restrict available funds for capital investment. Managers may prefer slower organic growth to a sudden increase in size arising from accepting several large investment projects. This reason might apply in a family-owned business that wishes to avoid hiring new managers. Managers may wish to avoid raising further equity finance if this will dilute the control of existing shareholders. Managers may wish to avoid issuing new debt if their expectations of future economic conditions are such as to suggest that an increased commitment to fixed interest payments would be unwise.

One of the main reasons suggested for soft capital rationing is that managers wish to create an internal market for investment funds. It is suggested that requiring investment projects to compete for funds means that weaker or marginal projects, with only a small chance of success, are avoided. This allows a company to focus on more robust investment projects where the chance of success is higher. This cause of soft capital rationing can be seen as a way of reducing the risk and uncertainty associated with investment projects, as it leads to accepting projects with greater margins of safety.

33 ASOP CO

Key answer tips

This question encompasses two of the more fringe topics within the investment appraisal part of the syllabus; lease v buy and equivalent annual costs. It is a fair question, which well prepared students (those who have studied the syllabus in detail) should handle well.

The highlighted words are key phrases that markers are looking for.

(a)   After-tax cost of borrowing = 8.6 × (1 − 0.3) = 6% per year

Evaluation of leasing

Year	Cash flow	Amount ($)	6% Discount factors	Present value ($)
0–3	Lease rentals	(380,000)	1.000 + 2.673 = 3.673	(1,395,740)
2–5	Tax savings	114,000	4.212 − 0.943 = 3.269	372,666
				─────────
				(1,023,074)
				─────────

Present value of cost of leasing = $1,023,074

Evaluation of borrowing to buy

Year	Capital	Licence fee	Tax benefits	Net cash flow	6% discount factors	Present value
	$	$	$	$	$	$
0	(1,000,000)			(1,000,000)	1.000	(1,000,000)
1		(104,000)		(104,000)	0.943	(98,072)
2		(108,160)	106,200	(1,960)	0.890	(1,744)
3		(112,486)	88,698	(23,788)	0.840	(19,982)
4	100,000	(116,986)	75,934	58,948	0.792	46,687
5			131,659	131,659	0.747	98,349
						————
						(974,762)
						————

Present value of cost of borrowing to buy = $974,762

Workings

Year	TA depreciation	Tax benefits	Licence fee tax benefits	Total
	$	$	$	$
2	1,000,000 × 0.25 = 250,000	75,000	31,200	106,200
3	750,000 × 0.25 = 187,500	56,250	32,448	88,698
4	562,500 × 0.25 =140,625	42,188	33,746	75,934
5	421,875 – 100,000 = 321,875	96,563	35,096	131,659

ASOP Co should buy the new technology, since the present cost of borrowing to buy is lower than the present cost of leasing.

(b) **Nominal terms net present value analysis**

Year	1	2	3	4	5
	$	$	$	$	$
Cost savings	365,400	479,250	637,450	564,000	
Tax liabilities		(109,620)	(143,775)	(191,235)	(169,200)
	————	————	————	————	————
Net cash flow	365,400	369,630	493,675	372,765	(169,200)
Discount at 11%	0.901	0.812	0.731	0.659	0.593
	————	————	————	————	————
Present values	329,225	300,140	360,876	245,652	(100,336)
	————	————	————	————	————

Present value of benefits	1,135,557
Present cost of financing	(974,762)
	————
Net present value	160,795
	————

The investment in new technology is acceptable on financial grounds, as it has a positive net present value of $160,795.

Workings

Year	1	2	3	4
	$	$	$	$
Operating cost saving ($/unit)	6.09	6.39	6.71	7.05
Production (units/year)	60,000	75,000	95,000	80,000
Operating cost savings ($/year)	365,400	479,250	637,450	564,000
Tax liabilities at 30% ($/year)	109,620	143,775	191,235	169,200

(Examiner's note: Including the financing cash flows in the NPV evaluation and discounting them by the WACC of 11% is also acceptable)

(c) The equivalent annual cost or benefit method can be used to calculate the equal annual amount of cost or benefit which, when discounted at the appropriate cost of capital, produces the same present value of cost or net present value as a set of varying annual costs or benefits.

For example, the net present value (NPV) of investing in the new technology of $160,795 in part (b) was calculated using a weighted average cost of capital (WACC) of 11% over an expected life of four years. The annuity factor for 11% and four years is 3.102. The equivalent annual benefit (EAB) is therefore 160,795/3.102 = $51,835.9 per year. This can be checked by multiplying the EAB by the annuity factor, i.e. 51,835.9 × 3.102 = $160,795.

If an alternative investment in similar technology over five years had a lower EAB, the four-year investment would be preferred as it has the higher EAB.

ACCA marking scheme		Marks
(a) Present value of lease rentals	2	
Present value of lease rental tax benefits	1	
Present value of cost of leasing	1	
Investment and scrap values	1	
Licence fee	1	
TA depreciation tax benefits	2	
Licence fee tax benefits	1	
Present value of cost of borrowing to buy	1	
Appropriate decision on leasing versus buying	1	
		11
(b) Inflated cost savings	2	
Tax liabilities	1	
Present values of net cash flows	1	
Net present value	1	
Advice on acceptability of investment	1	
		6
(c) Definition of equivalent cost or benefit	1	
Relevant discussion	1	
Appropriate illustration	1	
		3
Total		20

Examiner's comments

Many students were able to do well in this question, especially in part (b).

In part (a), candidates were asked to calculate and determine whether a company should lease or buy new technology. Since this was a financing decision, candidates were instructed to use only financing cash flows. The lease versus borrowing to buy decision is covered in the Study Texts that support students studying Paper F9.

From a leasing perspective, candidates needed to calculate the present value of correctly-timed annual lease rental payments and their tax benefits, discounted by the after-tax cost of debt.

From a buying perspective, candidates needed to calculate the present value of the purchase price of the new technology and related tax allowable depreciation tax benefits, and the annual licence fees and their associated tax benefits, discounted by the after-tax cost of debt.

Many candidates did not follow the instruction to use financing cash flows only and included in their evaluation the reduced operating costs arising from using the new technology.

Common errors were splitting the licence fee out of the lease rental payments: using the weighted average cost of capital of the company as the discount rate, rather than the after-tax cost of debt; including interest payments in the evaluation, when these are taken account of by the discount rate: omitting the tax benefit arising on lease rental payments; incorrect timing of lease rental payments or tax benefits; including loan repayments or repayment of principal; and not using a present value approach to comparing the two financing choices. The correct approach can be found in the suggested answers to this examination.

Part (b) required calculating the net present value of buying the new technology using a nominal terms approach, and offering advice on the acceptability of the investment.

The net present value calculation included the nominal value of the operating cost reductions and their associated tax benefits, discounted by the weighted average cost of capital of the company, less the present value of the financing cash flows. Some candidates used the Fisher equation and the inflation rate of the costs savings to calculate a 'nominal' discount rate, but specific inflation cannot be used in this way and no other inflation rate was given in the question. The weighted average cost of capital could therefore be assumed to be in nominal terms.

While some answers included the net present value calculation with the financing evaluation by combining parts (a) and (b) of the question, many answers to this part of question one were of a good standard.

Part (c) asked candidates to discuss and illustrate how equivalent annual cost or equivalent annual benefit could be used to choose between technologies with different expected lives. Candidates who had studied the equivalent annual cost method were able to gain full marks on this part of question one.

Weaker answers discussed new technology or the need for cost-benefit analysis rather than meeting the requirement of the question.

While many answers gave a suitable illustration, such as dividing the net present value calculated in part (b) by a suitable annuity factor, some answers provided illustrations that were much longer than necessary and therefore wasted valuable time, given that this part of question 1 was worth only three marks.

BUSINESS FINANCE AND COST OF CAPITAL

34   FMY

Key answer tips

The requirement in part (a) is fairly general so to provide a comprehensive answer you will need to think through the different theories of business valuation and what influences it.

Part (c) offers an opportunity to pick up some easier marks provided you tailor your comments to the scenario presented.

The highlighted words in the written sections are key phrases that markers are looking for.

(a)   **The effect of method of financing on company value**

Tutor's top tips

Before starting to answer this section you should think about what factors you know that will influence business valuation. Don't confine yourself to just the business valuation part of the syllabus; try to think more broadly and consider how different elements of the syllabus inter-relate. The sorts of things you should identify are:

–   *TERP calculations (rights issues only)*

–   *P/E ratio method (with a focus on changes in earnings and the market forces that will influence the P/E ratio)*

–   *Discounted future cash flows (and the as capital structure changes so to may the WACC leading to changes in business valuation)*

–   *Market efficiency*

Rights issue

If the funds were raised via a rights issue, the theoretical ex-rights price (TERP) can be calculated as:

Current share price = $2.20 per share

Current number of shares = 10 million shares

Finance to be raised = $5m

Number of shares issued = 10m ÷ 4 = 2.5 million shares

Theoretical ex rights price per share = ((10m × 2.20) + $5m) / (10m + 2.5m) = $2.16 per share

The share price would theoretically fall from $2.20 to $2.16 per share although there would be no effect on overall shareholder wealth and total market capitalisation would only increase by the proceeds raised.

However, this does not take account of the benefits of the project. The investment made would result in an overall increase in shareholder wealth equal to the NPV of the project. This could be expected to increase the value of each share by a further 10 cents ($1.2m ÷ 12.5m shares).

Tutorial note

You would never be expected to include the NPV of a project in a TERP calculation but, as we see here, you may be required to recognise that investing in a project will lead to an increase in shareholder wealth equal to the value of the positive NPV.

Effect of rights issue on earnings per share

Current EPS = $4.5m ÷ 10m = 45 cents per share

Revised EPS = ($4.5m + $1.0m) ÷ 12.5m = 44 cents per share

The EPS would fall from 45 cents per share to 44 cents per share. As mentioned earlier, there would be no effect on shareholder wealth in the short term, although in the longer term, a fall in this key investor ratio could lead to some investors disposing of their shares, which would cause the share price to fall.

FMY would therefore have to persuade investors of the benefits of the project and of management's ability to deliver these on schedule. This is really an issue of investors' faith in management competence. If investors are convinced then the current P/E ratio of 4.9 ($0.45 ÷ $2.20) might be expected to increase to reflect the expectation of higher growth rates in the future.

Effect of rights issue on the debt/equity ratio

The company is currently 100% finance by equity. A rights issue would preserve this meaning there would be no change in the company's cost of capital, and therefore no additional movements in the valuation of the business other than those noted above.

Issue of debt

Effect of debt issue on earnings per share

Tutorial note

The trick with this calculation is to recognise the impact of the additional interest on the post-tax earnings of the business.

Interest payments on debt finance = $5m × 8.6% = $0.43m

Post tax fall in earnings = $0.43m × (1 − 0.3) = $0.3m

Revised EPS = ($4.5m + $1.0m − $0.3m) ÷ 10m = 52 cents per share

The EPS would increase from 45 cents per share to 52 cents per share. As mentioned earlier, there would be no effect on shareholder wealth in the short term, although in the longer term, an increase in this key investor ratio could attract investors and cause the share price to rise.

Effect of debt issue on the debt/equity ratio

In theory, the value of the firm is found by discounting all post-tax operating cash flows available for investors at the company's WACC. The method of financing has an impact as if it is possible to reduce the WACC, the value of the company will be increased.

The company is currently ungeared (100% equity financed).

Assuming the market value of equity remained unchanged, the revised debt/equity ratio would be: $5m ÷ (10m × $2.20) = 23%

Capital structure theories provide a useful guide to assessing the impact of methods of financing on the value of the firm.

The traditional view

The traditional view is that as a company first introduces debt into its capital structure, the impact of the cheap debt exceeds the impact of any increase in the cost of equity or debt due to the increased financial risk. Hence, the final impact is that WACC will fall.

As FMY is currently all equity financed, raising more equity is likely to maintain the current WACC and company value. If debt was raised, WACC is likely to fall and company value will be raised.

Modigliani & Miller (M&M)

M&M originally claimed that company value was independent of capital structure. However, once they considered the impact of tax relief that is available when debt interest is paid, they concluded that the WACC of a company would be minimized and its value maximised if debt made up 99.9% of a company's capital. Whilst real world factors such as bankruptcy risk preclude such high levels of gearing, FMY currently has no gearing. Hence, M&M's theory would also support the idea that raising more equity is likely to maintain the current WACC and company value, but that if debt was raised WACC is likely to fall and company value will be raised.

Conclusion

The company should investigate further the use of debt finance as this could enhance the value of the company.

(b) **Islamic finance**

Islamic finance rests on the application of Islamic, or Shariah, law.

The main principles of Islamic finance are that:

* Wealth must be generated from legitimate trade and asset-based investment. The use of money for the purposes of making money is forbidden.
* Investment should also have a social and an ethical benefit to wider society beyond pure return.
* Risk should be shared.
* Harmful activities (such as gambling, alcohol and the sale of certain foods) should be avoided.

The issue of debt finance as proposed by FMY Co (where the lender would make a straight interest charge, irrespective of how the underlying assets fare) would violate the principle of sharing risk and of not using money for the purposes of making money. Under Islamic finance, the charging and receiving of interest (riba) is strictly prohibited. This is in stark contrast to more conventional, western forms of finance.

One alternative form of finance would be Murabaha, a form of trade credit for asset acquisition. Here the provider of finance would buy the item and then sell it on to FMY Co at a price that includes an agreed mark-up for profit. The mark-up is fixed in advance and cannot be increased and the payment is made by instalments.

Another form of finance would be Islamic bonds, known as sukuk. To be Shariah-compliant, the sukuk holders must have a proprietary interest in the assets which are being financed. The sukuk holders' return for providing finance is a share of the income generated by the assets. The key distinction between sukuk and murabaha is that sukuk holders have ownership of the cash flows but not the assets themselves.

35 FENCE CO

Key answer tips

A well-rehearsed candidate should not struggle with the calculations here but layout is key so the marker can follow the method used.

Part (c) is standard textbook knowledge where some easy marks could be gained.

The highlighted words in the written sections are key phrases that markers are looking for.

(a) **Cost of equity**

The current cost of equity can be calculated using the capital asset pricing model.

Equity or market risk premium = 11 − 4 = 7%

Cost of equity = 4 + (0.9 × 7) = 4 + 6.3 = 10.3%

After-tax cost of debt

After-tax interest payment = 100 × 0.07 × (1 − 0.2) = $5.60 per bond

Year	Cash flow	$	5% discount	PV ($)	4% discount	PV ($)
0	market value	(107.14)	1.000	(107.14)	1.000	(107.14)
1 – 7	interest	5.60	5.786	32.40	6.002	33.61
7	redemption	100.00	0.711	71.10	0.760	76.00
				(3.64)		2.47

After-tax cost of debt = IRR = 4 + ((5 − 4) × 2.47)/(2.47 + 3.64) = 4 + 0.4 = 4.4%

Market value of equity = 10,000,000 × 7.50 = $75 million

Market value of Fence Co debt = 14 million × 107.14/100 = $15 million

Total market value of company = 75 + 15 = $90 million

WACC = ((10.3 × 75) + (4.4 × 15))/90 = 9.3%

(b)   Since the investment project is different to business operations, its business risk is different to that of existing operations. A cost of equity for appraising it can be therefore be found using the capital asset pricing model.

Ungearing proxy company equity beta

Asset beta = 1.2 × 54/(54 + (12 × 0.8)) = 1.2 × 54/63.6 = 1.019

Regearing asset beta

Market value of debt = $15m (calculated in part (a))

Regeared asset beta = 1.019 x (75 + (15 × 0.8))/75 = 1.019 × 87/75 = 1.182

Using the CAPM

Equity or market risk premium = 11 − 4 = 7%

Cost of equity = 4 + (1.182 × 7) = 4 + 8.3 = 12.3%

(c)   Portfolio theory suggests that the total risk of a portfolio of investments can be reduced by diversifying the investments held in the portfolio, e.g. by investing capital in a number of different shares rather than buying shares in only one or two companies.

Even when a portfolio has been well-diversified over a number of different investments, there is a limit to the risk-reduction effect, so that there is a level of risk which cannot be diversified away. This undiversifiable risk is the risk of the financial system as a whole, and so is referred to as systematic risk or market risk. Diversifiable risk, which is the element of total risk which can be reduced or minimised by portfolio diversification, is referred to as unsystematic risk or specific risk, since it relates to individual or specific companies rather than to the financial system as a whole.

Portfolio theory is concerned with total risk, which is the sum of systematic risk and unsystematic risk. The capital asset pricing model assumes that investors hold diversified portfolios, and so is concerned with systematic risk alone.

(d)   Capital market efficiency is concerned with pricing efficiency when weak form, semi-strong form and strong form efficiency are being discussed.

In relation to pricing efficiency, the efficient markets hypothesis (EMH) suggests that share prices fully and fairly reflect all relevant and available information. Relevant and available information can be divided into past information, public information and private information.

Significance of EMH to financial managers

If the EMH is correct and share prices are fair, there is no point in financial managers seeking to mislead the capital market, because such attempts will be unsuccessful. Window-dressing financial statements, for example, in order to show a company's performance and position in a favourable light, will be seen through by financial analysts as the capital market digests the financial statement information in pricing the company's shares.

Another consequence of the EMH for financial managers is that there is no particular time which is best for issuing new shares, as share prices on the stock market are always fair.

Because share prices are always fair, there are no bargains to be found on the stock market, i.e. companies whose shares are undervalued. An acquisition strategy which seeks to identify and exploit such stock market bargains is pointless if the EMH is correct.

It should be noted, however, that if real-world capital markets are semi-strong form efficient rather than strong form efficient, insider information may undermine the strength of the points made above. For example, a company which is valued fairly by the stock market may be undervalued or overvalued if private or insider information is taken into account.

ACCA marking scheme		Marks
(a)	Calculation of equity risk premium	1
	Calculation of cost of equity	1
	After-tax interest payment	1
	Setting up IRR calculation	1
	Calculating after-tax cost of debt	1
	Market value of equity	0.5
	Market value of debt	0.5
	Calculating WACC	1
	Maximum	**7**
(b)	Ungearing proxy company equity beta	2
	Regearing equity beta	1
	Calculation of cost of equity	1
	Maximum	**4**
(c)	Risk diversification	1–2
	Systematic risk	1–2
	Unsystematic risk	1–2
	Portfolio theory and the CAPM	1–2
	Maximum	**4**
(d)	Nature of capital market efficiency	1–2
	Significance of EMH for financial manager	2–3
	Maximum	**5**
		20

Examiner's comments

Part (a) of this question asked candidates to calculate the weighted average cost of capital of a company. Many answers gained very good marks here. Some candidates wrongly used the average return on the market (11%) as the equity or market risk premium in calculating the cost of equity using the capital asset pricing model (CAPM). More common were errors in calculating the after-tax cost of debt of the 7% bond, including:

– taking incorrect values from the discount and annuity tables

– using nominal value as market value

– using market value as nominal value

– calculating the after-tax interest payment with an incorrect corporation tax rate

– employing the before-tax interest payment in calculating the after-tax cost of debt

– making calculation errors when using the internal rate of return formula.

It should be mentioned that candidates, when calculating the after-tax cost of debt, should be seeking to make their answers reasonably accurate. Consequently, if the first estimate of the cost of debt produces a negative NPV when interpolating the internal rate of return, the second estimate of the cost of debt should be lower, as the first estimate was too high.

Choosing a higher rate rather than a lower rate indicates an intention to extrapolate rather than interpolate, and to seek inaccuracy rather than accuracy. Having a wide spread between the estimated costs of debt also increases inaccuracy, so choosing 1% and 20% indicates an unwillingness to think about what the value of the after-tax cost of debt might roughly be. A bond approximation model (correctly used) can provide an initial estimate of the cost of debt as a guide to selecting discount rates for linear interpolation.

Part (b) required candidates to calculate a project-specific cost of equity. First, the beta of a proxy company had to be ungeared to give an asset beta. Second, the asset beta had to be regeared to give a project-specific equity beta. Finally, the project-specific cost of equity could be calculated using the CAPM.

Many candidates gained very good marks here. One error that some candidates made was to omit the tax effect from the calculation, which was surprising, as the equation required was given in the formulae sheet.

Part (c) asked to explain the difference between systematic and unsystematic risk in relation to portfolio theory and the capital asset pricing model (CAPM). Many answers struggled to gain good marks, essentially due to a lack of knowledge.

Systematic risk cannot be reduced by portfolio diversification, while unsystematic risk can be reduced by portfolio diversification. Some candidates got this the wrong way round and said that systematic risk could be reduced by portfolio diversification.

Systematic risk includes both business risk and financial risk (as illustrated by the equity beta in the CAPM), however some candidates wrongly identified systematic risk with business risk and unsystematic risk with financial risk.

Investors can reduce risk by portfolio diversification and the CAPM assumes that investors have diversified portfolios, yet many answers suggested that companies should reduce unsystematic risk by diversifying business operations.

Some candidates discussed unnecessary material in their answers, for example the process whereby a proxy equity beta can be ungeared and regeared in calculating a project-specific cost of equity or a project-specific weighted average cost of capital.

36 RWF

Key answer tips

This is a very common style question and the open-ended nature of part (a) of the requirement will require a logical and methodical approach to ensure you capture all of the marks. Make sure you balance the calculation of ratios with a discussion of their meaning.

The highlighted words in the written sections are key phrases that markers are looking for.

(a)   **Impact on corporate objectives**

Financial gearing:

Current   50,000/90,000 = 55.5%

Proposed – Debt issue   (50,000 + 9,000)/(90,000 + 6,670) = 61.0%

Proposed – Rights issue   (50,000/(90,000 + 9,000 + 6,800) = 47.3%

Earnings per share:

Current $6.3m/12m = 52.5c

Proposed – debt issue $9.17m/12m = 76.4c

New shares to be issued if rights issue used – $9m/$6 = 1.5m

Proposed – rights issue $9.8/(12 + 1.5) = 72.6c

Impact on other key ratios

Required:

Operating gearing:

Using fixed costs/total costs:

Current   (9,000 + 16,000)/(32,000 + 9,000 + 16,000) = 43.9%

Proposed   (16,000 + 17,000)/(34,000 + 16,000 + 17,000) = 49.3%

This will be the same for either financing option.

The administration costs are assumed to be fixed in nature.

Tutorial note:

Credit will be given for a further 2 relevant ratios only. It is possible that students may have attempted other ratios than those shown below.

ROCE (based on opening capital employed):

Current   13,000/(90,000+50,000-4,300) = 9.58%

Proposed – Debt issue or rights issue   18,000/(90,000+50,000+9,000) = 12.08%

Interest cover:

Current   13,000/4,000 = 3.25 times

Proposed – Debt issue   18,000/4,900 = 3.67 times

Proposed – Rights issue   18,000/4,000 = 4.5 times

Comment

The financial gearing is currently within the target of 60% and will fall if a rights issue is made. However it will increase marginally above the 60% target if debt is raised. Furthermore at the start of the forecast period when the debt has been raised but no profits have yet been earned the gearing will be as high as (59,000/90,000) 65.6%.

The EPS will rise irrespective of the type of finance used. The greatest rise is if a debt issue is made. Whilst this is good for the shareholders they will of course be taking more financial risk than if a rights issue is used. The percentage rise in EPS is 46% if debt is raised and 38% if a rights issue is used. As both of these exceed the 5% inflation rate the company will achieve its target of providing real growth in EPS.

The operational gearing will rise as a result of undertaking the project. Hence the operational or business risk of the company will increase due to the company having a higher proportion of fixed costs. As a result of this the company may be wary of taking on more financial risk.

ROCE is an important performance measure which is often used by investors. The expansion project will significantly increase ROCE albeit from a rather low level.

If financial risk is measured by interest cover the situation improves if either a rights issue or the debt is used. This may suggest that the company could afford to take on more debt/financial risk.

In order to comment further it would be useful to know industry average data as considering RWF Co in isolation is of limited use.

Recommendation

In order to keep the financial gearing within the target set by the company and as a result of the expected increase in operating gearing I suggest that the new finance required is raised by means of a rights issue.

(b)   **Criticisms of the corporate objectives stated include:**

Although the objectives focus on two separate and critical areas of performance (profitability and gearing), they are both financial in nature. A company should set both financial and non-financial objectives.

Depending upon the industry average gearing or the optimal gearing for RWF Co the gearing objective may be inappropriate.

Only having two objectives could promote manipulation especially if the achievement of these objectives results in the payment of bonuses.

Neither objective will necessarily result in the company maximising the wealth of shareholders which should be the primary objective of a company.

Recommendations

It is recommended that RWF Co adopts the corporate objective of maximising shareholder wealth subject to satisficing other key stakeholders.

In order to ensure this objective is met the company should adopt a broad range of performance measures and these should be both financial and non-financial.

37   BAR CO

Key answer tips

This question presents a fairly unusual way of testing this syllabus area. The answers to parts (a) and (c) should be easily achieved. Part (b) however required a mix of both calculations and discussion, combined with a fair amount of forethought in order to answer the requirement. Students who struggle in this area should pay particular attention to the calculations shown in the marking guide that are necessary to generate a relevant discussion.

The highlighted words are key phrases that markers are looking for.

(a)   **Theoretical ex rights price**

Rights issue price = 7.50 × 0.8 = $6.00 per share

Number of shares issued = $90m/6.00 = 15 million shares Number of shares currently in issue = 60 million shares

The rights issue is on a 1 for 4 basis

Theoretical ex rights price = ((4 × 7.50) + (1 × 6.00))/5 = $7.20 per share

Alternatively, theoretical ex rights price = ((60m × 7.50) + (15m × 6.00))/75m = $7.20 per share, where 75 million is the number of shares after the rights issue.

(b)   **Financial acceptability to shareholders of buying back loan notes**

The financial acceptability to shareholders of the proposal to buy back loan notes can be assessed by calculating whether shareholder wealth is increased or decreased as a result.

The loan notes are being bought back by Bar Co at their market value of $112.50 per loan note, rather than their nominal value of $100 per loan note. The total nominal value of the loan notes redeemed will therefore be less than the $90 million spent redeeming them.

Nominal value of loan notes redeemed = 90m × (100/112.50) = $80 million

Interest saved by redeeming loan notes = 80m × 0.08 = $6.4 million per year

Earnings per share will be affected by the redemption of the loan notes and the issue of new shares.

Revised profit before tax = 49m − (10m − 6.4m) = $45.4 million

Revised profit after tax (earnings) = 45.4m × 0.7 = $31.78 million

Revised earnings per share = 100 × (31.78m/75m) = 42.37 cents per share

Current earnings per share = 100 × (27m/60m) = 45 cents per share

Current price/earnings ratio = 750/45 = 16.7 times

The revised earnings per share can be used to calculate a revised share price if the price/earnings ratio is assumed to be constant.

Revised share price = 16 – 7 × 42 – 37 = 708 cents or $7 – 08 per share

This share price is less than the theoretical ex rights price per share ($7.20) and so the effect of using the rights issue funds to redeem the loan notes is to decrease shareholder wealth. From a shareholder perspective, therefore, this use of the funds cannot be recommended.

However, this conclusion depends heavily on the assumption that the price/earnings ratio remains constant, as this ratio was used to calculate the revised share price from the revised earning per share. In reality, the share price after the redemption of loan notes will be set by the capital market and it is this market-determined share price that will determine the price/earnings ratio, rather than the price/earnings ratio determining the share price. Since the financial risk of Bar Co has decreased following the redemption of loan notes, the cost of equity is likely to fall and the share price is likely to rise, leading to a higher price/earnings ratio. If the share price increases to above the theoretical ex rights price per share, corresponding to an increase in the price/earnings ratio to more than 17 times (720/42.37), shareholders will experience a capital gain and so using the cash raised by the rights issue to buy back loan notes will become financially acceptable from their perspective.

(c) A key financial objective for a stock exchange listed company is to maximise the wealth of shareholders. This objective is usually replaced by the objective of maximising the company's share price, since maximising the market value of the company represents the maximum capital gain over a given period. The need for dividends can be met by recognising that share prices can be seen as the sum of the present values of future dividends.

Maximising the company's share price is the same as maximising the equity market value of the company, since equity market value (market capitalisation) is equal to number of issued shares multiplied by share price. Maximising equity market value can be achieved by maximising net corporate cash income and the expected growth in that income, while minimising the corporate cost of capital. Listed companies therefore have maximising net cash income as a key financial objective.

Not-for-profit (NFP) organisations seek to provide services to the public and this requires cash income. Maximising net cash income is therefore a key financial objective for NFP organisations as well as listed companies. A large charity seeks to raise as much funds as possible in order to achieve its charitable objectives, which are non-financial in nature.

Both listed companies and NFP organisations need to control the use of cash within a given financial period, and both types of organisations therefore use budgets. Another key financial objective for both organisations is therefore to keep spending within budget.

The objective of value for money (VFM) is often identified in connection with NFP organisations. This objective refers to a focus on economy, efficiency and effectiveness. These three terms can be linked to input (economy refers to securing resources as economically as possible), process (resources need to be employed efficiently within the organisation) and output (the effective use of resources in achieving the organisation's objectives).

Described in these terms, it is clear that a listed company also seeks to achieve value for money in its business operations. There is a difference in emphasis, however, which merits careful consideration. A listed company has a profit motive, and so VFM for a listed company can be related to performance measures linked to output, e.g. maximising the equity market value of the company. An NFP organisation has service-related outputs that are difficult to measure in quantitative terms and so it focuses on performance measures linked to input, e.g. minimising the input cost for a given level of output.

Both listed companies and NFP organisations can use a variety of accounting ratios in the context of financial objectives. For example, both types of organisation may use a target return on capital employed, or a target level of income per employee, or a target current ratio.

Comparing and contrasting the financial objectives of a stock exchange listed company and a not-for-profit organisation, therefore, shows that while significant differences can be found, there is a considerable amount of common ground in terms of financial objectives.

ACCA marking scheme		Marks
(a)	Rights issue price	1
	Theoretical ex rights price	2
	Maximum	3
(b)	Nominal value of bonds redeemed	1
	Interest saved on redeemed bonds	1
	Earnings per share after redemption	1
	Current price/earnings ratio	1
	Revised share price	1
	Comment on acceptability to shareholders	1–2
	Comment on constant price/earnings ratio	1–2
	Maximum	7
(d)	Maximising shareholder wealth	2–3
	Maximising cash income	2–3
	Controlling spending with budgets	2–3
	Value for money	2–3
	Other relevant discussion	2–3
	Maximum	10
		20

Examiner's comments

There were a number of points that could have been discussed, including the finance director's view that the dividend per share 'should be increased by 20% in order to make the company more attractive to equity investors'. Increases in dividends usually lag behind increases in earnings and depend on the dividend policy of a company. It is debatable whether increasing the dividend per share makes a company more attractive to investors. It could be argued, for example, that its existing dividend clientele are satisfied by its current dividend policy. It could also be argued that making a dividend decision without also considering investment and financing needs is foolish

Candidates were asked, in part (a) to calculate the theoretical ex rights price per share and most answers did this correctly.

Part (b) required candidates to calculate and discuss whether using the rights issue cash to buy back loan notes was acceptable to shareholders, commenting on the belief that the price/earnings ratio would remain constant.

Good answers calculated the current price/earnings ratio: the nominal value of the loan notes redeemed ($80 million); the nominal value of the loan notes remaining in the statement of financial position ($45 million); the reduction in the interest payable each year (down from $10 million to $3.6 million); the revised earnings and earnings per share values; and the revised share price (by multiplying the revised earnings per share by the current price/earnings ratio). The revised share price could then be compared with the theoretical ex rights price per share to assess the effect on shareholder wealth (a capital loss).

Answers lost marks to the extent that they did not achieve the elements described above. Answers that did not calculate the effect of redeeming $80 million of loan notes could discuss in general terms only whether buying back loan notes would be acceptable to shareholders. Many answers used the assumption of a constant price/earnings ratio, together with the theoretical ex rights price per share, to calculate implied earnings per share figure, but this serves no purpose and does not take account of buying back loan notes. Although the question said that the company planned to use the rights issue funds to pay off some of its debt, some answers assumed incorrectly that all of the loan notes were to be bought (using reserves to finance the difference, even though these are not cash).

Some answers calculated a revised price/earnings ratio using the theoretical ex rights price per share, but the statement that the price/earnings ratio was expected to remain constant meant that a revised share price could be calculated from the revised earnings per share. The theoretical ex rights price per share is the share price before the rights issue funds are used: once these funds are used, the share price will change, so the theoretical ex rights price per share cannot be used to calculate a revised price/earnings ratio.

Part (c) asked candidates to compare and contrast the financial objectives of a stock exchange listed company and a not-for-profit (NFP) organisation. In general, the answers to this part of question 4 were often quite weak. One reason for this is that many answers spent a lot of time discussing non-financial objectives, even though the question asked clearly for a discussion of financial objectives. A second reason for this is that many answered showed a general lack of awareness of financial objectives as such: some answers were not able to offer much more than shareholder wealth maximisation and increasing profit as financial objectives. A third reason is that some answers picked up on "compare and contrast" while ignoring financial objectives, and therefore offered a general comparison of the key features or decision areas of the two organisations. For example, the functional areas of the organisations might be compared and contrasted, or their stakeholders, or their personnel. This is not what the question was looking for..

38 NUGFER

Key answer tips

This question combines business finance with financial ratios, interest rates and market efficiency. It is an excellent example of the current examiner's style, especially part (a) where the requirement is deliberately left fairly open. The highlighted words are key phrases that markers are looking for.

(a)

Tutor's top tips

Before starting to answer this section you should think about what sources of finance you can think of, and what might be the deciding factors regarding whether they would be suitable or not. Key to this will be the current financial position of the company (existing gearing levels in particular) and how the company has performed recently. Take your steer from the information provided in the scenario – for every item consider why the examiner might have told you that, and how you can use this in your answer.

Nugfer Co is looking to raise $200m in cash in order to acquire a competitor. Any recommendation as to the source of finance to be used by the company must take account of the recent financial performance of the company, its current financial position and its expected financial performance in the future, presumably after the acquisition has occurred.

Recent financial performance

The recent financial performance of Nugfer Co will be taken into account by potential providers of finance because it will help them to form an opinion as to the quality of the management running the company and the financial problems the company may be facing. Analysis of the recent performance of Nugfer Co gives the following information:

Year	2007	2008	2009	2010
Operating profit	$41.7m	$43.3m	$50.1m	$56.7m
Net profit margin	34%	34%	32%	30%
Interest coverage ratio	7 times	7 times	4 times	3 times
Revenue growth		3.8%	23.0%	20.9%
Operating profit growth		3.8%	15.7%	13.2%
Finance charges growth		3.3%	101.6%	50.4%
Profit after tax growth		4.0%	1.2%	0.8%

Geometric average growth in turnover = $(189.3/122.6)^{0.33} - 1 = 15.6\%$

Geometric average operating profit growth = $(56.7/41.7)^{0.33} - 1 = 10.8\%$

One positive feature indicated by this analysis is the growth in revenue, which grew by 23% in 2009 and by 21% in 2010. Slightly less positive is the growth in operating profit, which was 16% in 2009 and 13% in 2010. Both years were significantly better in revenue growth and operating profit growth than 2008. One query here is why growth in operating profit is so much lower than growth in revenue. Better control of operating and other costs might improve operating profit substantially and decrease the financial risk of Nugfer Co.

The growing financial risk of the company is a clear cause for concern. The interest coverage ratio has declined each year in the period under review and has reached a dangerous level in 2010. The increase in operating profit each year has clearly been less than the increase in finance charges, which have tripled over the period under review. The reason for the large increase in debt is not known, but the high level of financial risk must be considered in selecting an appropriate source of finance to provide the $200m in cash that is needed.

Current financial position

The current financial position of Nugfer Co will be considered by potential providers of finance in their assessment of the financial risk of the company. Analysis of the current financial position of Nugfer Co shows the following:

Debt/equity ratio = long-term debt/total equity = $100 \times (100/221)$ = 45%

Debt equity/ratio including short-term borrowings = $100 \times ((100 + 160)/221)$ = 118%

The debt/equity ratio based on long-term debt is not particularly high. However, the interest coverage ratio indicated a high level of financial risk and it is clear from the financial position statement that the short-term borrowings of $160m are greater than the long-term borrowings of $100m. In fact, short-term borrowings account for 62% of the debt burden of Nugfer Co. If we include the short-term borrowings, the debt/equity ratio increases to 118%, which is certainly high enough to be a cause for concern. The short-term borrowings are also at a higher interest rate (8%) than the long-term borrowings (6%) and as a result, interest on short-term borrowings account for 68% of the finance charges in the statement of profit or loss.

It should also be noted that the long-term borrowings are bonds that are repayable in 2012. Nugfer Co needs therefore to plan for the redemption and refinancing of $100m of debt in two years' time, a factor that cannot be ignored when selecting a suitable source of finance to provide the $200m of cash needed.

Recommendation of suitable financing method

There are strong indications that it would be unwise for Nugfer Co to raise the $200m of cash required by means of debt finance, for example the low interest coverage ratio and the high level of gearing.

If no further debt is raised, the interest coverage ratio would improve after the acquisition due to the increased level of operating profit, i.e. $(56.7m + 28m)/18.8$ = 4.5 times. Assuming that $200m of 8% debt is raised, the interest coverage ratio would fall to $(84.7/(18.8 + 16))$ = 2.4 times and the debt/equity ratio would increase to $100 \times (260 + 200)/221$ = 208%.

If convertible debt were used, the increase in gearing and the decrease in interest coverage would continue only until conversion occurred, assuming that the company's share price increased sufficiently for conversion to be attractive to bondholders. Once conversion occurred, the debt capacity of the company would increase due both to the liquidation of the convertible debt and to the issuing of new ordinary shares to bond holders. In the period until conversion, however, the financial risk of the company as measured by gearing and interest coverage would remain at a very high level.

If Nugfer Co were able to use equity finance, the interest coverage ratio would increase to 4.5 times and the debt/equity ratio would fall to $100 \times (260/(221 + 200))$ = 62%. Although the debt/equity ratio is still on the high side, this would fall if some of the short-term borrowings were able to be paid off, although the recent financial performance of Nugfer Co indicates that this may not be easy to do. The problem of redeeming the current long-term bonds in two years also remains to be solved.

However, since the company has not paid any dividend for at least four years, it is unlikely that current shareholders would be receptive to a rights issue, unless they were persuaded that dividends would be forthcoming in the near future. Acquisition of the competitor may be the only way of generating the cash flows needed to support dividend payments.

A similar negative view could be taken by new shareholders if Nugfer Co were to seek to raise equity finance via a placing or a public issue.

Sale and leaseback of non-current assets could be considered, although the nature and quality of the non-current assets is not known. The financial position statement indicates that Nugfer Co has $300m of non-current assets, $100m of long-term borrowings and $160m of short-term borrowings. Since its borrowings are likely to be secured on some of the existing non-current assets, there appears to be limited scope for sale and leaseback.

Venture capital could also be considered, but it is unlikely that such finance would be available for an acquisition and no business case has been provided for the proposed acquisition.

While combinations of finance could also be proposed, the overall impression is that Nugfer Co is in poor financial health and, despite its best efforts, it may not be able to raise the $200m in cash that it needs to acquire its competitor.

(b)   When a new issue of bonds is made by a company, the interest rate on the bonds will be influenced by factors that are specific to the company, and by factors that relate to the economic environment as a whole.

Company-specific factors

The interest rate charged on a new issue of bonds will depend upon such factors as the risk associated with the company and any security offered.

The risk associated with the company will be assessed by considering the ability of the company to meet interest payments in the future, and hence its future cash flows and profitability, as well as its ability to redeem the bond issue on maturity.

Where an issue of new bonds is backed by security, the interest rate charged on the issue will be lower than for an unsecured bond issue. A bond issue will be secured on specific non-current assets such as land or buildings, and as such is referred to as a fixed-charge security.

Economic environment factors

As far as the duration of a new issue of bonds is concerned, the term structure of interest rates suggests that short-term debt is usually cheaper than long-term debt, so that the yield curve slopes upwards with increasing term to maturity. The longer the duration of an issue of new bonds, therefore, the higher will be the interest rate charged. The shape of the yield curve, which can be explained by reference to liquidity preference theory, expectations theory and market segmentation theory, will be independent of any specific company.

The rate of interest charged on a new issue of bonds will also depend on the general level of interest rates in the financial system. This is influenced by the general level of economic activity in a given country, such as whether the economy is in recession (when interest rates tend to fall) or experiencing rapid economic growth (when interest rates are rising as capital availability is decreasing). The general level of interest rates is also influenced by monetary policy decisions taken by the government or the central bank. For example, interest rates may be increased in order to exert downward pressure on demand and hence decrease inflationary pressures in an economy.

Tutorial note

The above answer is longer than would be expected from a candidate under examination conditions.

	ACCA marking scheme		
			Marks
(a)	Analysis of recent financial performance		1–3
	Discussion of recent financial performance		1–3
	Analysis of current financial position		1–3
	Discussion of current financial position		1–2
	Consideration of suitable sources of finance		4–6
	Recommendation of suitable source of finance		1
		Maximum	16
(b)	Company-specific factors		2–3
	Economic environment factors		2–3
		Maximum	4
Total			25

Examiner's comments

Many students gained good marks on part (b) of this question, while not doing very well on part (a).

In part (a) of this question, candidates were provided with financial information for a company and asked to evaluate suitable methods for it to raise $200 million, using both analysis and critical discussion. Many answers struggled to gain good marks for reasons such as poor understanding of sources of finance, a lack of analysis or errors in analysis, misunderstanding of the financial position and performance of the company, and a shortage of discussion.

The question said that the current assets of the company did not include any cash, but many answers suggested that $121 million of the $200 million needed could be provided from $121 million of retained earnings in the statement of financial position. As the company had no cash, this was of course not possible and shows a misunderstanding of the nature of retained earnings.

Some answers suggested asking the bank to increase the $160 million overdraft to $360 million in order to provide the finance for the $200 million acquisition. Since the acquisition was a long-term investment, short term finance could not be used under the matching principle. Suggestions of using lease finance were also not appropriate, although discussion of the sale and leaseback of the company's non-current assets was relevant. Some answers discussed business angels, government grants and venture capital, but these sources of finance are not relevant to a $200 million acquisition.

Analysis of the financial information given in the question was needed to support any critical discussion of ways of raising the $200 million required. Some answers gave no analysis or very little analysis and so were quite general in nature, outlining for example the differences between equity finance and debt finance. Errors in ratio calculations were common, highlighting the need for candidates to understand accounting ratio definitions. Four years of profitability information was provided, allowing trends and growth rates to be calculated, although some answers considered only information from the first year and the last year. The information, when analysed, gave a very gloomy picture and indicated that the company would have difficulty raising the cash it needed, whether from debt finance or equity finance. Taking on more debt would cause gearing, interest cover and financial risk to rise to dangerous levels, while existing and potential shareholders would not look favourably on a company that had not paid dividends for four years, especially one whose growth in profitability was on a downward trend.

Part (b) asked candidates to briefly explain the factors that influence the interest rate charged on a new issue of bonds, i.e. traded debt. Good answers discussed such factors as the period to redemption, the risk of the issuing company, the general level of interest rates in the economy, expectations of future inflation, redemption value and so on, and easily gained full marks. Poorer answers did not show understanding of the relationship for a bond between market value, interest rate, period to redemption, redemption value and cost of debt.

39   SPOT CO

Key answer tips

Students should be well equipped with the tools required for the evaluation in part (a). Care needs to be taken when choosing relevant numbers from the scenario to use in the **Workings**.

Part (b) should provide some easy marks for straight forward knowledge on this relatively new part of the syllabus.

(a)   In order to evaluate whether Spot Co should use leasing or borrowing, the present value of the cost of leasing is compared with the present value of the cost of borrowing.

Leasing

The lease payments should be discounted using the cost of borrowing of Spot Co. Since taxation must be ignored, the before-tax cost of borrowing must be used. The 7% interest rate of the bank loan can be used here.

The five lease payments will begin at year 0 and the last lease payment will be at the start of year 5, i.e. at the end of year 4. The appropriate annuity factor to use will therefore be 4.387 (1.000 + 3.387).

Present value of cost of leasing = 155,000 × 4.387= $679,985

Borrowing

The purchase cost and the present value of maintenance payments will be offset by the present value of the future scrap value. The appropriate discount rate is again the before-tax cost of borrowing of 7%.

Year	Cash flow	$	7% Discount factor	Present value ($)
0	Purchase	(750,000)	1.000	(750,000)
1 – 5	Maintenance	(20,000)	4.100	(82,000)
5	Scrap value	75,000	0.713	53,475

Present value of cost of borrowing = 750,000 + 82,000 – 53,475 = $778,525

The cheaper source of financing is leasing, since the present value of the cost of leasing is $98,540 less than the present value of the cost of borrowing.

(b)   Operating leasing can act as a source of short-term finance, while finance leasing can act as a source of long-term finance.

Operating leasing offers a solution to the obsolescence problem, whereby rapidly aging assets can decrease competitive advantage. Where keeping up-to-date with the latest technology is essential for business operations, operating leasing provides equipment on short-term contracts which can usually be cancelled without penalty to the lessee. Operating leasing can also provide access to skilled maintenance, which might otherwise need to be bought in by the lessee, although there will be a charge for this service.

Both operating leasing and finance leasing provide access to non-current assets in cases where borrowing may be difficult or even not possible for a company. For example, the company may lack assets to offer as security, or it may be seen as too risky to lend to. Since ownership of the leased asset remains with the lessor, it can be retrieved if lease rental payments are not forthcoming.

(c)   Interest (riba) is the predetermined amount received by a provider of finance, over and above the principal amount of finance provided. Riba is absolutely forbidden in Islamic finance. Riba can be seen as unfair from the perspective of the borrower, the lender and the economy. For the borrower, riba can turn a profit into a loss when profitability is low. For the lender, riba can provide an inadequate return when unanticipated inflation arises. In the economy, riba can lead to allocational inefficiency, directing economic resources to sub-optimal investments.

Islamic financial instruments require that an active role be played by the provider of funds, so that the risks and rewards of ownership are shared. In a Mudaraba contract, for example, profits are shared between the partners in the proportions agreed in the contract, while losses are borne by the provider of finance. In a Musharaka contract, profits are shared between the partners in the proportions agreed in the contract, while losses are shared between the partners according to their capital contributions. With Sukuk, certificates are issued which are linked to an underlying tangible asset and which also transfer the risk and rewards of ownership. The underlying asset is managed on behalf of the Sukuk holders.

In a Murabaha contract, payment by the buyer is made on a deferred or instalment basis. Returns are made by the supplier as a mark-up is paid by the buyer in exchange for the right to pay after the delivery date. In an Ijara contract, which is equivalent to a lease agreement, returns are made through the payment of fixed or variable lease rental payments.

ACCA marking scheme

		Marks
(a)	Timing of lease payments	1
	Present value of cost of leasing	1
	Present value of maintenance costs	1
	Present value of salvage value	1
	Present value of cost of borrowing	2
	Evaluation of financing choice	1
	Explanation of evaluation of financing method	3
	Maximum	10
(b)	Attractions of leasing as short-term finance source	2–3
	Attractions of leasing as long-term finance source	2–3
	Maximum	5
(c)	Explanation of interest (riba)	1–2
	Explanation of returns on Islamic financial instruments	3–4
	Maximum	5
Total		20

40   ECHO CO *Walk in the footsteps of a top tutor*

Key answer tips

The key learning points from this question are the benefits of answering requirements in an order that best suits you as well as the need to take guidance from the specific words used in both the scenario and the requirement itself. The highlighted words are key phrases that markers are looking for.

Tutor's top tips:

Start by reading the requirement. Having a good understanding of what is expected from you will allow you to read the scenario more effectively, processing the information as you go. Scribble you thoughts in the margins on what each piece of information could be used for in relation to the requirements.

The first thing that should strike you is this question has 4, very independent requirements. This means you can pick the order in which to tackle them to suit your strengths. For the majority, part (d) should be attempted first. The question is very generic and requires little more than regurgitation of knowledge from the syllabus.

Of the remaining three parts, part (c) has the most guidance on the structure and content of your answer. These therefore represent the easiest of the remaining marks. The layout of the scenario means you can immediately re-read the information on proposal C and then consider what additional information you will need.

Tutor's top tips:

The slightly different requirements in part (a) and part (b) is reflected in the mark allocation. In part (a) the requirement is to 'analyse' and 'discuss' compared to 'evaluate' and 'discuss' in part (b). Part (b) will therefore require some further calculations.

In part (a) you need to link back to the scenario where we're told the aim of proposal A is to make the company more attractive to equity investors. A sensible approach is to consider what makes a share attractive. You should immediately highlight the dividend payment, discussion of which would lead on to Modigliani & Miller's theories on dividend policy and efficient markets hypothesis.

(a)   Echo Co paid a total dividend of $2 million or 20c per share according to the statement of profit or loss information. An increase of 20% would make this $2.4 million or 24c per share and would reduce dividend cover from 3 times to 2.5 times. It is debatable whether this increase in the current dividend would make the company more attractive to equity investors, who use a variety of factors to inform their investment decisions, not expected dividends alone. For example, they will consider the business and financial risk associated with a company when deciding on their required rate of return.

It is also unclear what objective the finance director had in mind when suggesting a dividend increase. The primary financial management objective is the maximisation of shareholder wealth and if Echo Co is following this objective, the dividend will already be set at an optimal level. From this perspective, a dividend increase should arise from increased maintainable profitability, not from a desire to 'make the company more attractive'. Increasing the dividend will not generate any additional capital for Echo Co, since existing shares are traded on the secondary market.

Furthermore, Miller and Modigliani have shown that, in a perfect capital market, share prices are independent of the level of dividend paid. The value of the company depends upon its income from operations and not on the amount of this income which is paid out as dividends. Increasing the dividend would not make the company more attractive to equity investors, but would attract equity investors who desired the new level of dividend being offered. Current shareholders who were satisfied by the current dividend policy could transfer their investment to a different company if their utility had been decreased.

The proposal to increase the dividend should therefore be rejected, perhaps in favour of a dividend increase in line with current dividend policy.

Tutor's top tips:

In part (b), the scenario directs us towards the differences between short term and long term interest rates. As in part (c) the impact on gearing and interest cover can be highlighted and the lack of any investment opportunity should by highlighted as a problem.

(b)   The proposal to raise $15 million of additional debt finance does not appear to be a sensible one, given the current financial position of Echo Co. The company is very highly geared if financial gearing measured on a book value basis is considered. The debt/equity ratio of 150% is almost twice the average of companies similar to Echo Co. This negative view of the financial risk of the company is reinforced by the interest coverage ratio, which at only four times is half that of companies similar to Echo Co.

Raising additional debt would only worsen these indicators of financial risk. The debt/equity ratio would rise to 225% on a book value basis and the interest coverage ratio would fall to 2.7 times, suggesting that Echo Co would experience difficulty in making interest payments.

The proposed use to which the newly-raised funds would be put merits further investigation. Additional finance should be raised when it is needed, rather than being held for speculative purposes. Until a suitable investment opportunity comes along, Echo Co will be paying an opportunity cost on the new finance equal to the difference between the interest rate on the new debt (10%) and the interest paid on short-term investments. This opportunity cost would decrease shareholder wealth. Even if an investment opportunity arises, it is very unlikely that the funds needed would be exactly equal to $15m.

The interest charge in the statement of profit or loss information is $3m while the interest payable on the 8% loan notes is $2.4m (30 × 0.08). It is reasonable to assume that $0.6m of interest is due to an overdraft. Assuming a short-term interest rate lower than the 8% loan note rate – say 6% – implies an overdraft of approximately $10m (0.6/0.06), which is one-third of the amount of the long-term debt. The debt/equity ratio calculated did not include this significant amount of short-term debt and therefore underestimates the financial risk of Echo Co.

The bond issue would be repayable in eight years' time, which is five years after the redemption date of the current loan note issue. The need to redeem the current $30m loan note issue cannot be ignored in the financial planning of the company. The proposal to raise £15m of long-term debt finance should arise from a considered strategic review of the long-term and short-term financing needs of Echo Co, which must also consider redemption or refinancing of the current loan note issue and, perhaps, reduction of the sizeable overdraft, which may be close to, or in excess of, its agreed limit.

In light of the concerns and considerations discussed, the proposal to raise additional debt finance cannot be recommended.

Analysis

Current gearing (debt/equity ratio using book values) = 30/20 = 150%

Revised gearing (debt/equity ratio using book values) = (30 + 15)/20 = 225%

Current interest coverage ratio = 12/3 = 4 times

Additional interest following debt issue = 14m × 0.1 = $1.5m

Revised interest coverage ratio = 12/(3 + 1.5) = 2.7 times

Tutorial note:

The industry gearing has been calculated as debt / equity. You must ensure your calculation is consistent with this otherwise an effective comparison could not be made.

Tutor's top tips:

To calculate the theoretical ex-rights price (TERP), you will need the current share price, the subscription price and the basis of the issue. All are contained in the paragraph labelled 'Proposal C'. To calculate the amount of finance that would be raised, you also need to know the number of shares to be issued. This can be worked out based on the current number of shares in issue given in the Statement of financial position information. Be careful to read this carefully. There is $5m of share capital but as the nominal value of each share is 50c, this means there are 10m in issue.

Both of these are simple calculations and will most likely attract 1 mark each. This therefore leaves 5 marks for your evaluation and discussion of the proposal.

A requirement to 'evaluate' implies some further calculations will be needed, this time relating to gearing and financial risk. Start by reviewing the information given in the scenario and consider what calculations would be both possible and useful. You should identify:

— *Gearing calculations. Whilst you have market values for equity, you only have the book value of debt. To be consistent you should therefore use book values of both to calculate gearing. In order to discuss the proposal, you will need to know the existing gearing and the new gearing under the proposal. Both can be usefully compared to the industry average.*

— *You have also been provided with average data on interest cover. This signals that calculation of current and projected interest cover will be a source of further marks. Some further calculations need to be done by assuming the proceeds from the rights issue are able to earn the same rate of return as existing funds. This will therefore give an estimate of the new level of profitability. These calculations might not seem obvious and are not essential to passing the question.*

When discussing the impact of the proposal on gearing and financial risk it is essential to highlight that there doesn't appear to be a need to raise this finance as there is no plan on how it will be spent.

(c) **Analysis**

Rights issue price = 2.30 × 0.8 = $1.84

Theoretical ex rights price = (1.84 + (2.30 × 4))/5 = $2.21 per share

Number of new shares issued = (5/0.5)/4 = 2.5 million

Cash raised = 1.84 × 2.5m = $4.6 million

Number of shares in issue after rights issue = 10 + 2.5 = 12.5 million

Current gearing (debt/equity ratio using book values) = 30/20 = 150%

Revised gearing (debt/equity ratio using book values) = 30/24.6 = 122%

Current interest coverage ratio = 12/3 = 4 times

Current return on equity (ROE) = 6/20 = 30%

In the absence of any indication as to the return expected on the new funds, we can assume the rate of return will be the same as on existing equity, an assumption consistent with the calculated theoretical ex rights price. After-tax return on the new funds = 4.6m × 0.3 = $1.38 million Before-tax return on new funds = 1.38m × (9/6) = $2.07 million Revised interest coverage ratio = (12 + 2.07)/3 = 4.7 times

The current debt/equity and interest coverage ratios suggest that there is a need to reduce the financial risk of Echo Co. A rights issue would reduce the debt/equity ratio of the company from 150% to 122% on a book value basis, which is 50% higher than the average debt/equity ratio of similar companies. After the rights issue, financial gearing is still therefore high enough to be a cause for concern.

The interest coverage ratio would increase from 4 times to 4.7 times, again assuming that the new funds will earn the same return as existing equity funds. This is still much lower than the average interest coverage ratio of similar companies, which is 8 times. While 4.7 times is a safer level of interest coverage, it is still somewhat on the low side.

No explanation has been offered for the amount to be raised by the rights issue. Why has the Finance Director proposed that $4.6m be raised? If the proposal is to reduce financial risk, what level of financial gearing and interest coverage would be seen as safe by shareholders and other stakeholders? What use would be made of the funds raised? If they are used to redeem debt they will not have a great impact on the financial position of the company, in fact it appears likely that the overdraft is twice as big as the amount proposed to be raised by the rights issue. The refinancing need therefore appears to be much greater than $4.6m. If the funds are to be used for investment purposes, further details of the investment project, its expected return and its level of risk should be considered.

There seems to be no convincing rationale for the proposed rights issue and it cannot therefore be recommended, at least on financial grounds.

ACCA marking scheme		Marks
(a)	Discussion of proposal to increase dividend	
		5
(b)	Evaluation of debt finance proposal	3–4
	Discussion of debt finance proposal	4–5
		8
(c)	Theoretical ex rights price per share	1
	Amount of finance raised	1
	Evaluation of rights issue proposal	2–3
	Discussion of rights issue proposal	3–4
		7
Total		25

Examiner's comments

Part (a) asked candidates to analyse and discuss a proposal to increase dividend per share. Many candidates calculated correctly the increased dividend per share and then offered very little by way of discussion in order to gain any further marks.

There were a number of points that could have been discussed, including the finance director's view that the dividend per share 'should be increased by 20% in order to make the company more attractive to equity investors'. Increases in dividends usually lag behind increases in earnings and depend on the dividend policy of a company. It is debatable whether increasing the dividend per share makes a company more attractive to investors. It could be argued, for example, that its existing dividend clientele are satisfied by its current dividend policy. It could also be argued that making a dividend decision without also considering investment and financing needs is foolish: paying an increased dividend and then borrowing to meet investment plans is not advisable for a company as highly geared as the one under consideration here. Other points are discussed in the suggested answer to this question.

Part (b) asked for evaluation and discussion of a proposal to make a $15m bond issue and to invest the funds raised on a short-term basis until a suitable investment opportunity arose.

Candidates were expected to be aware that finance should be raised in order to meet a specific need and that investing long-term funds on a short-term basis would incur an unnecessary net interest cost. In this case, a highly-geared company would be choosing to increase its gearing and financial risk, without the prospect of investing the funds in a project offering returns greater than the increased financing cost.

The sector average debt/equity ratio (D/E) was provided, but many candidates chose to calculate capital gearing (D/(D + E)) in the mistaken belief that this was the debt to equity ratio. Comparison with the sector average gearing was therefore pointless, since the gearing ratios were on a different basis. Some candidates also calculated incorrectly the interest coverage, dividing interest into profit before tax or profit after tax, rather than into profit before interest and tax.

There were some lucid discussions of the dangers attached to the proposal to make a bond issue and these gained high marks.

It was surprising to see many candidates attempting to calculate the cost of debt (internal rate of return) of the bond issue. The bonds were to be issued and redeemed at par and so their cost of debt was the same as their interest rate, as these unnecessary calculations confirmed (where they were made correctly).

In part (c), candidates were asked to calculate the theoretical ex rights price per share and the amount of finance to be raised by a proposed rights issue, which was intended to reduce gearing and financial risk.

Many candidates were able to calculate the theoretical ex rights price and the finance raised, and went on to calculate the effect of the rights issue on the gearing of the company. Some candidates mistakenly assumed that the proceeds of the right issue would be used to redeem some of the existing debt, but the question did not specify this and in practice this might not be possible. Very few candidates recognised that, just as with the proposal to make a bond issue, there had been no evaluation of the funding needs of the company. Why raise $4.6m? Why not $10m? What were the rights issue funds going to be used for? A more concrete plan than raising cash to reduce gearing was needed if shareholder wealth was going to be maximised.

41 ZIGTO CO (JUNE 2012 - MODIFIED)

Key answer tips

This question presents an opportunity to gain some easy marks, provided that , in part (a), you focus on "the factors to be considered", such as interest rate, security, maturity, risk, profitability and so on, and do not focus instead on the different sources of finance. Similarly part (b) should bring out some fairly straight forward knowledge on this relatively new part of the syllabus.

The highlighted words are key phrases that markers are looking for.

(a)   **Factors to consider when choosing a source of debt finance:**

There are a number of factors that should be considered when choosing a suitable source of debt finance. Essentially a company should look to match the characteristics of the debt finance with its corporate needs.

Cost

Zigto Co should consider both issue costs and the rate of interest to be charged on the funds borrowed. The company should also consider the repayment terms. With a bank loan, for example, there may be an annual capital payment in addition to the annual interest payment. Additionally, some types of debt have early repayment penalties.

Maturity

The period over which the debt is taken should be matched against the period for which the company needs the finance and the ability of the company to meet the financial commitments associated with the debt finance selected. Another factor to consider is that short-term finance can be more flexible than long-term finance. If a company takes on long-term debt finance it takes on a long-term commitment to which it has a contractual obligation.

Financial risk

Debt will increase gearing and hence the financial risk of Zigto Co. The company should consider how gearing will change over the life of the debt finance selected and how the company will be viewed from a risk perspective by future investors.

Availability

The kinds of debt finance available to Zigto Co will depend upon the relative size of the company, its relationship with its bank and the capital markets to which it has access. It is likely that a bank loan, rather than any other kind of debt finance, will be selected by Zigto Co, since very few SMEs are able to issue traded loan notes.

Factors to be considered by providers of finance:

There are a number of factors that may be considered by providers of finance in deciding how much to lend to a company.

Risk and the ability to meet financial obligations

When considering the amount and the terms of the funds to be made available to Zigto Co, providers of debt finance will assess the ability of the company to meets its future financial obligations and the risk of the company. The previous record of the company can be used as a guide to the ability of its board of directors to manage its finances in a responsible and effective manner. The business plan of Zigto Co relating to the proposed business expansion will be carefully scrutinised by potential investors in order to make sure that it rests on reasonable assumptions and that the forecast cash flows can be achieved. This helps to reduce the uncertainty associated with the proposed expansion.

Security

The amount of funds made available to Zigto Co will also depend on the availability of assets to offer as security. Debt investors will expect security in order to reduce the risk of the investment from their point of view. If security is not available or is limited, Zigto Co will have to pay a higher rate of interest in compensation for the higher level of risk.

Legal restrictions on borrowing

Another factor to consider is whether there are any legal restrictions on the amount of debt that the company can take on, for example in existing debt contracts (restrictive or negative covenants), or in the company's memorandum or articles of association.

(b)   One central principle of Islamic finance is that making money out of money is not acceptable, i.e. interest is prohibited. A mudaraba contract, in Islamic finance, is a partnership between one party that brings finance or capital into the contract and another party that brings business expertise and personal effort into the contract. The first party is called the owner of capital, while the second party is called the agent, who runs or manages the business. The mudaraba contract specifies how profit from the business is shared proportionately between the two parties. Any loss, however, is borne by the owner of capital, and not by the agent managing the business. It can therefore be seen that three key characteristics of a mudaraba contract are that no interest is paid, that profits are shared, and that losses are not shared.

If Zigto Co were to decide to seek Islamic finance for the planned business expansion and if the company were to enter into a mudaraba contract, the company would therefore be entering into a partnership as an agent, managing the business and sharing profits with the Islamic bank that provided the finance and which was acting as the owner of capital. The Islamic bank would not interfere in the management of the business and this is what would be expected if Zigto Co were to finance the business expansion using debt such as a bank loan. However, while interest on debt is likely to be at a fixed rate, the mudaraba contract would require a sharing of profit in the agreed proportions.

(c)   **Forward exchange contract**

Zigto Co needs to use the six-month forward exchange rate to hedge its six-month euro receipt.

Dollar value in six months' time = 500,000/1.990 = $251,256

Money market hedge

The six-month euro receipt is a future asset and needs to be hedged by a future euro liability. Zigto Co needs to borrow sufficient euros now so that in six months' time the debt is equal to €500,000. The six month euro borrowing rate is 2.5% (5%/2).

Euros borrowed now = 500,000/1.025 = €487,805

Dollar value of this euro debt = 487,805/2.000 = $243,903

The six-month dollar deposit rate is 2% (4%/2)

Future value of these dollars placed on deposit = 243,903 × 1.02 = $248,781

The forward contract gives the higher value and hence is preferred to the money market hedge.

(d)   **Expected (future) spot exchange rate**

Using purchasing power parity, the expected (future) spot exchange rate can be calculated from the relative inflation rates, i.e. expected spot rate = 2.00 × (1.03/1.045) = €1.971 per $. The change in the spot rate over time can therefore, according to purchasing power parity, be related to relative inflation rates. This expected spot rate can be compared with the current twelve-month forward rate of €1.981 per $

Relationship between the expected (future) spot rate and the current forward rate

The twelve-month forward exchange rate is a rate currently offered in the forward exchange market and a company can lock into this rate using a forward exchange contract. Forward rates are set using interest rate parity, i.e. by relative interest rates between two countries.

If there were equilibrium between relative inflation rates and relative interest rates between two countries, the expected spot rate and the current forward rate would be the same. This is referred to as expectations theory. In practice, purchasing power parity tends to hold over long periods of time, and the existence of short-term disequilibrium leading to a difference between the expected spot rate and the current forward rate is not unusual.

ACCA marking scheme		
		Marks
(a)	Factors to consider when choosing source of debt	4–5
	Factors considered by providers of finance	4–5
	Maximum	7
(b)	Nature of a murdaraba contract	3
	Financing business expansion using murdaraba	2
		5

(c)	Calculated value of a forward exchange contract		1
	Calculated value of a money market hedge		3
	Comment on hedge to select		1
		Maximum	5
d)	Calculation of one-year future spot rate		1
	Link between future spot rate and forward rate		2
		Maximum	3
Total			**20**

42 PAVLON

Key answer tips

This is a difficult question that requires some imaginative thinking in order to tackle efficiently. The idea of calculating the dividend payout ratio for part (a) is one which seems logical when you review the answer but might not necessarily have occurred to you when attempting the question under timed conditions.

Part (b) is a more clear cut application of the dividend valuation model with the change in growth rate being the only complication. The highlighted words are key phrases that markers are looking for.

(a) (i) The first step is to try to determine exactly what is Pavlon's current dividend policy.

Year prior to listing	Number of shares	EPS	Growth over previous year	Dividend per share	Payout ratio
5	21,333,333	8.44¢	–	3.6¢	42.7%
4	21,333,333 (Note 2)	11.25¢	33%	4.8¢	42.7%
3	26,666,667	14.44¢	28%	6.16¢	42.7%
2	26,666,667	15.38¢	6%	6.56¢	42.7%
1	26,666,667 (Note 1)	16.69¢	8.5%	7.12¢	42.7%
Current	40,000,000	13.75¢ (est)	-18%	5.5¢ (proposed)	40%

Note 1 $\dfrac{40,000,000}{1.5} = 26,666,667$

Note 2 $\dfrac{26,666,667}{1.25} = 21,333,333$

Pavlon appears to be adopting a policy of a fixed payout ratio of 42.7% pa over the five year period. In general such a policy can lead to wide variations in dividends per share. In Pavlon's case over the last five years earnings have been rising and a continual (though declining) growth in dividend has resulted.

If it is believed that share price is affected by dividend policy then these fluctuations in dividends and the decline in growth could depress equity value.

Most listed companies attempt to adopt a stable or rising level of dividend per share even in the face of fluctuating earnings. This approach is taken in order to maintain investor confidence. If Pavlon were to continue with its present policy and earnings were to decline the resultant dividend could have serious repercussions for share price.

(ii) The proposed final dividend gives a total for the year of 5.5¢. This is a significant fall in dividend per share and a small decline in the dividend payout ratio. In the absence of market imperfections such as taxation and transaction costs, it could be argued that dividend policy has no impact on shareholder wealth. It is the firm's future earnings stream that is of importance, not the way in which it is split between dividend and retentions.

However, once market imperfections are introduced dividend policy can be shown to have an impact on investor wealth.

Private individuals may pay income tax at a higher rate than capital gains tax due to available CGT annual exemptions. They would therefore prefer retentions to distributions. Any income required could be generated by selling shares to manufacture 'home made' dividends (note however the problem of transaction costs).

If the reduction in dividend payout were carefully explained it might therefore be acceptable to wealthy individuals.

The tax position of institutional shareholders varies and so therefore will their attitude to dividend policy. Most, however, require a steady flow of income to meet their day-to-day obligations (pensions, insurance claims etc) and may not wish (or be able) to generate homemade dividends.

It could be argued that new investors have bought shares in Pavlon with full knowledge of its dividend policy and should therefore not be surprised if it sticks to a policy of a 40% payout. However, many shareholders might expect it to change its policy now that it has obtained a listing.

A further factor to consider is the informational content of dividends. The proposed dividend cut might be seen as a signal of poor earnings in the future and lead to investors of either group selling shares.

Overall there is no conclusive evidence on what makes for an optimal dividend policy. Pavlon should however consider the tax position of its investors and the potential reaction of the market to a cut in dividend.

(b) If the company's profits and dividends are expected to increase initially by 15% pa then investors will expect this year's dividend to be 7.12¢ × 1.15 = 8.188¢

Value of first three years' dividend

Year	Dividend			PV factor 12%	Present value
Current	7.12 × 1.15	=	8.188	0.893	7.312
2	8.188 × 1.15	=	9.416	0.797	7.505
3	9.416 × 1.15	=	10.829	0.712	7.710
					22.527

Note for simplicity we assume that the current dividend is one year hence.

Value of dividends years 4 – ∞

$$= \frac{d(1+g)}{i-g} = \frac{10.829(1.08)}{0.12-0.08} = 292.383$$

This gives the value of the perpetuity as at year 3. To obtain year 0 values we must discount back.

$$292.383 \times 0.712 = 208.2$$

Value of share at time 0 = 22.527 + 208.2 = 231¢

Since the current market value of Pavlon's shares is $78m/40m = $1.95 the share appears to be undervalued.

43 ARWIN

Key answer tips

Part (a) should be straightforward, except that you need to be careful with the calculation of the fixed costs in the cost of sales. These are not expected to rise next year, and so should be calculated using the current year figures. For part (b), the question does not state how financial gearing or operational gearing should be measured: there are different methods of calculation. Make clear the method of calculation you are using. (The solution here gives two methods of measuring financial gearing and three methods of measuring operational gearing, but your answer only needs one of each.) For part (c), you need to consider the link between operating gearing and financial gearing as measures of risk. The highlighted words are key phrases that markers are looking for.

(a)   The forecast statement of profit or loss are as follows:

	Debt finance $000	Equity finance $000
Sales revenue (50,000 × 1.12)	56,000	56,000
Variable cost of sales (85% × sales)	28,560	28,560
Fixed cost of sales (15% × 30,000)	4,500	4,500
Gross profit	22,940	22,940
Administration costs (14,000 × 1.05)	14,700	14,700
Profit before interest and tax	8,240	8,240
Interest (see working)	800	300
Profit before tax	7,440	7,940
Taxation at 30%	2,232	2,382
Profit after tax	5,208	5,558
Note: Dividends paid (60%)	3,125	3,335
Net change in equity (retained profit)	2,083	2,223

Working

Interest under debt financing = $300,000 + ($5,000,000 × 0.10) = $800,000.

(b)   **Financial gearing**

If financial gearing is measured as the debt: equity ratio:

Using debt/equity ratio:	Current	Debt finance	Equity finance
Debt	2,500	7,500	2,500
Share capital and reserves	22,560	24,643	29,783
Debt/equity ratio (%)	11.1	30.4	8.4

Workings:

Share capital and reserves (debt finance) = 22,560 + 2,083 = $24,643

Share capital and reserves (equity finance) = 22,560 + 5,000 + 2,223 = $29,783.

If financial gearing is measured as the ratio of debt capital to total capital:

Using capital (total) gearing:	Current	Debt finance	Equity finance
Debt	2,500	7,500	2,500
Total long-term capital	25,060	32,143	32,283
Capital (total) gearing (%)	10.0	23.3	7.7

Operational gearing:

If operational gearing is measured as the ratio of fixed costs to total costs:

Using fixed costs/total costs:	Current	Debt finance	Equity finance
Fixed costs	18,500	19,200	19,200
Total costs	44,000	47,760	47,760
Operational gearing (%)	42.0%	40.2%	40.2%

Total costs are assumed to consist of cost of sales plus administration costs.

If operational gearing is measured as the ratio of fixed costs to variable costs:

Using fixed costs/variable costs:	Current	Debt finance	Equity finance
Fixed costs	18,500	19,200	19,200
Variable costs	25,500	29,560	28,560
Operational gearing (%)	0.73	3.3	3.3

If operational gearing is measured as the ratio of contribution to profit before interest and tax (PBIT):

Using contribution/PBIT	Current	Debt finance	Equity finance
Contribution	24,500	27,440	27,440
PBIT	6,000	8,240	8,240
Operational gearing	4.1	3.3	3.3

Contribution is sales revenue minus the variable cost of sales.

Interest cover:

	Current	Debt finance	Equity finance
Profit before interest and tax	6,000	8,240	8,240
Debt interest	300	800	300
Interest cover	20	10.3	27.5

Earnings per share:

	Current	Debt finance	Equity finance
Profit after tax	3,990	5,208	5,558
Number of shares	10,000	10,000	11,250
Earnings per share (cents)	39.9	52.1	49.4

Comment:

The debt finance proposal leads to the largest increase in earnings per share, but results in an increase in financial gearing and a decrease in interest cover. Whether these changes in financial gearing and interest cover are acceptable depends on the attitude of both investors and managers to the new level of financial risk; a comparison with sector averages would be helpful in this context. The equity finance proposal leads to a decrease in financial gearing and an increase in interest cover. The expansion leads to a decrease in operational gearing, whichever measure of operational gearing is used, indicating that fixed costs have decreased as a proportion of total costs.

(c) As operational gearing increases, a business becomes more sensitive to changes in sales revenue and the general level of economic activity, and profit before interest becomes more volatile. From this perspective, operational gearing is a measure of business risk.

Financial risk in the context of this question can be described as the possibility of a company experiencing changes in the level of its distributable earnings as a result of the need to make interest payments on debt finance. The earnings volatility of companies in the same business will therefore depend not only on business risk, but also on the proportion of debt finance each company has in its capital structure.

It is likely that a business with high operational gearing will have low financial gearing, and a business with high financial gearing will have low operational gearing. This is because managers will be concerned to avoid excessive levels of total risk, i.e. the sum of business risk and financial risk. A business with a combination of high operational gearing and high financial gearing clearly runs an increased risk of experiencing liquidity problems, making losses and becoming insolvent.

44 ASSOCIATED INTERNATIONAL SUPPLIES CO

Key answer tips

The best starting point for part (a) is to prepare the appendix to your report. You will need to calculate all the main groups of ratios; be led by the scenario and consider why each piece of information has been provided. You can use the requirement to help structure your report. In this instance you have been asked to comment on growth, liquidity and the capacity to continue trading. These would therefore make excellent sub-headings.

Part (b) is very generic and should have been tackled before part (a). The requirement is to 'explain' and 'evaluate' so make sure you draw out the advantages and disadvantages of each source of finance as well as just identifying them should. For 5 marks you have aimed for at least three sources of equity. The highlighted words are key phrases that markers are looking for.

(a) **Analysis of company position**

Associated International Supplies Co

Circulation: Associated International Supplies Co (AIS Co)

Author:

Date: xx/xx/xx

General appraisal

The first point to note is that, by most standards, the company would be regarded as small, and is therefore likely to exhibit many of the problems typical of the small company sector. Generally, small companies which are characterised by strong growth also usually exhibit substantial borrowings in relation to equity funds. It is likely, therefore, that the appropriate mix of financing for the business becomes a critical issue in the appraisal of AIS Co.

Growth and liquidity

In the five year period from 20X4 to 20X9 sales for AIS have grown by 151%. In terms of supporting the business with adequate working capital, the pressures of such growth can be substantial. Thus, in the same period we see that current assets have expanded by 54% and current liabilities by 91%. Whilst this aspect of the business will be dealt-with in more detail below, it is worthwhile questioning at this stage whether sufficient funding for working capital is available to support the growth in sales.

Whilst there has been significant growth in sales during the period, profit before tax (PBT) as a percentage of sales has actually declined from 8% to about 5%. This must call into question either the management of costs (operational or financial) or whether the company is unable to force price increases on to customers. Given the information available, the most likely source of this problem appears to relate to interest costs. Both current and non-current liabilities have increased substantially (91% and 276%, respectively) against a background of barely increased equity funding. Debt funding (both long and short term) looks to have increased (see detail below) and this will have an associated interest burden. This has an importance in relation to the sustainability of the business.

Earnings retentions do not appear sufficient to fund business growth, and hence it is clear that borrowings have been increased to deal with this problem. However, a balance must be kept in the business between its earnings capability and its capacity to service its debt commitments. Whilst PBT has increased by 53% over the period, retentions have declined by about 74%. This may be partly explained by an increased tax burden, but is obviously due mainly to excessive distributions. In other words, not enough funds are being retained in the business to support its growth or funded from increased equity issues.

The impact of excessive growth in relation to its funding base might have a severe impact on liquidity. Net current assets are not seriously out of line if a ratio of current assets to current liabilities of 1.0 (unity) is considered acceptable. However, when current assets are looked at in relation to sales a different picture emerges. The ratio was 54% in 20X4 and only 33% in 20X9. This suggests, in combination with the other information, that inventories, receivables and cash resources might be insufficient to support the volume of sales. It might be argued that this reflects greater efficiency in current asset management. This is indeed the case when receivables days are compared over the period (they declined from 99 to 61), but it is not in relation to payables days which also declined (from 88 to 67 during the period). When working capital is measured as a proportion of sales, we observe a decline from 11.4% in 20X4 to 0.5% in 20X9. This appears to be a reflection of reduced current asset investment and overdraft increases.

Because it is debt rather than equity funding that has grown, the business faces a potentially critical situation. We know that current assets consist mainly of inventory and receivables (because the business has substantial borrowings, it is unlikely to simultaneously have large cash balances) and that this is being funded by borrowing rather than retained earnings. The reason why this is the case is because the business is not generating adequate profits and it is distributing too much of post tax earnings. The outlook is for greater borrowing. The poor profit figures suggest that a critical point has been reached in terms of liquidity and solvency. This is reflected in debt/equity ratios which have increased from 2.19 in 20X4 to 4.22 in 20X9 (current and non-current liabilities used as debt and capital and reserves used as equity). Unless a capital reorganisation can take place quickly, either through injected funds or conversion of debt into equity, the business is likely to become insolvent.

Company capacity to continue trading

Given the points made above, it is unlikely that the business can continue in its current form. The trading performance is obviously very strong when measured in terms of its sales capacity and growth. This indicates a good customer base and the ability to service customer needs. The markets the company serves suggest a long-term future for its product or service.

However, it is likely that the company's cost base will be overwhelmed by interest charges, which is resulting in reduced PBT/Sales ratios over the period in spite of significant sales growth. If that is the case, it may well be that the underlying trading profitability is good. If it is not found to be good after further investigation then additional action may need to be taken. For example if low profitability is due to aggressive pricing, an investigation into alternative marketing strategies may be appropriate. In addition, given the significant growth, it may now be an appropriate time to look at the customer base and withdraw service from those customers who are either unprofitable or otherwise difficult (late payers, for example). Product mix might be usefully assessed to focus on higher-margin sales activities and to decrease effort on lower-margin activities. A business plan describing the customer base and the strategy for greater profitability will underpin any bid for a reorganisation of AIS Co's finances.

Bank support is crucial to long term survival if the debt is in the form of bank related lending. Alternative sources of finance should also be considered, particularly in the form of equity which is required to re-balance the business.

Other factors

(i)   Venture capitalists might be interested in the business because of its significant growth but poorly structured finance. An equity injection would stabilise the business' finances.

(ii) Future projections of growth might provide a clearer picture of how to respond to the situation the business is now in.

(iii) The maturity of the debt obligations would indicate any critical repayments that may be due.

(iv) Comparisons with other businesses in the sector may provide some assurance as to the debt levels if high debt is a characteristic of the sector.

(v)   Investigation of possible renegotiation of the debt to ease the interest burden.

(vi)   Investigation of potential sale of the business or merger with a large partner with a view to securing a realistic equity base.

(vii)   Information on detailed trading results would enable an accurate assessment of the profitability of AIS Co.

(viii)   Working capital management needs to be investigated to assess if it is being efficiently organised.

Appendix to report: Ratio calculations

Sales growth: (3,010 – 1,200)/1,200 = 151%

Current asset growth: (1,000 – 650)/650 = 54%

Current liability growth: (982 – 513)/513 = 91%

Non-current liabilities growth: (158 – 42)/42 = 276%

PBT growth: (150 – 98)/98 = 53%

Retained earnings decline: (65 – 17)/65 = 74%

	20X4	20X9
PBT/Sales	98/1,200 = 8%	150/3,010 = 5%
Current assets/Current liabilities	650/513 = 1.3	1,000/982 = 1.0
Current assets/Sales	650/1,200 = 54%	1,000/3,010 = 33%
Working capital/Sales	(650–513)/1,200 = 11.4%	(1,000–982)/3,010 = 0.5%
Debt/Equity	(513 + 42)/210 = 2.64	(982 + 158)/270 = 4.22
Receivables at 50% of current assets	$325,000	$500,000
Sales per day (365 days)	$3,288	$8,247
Receivables days	325,000/3,288 = 99	500,000/8,247 = 61
Payables at 25% of current liabilities	$128,000	$245,500
Cost of sales per day (365 days)	$1,452	$3,643
Payables days	128,000/1,452 = 88	245,500/3,643 = 67

(b)   **General**

The most significant barrier to secure external equity funding for small firms is the lack of liquidity, or the inability to either find a market or buyer for the shares when the time arrives when the investor wishes to sell.

Sources of finance

No details are given concerning the nature of a business to comment on, and hence only general recommendations can be made. Below are listed some ideas of what might be most suitable:

(i)   If the non-current asset is substantial, such as a new building, or tooling for a new product, then a smaller stock market, such as the Alternative Investment Market in the UK, may be suitable. AIM is directed largely at small and growing companies who do not qualify for the main stock market. The restrictions for admission are not that binding and may suit a company such as AIS Co.

(ii)   Venture capital may also be suitable. This would be desirable from the point of view that, whilst venture capitalists may take an equity participation, they are likely to liquidate their shareholders to the owners of the business and hence ownership dilution would not occur.

(iii) Cash or dividend retentions. This would clearly take time for major asset purchases and may not be suitable for companies that face a funding shortfall in any case (the costs required in asset purchase may simply be too big for any realistic retention timescale).

(iv) Entering a merger or partnership, or accessing 'Business Angel' funding.

45 AMH CO

Key answer tip

Part (a) requires some standard WACC Workings but care needs to be taken to give a clear layout as there are several stages involved. Similarly the key to answering part (b) is to set out the steps clearly and logically. This part of the question involves no application so could have been attempted first for some easier marks. It is important to be guided by the mark allocation as to the length of your discussion.

The highlighted words are key phrases that markers are looking for.

(a) **Cost of equity**

The geometric average dividend growth rate in recent years:

(36.3/30.9)0.25 – 1 = 1.041 – 1 = 0.041 or 4.1% per year

Using the dividend growth model:

Ke = 0.041 + [(36.3 × 1.041)/470] = 0.041 + 0.080 = 0.121 or 12.1%

Cost of preference shares

As the preference shares are not redeemable:

Kp = 100 × [(0.04 × 100)/40] = 10%

Cost of debt of loan notes

The annual after-tax interest payment is 7 × 0.7 = $4.9 per loan note.

Using linear interpolation:

Year	Cash flow	$	5% DF	PV ($)	4% DF	PV ($)
0	Market price	(104.50)	1.000	(104.50)	1.000	(104.5)
1 – 6	Interest	4.9	5.076	24.87	5.242	25.69
6	Redemption	105	0.746	78.33	0.790	82.95
				(1.30)		4.14

After-tax cost of debt = 4 + [((5 – 4) × 4.14)/(4.14 + 1.30)] = 4 + 0.76 = 4.8%

Cost of debt of bank loan

If the bank loan is assumed to be perpetual (irredeemable), the after-tax cost of debt of the bank loan will be its after-tax interest rate, i.e. 4% × 0.7 = 2.8% per year.

Market values

Number of ordinary shares = 4,000,000/0.5 = 8 million shares

	$000
Equity: 8m × 4.70 =	37,600
Preference shares: 3m × 0.4 =	1,200
Redeemable loan notes: 3m × 104.5/100 =	3,135
Bank loan (book value used)	1,000
Total value of AMH Co	42,935

WACC calculation

[(12.1 × 37,600) + (10 × 1,200) + (4.8 × 3,135) + (2.8 × 1,000)]/42,935 = 11.3%

(b) The capital asset pricing model (CAPM) assumes that investors hold diversified portfolios, so that unsystematic risk has been diversified away. Companies using the CAPM to calculate a project-specific discount rate are therefore concerned only with determining the minimum return that must be generated by an investment project as compensation for its systematic risk.

The CAPM is useful where the business risk of an investment project is different from the business risk of the investing company's existing business operations. In such a situation, one or more proxy companies are identified that have similar business risk to the investment project. The equity beta of the proxy company represents the systematic risk of the proxy company, and reflects both the business risk of the proxy company's business operations and the financial risk arising from the proxy company's capital structure.

Since the investing company is only interested in the business risk of the proxy company, the proxy company's equity beta is 'ungeared' to remove the effect of its capital structure. 'Ungearing' converts the proxy company's equity beta into an asset beta, which represents business risk alone. The asset betas of several proxy companies can be averaged in order to remove any small differences in business operations.

The asset beta can then be 'regeared', giving an equity beta whose systematic risk takes account of the financial risk of the investing company as well as the business risk of an investment project. Both ungearing and regearing use the weighted average beta formula, which equates the asset beta with the weighted average of the equity beta and the debt beta.

The project-specific equity beta resulting from the regearing process can then be used to calculate a project-specific cost of equity using the CAPM. This can be used as the discount rate when evaluating the investment project with a discounted cash (DCF) flow investment appraisal method such as net present value or internal rate of return. Alternatively, the project-specific cost of equity can be used in calculating a project-specific weighted average cost of capital, which can also be used in a DCF evaluation.

ACCA marking scheme

		Marks
(a)	Calculation of historic dividend growth rate	1
	Calculation of cost of equity using DGM	2
	Calculation of cost of preference shares	1
	Calculation of after-tax interest payment on bond	1
	Setting up linear interpolation calculation	1
	Calculation of after-tax cost of debt of bond	1
	Calculation of after-tax cost of debt of bank loan	1
	Calculation of market values	2
	Calculation of WACC	2
	Maximum	12
(b)	Ungearing proxy company equity beta	1–2
	Averaging and regearing asset betas	1–2
	Project-specific cost of equity using CAPM	1–2
	Project-specific WACC	1–2
	Appropriate reference to business risk	1
	Appropriate reference to financial risk	1
	Maximum	8
Total		**20**

Examiner's comments

Candidates were asked here to calculate the market value weighted average cost of capital (WACC) of a company. Most candidates did well on this question.

As the question asked for market values to be used, no marks were given to using book values as weights. Most candidates calculated market values correctly for ordinary shares, preference shares and loan notes, although some candidates forgot that the loan note market price related to a nominal value per loan note of $100.

Some candidates incorrectly omitted the long-term bank loan from the WACC calculation. Although the bank loan had no market value, its book value could be used instead and due to its significance as a long-term source of finance in this case, it had to be included in the WACC calculation.

The historical dividend growth rate needed to be calculated for use in the dividend growth model (DGM) and some candidates had difficulty here, using either the wrong dividend or the wrong base period. Most candidates were able to calculate the cost of equity using the DGM and where this was not the case, a lack of understanding was usually in evidence.

Most candidates calculated the cost of preference shares correctly, although some candidates lost marks by making it an after-tax value. Since preference shares pay a dividend, which is a distribution of after-tax profit, there is no tax effect to consider.

Most candidates calculated the cost of debt of the loan notes either correctly or reasonably well. Errors that were made in the internal rate of return calculation included:

– Redemption at nominal value rather than at a 5% premium to nominal value.

– Using nominal value as the purchase price of the loan note rather than market value.

– Treating the purchase price as income and interest and redemption value as expenditure.

- Using the before-tax interest payment in the calculation instead of the after-tax interest payment.

- Interpolating when the calculated net present values called for extrapolation.

Some candidates used the before-tax interest rate on the bank loan as its cost of debt, when the after-tax interest rate should have been used. Alternatively (with explanation), the after-tax cost of debt of the loan notes could have been used as the cost of debt of the bank loan.

Part (b) asked candidates to discuss how the capital asset pricing model (CAPM) could be used to calculate a project-specific cost of capital. The requirement gave a strong hint as to how this might be done by requiring the discussion to refer to systematic risk, business risk and financial risk.

Answers to this question were of variable quality. The key concept here is risk and better answers addressed the following points.

- Related project risk to the business risk of the proxy company.

- Discussed the need to un-gear the equity beta of the proxy company to an asset beta, in order to remove the effect of its financial risk element.

- Discussed the need to re-gear the asset beta to an equity beta, in order to reflect the financial risk of the investing company.

- Noted the need to use the CAPM to calculate a project-specific cost of equity.

- Discussed how the final step would be in calculating a project-specific WACC.

Weaker answers limited themselves to saying something about each of the three kinds of risk mentioned in the question requirement, and saying little about how to calculate a project-specific cost of capital.

Definitions of business risk and financial risk were often quite vague. In the context of the question, both business risk and financial risk relate the variability of returns to the shareholder, since the CAPM calculates the cost of equity. Business risk relates to the variability of shareholder returns due to operational factors, which are factors that influence profit before interest and tax (PBIT). Financial risk relates to the variability of shareholder returns due to how a company finances its operations, which affects the relationship between profit before tax and PBIT. Business risk can be measured by operational gearing, while financial risk can be measured by statement of financial position gearing or by interest cover. When risk is seen from this perspective, the CAPM makes much more sense as a way of calculating the cost of equity.

46   GTK CO *Walk in the footsteps of a top tutor*

Key answer tip

Both parts (a) & (b) are relatively straightforward investment appraisal calculations which shouldn't pose many problems. In part (c) it is essential that you read the requirement carefully. As you have to make a recommendation you must ensure any advantages or disadvantages you note are relevant to the scenario given. The highlighted words are key phrases that markers are looking for.

(a)   **Expected net present value of Proposed 1**

Tutor's top tips:

It's worthwhile giving some quick consideration to the best way to layout your answer to this part of the requirement. A columnar format, like that presented here, will often be the most efficient and will reduce the amount of information you need to write more than once. This is particularly important here since your answer to part (i) will naturally lead into your answer to part (ii).

Don't forget the requirement to comment on your findings. In situation involving expected values, your comments should generally focus on the reliability of the probability estimates and the risk involved (look at the variability between the best result and the worst).

	Scenario 1	Scenario 2	Scenario 3
Number of sunny days	100	125	150
Saving ($/day)	700	700	700
Annual saving ($)	70,000	87,500	105,000
Costs	(24,000)	(24,000)	(24,000)
Net annual savings	46,000	63,500	81,000
Present value of net savings at 10%	460,000	635,000	810,000
Investment	500,000	500,000	500,000
Net present value	(40,000)	135,000	310,000
Probability	30%	60%	10%

Expected net present value = (−40,000 × 0.3) + (135,000 × 0.6) + (310,000 × 0.1) = $100,000

The ENPV is $100,000 so if the investment is evaluated on this basis, it is financially acceptable. In reaching a decision, however, the company should consider that there is a 30% chance of making a loss. This may be seen as an unacceptably high risk. Furthermore, the number of sunny days each year will not be constant, as assumed here, and may or may not be exactly 100, 125 or 150 days. It is possible the net present values of Scenarios 1 and 3 represent extremes in terms of expectations, and that the net present value of Scenario 2 may be most useful as representing the most likely outcome, even on a joint probability basis. It is also worth noting that inflation has not been taken into account and that the ever-increasing cost of energy may make the proposed investment much more financially attractive if it were factored into the analysis.

Workings

Present values must be calculated with the before-tax cost of capital of 10%, since before-tax cash flows are being evaluated here. The present value of a perpetuity is found by dividing the constant annual cash flow by the cost of capital.

Present value of net savings, Scenario 1 = 46,000/0.10 = $460,000

Present value of net savings, Scenario 2 = 63,500/0.10 = $635,000

Present value of net savings, Scenario 3 = 81,000/0.10 = $810,000

Tutor's top tips:

You are asked how equity finance or traded debt might be raised and will therefore need to discuss the different methods of issuing shares (rights issue, and placing being the most suitable here) and different things to consider when issuing debt.

(c)   GTK Inc is a company with a small overdraft and no long-term debt. The $1.1 million could be raised as follows:

Equity finance

The equity financing choices available to GTK Inc are a rights issue or a placing.

Rights issue

In this method of raising new equity finance, new shares are offered to existing shareholders pro rata to their existing shareholdings, meeting the requirements of company law in terms of shareholders' pre-emptive rights. Since GTK Inc has several million dollars of shareholders' funds, it may be able to raise $1.1 million through a rights issue, but further investigation will be needed to determine if this is possible. Factors to consider in reaching a decision will include

- the number of shareholders, the type of shareholders (institutional shareholders may be more willing to subscribe than small shareholders),
- whether a recent rights issue has been made,
- the recent and expected financial performance of GTK Inc, and
- the effect of a rights issue on the company's cost of capital.

A rights issue would not necessarily disturb the existing balance of ownership and control between shareholders. Approximately half of the finance needed is for a permanent investment and the permanent nature of equity finance would match this.

Placing

This way of raising equity finance involves allocating large amounts of ordinary shares with a small number of institutional investors. Existing shareholders will need to agree to waive their pre-emptive rights for a placing to occur, as it entails issuing new shares to new shareholders. The existing balance of ownership and control will therefore be changed by a placing. Since GTK Inc is a listed company, it is likely that a significant percentage of its issued ordinary share capital will be in public hands and the effect of a placing on this fraction will need to be considered. There may be a change in shareholder expectations after the placing, depending on the extent to which institutional investors are currently represented among existing shareholders, but since the company is listed there is likely to be a significant institutional representation.

Traded debt

A new issue of traded debt could be redeemable or irredeemable, secured or unsecured, fixed rate or floating rate, and may perhaps be convertible. Deep discount bonds and zero coupon bond are also a possibility, but much rarer. The effect of an issue of debt on the company's cost of capital should also be considered.

Security

Bonds may be secured on assets in order to reduce the risk of the bond from an investor point of view. Fixed charge debt is secured on specified non-current assets, such as land or buildings, while floating charge debt is secured on all assets or on a particular class of assets. In the event of default, holders of secured debt can take action to recover their investment, for example by appointing a receiver or by enforcing the sale of particular assets.

Redemption

Irredeemable corporate debt is very rare and a new issue of traded debt by GTK Inc would be redeemable, i.e. repayable on a specified future date. The project life of two of the proposed capital investments suggests that medium-term debt would be appropriate.

Fixed rate and floating rate

Fixed rate debt gives a predictable annual interest payment and, in terms of financial risk, makes the company immune to changes in the general level of interest rates. If interest rates are currently low, GTK Inc could lock into these low rates until its new debt issue needs to be redeemed. Conversely, if interest rates are currently high and expected to fall in the future, GTK Inc could issue floating rate debt rather than fixed rate debt, in the expectation that its interest payments would decrease as interest rates fell.

Cost of capital

GTK Inc has no long-term debt and only a small overdraft. Since debt is cheaper than equity in cost of capital terms, the company could reduce its overall cost of capital by issuing traded debt. A decrease in the overall cost of capital could benefit the company and its shareholders in terms of an increase in the market value of the company, and an increase in the number of financially acceptable investment projects.

47   TFR

Key answer tips

Provided you have carefully read the details of the scenario, the calculations in part (a) should be relatively uncomplicated. Part (b) requires you to be more practical. The key element in part (b) is the implications for cash flow. An estimate of this would therefore be useful. The highlighted words are key phrases that markers are looking for.

(a)   **Statement of profit or loss for TFR for the five-year period**

Year	Current	Year 1	Year 2	Year 3	Year 4	Year 5
	$	$	$	$	$	$
Sales revenue	210,000	255,000	300,000	345,000	390,000	390,000
Expenses	168,000	204,000	240,000	276,000	312,000	312,000
Net profit	42,000	51,000	60,000	69,000	78,000	78,000
Interest	2,000	11,000	8,750	6,500	4,250	2,000
Profit before tax	40,000	40,000	51,250	62,500	73,750	76,000
Tax	10,000	10,000	12,813	15,625	18,438	19,000
Profit after tax	30,000	30,000	38,438	46,875	55,313	57,000
Finance						
Dividend	15,000	15,000	19,219	23,438	27,656	28,500
Retained profit	15,000	15,000	19,219	23,438	27,656	28,500
Equity finance	200,000	215,000	234,219	257,656	285,313	313,813
Debt finance	Nil	75,000	50,000	25,000	Nil	Nil
Ratios						
Interest cover (times)	21.0	4.6	6.9	10.6	18.4	39
Debt/equity (%)	Nil	35	21	10	Nil	Nil
ROE (%)	15	14	16	18	19	18
ROCE (%)	21	18	21	24	27	25
ROCE (%)*	19	16	20	23	26	23

*Including the existing and continuing overdraft in capital employed.

Workings

Annual interest (assuming the continuing overdraft is maintained at the current level)

Year 1 interest payment = 100,000 × 0.09 = 9,000 + 2,000 = $11,000

Year 2 interest payment =   75,000 × 0.09 = 6,750 + 2,000 = $8,750

Year 3 interest payment =   50,000 × 0.09 = 4,500 + 2,000 = $5,500

Year 4 interest payment =   25,000 × 0.09 = 2,250 + 2,000 = $4,250

Year 5 interest payment = $2,000

Note: in year 5, we have assumed that no further growth in sales revenue occurs after the fourth year

(b)   **Financial implications for TFR of accepting bank loan**

Cash flow

A key consideration is whether TFR will be able to meet the annual payments of interest and capital. It is assumed, in preparing a cash flow forecast, that there is no difference between profit and cash, and that inflation can be ignored. The annual cash surplus after meeting interest and tax payments is therefore assumed to be equal to retained profit.

Year	1	2	3	4
Net change in equity (retained profit)	15,000	19,219	23,438	27,656
Capital repayment	25,000	25,000	25,000	25,000
Net cash flow	(10,000)	(5,781)	(1,563)	2,656

TFR is clearly not able to meet the annual capital repayments as things stand

Dividend policy

One way to try to address this would be to change the dividend policy.

It appears that TFR have maintained a policy of paying out a constant proportion of profit after tax as dividends. One possible course of action is to cut its dividend now and then increase it in the future as profitability allows. Since TFR is owner-managed, a change in dividend policy may be possible, depending of course on the extent to which the owner or owners rely on dividend income.

The annual cash flow shortfall is less than the annual dividend payment, so a change in dividend policy would probably allow the loan to be accepted.

Year	1	2	3	4
Profit after tax	30,000	38,438	46,875	55,313
Capital repayment	25,000	25,000	25,000	25,000
Available funds	5,000	13,438	21,875	30,313

It is useful to consider key financial information after the loan has been paid off.

Financial risk

The effect on financial risk of taking on the loan can be examined. If the interest and capital payments are kept up, financial risk will be lower than its current level at the end of four years, all things being equal. Interest cover increases from its current level after five years, from 21 times to 39 times, but is on the low side at the end of the first year (4.6 times), although an improved level is reached at the end of the second year (6.9 times), with further increases in subsequent years. The debt/equity ratio peaks at 35% at the end of the first year and falls rapidly thereafter, at no time looking dangerous, and TFR returns to its current ungeared position after five years. The bank, as provider of debt finance, would be interested in the trend in these ratios, as well as in the ongoing cash flow position.

Both return on equity (ROE) and return on capital employed (ROCE) improve with growth in sales revenue, but are lower than current levels in the first and second years following taking on the loan. At the end of five years ROE has improved to 18% from 15% and ROCE from 19% to 23%. Interest and capital payments would not increase with inflation.

Provided TFR can meet the interest and capital repayments, business expansion using debt finance may be financially feasible. However, this analysis has ignored any potential pressure for reduction or repayment of the overdraft. An average overdraft of $20,000 is quite large for a company with an annual sales revenue of $210,000 and therefore cannot be ignored in any assessment of financial risk. TFR may therefore consider asking for a longer repayment period, with lower annual capital repayments, if it plans to reduce the size of the overdraft or if it is concerned about future cash flow problems.

48 GXG CO

Key answer tips

This is a nice, relatively simple business finance question. It is vital to note that the first two requirements ask the student to comment on their findings.

The highlighted words are key phrases that markers are looking for.

(a) The dividend growth model can give a value of GXG Co at the end of the second year of not paying dividends, based on the dividends paid from the end of the third year onwards. The company has 10 million shares in issue ($5 million/50 cents nominal value) and so the total dividend proposed at the end of the third year will be $2.5 million (25 cents per share × 10m). If these dividends increase by 4% per year in subsequent years, their capital value at the end of the second year will be:

$2.5/(0.09 - 0.04) = \$50$ million

The dividend valuation model value (the capital value of the dividends at year 0) will be:

$50/1.09^2 = \$42.1$ million

The current present value of dividends to shareholders, using the existing 3% dividend growth rate:

$(1.6 \times 1.03)/(0.09 - 0.03) = \$27.5$ million

The proposal will increase shareholder wealth by $42.1 - 27.5 = \$14.6$ million and so is likely to be acceptable to shareholders.

Examiner note:

Calculations on a per share basis could also be used to evaluate the effect of the proposal on shareholder wealth).

(b)   Increase in before-tax income = 0.18 × 3.2m = $576,000

Revised operating profit = 576,000 + 3,450,000 = $4,026,000

Interest on new debt = 3,200,000 × 0.06 = $192,000

Revised interest = 192,000 + 200,000 = $392,000

Revised profit before tax = 4,026,000 − 392,000 = $3,634,000

Revised profit after tax = 3,634,000 × 0.8 = $2,907,200

Revised earnings per share = 100 × (2,907,200/10,000,000) = 29.1 cents per share

Earnings per share would increase by 3.1 cents per share.

Current interest cover = 3,450,000/200,000 = 17 times

Revised interest cover = 4,026,000/392,000 = 10 times

The increase in earnings per share would be welcomed by shareholders, but further information on the future of the company following the investment in research and development would be needed for a more comprehensive answer. The decrease in interest cover is not serious and the increase in financial risk is unlikely to upset shareholders.

(c)   Traded bonds are debt securities issued onto the capital market in exchange for cash received by the issuing company. The cash raised must be repaid on the redemption date, usually between five and fifteen years after issue. Bonds are usually secured on non-current assets of the issuing company, which reduces the risk to the lender. In the event of default on interest payments by the borrower, the bond holders can appoint a receiver to sell the assets and recover their investment. Interest paid on the bonds is tax-deductible, which reduces the cost of debt to the issuing company. Provided the borrower continues to pay the interest, however, bond finance is a low risk financing choice by the issuer.

There are a number of differences between bond finance and a new equity issue via a placing that will influence the choice between them. Equity finance does not need to be redeemed, since ordinary shares are truly permanent finance. While bond interest is usually fixed, the return to shareholders in the form of dividends depends on the dividend decision made by the directors of a company, and so these returns can increase, decrease or be passed. Furthermore, since dividends are a distribution of after-tax profit, they are not tax-deductible like interest payments, and so equity finance is not tax-efficient like debt finance.

Venture capital is found in specific financing situations, i.e. where risk finance is needed, for example, in a management buyout. Both equity and debt finance can be part of a venture capital financing package, but the return expected on venture capital is very high because of the level of risk faced by the investor.

ACCA marking scheme		Marks
(a)	Value of company at end of two years using DGM	2
	Value of company at year zero	1
	Current value of company using Dividend Valuation Model	2
	Acceptability of option 1 to shareholders	1
	Comment on findings	1
	Maximum	6

(b)		
	Revised operating profit	0.5
	Revised interest	0.5
	Revised profit after tax	0.5
	Revised earnings per share	0.5
	Current interest cover	0.5
	Revised interest cover	0.5
	Comment on earnings per share	1
	Comment on findings	1
	Comment on findings	1
	Maximum	5
(c)		
	Discussion of bond finance	3–4
	Discussion of equity finance via placing	3–4
	Discussion of venture capital	3–4
	Comment on findings	1
	Maximum	9
Total		**20**

Examiner's comments

Candidates tended to struggle with part (a), although some scored full marks. In this question, the proposal was to suspend dividends for two years, before paying higher dividends at a higher growth rate than the current one from the third year onwards. The DGM could be used to calculate a share price (the present value of future dividends from the third year onwards) at the end of the second year. This share price could then be discounted for two years to give a current share price. Some candidates adopted a different, but equally valid, approach of discounting the year 3 dividend to the end of year 1 or to year 0, and then applying the DGM. How then would we know if the proposal was acceptable? By comparing the share price for the proposal to the current share price, calculated using the current dividend, the current dividend growth rate and the DGM.

General comments about whether shareholders would accept a two-year dividend suspensions, for example from the perspective of dividend relevance or irrelevance theory, were give some credit in the marking process. However, the expectation was that the comment on acceptability would refer to the comparison of the values discussed above.

The requirement in part (b) was to calculate the effect on earnings per share and interest cover of a proposal to raise finance by a loan note issue, commenting on the findings. The key points here were:

– Investing the funds at 18% before tax would increase operating profit;

– Financing the investment with debt would result in an increase in interest payments;

– Financing the investment with debt meant that the number of issued shares would not change.

Some answers calculated correctly the interest on the new debt, but ignored interest payable on the current debt when calculating interest cover. Another error was ignoring the return on the new funds invested, so that both current and revised interest cover were calculated using the same operating profit. Some answers calculated interest cover using profit before tax, or profit after tax, indicating a lack of understanding of accounting ratios. Credit was given for sensible comments on findings, even where the findings contained errors.

Answers to part (c) were of variable quality, indicating that some candidates were lacking on knowledge in this area of the syllabus. A number of answers, for example, showed limited understanding of placing venture capital. Some answers limited themselves to discussing each source of finance separately, without addressing the requirement to discuss the factors to be considered in choosing between them, and so could not be awarded full marks. At the other extreme, some answers discussed a number of factors, but related these very loosely, if at all, to the three sources of finance to which the question referred. For example, saying that a company should consider maturity, without indicating how maturity is a feature of the three sources of finance, does not help in choosing between them. A balanced discussion was therefore needed for full marks

49   ILL COLLEAGUE

Key answer tips

A solid understanding of the basics of calculating the weighted average cost of capital will be sufficient to answer part (a). Part (b) represents more of a challenge and requires you to be competent in gearing and ungearing betas. Part (c) could have been attempted first as it gave an opportunity to gain some easy marks.

(a)   (i)   **Dividend valuation model**

If we assume a constant growth in dividends, we may estimate the cost of equity by using:

$$K(e) = \frac{D_0(1+g)}{P_0} + g$$

where: D_0 = \$2.14m/10m shares = 21.4c

P_0 = 321c

g   = 11%

Therefore:

$K(e)$ = (21.4c × 1.11 / 321c) + 0.11 = 0.184, or 18.4%

Kd(1-t)

As the question tells us to assume that 'corporate debt is risk-free', we can therefore assume that the cost of debt equals the risk free rate:

Kd (1-t)   = 12% × (1 − 0.35) = 7.8%

The weighted average cost of capital (WACC) is therefore:

WACC   = 18.4% × $\frac{2}{3}$ + 7.8% × $\frac{1}{3}$

= 14.87%

(ii)   **Capital asset pricing model**

R SHARES   = R_f + βSHARES × [R_m − R_f]

Beta   = 1.4

R_f = 12%

R_m = 16%

Therefore:

R SHARES $= 12\% + [16\% - 12\%] \times 1.40 = 17.6\%$

Kd $= 7.8\%$ as in part (i)

WACC $= 17.6\% \times \frac{2}{3} + 7.8\% \times \frac{1}{3}$

$= 14.33\%$

The cost of equity may be estimated using either the dividend valuation model or the capital asset pricing model. In theory the two models should provide the same estimate of the cost of equity. In many instances, because of market imperfections and problems in the estimation of an appropriate growth rate in the dividend valuation model, the two models often give different results. CAPM is normally considered to be the better alternative. However, this model also has theoretical weaknesses and there may be problems in obtaining data to input into the model.

(b)   A major diversification into a new industry is likely to involve a different level of systematic risk from that of the company's existing investment portfolio. In these circumstances a project specific discount rate should be estimated, and the company's weighted average cost of capital is not appropriate. The project specific discount rate will need to reflect both the systematic risk (business risk) of operating cash flows and the financial gearing (financial risk) of the company as a whole.

A pragmatic way of identifying the systematic business risk is to use the published equity beta coefficients of other companies within the industry. These equity betas are considered to reflect the systematic risk of our company's major investment in the industry. However, if the average gearing level of the companies in the industry differs from our company's gearing, the beta will need to be adjusted (degeared and regeared) to reflect the gearing level (financial risk) of our company.

The β equity of the industry is 1.50.

Using β asset $\quad = \beta$ equity $\dfrac{E}{E+D(1-t)} + \beta$ debt $\dfrac{D(1-t)}{E+D(1-t)}$

As β debt is 0.

β asset $\quad = 1.50 \times \dfrac{3}{3+1(1-0.35)} + 0$

β asset $\quad (= \beta$ equity for an ungeared project$) = 1.23$

Adjustment for the company's gearing level may be achieved by 're-gearing' the β asset.

Asset beta $\quad =$ Equity beta $\times \dfrac{E}{E+D(1-t)}$

1.23 $\quad =$ Equity beta $\times \dfrac{2}{2+1(1-0.35)}$

Equity beta $\quad = 1.23/0.75 = 1.64$

Project E(r equity) $= 12 + (16 - 12) \times 1.64$

$= 18.56\%$

(c) **Practical problems estimating data inputs for the CAPM**

The CAPM is an ex-ante model. It is difficult, if not impossible, to forecast accurate future returns of the company, project, or market. For practical purposes, ex-post data is normally used in the CAPM.

Even if the use of ex-post data is considered to be acceptable, it is difficult to estimate the appropriate data inputs:

Rf – What is the appropriate risk-free rate? A short-term government bill? A long-term government stock?

Rm – What is the market return? Do returns on companies comprising the FTSE All Share Index (or similar) provide a satisfactory estimate of returns on the market as a whole?

Beta – The use of an historical beta assumes that future risk is the same as past risk. Evidence for individual companies suggests that this is not the case.

Timescales – Over what period should historic data be considered? How frequently should returns be calculated?

50 AQR CO

Key answer tips

A solid understanding of the basics of calculating the weighted average cost of capital will be sufficient to answer part (a). Part (b) would have seemed more familiar but care must be taken to answer the perspective taken in the question

The highlighted words are key phrases that markers are looking for.

(a) **Cost of equity**

Geometric average dividend growth rate = (21.8/19.38)0.25 – 1 = 0.0298 or 3%

Using the dividend growth model, ke = 0.03 + ((21.8 × 1.03)/250) = 0.03 + 0.09 = 12%

Market values of equity and debt

Market value of equity = Ve = 100m × 2.50 = $250 million

Market value of loan notes = Vd = 60m × (104/100) = $62.4 million

Total market value of AQR Co = Ve + Vd = 250 + 62.4 = $312.4 million

Current WACC calculation

The current after-tax cost of debt is 7%

WACC = ((ke × Ve) + (kd(1 – T) × Vd)/(Ve + Vd)) = ((12 × 250m) + (7 × 62.4m))/312.4m = 11%

The weighted average after-tax cost of capital before the new issue of loan notes is 11%

After-tax cost of debt of new loan note issue

After-tax interest rate = 8 × (1 – 0.3) = 5.6% per year

Using linear interpolation:

Year	Cash flow	$	5% Discount	PV ($)	6% Discount	PV ($)
0	Market value	(100)	1.000	(100.00)	1.000	(100.00)
1–10	Interest	5.6	7.722	43.24	7.360	41.22
10	Redemption	105	0.614	64.47	0.558	58.59
				7.71		(0.19)

After-tax cost of debt = 5 + [((6 – 5) × 7.71)/(7.71 + 0.19)] = 5 + 0.98 = 5.98% or 6%

Examiner's note: other methods of calculating the after-tax cost of redeemable debt are acceptable.

Revised WACC calculation

The market value of the new issue of loan notes is $40 million

The total market value of AQR Co increases to 312.4 + 40 = $32.4 million

WACC = ((12 × 250m) + (7 × 62.4m) + (6 × 40))/352.4m = 10.4%

After the new issue of loan notes, the weighted average after-tax cost of capital has decreased from 11% to 10.4% because the proportion of debt finance, which has a lower required rate of return than equity finance, has increased. Gearing on a market value basis has increased from 20% (62.4/312.4) to 29% (102.4/352.4).

The WACC calculation assumes that the cost of equity has not changed, when in reality the cost of equity might be expected to rise in response to the increase in financial risk caused by the new issue of debt. The share price of the company has also been assumed to be constant.

(b) There is certainly a relationship between the weighted average cost of capital (WACC) and the market value of the company, since the market value can be expressed as the present value of future corporate cash flows, discounted by the WACC.

Marginal and average cost of debt

As for decreasing the WACC by issuing traded bonds, if the marginal cost of capital, in this case the cost of debt of the new bond issue, is less than the weighted average cost of capital (WACC), it would seem logical to expect the WACC to decrease. However, as noted in an earlier discussion, increasing gearing will increase financial risk and may lead to an increase in the cost of equity, offsetting the effect of the cheaper debt. The relationship between capital structure and WACC has been debated for many years.

Traditional view of capital structure

In the traditional view of capital structure, there is a non-linear relationship between the cost of equity and financial risk, as measured by gearing. Equity investors are indifferent to the addition of small amounts of debt, so as a company gears up by replacing expensive equity with cheaper debt, the WACC initially decreases. Debt is cheaper than equity because of the relative positions of the two sources of finance in the creditor hierarchy (the traditional view of capital structure ignores taxation). As equity investors start to respond to increasing financial risk, however, the cost of equity begins to increase until a point is reached where WACC ceases to fall. This corresponds to an optimal capital structure, since at this point WACC is at a minimum and hence the market value of the company is at a maximum. After this point, the WACC starts to increase as the company continues to gear up, rising more quickly at very high levels of gearing due to the appearance of bankruptcy risk. Under the traditional view the finance director might be correct in his belief that issuing debt will decrease WACC, depending on the position of the company relative to its optimal capital structure.

Miller and Modigliani

Miller and Modigliani showed that in a perfect capital market without corporate taxation, the replacement of expensive equity with cheaper debt did not lead to a decrease in the WACC, since the effect of adding in cheaper debt was exactly offset by the increase in the cost of equity, which had a linear relationship with financial risk, as represented by gearing. This meant that the market value of the company was independent of its capital structure (financial risk) and depended only on its business operations (business risk).

In their second paper on capital structure Miller and Modigliani showed that, if taxation were allowed (so that the after-tax cost of debt was considered, rather than the before-tax cost of debt), replacing equity with debt led to a linear decrease in the WACC, because of the tax shield on profits gained by interest payments being an allowable deduction in calculating tax liability. Under this contribution to capital structure theory, gearing up as much as possible would maximise the market value of the company and the finance director would be correct in his belief that issuing traded bonds would decrease the WACC of AQR Co.

Market imperfections view

In reality, it was noted that companies do not gear up as much as possible because of the dangers of high gearing. Further market imperfections, relative to the idea of a perfect capital market in Miller and Modigliani's first paper on capital structure, included bankruptcy risk and the costs of financial distress at high levels of gearing. These reduced and finally reversed the tax shield effect noted by Miller and Modigliani, resulting in an optimal capital structure at the point where the WACC was at its lowest and the value of the company was at its highest.

Pecking order theory

In practice it has been noticed that companies do not appear to base their financing decisions on the objective of achieving an optimal capital structure, but rather have a preference for sources of finance in the order of retained earnings, bank loans, ordinary debt, convertible debt and equity. A number of reasons have been suggested for this 'pecking order'.

ACCA marking scheme		Marks
(a)	Calculation of historic dividend growth rate	1
	Calculation of cost of equity using DGM	2
	Calculation of market weights	1
	Calculation of pre-issue WACC	2
	Correct use of tax as regards new debt	1
	Setting up linear interpolation calculation	1
	Calculating after-tax cost of debt of new debt	1
	Calculation of post-issue WACC	2
	Comment	1
	Maximum	12
(b)	Marginal and average cost of debt	1–2
	Traditional view of capital structure	1–2
	Miller and Modigliani 1 and 2	1–3
	Market imperfections view	1–2
	Pecking order theory	1–2
	Other relevant discussion	1–2
	Maximum	8
Total		20

Examiner's comments

Part (a) asked for the calculation of the market value after-tax weighted average cost of capital (WACC) before and after a new issue of loan notes. Many candidates gained full marks for the two WACC calculations and most students were able to gain some credit by some of the subsidiary calculations. Some students ignored the market value of existing loan notes given in the question and calculated a market value based on the present value of future interest payments and redemption at par (nominal value). This was not actually possible, since the question provided neither the interest rate nor the maturity of the existing loan notes. Some answers ignored the after-tax cost of debt given in the question and calculated a new (incorrect) after-tax cost of debt. For example, some answers treated existing loan notes as irredeemable and used the after-tax cost of debt provided as a before-tax interest rate. This implies learning a WACC calculation method without understanding the underlying principles, leading to an attempt to make the information provided fit the calculation method learned.

A surprising number of candidates could not calculate the dividend growth rate, whether on a geometric or an arithmetic basis. Both methods were acceptable. There were also a significant number of errors in calculating the cost of equity using the dividend growth model. Alarm bells should sound if the calculated cost of equity is less than the cost of debt, or if the calculated cost of equity is quite large. A glance through past examination papers will show that a realistic approach has been used, with the cost of equity lying between say 5% and 15%. Alarm bells should also sound if the calculated WACC is greater than the highest cost of capital being averaged, or less than the lowest cost of capital being averaged, since logically an average value must lie between the highest and lowest values being averaged.

The cost of debt of the new loan note issue could be found through linear interpolation. The correct way to treat taxation here is to use the after-tax interest payment in the interpolation calculation, with the redemption value being unaffected by profit tax. Many candidates were able to use linear interpolation correctly.

Following the calculation of the revised WACC, some comment was required on findings. If the calculations had been similar to those in the suggested answer, a decrease in WACC had been found. Better answers noted that this decrease rested on assumptions such as that the cost of equity had not increased, despite the rise in financial risk, and that the share price had not changed.

In part (b), candidates were asked for a discussion of the suggestion that issuing bonds will decrease WACC and increase the market value of a company. Better answers to this question looked at capital structure theory, including the traditional view, the views of Miller and Modigliani, the market imperfections view and pecking order theory. Other answers gained credit by using a practical perspective, noting that issuing debt without having an investment purpose was poor financial management and that the shareholder response to increased financial risk could not be ignored. Weaker answers struggled to discuss the relationship between WACC, company market value, the cost of equity, the cost of debt and taxation, perhaps discussing instead the different ways of valuing a company, which was not required by the question.

51 CARD CO

Key answer tips

Parts (a) and (c) require the use of models that students should feel comfortable with. Care must be taken to extract the relevant information from the scenario and a clear layout must be used in order for marks to be allocated where due.

Part (d) is standard fare in terms of a discussion about the impact of changing capital structure on the value of the company. Students must be well prepared for this common requirement.

The highlighted words are key phrases that markers are looking for.

(a) **Cost of equity of Card Co using DGM**

The average dividend growth rate in recent years is 4%:

$(62.0/55.1)0.333 - 1 = 1.040 - 1 = 0.04$ or 4% per year

Using the dividend growth model:

$Ke = 0.04 + [(62 \times 1.04)/716] = 0.04 + 0.09 = 0.13$ or 13%

(b) The dividend growth model calculates the apparent cost of equity in the capital market, provided that the current market price of the share, the current dividend and the future dividend growth rate are known. While the current market price and the current dividend are readily available, it is very difficult to find an accurate value for the future dividend growth rate. A common approach to finding the future dividend growth rate is to calculate the average historic dividend growth rate and then to assume that the future dividend growth rate will be similar. There is no reason why this assumption should be true.

The capital asset pricing model tends to be preferred to the dividend growth model as a way of calculating the cost of equity as it has a sound theoretical basis, relating the cost of equity or required return of well-diversified shareholders to the systematic risk they face through owning the shares of a company. However, finding suitable values for the variables used by the capital asset pricing model (risk-free rate of return, equity beta and equity risk premium) can be difficult.

(c)   First, the proxy company equity beta must be ungeared:

Asset beta = (1.038 × 0.75)/(0.75 + (0.25 × 0.7)) = 0.842

The asset beta must then be regeared to reflect the financial risk of Card Co:

Equity beta = 0.842 × (57,280 + (5,171 × 0.7))/57,280 = 0.895

Project-specific cost of equity = 4 + (0.895 × 5) = 8.5%

Workings

Market values

	$000
Equity: 8m × 7.16 =	57,280
Loan notes: 5m × 103.42/100 =	5,171
Total value of Card Co	62,451

(d)   The value of a company can be expressed as the present value of its future cash flows, discounted at its weighted average cost of capital (WACC). The value of a company can therefore theoretically be maximised by minimising its WACC. If the WACC depends on the capital structure of a company, i.e. on the balance between debt and equity, then the minimum WACC will arise when the capital structure is optimal.

The idea of an optimal capital structure has been debated for many years. The traditional view of capital structure suggests that the WACC decreases as debt is introduced at low levels of gearing, before reaching a minimum and then increasing as the cost of equity responds to increasing financial risk.

Miller and Modigliani originally argued that the WACC is independent of a company's capital structure, depending only on its business risk rather than on its financial risk. This suggestion that it is not possible to minimise the WACC, and hence that it is not possible to maximise the value of a company by selecting a particular capital structure, depends on the assumption of a perfect capital market with no corporate taxation.

However, real world capital markets are not perfect and companies pay taxes on profit. Since interest is a tax-allowable deduction in calculating taxable profit, debt is a tax-efficient source of finance and replacing equity with debt will decrease the WACC of a company. In the real world, therefore, increasing gearing will decrease the WACC of a company and hence increase its value.

At high levels of gearing, the WACC of a company will increase due, for example, to increasing bankruptcy risk. Therefore, it can be argued that use of debt in a company's capital structure can reduce its WACC and increase its value, provided that gearing is kept to an acceptable level.

ACCA marking scheme			Marks
(a)	Calculation of historic dividend growth rate		1
	Calculation of cost of equity using DGM		2
			———
		Maximum	**3**
			———
(b)	Dividend growth model discussion		2–3
	Capital asset pricing model discussion		2–3
			———
		Maximum	**5**
			———
(c)	Ungearing proxy company equity beta		1
	Regearing asset beta		1
	Project-specific cost of equity using CAPM		2
			———
		Maximum	**4**
			———
(d)	Traditional view of capital structure		1–2
	Miller and Modigliani views of capital structure		3–4
	Market imperfections view of capital structure		2–3
	Other relevant discussion		1–2
			———
		Maximum	**8**
			———
Total			**20**
			———

52 IRQ CO

Key answer tips

Part (a) represents a fairly straightforward WACC calculation and should give an early opportunity to pick up some easy marks.

Part (b) focusses on the interest rate risk management section of the syllabus. As a less frequently examined area, this is one that can often cause difficulties for students due to lack of knowledge. Make sure you're able to handle these requirements in case something comes up in your exam.

To score well in part (c) you must talk about the key principles underpinning Islamic finance and give some examples that would be suitable given the scenario.

The highlighted words in the written sections are key phrases that markers are looking for.

(a)   Cost of equity:

Cost = 4% + (1.1 × 7%) = 4% + 7.7% = 11.7%

Cost of irredeemable loan notes:

Post tax cost = $100 × 6% × (1 – 0.28) ÷ $107 = 4.0%

Cost of the variable rate bank loan:

Cost = 5% × (1 – 0.28) = 3.6%

Total market values:

Equity – $400m ÷ 0.5 × $2.30 = $1,840m

Irredeemable loan notes – $600m × $107 ÷ $100 = $642m

Variable rate bank loan – use book value – $100m

Total market value of finance – $2,582m (1,840 + 642 + 100)

WACC = (11.7% × 1,840/2,582) + (4.0% × 642/2,582) + (3.6% × 100/2,582) = 9.5%

(b)   The over-the-counter methods of interest rate hedging include:

A forward rate agreement (FRA) – this effectively fixes the amount of interest to be paid by a borrower such as IRQ Co.

An interest rate guarantee (IRG) – this is effectively an option on a forward rate agreement. Hence if an adverse interest rate movement arises the IRG will be exercised and will fix the maximum amount a borrower will pay. However if a favourable interest rate movement arises the IRG will be allowed to lapse and a borrower will be able to benefit from the fall in interest rates.

The exchange traded methods of interest rate hedging include:

Futures – like an FRA this effectively fixes the interest rate.

Options on futures – like an IRG this lets a company take advantage of a favourable move in interest rates but provides protection against adverse interest rate moves.

As both the IRG and options on futures provide flexibility they are costly and a premium will be payable.

The exchange traded methods use the standardised contracts available on the futures market and hence it may not be possible to hedge exactly the amount you want to hedge.

Tutorial note:

Any sensible illustration will be given credit if it shows the workings of an FRA.

FRA illustration:

Assume that IRQ Co identifies the need to borrow an additional $40m in 5 months time for a period of 6 months.

Assume a 5v11 FRA at 5.20 – 5.30 is available.

If IRQ Co takes up this FRA they are effectively fixed into paying a rate of 5.3% on the borrowings.

If the commercial rate in 5 months is 5.7% then the following cash flows will arise:

Interest paid on commercial borrowings – $40m × 5.7% × 6/12 = $1.14m

Compensation received from the FRA provider – $40m × 0.4% × 6/12 = $0.08m

(0.4% is the difference between the commercial rate and the rate agreed in the FRA)

Net cost – $1.06m (1.14 – 0.08) – this is $40m × 5.3% × 6/12

If the interest is lower than 5.3% in 5 months time the cash flows will be calculated in a similar way but compensation will be paid to the FRA provider.

(c)   The key principles of Islamic Finance are that the risk and reward should be shared between the investor and the user of the funds. Making money with money is deemed immoral and hence interest (riba) is forbidden. As a result, the profitability of a bank is more closely tied to that of its clients than is the case with conventional banking.

As interest is forbidden a conventional variable rate bank loan would not be allowed. Instead a murabaha contract could be used. Under such a contract the bank buys the assets and then sells them to the company. The company then pays the bank by way of a deferred payment or makes payments by instalments. The assets involved could be both non-current assets such as machinery or current assets such as raw materials. However the assets must actually exist/be tangible. Hence the company can use the assets to generate a profit and use this profit to repay the bank. Hence Murabaha is similar in nature to a loan.

Tutorial note:

Marks would also be awarded for discussing a sukuk contract.

BUSINESS VALUATIONS

53   KFP CO

Key answer tips

This is an excellent example of the examiner's style and in particular the way he combines two or more areas of the syllabus into one question.

(a)   **Weighted average cost of capital (WACC) calculation**

Cost of equity of KFP Co = 4.0 + (1.2 × (10.5 − 4.0)) = 4.0 + 7.8 = 11.8% using the capital asset pricing model

To calculate the after-tax cost of debt, linear interpolation is needed

After-tax interest payment = 100 × 0.07 × (1 − 0.3) = $4.90

Year	Cash flow	$	10% discount	PV ($)	5% discount	PV ($)
0	Market value	(94.74)	1.000	(94.74)	1.000	(94.74)
1 to 7	Interest	4.9	4.868	23.85	5.786	28.35
7	Redemption	100	0.513	51.30	0.711	71.10
				(19.59)		4.71

After-tax cost of debt = 5 + ((10 − 5) × 4.71)/(4.71 + 19.59) = 5 + 1.0 = 6.0%

Number of shares issued by KFP Co = $15m/0.5 = 30 million shares

Market value of equity = 30m × 4.2 = $126 million

Market value of bonds issued by KFP Co = 15m × 94.74/100 = $14.211 million

Total value of company = 126 + 14.211 = $140.211 million

WACC = ((11.8 × 126) + (6.0 × 14.211))/140.211 = 11.2%

(b) (i) **Price/earnings ratio method**

Earnings per share of NGN = 80c per share

Price/earnings ratio of KFP Co = 8

Share price of NGN = 80 × 8 = 640c or $6.40

Number of ordinary shares of NGN = 5/0.5 = 10 million shares

Value of NGN = 6.40 × 10m = $64 million

However, it can be argued that a reduction in the applied price/earnings ratio is needed as NGN is unlisted and therefore its shares are more difficult to buy and sell than those of a listed company such as KFP Co. If we reduce the applied price/earnings ratio by 10% (other similar percentage reductions would be acceptable), it becomes 7.2 times and the value of NGN would be (80/100) × 7.2 × 10m = $57.6 million

(ii) **Dividend growth model**

Dividend per share of NGN = 80c × 0.45 = 36c per share

Since the payout ratio has been maintained for several years, recent earnings growth is the same as recent dividend growth, i.e. 4.5%. Assuming that this dividend growth continues in the future, the future dividend growth rate will be 4.5%.

Share price from dividend growth model = (36 × 1.045)/ (0.12 − 0.045) = 502c or $5.02 Value of NGN = 5.02 × 10m = $50.2 million

(c) When evaluating the suggestion that debt could be used to finance a cash bid for NGN, the current and post acquisition capital structures and their relative gearing levels should be considered, as well as the amount of debt finance that would be needed.

Earlier calculations suggest that at least $58m would be needed, ignoring any premium paid to persuade target company shareholders to sell their shares. The current debt/equity ratio of KFP Co is 60% (15m/25m). The debt of the company would increase by $58m in order to finance the bid and by a further $20m after the acquisition, due to taking on the existing debt of NGN, giving a total of $93m. Ignoring other factors, the gearing would increase to 372% (93m/25m).

KFP Co would need to consider how it could service this dangerously high level of gearing and deal with the significant risk of bankruptcy that it might create.

It would also need to consider whether the benefits arising from the acquisition of NGN would compensate for the significant increase in financial risk and bankruptcy risk resulting from using debt finance.

ACCA marking scheme		
		Marks
(a) Cost of equity calculation	2	
Correct use of taxation rate	1	
Cost of debt calculation	3	
Market value of equity	1	
Market value of debt	1	
WACC calculation	1	
		9
(b) Price/earnings value of company	2	
Current dividend per share	1	
Dividend growth model value of company	2	
		6
(c) Comment on debt finance for cash offer	5	
	Maximum	5
Total		20

Examiner's comments

In part (a), candidates were asked to calculate the weighted average cost of capital (WACC) of a company. Many candidates gained full marks for their calculations. Some answers lost marks because they included the debt of the target company in their calculation. The WACC of one company is clearly independent of the debt of another company.

Information provided in the question enabled the cost of equity to be found using the CAPM formula. Some candidates ignored this information and attempted to use the dividend growth model instead. Other candidates un-geared and re-geared the equity beta of the company, even though this was unnecessary since the equity beta was not from a proxy company. Most candidates calculated the cost of equity correctly.

The cost of debt had to be calculated using linear interpolation and most answers did this more or less successfully. Where errors arose, these involved using a shorter bond maturity than that in the question (7 years), exchanging the market value and the par value in the interpolation calculation, omitting to make the interest payment after-tax, and mixing total values and per share values in the same calculation.

Most candidates correctly used market values as weights.

Part (b) called for the calculation of the value of the target company using the PER (price/earnings ratio) method and the dividend growth model (DGM). These were not complicated calculations, although it was necessary to assume with the DGM that the dividend growth rate was the same as the earnings per share growth rate given in the question. This was a reasonable assumption, as the earnings per share growth rate and the dividend payout ratio had both been constant for several years.

Even though the question gave both the earnings per share (EPS) of the target company and an instruction to use the PER provided, some candidates made life difficult for themselves by doing something other than multiplying the earnings per share by the PER. The most common error was using the retained earnings of the target company instead of the EPS provided. Another common error was trying to calculate a PER value, rather than using the one given.

Many candidates had difficulty in calculating the dividend per share for using in the DGM. Since the target company EPS and payout ratio were provided in the question, this can only be explained by a lack of understanding of the payout ratio.

Part (c) asked candidates to comment on the use of debt to finance the acquisition. Some answers were very general in nature, discussing the attractions of debt as a source of finance. Better answers calculated the current gearing of the bidding company and then considered the effect on that gearing of adding debt equal to the value of the target company calculated earlier.

54 CLOSE CO

Key answer tips

It is important to take note of how succinctly the model answer arrives at the answers for each element of part (a) as time can easily be wasted with more long-winded approaches.

Part (c) is a standalone requirement which could have been attempted first to gain some easy marks relatively quickly.

The highlighted words are key phrases that markers are looking for.

(a) **Net asset valuation**

In the absence of any information about realisable values and replacement costs, net asset value is on a book value basis. It is the sum of non-current assets and net current assets, less long-term debt, i.e. 595 + 125 – 70 – 160 = $490 million.

Dividend growth model

Total dividends of $40 million are expected to grow at 4% per year and Close Co has a cost of equity of 10%. Value of company = (40m × 1.04)/(0.1 – 0.04) = $693 million

Earnings yield method

Profit after tax (earnings) is $66.6 million and the finance director of Close Co thinks that an earnings yield of 11% per year can be used for valuation purposes.

Ignoring growth, value of company = 66.6m/0.11 = $606 million

Alternatively, profit after tax (earnings) is expected to grow at an annual rate of 5% per year and earnings growth can be incorporated into the earnings yield method using the growth model. Value of company = (66.6m × 1.05)/(0.11 – 0.05) = $1,166 million

Examiner's note: full credit would be gained whether or not growth is incorporated in the earnings yield method.

(b) **Market value of equity**

Close Co has 80 million shares in issue and each share is worth $8.50 per share. The market value of equity is therefore 80 × 8.50 = $680 million

Cost of equity

This is given as 10% per year.

Market value of 8% bonds

The market value of each bond will be the present value of the expected future cash flows (interest and principal) that arise from owning the bond. Annual interest is 8% per year and the bonds will be redeemed at their nominal value of $100 per bond in six years' time. The before-tax cost of debt is given as 7% per year and this is used as a discount rate.

Present value of future interest = (8 × 4.767) = $38.14

Present value of future principal payment = (100 × 0.666) = $66.60

Ex interest bond value = 38.14 + 66.60 = $104.74 per bond

Market value of bonds = 120m × (104.74/100) = $125.7 million

After-tax cost of debt of 8% bonds

The before-tax cost of debt of the bonds is given as 7% per year.

After-tax cost of debt of bonds = 7 × (1 – 0.3) = 7 × 0.7 = 4.9% per year

Value of the 6% bank loan

The bank loan has no market value and so its book value of $40 million is used in calculating the weighted average cost of capital.

After-tax cost of debt of 6% bank loan

The interest rate of the bank loan can be used as its before-tax cost of debt. After-tax cost of debt of bank loan = 6 × (1 – 0.3) = 6 × 0.7 = 4.2% per year

Calculation of weighted average after-tax cost of capital (WACC)

Total value of company = 680m + 125.7m + 40m = $845.7m

After-tax WACC = ((680m × 10) + (125.7m × 4.9) + (40 × 4.2))/845.7 = 9.0 % per year

> *Examiner's note: the after-tax cost of debt of the 8% bonds could have been calculated using linear interpolation, although the result would be close to 4.9%.*

(c) The weighted average cost of capital (WACC) is the average return required by current providers of finance. The WACC therefore reflects the current risk of a company's business operations (business risk) and way in which the company is currently financed (financial risk). When the WACC is used as discount rate to appraise an investment project, an assumption is being made that the project's business risk and financial risk are the same as those currently faced by the investing company. If this is not the case, a marginal cost of capital or a project-specific discount rate must be used to assess the acceptability of an investment project.

The business risk of an investment project will be the same as current business operations if the project is an extension of existing business operations, and if it is small in comparison with current business operations. If this is the case, existing providers of finance will not change their current required rates of return. If these conditions are not met, a project-specific discount rate should be calculated, for example by using the capital asset pricing model.

The financial risk of an investment project will be the same as the financial risk currently faced by a company if debt and equity are raised in the same proportions as currently used, thus preserving the existing capital structure. If this is the case, the current WACC can be used to appraise a new investment project. It may still be appropriate to use the current WACC as a discount rate even when the incremental finance raised does not preserve the existing capital structure, providing that the existing capital structure is preserved on an average basis over time via subsequent finance-raising decisions.

Where the capital structure is changed by finance raised for an investment project, it may be appropriate to use the marginal cost of capital rather than the WACC.

ACCA marking scheme			Marks
(a)	Net asset value		1
	Dividend growth model value		2
	Earnings yield method		2
			―――
		Maximum	5
			―――
(b)	Market value of equity		1
	Market value per bond		2
	Market value of bonds		1
	After-tax cost of debt		1
	After-tax cost of bank loan		1
	Weighted average cost of capital		2
			―――
		Maximum	8
			―――
(c)	Business risk		2–3
	Financial risk		2–3
	Project-specific discount rate		1–2
	Marginal cost of capital		1–2
			―――
		Maximum	7
			―――
Total			20
			―――

Examiner's comments

Candidates were asked here to calculate the value of a company using net asset value, the dividend growth model and the earnings yield method.

It was surprising how many answers struggled to calculate net asset value from the statement of financial position figures provided in the question. This calculation is a relatively straightforward one.

Most candidates were able to calculate correctly the value of the company using the dividend growth model. Some answers wasted time calculating the value per share, but the question did not ask for this, rather it asked for the value of the company.

Fewer candidates were able to calculate correctly the value of the company using the earnings yield method, whether without earnings growth (earnings divided by earnings yield) or with earnings growth (using the growth model). Some answers converted the earnings yield figure given in the question into a price/earnings ratio (the one is the reciprocal of the other), but the price/earnings ratio valuation method was not asked for here. Some answers substituted the cost of equity for the earnings yield, or incorrectly used dividends rather than earnings.

The requirement in part (c) was to calculate the weighted average cost of capital (WACC) of a company. The cost of equity and the before-tax cost of debt were given in the question.

Some answers seemed to follow a learned routine for calculating WACC, without noting the information given by the question. This is the only reason I can offer to explain why some answers calculated the cost of equity, even though this was stated to be 10%.

In order to calculate the WACC, the market values of equity and the 8% bonds were needed. Most answers calculated correctly the market value of equity. Many answers then assumed that the market value of the bonds was $120 million, but this was in fact the nominal (par) value of the bonds in the statement of financial position. The information needed to calculate the market value per bond was given in the question: interest rate, redemption value, maturity and cost of debt. Some answers calculated the market value using the after-tax interest payments, when the interest payments should have been before tax.

The after-tax cost of debt could be calculated by multiplying the before-tax cost of debt by one minus the tax rate, or by linear interpolation. Many answers used linear interpolation, but if the market value of the bonds had not been calculated, the interpolation calculation had no purpose. Candidates should be aware that if a bond is trading at nominal value ($100) and is to be redeemed at nominal value ($100), then the interest rate is the same as the cost of debt. A linear interpolation calculation using these values to find the cost of debt simply goes round in a circle back to the interest rate.

While some answers ignored the bank loan, other answers correctly included it using the after-tax interest cost as its cost of debt, or explaining why it could be costed using the after-tax cost of debt of the 8% bonds.

A small number of answers added reserves to the market value of equity, but reserves are only of significance when using book values as weights.

Part(d) asked for a discussion of the circumstances under which WACC could be used as the discount rate in investment appraisal, together with a brief indication of alternative approaches that could be used where WACC was not appropriate.

Good answers identified and discussed the link between business risk, financial risk and WACC, along the lines covered by the suggested answer. Essentially, WACC can be used as the discount rate in investment appraisal if business risk and financial risk do not change. Some answers ignored the requirement to indicate briefly alternative approaches that could be adopted and discussed at length the use of the capital asset pricing model in investment appraisal.

55 MFZ CO

Key answer tips

Parts (a) and (b) should have been straightforward, involving a mixture of calculations and discussion. In part (c) make sure you answer the question set – only long term debt is referred to. The highlighted words are key phrases that markers are looking for.

(a) **Objective 1**

MFZ Co has stated an objective to achieve growth in profit before interest and tax of 4% per year. Analysis shows that profit before interest and tax growth was 3.4% in 2014 (18.3m/17.7m) and 3.5% in 2013 (17.7m/17.1m). MFZ Co has therefore not achieved this objective in either year.

Objective 2

Year	2014	2013	2012
Profit after tax	$12.8m	$12.4m	$12.0m
Number of shares	12m	12m	12m
Earnings per share	106.67c	103.33c	100.00c
Annual growth	3.2%	3.3%	

MFZ Co has stated an objective to achieve growth in earnings per share of 3.5% per year. Analysis shows that growth in earnings per share was 3.2% in 2014 (106.67c/103.33c) and 3.3% in 2013 (103.33c/100.00c). MFZ Co has therefore not achieved this objective in either year.

Objective 3

MFZ Co has stated an objective to achieve growth in total shareholder return (TSR) of 5% per year. Analysis shows that growth in TSR was 11.4% in 2014 and 11.7% in 2013. MFZ Co has therefore achieved this objective in both 2014 and 2013.

Year	2014	2013	2012
Equity market value	$56.4m	$55.2m	$54.0m
Number of shares	12m	12m	12m
Share price	$4.70	$4.60	$4.50
Dividends	$5.1m	$5.1m	$4.8m
Number of shares	12m	12m	12m
Dividend per share	42.5c	42.5c	40.0c

On a per share basis:

2014 TSR = 100 × (470 – 460 + 42.5)/460 = 11.4%

2013 TSR = 100 × (460 – 450 + 42.5)/450 = 11.7%

Alternatively, using total values:

2014 TSR = 100 × (56.4m – 55.2m + 5.1m)/55.2m = 11.4%

2013 TSR = 100 × (55.2m – 54.0m + 5.1m)/54.0m = 11.7%

(b) Historical dividends per share have been 42.5c (2014), 42.5c (2013) and 40.0c (2012). There has therefore been zero growth in dividend per share in 2014, 6.25% growth in dividend per share in 2013, and an average dividend growth rate of 3.1% over the two-year period from 2012 to 2014. The same result could be found by considering total dividend paid rather than dividend per share, since the number of shares has been constant over the two-year period. If historical dividend per share growth is assumed to be an indication of future dividend per share growth, it seems reasonable to use a dividend growth rate of 3.1% or zero in the dividend growth model (DGM).

Using zero future dividend growth, the 2014 share price using the DGM will be $3.54 per share (42.5/0.12) and the 2014 total equity market value will be $42.48m ($3.54 × 12m).

Using 3.1% dividend growth, the 2014 share price using the DGM will be $4.92 per share ((42.5 × 1.031)/(0.12 − 0.031)) and the 2014 total equity market value will be $59.04m ($4.92 × 12m).

The 2014 equity market value on the capital market is $56.4m. This is higher than the DGM value using zero future dividend growth and lower than the DGM value using 3.1% dividend growth. One reason for the difference between the 2014 equity market value and the values predicted by the DGM is that the capital market expects future growth in dividends to be different from the assumed value used in the DGM, e.g. slightly less than 3.1%.

The future cost of equity of MFZ Co may also differ from the current cost of equity of 12% used in the DGM calculation and the current market price may reflect an expectation of a future change in the cost of equity.

(c) There are a number of sources of long-term debt finance which may be available to a listed company such as MFZ Co, with a variety of characteristics.

Long-term bank loan

MFZ Co could obtain the $9.2m which it needs for investment purposes via a bank loan, from either a single bank or from a syndicate of banks. Interest payments on the bank loan could be annual, twice yearly or quarterly, and at either a fixed rate or a floating rate of interest. Repayments of capital may be required along with interest payments and it is possible that a constant cash amount would be regularly paid, with the amount of interest in the payment declining and the amount of capital in the payment increasing over time. It is likely that the bank loan would be secured against particular non-current assets of MFZ Co, so that the bank could recover its loan if the company defaults on interest payments.

Bonds or loan notes

Bonds or loan notes may be redeemable or irredeemable (permanent), although in recent years irredeemable corporate bonds have been very rare. Fixed rate or floating rate interest is paid on the bonds, either annually or half yearly, with the interest being based on nominal (par) value of the bonds rather than on their market value. Bonds, like ordinary shares, are mainly traded on the capital markets and can be issued in a variety of foreign currencies. Redemption of a large bond issue can pose a serious cash flow problem for a company and may call for refinancing rather than outright redemption. The return required on debt finance (the cost of debt) is lower than the return required on equity (the cost of equity), and so MFZ Co could reduce its average cost of capital by issuing debt finance, as it is currently financed by equity alone.

Convertible bonds or loan notes

Convertible bonds or loan notes are bonds which, at the option of the holder, can be converted into a specified quantity of ordinary shares (the conversion ratio) on a specified future date (the conversion date). They have the advantage for the issuing company that, assuming conversion terms are set appropriately, conversion will occur and so redemption can be avoided. If conversion occurs, there can be a significant reduction in the gearing of the issuing company. The future option to convert into equity has value to investors and as a consequence, the interest rate on convertible debt is lower than that on ordinary bonds. Convertible bonds can pay interest annually or twice annually, at a fixed or a floating rate of interest. If conversion does not take place, however, redemption of the bonds or loan notes will be required.

Deep discount bonds and zero coupon bonds

The return to a bond holder consists of regular interest payments (income) and repayment of the principle amount on redemption (capital). Investors may accept lower interest payments (lower income) in exchange for an increase in capital return. This can be achieved if the bond is issued at a deep discount to nominal value, but redeemed at nominal value. This kind of financial security is called a deep discount bond and may be suitable for companies which do not expect an immediate return on invested capital. A zero coupon bond goes a step further and pays no interest (coupon) at all, so that the return to the investor is entirely in the form of capital appreciation. Bonds like these are useful for companies which expect cash flows from invested capital to occur mainly later in the life of an investment project, rather than more evenly throughout its life.

ACCA marking scheme		Marks
(a)	Calculations of PBIT growth	1
	Comment on PBIT growth	1
	Calculations of EPS growth	1
	Comment on EPS growth 2014	1
	total shareholder return 2013	1
	total shareholder return	1
	Comment on TSR growth	1
	Maximum	**7**
(b)	Cash to be raised	1
	Rights issue price	1
	New shares issued	1
	Theoretical ex rights price per share	2
	Maximum	**5**
(c)	Long-term bank loan	1–2
	Bonds or loan notes	1–2
	Convertible bonds or loan notes	1–2
	Deep discount bonds and zero coupon bonds	1–2
	Other relevant discussion	1–2
	Maximum	**8**
Total		**20**

Examiner's comments

Part (a) asked candidates to analyse and discuss the extent to which a company had achieved each of three objectives during a two-year period. Overall performance was somewhat variable in quality.

The first objective related to profit before interest and tax (PBIT) and most candidates were able to calculate PBIT growth in each of two years, and discuss the extent to which the objective had been achieved. Some answers gave only a geometric mean growth rate, when annual growth rates were needed to discuss the extent to which the annual objectives had been achieved.

The second objective related to earnings per share (EPS) and some candidates were not able to calculate EPS, so the success rate (in terms of marks gained) for this objective was lower than for the first objective. Answers that calculated EPS correctly were usually able to discuss the extent to which the objective had been achieved.

The third objective related to total shareholder return (TSR) and a significant number of candidates had difficulty in calculating this. The success rate for this objective was therefore lower than for the first two objectives. TSR is the actual return to an investor for buying a share at the start of the year, so it is the sum of the capital gain and dividend for the year, expressed as a percentage of the opening share price. While dividend yield was therefore a useful figure to calculate, the dividend growth rate was not. Calculations could be made on a whole company or on a per share basis, as the number of shares in issue was constant over the two-year period. Answers that calculated TSR correctly were usually able to discuss the extent to which the objective had been achieved

The requirement for part (b) was to calculate the total equity market value of a company using the dividend growth model (DGM) and then to discuss why this value might differ from the current equity market value.

While most candidates were able to calculate the historic dividend growth rate, some candidates experienced difficulty in using the DGM. As discussed in previous examiner reports, some candidates wrote out the DGM in a format for calculating the cost of equity, and then either calculated a cost of equity (although the value of this was given in the question) or tried to rearrange the formula having inserted values for all variables other than the equity market value. Both approaches are surprising because the growth model is given in the formulae sheet.

Some candidates got into difficulties with magnitudes, e.g. calculating the total equity market value in millions of dollars using the DGM and then multiplying this value by the total number of shares as though it were in dollars per share.

Part (c) asked candidates to discuss the sources and characteristics of long-term debt finance available to the company in the question. Many candidates struggled to gain good marks.

One reason that some candidates struggled to gain marks was because they did not read the requirement carefully. Since a discussion of long-term debt finance was needed, no credit was given to discussions of short-term debt finance (e.g. overdrafts) or equity finance (such as ordinary shares and preference shares).

The suggested answer looks at long-term bank loans, bonds or loan notes, convertible bonds and loan notes, and deep discount bonds and zero coupon bonds. Credit was given to answers that discussed finance leasing and sale and leaseback. Credit was also given to answers that discussed the characteristics of long-term debt finance from a general perspective, rather than using the sources of debt finance perspective of the suggested answer.

56   NN CO

Key answer tips

A fairly straightforward question for this key syllabus area. The calculations in parts (a) to (c) shouldn't present many problems and the discursive part (d) on market efficiency was also straightforward. The highlighted words are key phrases that markers are looking for.

(a) Using the dividend growth model, the share price of NN Co will be the present value of its expected future dividends, i.e. (66 × 1.03)/(0.12 – 0.03) = 755 cents per share or $7.55 per share

Number of ordinary shares = 50/0.5 = 100m shares

Value of NN Co = 100m × 7.55 = $755m

Net asset value of NN Co = total assets less total liabilities = 143 – 29 – 20 – 25 = $69m

In calculating net asset value, preference share capital is included with long-term liabilities, as it considered to be prior charge capital.

Tutorial note:

Don't forget that you're trying to get back to the value of the company for the owners – meaning the ordinary shareholders. This is why you need to also deduct the value of preference shares, even though they are not shown as liabilities on the statement of financial position.

(b) The after-tax cost of debt of NN Co can be found by linear interpolation

The annual after-tax interest payment = 7 × (1 – 0.25) = 7 × 0.75 = $5.25 per year

Year	Cash flow ($)	5% Discount factor	Present value ($)
0	(103.50)	1.000	(103.50)
1–6	5.25	5.076	26.65
6	100	0.746	74.60
			(2.25)

Year	Cash flow ($)	4% Discount factor	Present value ($)
0	(103.50)	1.000	(103.50)
1–6	5.25	5.242	27.52
6	100	0.790	79.00
			3.02

After-tax cost of debt = 4 + [(1 × 3.02)/(3.02 + 2.25)] = 4 + 0.57 = 4.6%

Tutorial note:

The calculated value of the after-tax cost of debt will be influenced by the choice of discount rates used in the linear interpolation calculation and so other values would also gain credit here.

(c)   Annual preference dividend = 8% × 50 cents = 4 cents per share

Cost of preference shares = 100 × (4/67) = 6%

Number of ordinary shares = 50/0.5 = 100m shares

Market value of equity = V_e = 100m shares × 8.30 = $830m

Number of preference shares = 25/0.5 = 50m shares

Market value of preference shares = V_p = 0.67 × 50m = $33.5m

Market value of long-term borrowings = V_d = 20 × 103.50/100 = $20.7m

Total market value of company = ($V_e + V_d + V_p$) = (830 + 33.5 + 20.7) = $884.2m

WACC = ($k_e V_e + k_p V_p + k_d(1 - T)V_d$)/ ($V_e + V_p + V_d$) = (12 × 830 + 6 × 33.5 + 4.6 × 20.7)/884.2 = 11.6%

(d)   Market efficiency is usually taken to refer to the way in which ordinary share prices reflect information. Fama defined an efficient market as one in which share prices fully and fairly reflect all available information.

A semi-strong form efficient market is one where share prices reflect all publicly available information, such as past share price movements, published company annual reports and analysts' reports in the financial press.

A strong form market is one where share prices reflect all information, whether publicly available or not. Share prices would reflect, for example, takeover decisions made at private board meetings.

ACCA marking scheme			
			Marks
(a)	Share price using dividend growth model		2
	Value of company using dividend growth model		1
	Net asset value of company		2
		Maximum	5
(b)	Correct use of taxation		1
	Calculation of after-tax cost of debt		3
		Maximum	4
(c)	Cost of preference shares		1
	Market value of equity		1
	Market value of preference shares		1
	Market value of debt		1
	Weighted average cost of capital		2
		Maximum	6
(d)	Explanation of "efficiency"		1–2
	Semi-strong form		1–2
	Strong form		1–2
		Maximum	5
Total			20

Examiner's comments

Many candidates did well in parts (a)(i), (b) and (c), while doing poorly in part (a)(ii) and struggling to remain focused on the question asked in part (d).

In part (a) candidates were required to calculate the equity value of a company using the dividend growth model (DGM) and then the net asset value.

Many candidates calculated correctly the share price of the company using the DGM, although some candidates failed to multiply this share price by the number of shares to give the equity value of the company. Poorer answers re-arranged the DGM in order to calculate a cost of equity using the current share price, but this was unnecessary, as the cost of equity was given in the question.

The net asset value calculated by many candidates showed that they were uncertain as to the meaning of 'net asset value'. Some candidates gave a net asset value of $94 million, a figure which fails to treat preference share capital as prior charge capital and hence include it with long-term liabilities.

Part (b) asked candidates to calculate the after-tax cost of debt of a company. Many candidates gained full marks by calculating the after-tax interest payment, using two discount rates to calculate two net present values for investing in the bond, and using linear interpolation to calculate the after-tax cost of debt. Answers that did not gain full marks contained errors such as using the wrong tax rate (it was 25%), addition or multiplication errors, using the before-tax interest payment, or putting incorrect values to variables in the linear interpolation calculation.

Some answers calculated the cost of capital of preference shares in addition to calculating the after-tax cost of debt, and then attempted to average the two costs of capital. While preference shares are classed as prior charge capital, they pay a dividend, not interest, and preference shares are not debt.

In part (c), candidates were required to calculate the weighted average cost of capital (WACC) of a company. Candidates therefore needed to calculate the market values of ordinary shares, preference shares and bonds, and the preference share cost of capital, having already calculated the after-tax cost of debt and being given the cost of equity by the question.

The most common reason for not gaining full marks was calculating incorrectly the cost of capital of the preference shares. This can be found by dividing the preference dividend by the market price of the preference share, but many candidates used the dividend rate of the preference shares (8% per year) as the dividend, instead of calculating the preference dividend from the nominal value (par value), i.e. 8% of 50 cents giving a dividend of 4 cents per share.

Other reasons for losing marks included aggregating the market values of ordinary shares and preference shares, before applying the cost of equity to both: omitting the preference share capital from the WACC calculation; multiplying the after-tax cost of debt by (1 − t) (one minus the tax rate); and calculating a new cost of equity, even though the cost of equity was given in the question.

57   CORHIG CO

Key answer tips

To answer this question effectively you need a logical approach and an awareness of the calculations behind the valuation methods. A look down the formulae sheet will help to reveal the correct path.

The highlighted words are key phrases that markers are looking for.

(a)

Tutorial note:

On the face of it, the price/earnings ratio valuation method is simple. Find an earnings figure, or earnings per share (EPS) figure, multiply by a price/earnings ratio and you have either the value of the company (if you used earnings) or a share price (if you used EPS). The number of issued shares of Corhig Co was not given in the question and some answers invented a figure, but as the requirement was to calculate the value of the company, the number of shares was not needed.

Price/earnings ratio valuation

The value of the company using this valuation method is found by multiplying future earnings by a price/earnings ratio. Using the earnings of Corhig Co in Year 1 and the price/earnings ratio of similar listed companies gives a value of 3,000,000 × 5 = $15,000,000.

Using the current average price/earnings ratio of similar listed companies as the basis for the valuation rests on two questionable assumptions. First, in terms of similarity, the valuation assumes similar business operations, similar capital structures, similar earnings growth prospects, and so on. In reality, no two companies are identical. Second, in terms of using an average price/earnings ratio, this may derive from companies that are large and small, successful and failing, low-geared and high-geared, and domestic or international in terms of markets served. The calculated company value therefore has a large degree of uncertainty attached to it.

The earnings figure used in the valuation does not include expected earnings growth. If average forecast earnings over the next three years are used ($3.63 million), the price/earnings ratio value increases by 21% to $18.15 million (3.63 × 5). Although earnings growth beyond the third year is still ignored, $18.15 million is likely to be a better estimate of the value of the company than $15 million because it recognises that earnings are expected to increase by almost 50% in the next three years.

(b)

> *Tutorial note:*
>
> *A useful point to remember with questions such as this, is that it is essential to pin down the amount and the timing of future cash flows when calculating present values.*

Value of company using the dividend valuation model

The current cost of equity using the capital asset pricing model = 4 + (1.6 × 5) = 12%

Since a dividend will not be paid in Year 1, the dividend growth model cannot be applied straight away. However, dividends after Year 3 are expected to grow at a constant annual rate of 3% per year and so the dividend growth model can be applied to these dividends. The present value of these dividends is a Year 3 present value, which will need discounting back to year 0. The market value of the company can then be found by adding this to the present value of the forecast dividends in Years 2 and 3.

PV of year 2 dividend = $500{,}000/1.12^2$ = $398,597

PV of year 3 dividend = $1{,}000{,}000/1.12^3$ = $711,780

Year 3 PV of dividends after year 3 = (1,000,000 × 1.03)/(0.12 − 0.03) = $11,444,444

Year 0 PV of these dividends = $11{,}444{,}444/1.12^3$ = $8,145,929

Market value from dividend valuation model = 398,597 + 711,780 + 8,145,929 = $9,256,306 or approximately $9.3 million.

Alternative calculation of dividend valuation method market value

The year 3 dividend of $1m can be treated as D1 from the perspective of year 2

The year 2 value of future dividends using the dividend growth model will then be:

$1,000,000/(0.12 − 0.03) = $11,111,111

Year 0 PV of these dividends = 11,111,111/1.122 = $8,857,710

Adding the PV of the year 2 dividend gives a market value of 8,857,710 + 398,597 = $9,256,308 which, allowing for rounding, is the same as the earlier calculated value.

(c) **Current weighted average after-tax cost of capital**

Current cost of equity using the capital asset pricing model = 12%

After-tax cost of debt = 5 × (1 − 0.2) = 5 × 0.8 = 4%

Current after-tax WACC = (12 × 0.75) + (4 × 0.25) = 10% per year

Weighted average after-tax cost of capital after new debt issue

Revised cost of equity = K_e = 4 + (2.0 × 5) = 14%

Revised after-tax cost of debt = 6 × (1 − 0.2) = 6 × 0.8 = 4.8%

Revised after-tax WACC = (14 × 0.6) + (4.8 × 0.4) = 10.32% per year

Comment

The after-tax WACC has increased slightly from 10% to 10.32%. This change is a result of the increases in the cost of equity and the after-tax cost of debt, coupled with the change in gearing. Although the cost of equity has increased, the effect of the increase has been reduced because the proportion of equity finance has fallen from 75% to 60% of the long-term capital employed. Although the after-tax cost of debt has increased, the cost of debt is less than the cost of equity and the proportion of cheaper debt finance has increased from 25% to 40% of the long-term capital employed.

(d)   **Nature and assessment of business risk**

Business risk arises due to the nature of a company's business operations, which determines the business sector into which it is classified, and to the way in which a company conducts its business operations. It is the variability in shareholder returns that arises as a result of business operations.

Business risk can therefore be related to the way in which profit before interest and tax (PBIT or operating profit) changes as revenue or turnover changes. This can be assessed from a shareholder perspective by calculating operational gearing, which essentially looks at the relative proportions of fixed operating costs to variable operating costs.

Another measure of operational gearing that can be used is (100 × contribution/PBIT), although other measures are also used.

ACCA marking scheme		Marks
(a)	Price/earnings value using year 1 earnings	1
	Price/earnings value using average earnings	1
	Discussion of variables	2
	Maximum	4
(b)	Calculation of current cost of equity using CAPM	1
	PV of year 2 dividends	0.5
	PV of year 3 dividends	0.5
	Year 3 DGM value	2
	Year 0 PV of year 3 DGM value	1
	Company value using dividend valuation model	1
	Maximum	6
(c)	After-tax cost of debt	1
	After-tax WACC	1
	Revised cost of equity using CAPM	2
	Revised after-tax WACC	1
	Comment on change in WACC	1
	Maximum	6
(d)	Nature of business risk	1–2
	Assessment of business risk	1–2
	Maximum	4
Total		20

Examiner's comments

In part (a) the requirement was to calculate the value of a company (Corhig Co) using the price/earnings ratio (PER) method, discussing the usefulness of the variables used. Many students struggled with this question.

In reality, the PER method presents a number of problems, and this was illustrated by the question, which provided forecast earnings for the end of year 1, the end of year 2 and the end of year 3. What earnings figure should be used to give a PER value? It is better to use future earnings than past earnings and as the question shows, a value for future earnings should not be selected mechanically, but after careful thought.

Part (b) asked for a calculation of the current cost of equity of Corhig Co, and an estimate of the value of the company using the dividend valuation model.

Most answers correctly calculated the current cost of equity using the capital asset pricing model, although some answers confused the equity risk premium of 5% given in the question with the return on the market. Most answers struggled to use the dividend valuation model to value the company. Simply put, the dividend valuation model holds that the value of a company is equal to the present value of its future dividend. Most answers limited their valuation attempt to using the dividend growth model, ignoring the dividend expected in year 2. The dividend growth model can be used to provide a year 3 present value of the dividend stream expected after year 3. This year 2 present value then needed to be discounted back to year 0, and added to the present values of the dividend from years 2 and 3, to give the value of the company.

Part (c) asked candidates to calculate the current weighted average cost of capital (WACC) of Corhig Co, and then the revised WACC following a debt issue, commenting on the difference between the two values. Many answers gained high marks here, although some answers failed to offer a comment.

Many answers to part (d) showed the need to think about the nature of the risk faced by shareholders. Better answers gave evidence of an understanding of underlying concepts and used key terms.

58 MAT CO

Key answer tips

To answer part (a) effectively you need a logical approach and an awareness of the calculations behind the valuation methods. A look down the formulae sheet will help to reveal the correct path for part (a) (i).

This question is an excellent example of how calculations alone will not get you through this paper. Part (b) requires you to understand the meaning of the calculations so you can comment sensibly on your results. Finally, part (c) gives you an opportunity to demonstrate your knowledge about raising finance. If you are to score well on this section you must apply your comments to the specific scenario presented.

(a) (i) **Dividend growth model**

From the formulae sheet - $P_0 = \dfrac{Do(1+g)}{(r_e - g)}$

Tutorial note:

From the formulae sheet you can directly see that to calculate the share price (P_0) using the growth model, you will need three pieces of information: the dividend (D_0), the growth rate in dividends (g) and the cost of equity (r_e). Now you can look into the scenario and see how this information can be obtained.

1   You're told the dividend about to be paid is 5.0 cents.

2   You've been provided with information on the dividends paid in recent years. This means you can calculate the historic growth rate and assume this will continue in the future. Since we don't have any information on profitability, this will be only method of estimating dividend growth in this question.

3   You've been told that the return on government bonds (i.e. the risk free rate of return) is 5% and that the equity risk premium ($R_m - R_f$) is 8%. These pieces of information should trigger you to realise that CAPM can be used to calculate the cost of equity. In the formulae sheet you're given the correct formula to use.

To calculate the cost of equity (r_e) using CAPM, we have the formula (from the sheet)

$E(r)_j = R_f + \beta_j (E(r_m) - R_f)$

$r_e = 5\% + (1.15 \times 8\%) = 14.2\%$

Annual dividend growth (g) = $\sqrt[n]{\dfrac{\text{current dividend}}{\text{dividend n years ago}}} - 1$

$g = \sqrt[3]{\dfrac{5.0}{4.1}} - 1 = 0.0684$

Value per share = $\dfrac{5.0 \times 1.0684}{0.142 - 0.0684}$ = 72.6c

Total number of shares – $40m ÷ 0.25 = 160 million

Total equity value (ex div) – 160m × $0.726 = $116.16m

(b)

Summary of equity values:

Dividend growth model (from (a)(i) above)	$116.16m
Total market value of equity (ex div) (from the scenario):	
160m × ($0.66 – $0.05) =	$97.6m

Tutor's top tips:

To score well on this sort of requirement you must look at each number in turn and outline the arguments for and against the value as a basis. Remember, business valuation is not a precise science and many of the theories presented can be challenged when faced with reality.

Comments:

The dividend growth model value is just under $20m higher than the current market value.

A market value is often considered a highly relevant value but the current market value of MAT Co could be understated because the market is a secondary market and hence may not be so efficient and may not properly reflect the value of MAT Co. The market value may also be understated because the shares in the company are only traded infrequently and hence are not very liquid.

The dividend growth model could be incorrect and hence less relevant as it is very sensitive to changes in the inputs. For instance the forecast dividend growth rate is just based on recent growth and could prove wrong. The growth rate forecast of 6.84% does seem high given recent economic circumstances and could well prove unsustainable. Equally the cost of equity used is based on an estimate of the equity beta. This estimate could be incorrect.

(c)

Tutor's top tips:

Key to scoring well on this requirement is to relate your comments back to the scenario given. Simply writing a list of generic factors that any company should consider will not score highly.

The directors of MAT Co should take the following factors into account when considering how to raise additional finance:

Cost – Debt finance is cheaper and hence if the company has the capacity to raise more debt it could be advantageous. Indeed given the property value in the company of $65m and the long term debt of only $18m the company would seem capable of raising more debt.

Cash flows – Prior to raising more debt the company must forecast future cash flows to ensure sufficient cash will be generated to service any debt raised. Given the current cash balances the company does seem to be cash generative.

Risk – Prior to raising finance the directors must consider the risk of the company. For instance if future expansion is going to increase the business risk of the company they may be more wary of taking on more debt and increasing the financial risk. Equally the directors should consider the gearing/financial risk of similar companies and the appetite for risk of the shareholders.

Availability – The directors must consider the likely availability of finance.

As the shares do not seem very liquid raising new equity from new investors may be difficult. Equally they should question whether the existing shareholders have the ability to support a rights issue. Given the recent dividend growth and dividend yield they may be happy to invest more in the company.

More debt finance is likely to be available if the company can show good cash flow forecasts as plenty of security seems available.

Security & Covenants – The directors must be aware that additional debt finance is likely to require security and may require covenants. The directors must ensure they are happy to give any such guarantees before raising additional debt.

Control – The directors must consider that raising equity from new investors could have an impact upon the control of the company.

Duration – The directors must consider the term of any proposed finance and make sure it is appropriate given the nature of what it is to be invested in. Furthermore the investors should ensure that any new debt finance does not become repayable at the same time as the existing long term liability as this could put a large cash flow strain on the company.

Economic outlook – Prior to raising finance the directors should ensure that they have considered the outlook for the economy and the impact this could have on the trade of the company and the cost of finance. In particular the outlook for interest rates should be considered if debt finance is to be raised.

59   THP CO   *Walk in the footsteps of a top tutor*

Key answer tips

The key learning point from this question is the importance of making sure your marker can follow your answer. This will often involve explaining your thought process, including commenting on why the calculation you've performed is the right approach. The highlighted words are key phrases that markers are looking for.

Tutor's top tips:

In the 15 minutes reading time you should aim to have skim read the scenario, getting a feeling for the information you've been provided with and paying particular attention to names and dates. You should also have skim read the requirement, underlining the models referred to and noted the calculations that are being asked for. Look for any part of the question that relies purely on knowledge of the syllabus (i.e. no calculations) and flag these as a good place to start. Part (e) of this question falls into this category.

Once you've completed part (e) you should look at the other requirements. Is there a specific order you will need to do them in or can you choose your strongest area to do first. Here we'll need to tackle the requirements in order as you need the output of part (a) to answer part (b).

Tutor's top tips:

In part (a) you should follow the order presented in the requirement. It is leading you through the process. All the information is stated in the scenario or can be calculated without many complications. Part (iv) is the area most likely to cause problems (although you might not realise it at the time). The majority of situations the market capitalisation after an issue would be the TERP × new number of shares in issue. However, in this scenario, we've been told of some issue costs which must be deducted. Don't worry if you didn't spot this, it will only have been worth 2 marks (maximum). However, this does show the benefits of querying every piece of information provided by the examiner and asking "why has he told me that?"

(a)   **Rights issue price**

This is at a 20% discount to the current share price = 4.80 × 0.8 = $3.84 per share

New shares issued = 3m/3 = 1m

Cash raised = 1m × 3.84 = $3,840,000

Theoretical ex rights price = [(3 × 4.80) + 3.84]/4 = $4.56 per share

Market capitalisation after rights issue = 14.4m + 3.84m = $18.24 – 0.32m = $17.92m

This is equivalent to a share price of 17.92/4 = $4.48 per share

The issue costs result in a decrease in the market value of the company and therefore a decrease in the wealth of shareholders equivalent to 8c per share.

Tutor's top tips:

The key to part (b) is recognising that since CRX is in the same business sector as THP, you can use THP's P/E ratio as a proxy for CRX. Whilst you're not specifically told this, you do have the information to work it out. Make sure your answer explains what you're doing and why this is an acceptable approach.

(b)   **Price/earnings ratio valuation**

Price/earnings ratio of THP Co = 480/64 = 7.5

Earnings per share of CRX Co = 44.8c per share

Using the price earnings ratio method, share price of CRX Co = (44.8 × 7.5)/100 = $3.36

Market capitalisation of CRX Co = 3.36 × 1m = $3,360,000

(Alternatively, earnings of CRX Co = 1m × 0.448 = $448,000 × 7.5 = $3,360,000)

Tutor's top tips:

Part (c) starts by asking you to assume a semi-strong form efficient market. Your first thought should be to consider the implications of this, which is that only publicly available information will be reflected in the share price. Again, you should note down your thought process. Next you will need to identify what will affect the market capitalisation post acquisition. You should conclude this will be the market capitalisation of THP plus the market capitalisation of CRX less the price paid for CRX (since this cash has left the business). All of this information is available, either as a result of your previous calculations or given in the scenario. Only in part (ii) will we need to factor in the additional savings since this information has now been made public.

(c)   In a semi-strong form efficient capital market, share prices reflect past and public information. If the expected annual after-tax savings are not announced, this information will not therefore be reflected in the share price of THP Co. In this case, the post acquisition market capitalisation of THP Co will be the market capitalisation after the rights issue, plus the market capitalisation of the acquired company (CRX Co), less the price paid for the shares of CRX Co, since this cash has left the company in exchange for purchased shares. It is assumed that the market capitalisations calculated in earlier parts of this question are fair values, including the value of CRX Co calculated by the price/earnings ratio method.

Price paid for CRX Co = 3.84m – 0.32m = $3.52m

Market capitalisation = 17.92m + 3.36m – 3.52m = $17.76m

This is equivalent to a share price of 17.76/4 = $4.44 per share

The market capitalisation has decreased from the value following the rights issue because THP Co has paid $3.52m for a company apparently worth $3.36m. This is a further decrease in the wealth of shareholders, following on from the issue costs of the rights issue.

If the annual after-tax savings are announced, this information will be reflected quickly and accurately in the share price of THP Co since the capital market is semi-strong form efficient. The savings can be valued using the price/earnings ratio method as having a present value of $720,000 (7.5 × 96,000). The revised market capitalisation of THP Co is therefore $18.48m (17.76m + 0.72m), equivalent to a share price of $4.62 per share (18.48/4). This makes the acquisition of CRX Co attractive to the shareholders of THP Co, since it offers a higher market capitalisation than the one following the rights issue. Each shareholder of THP Co would experience a capital gain of 14c per share (4.62 – 4.48).

In practice, the capital market is likely to anticipate the annual after-tax savings before they are announced by THP Co.

Tutor's top tips:

Part (d) is an opportunity to score an easy 8 marks by discussing the relative things to consider when deciding between debt and equity. Be careful though, the requirement does specify that your points should be relevant to THP. So for example, don't just talk about the impact on gearing, work it out using the information provided. To ensure you don't spend too much time on this part of the question, you should think about the mark allocation. For 8 marks where you are being asked to 'discuss' you should be spend no more than 14 minutes (8 × 1.8 mins per mark) talking about 4 factors THP should consider. Contrast this with a requirement to 'state' or 'list' which is more likely to attract only 1 mark per relevant point.

(d)   There are a number of factors that should be considered by THP Co, including the following:

Gearing and financial risk

Equity finance will decrease gearing and financial risk, while debt finance will increase them. Gearing for THP Co is currently 68.5% and this will decrease to 45% if equity finance is used, or rise to 121% if debt finance is used. There may also be some acquired debt finance in the capital structure of CRX Co. THP Co needs to consider what level of financial risk is desirable, from both a corporate and a stakeholder perspective.

Target capital structure

THP Co needs to compare its capital structure after the acquisition with its target capital structure. If its primary financial objective is to maximise the wealth of shareholders, it should seek to minimise its weighted average cost of capital (WACC). In practical terms this can be achieved by having some debt in its capital structure, since debt is relatively cheaper than equity, while avoiding the extremes of too little gearing (WACC can be decreased further) or too much gearing (the company suffers from the costs of financial distress).

Availability of security

Debt will usually need to be secured on assets by either a fixed charge (on specific assets) or a floating charge (on a specified class of assets). The amount of finance needed to buy CRX CO would need to be secured by a fixed charge to specific fixed assets of THP Co. Information on these fixed assets and on the secured status of the existing 8% loan notes has not been provided.

Economic expectations

If THP Co expects buoyant economic conditions and increasing profitability in the future, it will be more prepared to take on fixed interest debt commitments than if it believes difficult trading conditions lie ahead.

Control issues

A rights issue will not dilute existing patterns of ownership and control, unlike an issue of shares to new investors. The choice between offering new shares to existing shareholders and to new shareholders will depend in part on the amount of finance that is needed, with rights issues being used for medium-sized issues and issues to new shareholders being used for large issues. Issuing traded debt also has control implications however, since restrictive or negative covenants are usually written into the bond issue documents.

Workings

Current gearing (debt/equity, book value basis) = 100 × 5,000/7,300 = 68.5%

Gearing if equity finance is used = 100 × 5,000/(7,300 + 3,840) = 45%

Gearing if debt finance is used = 100 × (5,000 + 3,840)/7,300 = 121%

ACCA marking scheme		
		Marks
(a)	Rights issue price	1
	Cash raised	1
	Theoretical ex rights price per share	1
	Market capitalisation	2
		──
		5
(b)	Calculation of price/earnings ratio	1
	Price/earnings ratio valuation	2
		──
		3
(c)	Calculations of market capitalisation	2–3
	Comment	3–4
		──
	Maximum	5
(d)	Relevant discussion	6–7
	Links to scenario in question	2–3
		──
	Maximum	7
Total		──
		20
		──

Examiner's comments

In part (a) candidates were asked to calculate the rights issue price per share, the cash raised by the rights issue, the theoretical ex rights price per share and the market capitalisation after the rights issue.

A significant number of candidates showed that they were unfamiliar with this part of the syllabus and gave answers that gained little credit. Candidates should be aware that rights issues will not be made at a discount to par value.

Part (b) required the use of the price/earnings ratio method to calculate a share price and market capitalisation. Answers to this part of question 2 were often incomplete or adopted an incorrect methodology, for example calculating the price/earnings ratio of the target company when the question did not give the information needed for this. The correct approach is to multiply an earnings per share figure (or total earnings) by a suitable price/earnings ratio (in this case that of the acquirer).

Part (c) asked candidates to calculate and comment on market capitalisation before and after an announcement of expected annual after-tax cost savings, assuming a semi-strong form efficient market. The key thing to remember here is that in such a market, share prices fully and fairly reflect all relevant past and public information. The market capitalisation after the announcement would include the present value of the expected savings, calculated for example by the price/earnings method or by the dividend growth model. Before the announcement, the market capitalisation would not include this information and would be the market capitalisation immediately after the rights issue had taken place, adjusted for issue costs and the market value of the company acquired. Many candidates did not offer any calculations to support their discussion here, or offered calculations that did not relate to the question asked. Please refer to the suggested answer to this question for more detailed information on appropriate discussion and calculations.

Part (d) asked for a discussion of the factors that should be considered in choosing between equity and debt, with the answer being related to the circumstances of the acquirer and its proposed cash offer. Good answers focused on the circumstances of the company, considered its current capital structure, and discussed such factors as financial risk, current and expected interest rates, security and servicing costs, while weak answers offered a brief list of points with no discussion.

60   DARTIG CO

Key answer tips

This question has a few trickier elements that may unnerve some students.

Part (e) gives the easiest opportunity to grab marks. A straightforward explanation of the agency problem as well as how share options could be used to reduce the issue should allow most students to score highly. Being unrelated to the other parts, it should be tackled first.

The other four parts to the question all require some degree of calculations. Part (a) is also straightforward, and should result in full marks for most candidates.

Part (d) should be reasonable for most candidates. The highlighted words are key phrases that markers are looking for.

(a)   Rights issue price = 2.5 × 0.8 = $2.00 per share

Theoretical ex rights price = ((2.50 × 4) + (1 × 2.00)/5=$2.40 per share

(Alternatively, number of rights shares issued = $5m/$2.00 = 2.5m shares

Existing number of shares = 4 × 2.5m = 10m shares

Theoretical ex rights price per share = ((10m × 2.50) + (2.5m × 2.00))/12.5m = $2.40)

Tutor's top tips:

In parts (b) and (c), students may be thrown by the assertion that "the expansion of existing business will allow the average growth rate of earnings per share over the last four years to be maintained". A rights issue would normally result in a fall in EPS due to the higher number of shares in issue. In this case though, the new finance from the rights issue will be invested and will earn a sufficiently high return to avoid the usual reduction. Indeed, growth of 4% is being predicted.

Some background calculations may help to illustrate this further:

$$\frac{\$5m}{\$2.50 \times 80\%} = 2.5 \text{ million new shares to be issued.}$$

A 1 for 4 rights issue therefore implies the company must have 10 million shares in issue at present and will have 12.5 million after the rights issue.

Current EPS = 32.4 cents. Total earnings is therefore 0.324 × 10 million = $3.24 million

New total earnings will be 12.5 million × $0.324 × 1.04 = $4.21 million.

> *In the cold light of day it is not unreasonable to expect the finance raised to increase earnings by this amount (an annual return of just under 20%). However, such rational thought often escapes candidates within the pressure of the exam hall.*

(b)   Current price/earnings ratio = 250/32.4 = 7.7 times

Average growth rate of earnings per share = $100 \times ((32.4/27.7)^{0.25} - 1) = 4.0\%$

Earnings per share following expansion = $32.4 \times 1.04 = 33.7$ cents per share

Share price predicted by price/earnings ratio method = $33.7 \times 7.7 = \$2.60$

Since the price/earnings ratio of Dartig Co has remained constant in recent years and the expansion is of existing business, it seems reasonable to apply the existing price/earnings ratio to the revised earnings per share value.

(c)   The proposed business expansion will be an acceptable use of the rights issue funds if it increases the wealth of the shareholders. The share price predicted by the price/earnings ratio method is \$2.60. This is greater than the current share price of \$2.50, but this is not a valid comparison, since it ignores the effect of the rights issue on the share price. The rights issue has a neutral effect on shareholder wealth, but the cum rights price is changed by the increase in the number of shares and by the transformation of cash wealth into security wealth from a shareholder point of view. The correct comparison is with the theoretical ex rights price, which was found earlier to be \$2.40. Dartig Co shareholders will experience a capital gain due to the business expansion of \$2.60 – 2.40 = 20 cents per share. However, these share prices are one year apart and hence not directly comparable.

If the dividend yield remains at 6% per year ($100 \times 15.0/250$), the dividend per share for 2008 will be 15.6 cents (other estimates of the 2008 dividend per share are possible). Adding this to the capital gain of 20 cents gives a total shareholder return of 35.6 cents or 14.24% ($100 \times 35.6/240$). This is greater than the cost of equity of 10% and so shareholder wealth has increased.

Tutor's top tips:

The model answer for both parts (b) and (c) both illustrate an approach to the question set but it is doubtful that many students actually produced the results presented, especially regarding the total shareholder return. However, even if you have difficulties getting your head around the situation, it is still possible to gather many of the marks. Method marks are available for any students who demonstrate a logical approach and utilise the basic price/earnings ratio method.

(d)   The primary financial management objective of a company is usually taken to be the maximisation of shareholder wealth. In practice, the managers of a company acting as agents for the principals (the shareholders) may act in ways which do not lead to shareholder wealth maximisation. The failure of managers to maximise shareholder wealth is referred to as the agency problem.

Shareholder wealth increases through payment of dividends and through appreciation of share prices. Since share prices reflect the value placed by buyers on the right to receive future dividends, analysis of changes in shareholder wealth focuses on changes in share prices. The objective of maximising share prices is commonly used as a substitute objective for that of maximising shareholder wealth.

The agency problem arises because the objectives of managers differ from those of shareholders: because there is a divorce or separation of ownership from control in modern companies; and because there is an asymmetry of information between shareholders and managers which prevents shareholders being aware of most managerial decisions.

One way to encourage managers to act in ways that increase shareholder wealth is to offer them share options. These are rights to buy shares on a future date at a price which is fixed when the share options are issued. Share options will encourage managers to make decisions that are likely to lead to share price increases (such as investing in projects with positive net present values), since this will increase the rewards they receive from share options. The higher the share price in the market when the share options are exercised, the greater will be the capital gain that could be made by managers owning the options.

Share options therefore go some way towards reducing the differences between the objectives of shareholders and managers. However, it is possible that managers may be rewarded for poor performance if share prices in general are increasing. It is also possible that managers may not be rewarded for good performance if share prices in general are falling. It is difficult to decide on a share option exercise price and a share option exercise date that will encourage managers to focus on increasing shareholder wealth while still remaining challenging, rather than being easily achievable.

ACCA marking scheme			
			Marks
(a)	Rights issue price	1	
	Theoretical ex rights price per share	2	
		—	
			3
(b)	Existing price/earnings ratio	1	
	Revised earnings per share	1	
	Share price using price/earnings method	1	
		—	
			3
(c)	Discussion of share price comparisons	3 – 4	
	Calculation of capital gain and comment	1 – 2	
		—	
			Max 5
(d)	Discussion of agency problem	4 – 5	
	Discussion of share option schemes	4 – 5	
		—	
			Max 9
Total			25

Examiner's comments

In part (a), candidates were asked to calculate a theoretical ex rights price per share. Many candidates gained full marks for their calculations. Weaker answers made errors as regards the form of the issue (it was 1 for 4, not 4 for 1), or thought the theoretical ex rights price was the rights issue price, or calculated the value of the rights.

Part (b) required the calculation of the share price after the business expansion, using the price/earnings ratio method. The first step was to calculate the current price/earnings ratio. The second step was to calculate the earnings per share (EPS) after the proposed business expansion. The final step was to calculate the future share price by multiplying the two together.

A number of candidates were not able to calculate the price/earnings ratio by dividing the current share price by the current EPS. Calculating the EPS after the expansion by multiplying the current EPS by the average historic EPS growth rate was also a problem for some candidates, who were unable to calculate average historic growth rate, or who applied the growth rate to the average EPS rather than the current EPS.

Some students were also unfamiliar with the PER valuation method, even though this is discussed in the study texts.

Part (c) asked for a discussion of whether the business expansion was an acceptable use of the rights issue funds, and an evaluation of the effect of the expansion on the wealth of shareholders. The two parts of the question are linked, since the question of whether the use made of the finance is acceptable depends on the effect on the wealth of shareholders.

If shareholder wealth increases, the proposed use of the finance is acceptable. Better answers therefore looked to compare the theoretical rights price per share (the share price before the rights issue funds were invested) with the share price after the investment had taken place (for example the share price calculated in part (b)), or to compare the return from the investment (for example, total shareholder return, which is the sum of capital gain and divided yield) with the cost of equity.

Part (d) required candidates to explain the nature of the agency problem and to discuss using share option schemes to reduce it in a stock-market listed company. The agency problem is that managers may act in ways that do not lead to the maximisation of shareholder wealth. Shareholder wealth increases through receiving dividends and through capital gains in share prices, and is usually assessed through changes in share prices. Better answers referred to these key financial management concepts.

Share option schemes, in making managers into shareholders, lead to convergence of objectives, if only on a shared focus on increased wealth through increasing share prices. Unfortunately, while share prices increases can arise from good managerial decisions, share price changes can arise for other reasons as well. There was scope here for candidates to discuss a range of issues relating to the difficulty of designing a share option scheme that rewarded managers for good performance, but not for poor performance.

61 PHOBIS

Key answer tips

This question has three discrete requirements which are of varying difficulty. To score well you must ensure you capture the easy marks quickly and don't get bogged down on one particular area meaning you run out of time, or worse still, run over time and limit your ability to get all marks on later questions. Part (b) is the most difficult of the three requirements. This should have been tackled last. The highlighted words are key phrases that markers are looking for.

(a)   (i)   **Price/earnings ratio method valuation**

       Earnings per share of Danoca Co = 40c

       Average sector price/earnings ratio = 10

       Implied value of ordinary share of Danoca Co = 40 × 10 = $4.00

       Number of ordinary shares = 5 million

       Value of Danoca Co = 4.00 × 5m = $20 million

(ii)   Dividend growth model

Earnings per share of Danoca Co = 40c

Proposed payout ratio = 60%

Proposed dividend of Danoca Co is therefore = 40 × 0.6 = 24c

If the future dividend growth rate is expected to continue the historical trend in dividends per share, the historic dividend growth rate can be used as a substitute for the expected future dividend growth rate in the dividend growth model. Average geometric dividend growth rate over the last two years = (24/22)1/2 = 1.045 or 4.5% (Alternatively, dividend growth rates over the last two years were 3% (24/23.3) and 6% (23.3/22), with an arithmetic average of (6 + 3)/2 = 4.5%)

Cost of equity of Danoca Co using the capital asset pricing model (CAPM)

= 4.6 + 1.4 × (10.6 − 4.6) = 4.6 + (1.4 × 6) = 13%

Value of ordinary share from dividend growth model = (24 × 1.045)/(0.13 − 0.045) = $2.95

Value of Danoca Co = 2.95 × 5m = $14.75 million

The current market capitalisation of Danoca Co is $16.5m ($3.30 × 5m).The price/earnings ratio value of Danoca Co is higher than this at $20m, using the average price/earnings ratio used for the sector. Danoca's own price/earnings ratio is 8.25. The difference between the two price/earnings ratios may indicate that there is scope for improving the financial performance of Danoca Co following the acquisition. If Phobis Co has the managerial skills to effect this improvement, the company and its shareholders may be able to benefit as a result of the acquisition.

The dividend growth model value is lower than the current market capitalisation at $14.75m. This represents a minimum value that Danoca shareholders will accept if Phobis Co makes an offer to buy their shares. In reality they would want more than this as an inducement to sell. The current market capitalisation of Danoca Co of $16.5m may reflect the belief of the stock market that a takeover bid for the company is imminent and, depending on its efficiency, may indicate a fair price for Danoca's shares, at least on a marginal trading basis. Alternatively, either the cost of equity or the expected dividend growth rate used in the dividend growth model calculation could be inaccurate, or the difference between the two values may be due to a degree of inefficiency in the stock market.

(b)   **Calculation of market value of each convertible bond**

Expected share price in five years' time = 4.45 × 1.065^5 = $6.10

Conversion value = 6.10 × 20 = $122

Compared with redemption at par value of $100, conversion will be preferred

The current market value will be the present value of future interest payments, plus the present value of the conversion value, discounted at the cost of debt of 7% per year.

Market value of each convertible bond = (9 × 4.100) + (122 × 0.713) = $123.89

Calculation of floor value of each convertible bond

The current floor value will be the present value of future interest payments, plus the present value of the redemption value, discounted at the cost of debt of 7% per year.

Floor value of each convertible bond = (9 × 4.100) + (100 × 0.713) = $108.20

Calculation of conversion premium of each convertible bond

Current conversion value = 4.45 × 20 = $89.00

Conversion premium = $123.89 – 89.00 = $34.89

This is often expressed on a per share basis, i.e. 34.89/20 = $1.75 per share

(c)   Stock market efficiency usually refers to the way in which the prices of traded financial securities reflect relevant information.

When research indicates that share prices fully and fairly reflect public information as well as past information, a stock market is described as semi-strong form efficient.

The significance to a listed company of its shares being traded on a stock market which is found to be semi-strong form efficient is that any information relating to the company is quickly and accurately reflected in its share price. Managers will not be able to deceive the market by the timing or presentation of new information, such as annual reports or analysts' briefings, since the market processes the information quickly and accurately to produce fair prices. Managers should therefore simply concentrate on making financial decisions which increase the wealth of shareholders.

ACCA marking scheme		
		Marks
(a)	Price/earnings ratio value of company	2
	Proposed dividend per share	1
	Average dividend growth rate	1
	Cost of equity using CAPM	1
	Dividend growth model value of company	2
	Discussion	4
		10
(b)	Conversion value	1
	Market value	2
	Floor value	2
	Conversion premium	1
		6
(c)	Definition of Semi-strong form efficiency	1–2
	Significance of semi-strong form efficiency	2–3
		4
Total		20

Examiner's comments

In part (a), candidates were asked to calculate the value of a company using the price/earnings ratio method and the dividend growth model, and to discuss the significance of calculated values, in comparison to the current market value of the company, to a potential buyer. Answers to this part of question 1 often failed to gain many marks, mainly because candidates did not calculate company values.

The prices/earnings ratio method calculates the value of a company by multiplying an earnings per share figure by a price/earnings ratio, and then multiplying by the number of issued shares. Alternatively, total earnings can be multiplied by a price/earnings ratio. Although the question provided an average sector price/earnings ratio to use in this context, many candidates simply calculated the current price/earnings ratio of the company and compared this with the sector value. Calculating a price/earnings ratio is not the same as calculating the value of a company. Candidates should also note that the price/earnings ratio is a multiple and neither a percentage nor a monetary amount.

The dividend growth model (DGM) formula is given in the formulae sheet in the examination paper. Many candidates rearranged the DGM formula in order to calculate a cost of equity, even though what was needed was to calculate a share price by inserting values for the current dividend, the cost of equity and the dividend growth rate into the DGM formula provided. The cost of equity could be calculated from the capital asset pricing model, using the formula given in the formulae sheet. The current dividend could be calculated using the dividend payout ratio and the current earnings per share value provided in the question. The future dividend growth rate could be calculated on an historical average basis, although there were many errors in its calculation. A number of candidates were unable to distinguish between some of the variables given in the question, for example confusing dividend per share with earnings per share, return on the market with cost of equity, and equity beta with retention ratio.

Even though the current market value of the company (number of shares multiplied by share price) was needed, a number of candidates failed to calculate it. The level of discussion was often limited, although some candidates demonstrated that they were aware of the weaknesses of the valuation models used.

Part (b) asked candidates to calculate the market value, floor value and conversion value of a $100 convertible bond. Many candidates either failed to answer this part of question 1, or showed in their answers that they did not understand how to calculate the present value of a stream of future cash flows (which is what the market value of a bond is equivalent to).

Candidates needed to calculate the present value of future interest payments plus the present value of the future conversion value (the market value, since conversion was financially preferable to redemption), and the present value of future interest payments plus the present value of the future redemption at par value (the floor value, since this stream of future cash flows is guaranteed). Some candidates were able to calculate the floor value, but called it the market value. Some candidates were able to calculate the current conversion value, but were not aware that this was used in calculating the conversion premium.

A number of candidates were not aware of the difference between interest rate, cost of debt and share price growth rate and used their values interchangeably. Some candidates introduced an assumed tax rate, when the question made no reference to taxation at all. There were indications of candidates learning a computation method, without acquiring an understanding of the concepts underlying it. Candidates must understand the importance, in financial management, of discounting future values in order to obtain present values, since this is used in investment appraisal, bond valuation, share valuation and company valuation.

Part (c) required candidates to discuss the significance to a listed company of its shares being traded on a semi-strong form efficient stock market.

A number of candidates did not understand and could not discuss market efficiency, and very few correctly discussed the significance of semi-strong market efficiency to a company. Overall, many answers were not of a pass standard.

RISK MANAGEMENT

62 NEDWEN

Key answer tips

This is a fairly straightforward question that has a good balance of discursive and mathematical elements. Parts (a) and (b) offer a chance to pick up some easy marks for simple 'learn and churn' type answers. To score well in parts (c) and (d) you need to be clear on the spot and forward rates provided to ensure you select the right ones The highlighted words are key phrases that markers are looking for.

(a)   **Transaction risk**

This is the risk arising on short-term foreign currency transactions that the actual income or cost may be different from the income or cost expected when the transaction was agreed. For example, a sale worth $10,000 when the exchange rate is $1.79 per £ has an expected sterling value is $5,587. If the dollar has depreciated against sterling to $1.84 per £ when the transaction is settled, the sterling receipt will have fallen to $5,435. Transaction risk therefore affects cash flows and for this reason most companies choose to hedge or protect themselves against transaction risk.

Translation risk

This risk arises on consolidation of financial statements prior to reporting financial results and for this reason is also known as accounting exposure. Consider an asset worth €14 million, acquired when the exchange rate was €1.4 per $. One year later, when financial statements are being prepared, the exchange rate has moved to €1.5 per $ and the statement of financial position value of the asset has changed from $10 million to $9.3 million, resulting an unrealised (paper) loss of $0.7 million. Translation risk does not involve cash flows and so does not directly affect shareholder wealth. However, investor perception may be affected by the changing values of assets and liabilities, and so a company may choose to hedge translation risk through, for example, matching the currency of assets and liabilities (e.g. a euro-denominated asset financed by a euro-denominated loan).

Economic risk

Transaction risk is seen as the short-term manifestation of economic risk, which could be defined as the risk of the present value of a company's expected future cash flows being affected by exchange rate movements over time. It is difficult to measure economic risk, although its effects can be described, and it is also difficult to hedge against it.

(b) **Forward market evaluation**

Net receipt in 1 month = $240,000 – $140,000 = $100,000

Nedwen Co needs to sell dollars at an exchange rate of 1.7829 + 0.003 = $1.7832 per £

Sterling value of net receipt = $100,000/1.7832 = £56,079

Receipt in 3 months = $300,000

Nedwen Co needs to sell dollars at an exchange rate of 1.7846 + 0.004 = $1.7850 per £

Sterling value of receipt in 3 months = $300,000/1.7850 = £168,067

(c) **Evaluation of money-market hedge**

Expected receipt after 3 months = $300,000

Dollar interest rate over three months = 5.4/4 = 1.35%

Dollars to borrow now to have $300,000 liability after 3 months = 300,000/1.0135 = $296,004

Spot rate for selling dollars = 1.7820 + 0.0002 = $1.7822 per £

Sterling deposit from borrowed dollars at spot = $296,004/1.7822 = £166,089

Sterling interest rate over three months = 4.6/ 4 = 1.15%

Value in 3 months of sterling deposit = £166,089 × 1.0115 = £167,999

The forward market is marginally preferable to the money market hedge for the dollar receipt expected after 3 months.

(d) A currency futures contract is a standardised contract for the buying or selling of a specified quantity of foreign currency. It is traded on a futures exchange and settlement takes place in three-monthly cycles ending in March, June, September and December, i.e. a company can buy or sell September futures, December futures and so on. The price of a currency futures contract is the exchange rate for the currencies specified in the contract.

When a currency futures contract is bought or sold, the buyer or seller is required to deposit a sum of money with the exchange, called initial margin. If losses are incurred as exchange rates and hence the prices of currency futures contracts change, the buyer or seller may be called on to deposit additional funds (variation margin) with the exchange. Equally, profits are credited to the margin account on a daily basis as the contract is 'marked to market'.

Most currency futures contracts are closed out before their settlement dates by undertaking the opposite transaction to the initial futures transaction, i.e. if buying currency futures was the initial transaction, it is closed out by selling currency futures. A gain made on the futures transactions will offset a loss made on the currency markets and vice versa.

Nedwen Co expects to receive $300,000 in three months' time and so is concerned that sterling may appreciate (strengthen) against the dollar, since this would result in a lower sterling receipt. The company can hedge the receipt by selling sterling futures contracts and since it is 1 April, would sell June futures contracts. In June, Nedwen Co would buy the same number of futures it sold in April and sell the $300,000 it received on the currency market.

ACCA marking scheme			
			Marks
(a)	Transaction risk	2 marks	
	Translation risk	2 marks	
	Economic risk	2 marks	
			6
(b)	Netting	1 mark	
	Sterling value of 3-month receipt	1 mark	
	Sterling value of 1-year receipt	1 mark	
			3
(c)	Evaluation of money market hedge	4 marks	
	Comment	1 mark	
			5
(d)	Definition of currency futures contract	1–2 marks	
	Initial margin and variation margin	1–2 marks	
	Buying and selling of contracts	1–2 marks	
	Hedging the three-month receipt	1–2 marks	
	Maximum		6
Total			20

63 BOLUJE CO

Key answer tips

Part (a) is a standard discussion on the benefits of debt finance. Part (b) may look complicated, dealing in foreign bonds denominated in pesos, but requires a straightforward application of the dividend valuation model using the base premise of the market value of an investment equalling the present value of the future cash flows.

Part (c) gives plenty of opportunity for students to cover familiar areas. The trick with the calculations (an illustration was requested) is to recognise that Boluje is hedging its interest payments only (and not the full amount of the foreign bonds).

Finally, for 8 marks part (d) should be a relatively easy discussion of other hedging methods primarily focussing on futures and options. The highlighted words are key phrases that markers are looking for.

(a)   Pecking order theory suggests that companies have a preferred order in which they seek to raise finance, beginning with retained earnings. The advantages of using retained earnings are that issue costs are avoided by using them, the decision to use them can be made without reference to a third party, and using them does not bring additional obligations to consider the needs of finance providers.

Once available retained earnings have been allocated to appropriate uses within a company, its next preference will be for debt. One reason for choosing to finance a new investment by an issue of debt finance, therefore, is that insufficient retained earnings are available and the investing company prefers issuing debt finance to issuing equity finance.

Debt finance may also be preferred when a company has not yet reached its optimal capital structure and it is mainly financed by equity, which is expensive compared to debt. Issuing debt here will lead to a reduction in the WACC and hence an increase in the market value of the company. One reason why debt is cheaper than equity is that debt is higher in the creditor hierarchy than equity, since ordinary shareholders are paid out last in the event of liquidation. Debt is even cheaper if it is secured on assets of the company. The cost of debt is reduced even further by the tax efficiency of debt, since interest payments are an allowable deduction in arriving at taxable profit.

Debt finance may be preferred where the maturity of the debt can be matched to the expected life of the investment project. Equity finance is permanent finance and so may be preferred for investment projects with long lives.

(b) Annual interest paid per foreign bond = 500 × 0.061 = 30.5 pesos

Redemption value of each foreign bond = 500 pesos

Cost of debt of peso-denominated bonds = 7% per year

Market value of each foreign bond = (30.5 × 4.100) + (500 × 0.713) = 481.55 pesos

Current total market value of foreign bonds = 16m × (481.55/500) = 15,409,600 pesos

(c) (i) Interest payment in one year's time = 16m × 0.061 = 976,000 pesos

A money market hedge would involve placing on deposit an amount of pesos that, with added interest, would be sufficient to pay the peso-denominated interest in one year. Because the interest on the peso-denominated deposit is guaranteed, Boluje Co would be protected against any unexpected or adverse exchange rate movements prior to the interest payment being made.

Peso deposit required = 976,000/ 1.05 = 929,524 pesos

Dollar equivalent at spot = 929,524/ 6 = $154,921

Dollar cost in one year's time = 154,921 × 1.04 = $161,118

(ii) Cost of forward market hedge = 976,000/6.07 = $160,790

The forward market hedge is slightly cheaper

(d) Boluje receives peso income from its export sales and makes annual peso-denominated interest payments to bond-holders. It could consider opening a peso account in the overseas country and using this as a natural hedge against peso exchange rate risk.

Boluje Co could consider using lead payments to settle foreign currency liabilities. This would not be beneficial as far as peso-denominated liabilities are concerned, as the peso is depreciating against the dollar. It is inadvisable to lag payments to foreign suppliers, since this would breach sales agreements and lead to loss of goodwill.

ACCA marking scheme			
			Marks
(a)	Relevant discussion		7
(b)	Market value of each foreign bond	3	
	Total market value of foreign bonds	1	
		—	
			4
(c)	(i) Explanation of money market hedge	2	
	Illustration of money market hedge	2	
		—	
			4
	(ii) Comparison with forward market hedge		2
(d)	Discussion of natural hedge	1 – 2	
	Description of leading/lagging	1 – 2	
		—	
			Max 3
			—
Total			**20**

LISHING 393

Examiner's comment

In part (a) of this question, candidates were asked to explain the reasons why a company might choose to finance a new investment by an issue of debt. Answers were of variable quality, with some candidates writing very little while others gained full marks.

Weaker answers discussed other sources of finance, such as leasing or preference shares, or focused on the disadvantages of equity finance, indicating perhaps that candidates had prepared for a question about equity, but were unprepared for a question about debt. Better answers covered such reasons as the lower cost of debt compared with other sources of finance, due to lower risk of debt finance and its tax efficiency: the relative ease with which debt finance could be raised; the potentially positive effect of the lower cost of debt on the weighted average cost of capital and the market value of the company; the place of debt finance in pecking order theory; and the matching of debt and asset maturity.

Part (b) required candidates to calculate the total market value (in pesos) of a foreign bond (denominated in pesos). The market value of a bond is the present value of future interest payments added to the present value of the future redemption value. Good answers calculated the interest payable in pesos on each bond, the market value of each bond as just described, and then the total market value by multiplying the market value per bond by the number of bonds issued. Weaker answers sought to calculate the internal rate of return of the bond, which was unnecessary as the cost of debt was given in the question. Internal rate of return is not equal to market value.

Part (c) asked for an explanation and an illustration of a money market hedge, and a comparison of the relative costs of a money market hedge and a forward market hedge. Answers were again of very variable quality.

Many candidates were unable to calculate the annual peso interest required by the illustration of the money market hedge. Both the interest rate and the par value of the bond issue were given in the question, and multiplying one by the other gives the amount of interest to be paid. Some candidates invented a cash flow to illustrate the money market hedge: candidates who invented a future peso receipt failed to notice that the interest rates given in the question could not then be used, since the peso rate was a deposit rate and the dollar rate was a borrowing rate. Weaker answers tried to hedge a future dollar payment, when the question stated that the dollar was the home currency.

Many candidates were able to calculate correctly the dollar value of a forward market hedge and indicate whether this hedge would be preferred to a money market hedge.

Many candidates gave good answers to part (d), even if some answers tended to be a list rather a description. The question was open-ended, asking for a description of methods (excluding derivatives) that could be used to hedge exchange rate risk. Many methods could be and were described, including netting, matching, invoicing in the home currency and leading and lagging.

64   EXPORTERS PLC *Walk in the footsteps of a top tutor*

Key answer tips

Another fairly standard question that combines knowledge with application. The highlighted words are key phrases that markers are looking for.

Tutor's top tips:

Don't feel you have to tackle the different parts of the requirement in order. Part (b) gives the best opportunities for some easy marks so is the best place to start.

(a)   **Exporters plc**

Tutor's top tips:

This first thing to appreciate about this part of the requirement is that it's asking a question that rarely gets asked in reality – what if we hadn't entered into that hedge? Remember, the purpose of hedging a transaction is to eliminate risk, and so it isn't often someone would bother looking back to calculate what would have happened if they hadn't bothered!

That said, to perform the calculation you need to keep in mind the following things:

1   *Forward rates will be determined by interest differentials (the question doesn't specify the forward rate the company is locking in to. It does however, give you the interest differentials that will allow you to work the forward rate out.*

2   *What does happen to interest rates in the future will be determined by many different factors – the rate that does occur in the future is unlikely to be the same as the future rate that was contacted. This will give rise to a gain or loss on the transaction.*

3   *If the £ gains in value (appreciates), you will get more Northland dollars for each £. Equally, if it losses value (depreciates or weakens) it will buy less Northland dollars.*

UK interest rates over 6 months are $\frac{1}{2} \times 12\%$ = 6%.

Northland interest rates over 6 months are $\frac{1}{2} \times 15\%$ = 7.5%

Implied forward rate for the £ after 6 months = $\frac{1.075}{1.06} \times 2.5$ = 2.5354.

> **Tutorial note:**
>
> *If you calculated your forward rate using the annual interest rates, you would only lose one mark. All further calculations will be based on the 'own figure rule' which means that, provided you used the right technique, your answer would be marked as correct, even though you have a different answer to that shown here.*

(1) If the £ has gained 4%, N's actual rate is 2.5 × 1.04 = 2.6 to the £.

$$\text{Hedged receipt} = \frac{\$500,000}{2.5354} = \qquad \pounds197,208$$

$$\text{Unhedged receipt} = \frac{\$500,000}{2.6} = \qquad \pounds192,308$$

∴ Gain from hedging = £197,208 − £192,308 = £4,900.

(2) If the £ has lost 2%, N's actual rate is 2.5 × 0.98 = 2.45 to the £

$$\text{Unhedged receipt} = \frac{\$500,000}{2.45} = \pounds204,082$$

∴ Loss from hedging = £204,082 − £197,208 = £6,874.

(3) If the £ has remained stable, N's actual rate is still 2.5 to the £.

$$\text{Unhedged receipt} = \frac{\$500,000}{2.5} = \pounds200,000$$

∴ Loss from hedging = £200,000 − £197,208 = £2,792.

(b) **Forward market currency hedge**

A company can use the foreign exchange markets to hedge exactly as shown in the question. A company due to receive foreign currency in 6 months time can sell that currency forward, i.e. agree an exchange rate now at which that amount of foreign currency will be exchanged into sterling. The cost involved will be paid to the bank arranging the transaction and will usually be built into the contract's exchange rate so that the foreign currency is quoted net. The benefits are peace of mind to the company that they have laid off the risks of exchange rate movements between the contract date and the date when the foreign currency will be paid or received. Part (a) illustrates a range of possible gains and losses on a forward market currency hedge depending on the actual currency movements before the contract matures.

Currency futures hedge

Currency futures contracts are traded on separate exchanges such as the London International Financial Futures and Options Exchange (LIFFE). Each contract provides a simultaneous right and obligation to buy or sell on a specific future date a standard amount of a particular currency at a price that is known at the time of entering the contract. Since the contracts are sold in standard amounts and have a limited number of maturity dates each year, they are highly standardised and a liquid market has developed to trade them.

A UK exporting company due to receive 500,000 Northland dollars in six months' time could only hedge its currency exposure by means of currency futures if contracts are available between Northland dollars and sterling, and then only could it create an exact hedge if 500,000 dollars happened to be a multiple of the standard contract size. But assuming that both these conditions are fulfilled, the company can buy contracts to sell Northland dollars into sterling at the required future time.

Currency options hedge

A call/put option gives the buyer of that option the right, but not the obligation, to buy/sell currency in the future at a particular exchange rate. A UK company which uses a forward or futures position avoids losing from adverse movements on currencies but also fails to gain from favourable movements. A currency option is suitable for a UK company which believes it knows the direction of future exchange rate movements, but is not sure and wishes to minimise the loss arising in the event of being proved incorrect.

The company in the question anticipates dollars receivable in six months' time. It can pay an option premium to buy sterling call options. These enable the company to benefit from the anticipated appreciating dollar while providing protection against the opposite movement.

65   ELECT CO

Key answer tips

This question is a good mixture of knowledge and application. Part (d) offers a good opportunity to pick up some easy marks and so should be attempted first. The calculations within parts (a) and (b) are reasonably straightforward although those in part (c) will require you to make some assumptions in order to answer in full.

The highlighted words in the written sections are key phrases that markers are looking for.

(a)   The value of a $100 par value bond can be calculated as follows:

	Cash flow $	10% AF/DF	PV $
T1-6 – annual interest	8	4.355	34.84
T6 – conversion value	100	0.564	56.40
Value			91.24

Total market value of Bond A: $10m × 91.24/100 = $9.12m

(b)   Cost of equity shares = 15% (per question)

Cost of bank loan = (3% + 1%) × (1 – 0.3) = 2.8%

After-tax cost of Bond A:

	Cash flow	5% DF	PV	10% DF	PV
T0 – market value	(91.24)	1	(91.24)	1	(91.24)
T1-6 – post tax interest	5.6	5.076	28.43	4.355	24.39
T6 – conversion value	100	0.746	74.60	0.564	56.40
			11.79		–10.45

Cost = IRR = 5 + (11.79/(11.79 + 10.45)) × (10 – 5) = 7.65%

Total market values:

Equity – $1.70 × 10m/2 =	$34.00m
Bond A – as above	$9.12m
Bank loan –	$5.00m
Total MV –	$48.12m

$$\text{WACC} = \left[\frac{34}{48.12}\right]15\% + \left[\frac{9.12}{48.12}\right]7.65\% + \left[\frac{5}{48.12}\right]2.8\% = 12.3\%$$

(c)   (i)   Assuming that the new equity finance does not affect the market value of each existing share, the impact on the WACC can be estimated as:

$$\text{WACC} = \left[\frac{(34+5)}{(48.12+5)}\right]15\% + \left[\frac{9.12}{(48.12+5)}\right]7.65\% + \left[\frac{5}{(48.12+5)}\right]2.8\% = 12.6\%$$

(ii)   Assuming that the additional debt finance does not result in a change to the cost of equity, the impact on the WACC can be estimated as:

WACC =

$$\left[\frac{34}{(48.12+5)}\right]15\% + \left[\frac{9.12}{(48.12+5)}\right]7.65\% + \left[\frac{5}{(48.12+5)}\right]2.8\% + \left[\frac{5}{(48.12+5)}\right]7\% = 11.8\%$$

(d)   **Factors affecting the choice between fixed and floating rate debt:**

Expected changes in interest rates

Obtaining a floating rate loan means a company will be affected by changes in interest rates. If rates increase, then the company will pay more interest on a loan; if rates fall, then the company pays less. If interest rates are expected to rise, then a fixed rate loan may be preferable as the company will not be affected by the rate increase; similarly, if rates are expected to fall, then a variable rate loan will be preferred to take advantage of falling rates of interest.

Amount of time the loan is required

Obtaining a fixed rate loan may be more risky if the loan is for a long period of time as the company will effectively be locked into this rate. Rate changes become more difficult to forecast in the long term. However, a fixed rate again provides certainty as to the amount of interest to be paid. If the loan is for a long period, then various hedging techniques will normally be considered.

Existing mix of fixed and variable loans

The finance director of Elect Co may require a portfolio of fixed and variable rates loans simply as a method of hedging risk. Given that the value of variable rate loans is currently lower than fixed loans then this may indicate a preference for variable rate loan.

Risk appetite

Elect Co will view the variable and fixed loans as having different levels of risk. If the company's risk appetite is low, then a lower risk alternative will be taken. However, treasurers will normally want a range of financial products to minimise risk for their company.

Methods of hedging interest rate risk

FRA

An FRA is an over-the-counter instrument that can be arranged with a bank, fixing the interest rate on a notional principal amount for a given period of time. FRAs are only available for quite large principal amounts (at least $1 million) and can be arranged up to about two years into the future.

A company wishing to fix an interest rate for borrowing should buy an FRA. The FRA is not an agreement to borrow the funds required. Elect Co must arrange to borrow the $5 million separately. Elect Co will borrow $5 million at the current market rate of interest, whatever this happens to be. The FRA would be settled by:

- a payment from the bank to Elect Co if the benchmark interest rate is higher than the FRA rate; or

- a payment from Elect Co to the bank if the benchmark rate is lower than the FRA rate.

The hedge works because the interest payment on the actual borrowing plus or minus the settlement amount for the FRA should fix the overall effective borrowing cost for Elect Co.

Interest rate futures

Short-term interest rate futures are exchange-traded instruments. A company wishing to fix a rate for borrowing should sell interest rate futures.

The interest rate is in the price of the future. Prices are quoted at 100 minus the interest rate, so if Elect Co were to sell futures, say, at 92.50, this would 'fix' its borrowing rate at 7.5%. As the future approaches settlement date, if the interest rate has risen (to say 9%), the market price of the futures should have moved to about 91.00. Elect Co could then close its position by buying futures, and making a profit of 1.50 (150 points) on each contract of its futures dealing. The net borrowing cost would be 9% less the value of the profit on futures trading (1.5%) giving a net effective interest cost of 7.5%.

Since interest rate futures are only available in standardised amounts and dates, they are less flexible than FRAs, and so possibly less attractive to Elect Co.

Interest rate guarantee

This is a type of borrower's option and unlike an FRA or futures which are binding contracts on both parties, it is not a binding commitment on the option holder. If Elect Co buys this instrument at a cap strike price of say 7%, it will exercise its option if the interest rate at expiry is higher than 7%. It will then receive the interest value of the difference between the actual interest rate and the cap rate of 7%.

However, if the interest rate was to fall, Elect Co would be able to walk away from the option.

The premiums payable on interest rate guarantees can be expensive and must be paid up-front.

66 CC CO

Key answer tips

Part (c) can easily be attempted in isolation and could be tackled first to capture the knowledge level marks early within your allotted time.

Part (b) is dependent on your answer to part (a) although the own figure rule will apply when part (b) is marked. A methodical approach should yield some easy marks

The highlighted words in the written sections are key phrases that markers are looking for.

(a) **Using a forward market hedge**

Dollar value of payment = €1.5m/0.698 = $2.149m

Using a money market hedge

Expected payment after 3 months = €1.5m

Euro interest rate over three months = 2.9/4 = 0.725%

Euros to invest now to have €1.5m asset after 3 months = €1.5m/1.00725 = €1.4892m

Spot rate for buying Euros = 0.70 €/$

Dollar loan needed for Euros deposited = €1.4892 / 0.7 = $2.127m

Dollar interest rate over three months = 5.5/ 4 = 1.375%

Value in 3 months of dollar loan = €2.127 × 1.01375 = $2.1567

The forward market is marginally preferable to the money market hedge for the Euro payment expected after 3 months.

(b)

Year	0	1	2	3	4	5
		$000	$000	$000	$000	$000
Contribution (W1)		1,330	2,830	2,408	1,280	
Fixed costs (W2)		(265)	(281)	(298)	(316)	
Taxable cash flow		1,065	2,549	2,110	964	
Taxation			(320)	(765)	(633)	(289)
Initial investment	(2,149)					
CA tax benefits (W3)			161	161	161	161
After-tax cash flow	(2,149)	1,065	2,390	1,506	492	(128)
Discount at 10% (W4)	1	0.909	0.826	0.751	0.683	0.621
Present values	(2,149)	968	1,974	1,131	336	(79)

Net present value = $2,181,000. The net present value is positive and so the investment is financially acceptable.

Workings

(W1) **Annual contribution**

Year	0	1	2	3	4
Sales volume (units/yr)		250,000	500,000	400,000	200,000
Selling price ($/unit)		12.60	13.23	13.89	14.59
Variable cost ($/unit)		7.28	7.57	7.87	8.19
Contribution ($/unit)		5.32	5.66	6.02	6.40
Contribution ($/yr)		1,330,000	2,830,000	2,408,000	1,280,000

(W2) **Fixed costs**

$250,000 inflating at 6% p.a. = $265,000 in T1 etc

(W3) **Tax allowable depreciation tax benefits**

Tax allowable depreciation is on a straight-line basis over the four-year life of the asset.

$2.149m ÷ 4 years = $537,250 per annum

Tax benefit = $537,250 × 30% = $161,175

(W4) **Discount factor**

$(1 + i) = (1 + r) \times (1 + h)$

$(1 + i) = (1 + 0.051) \times (1 + 0.047)$

$(1 + i) = 1.1004$

$i = 10\%$

(c)   A key effect of inflation on companies is the role it plays in determining exchange rates. Purchasing power parity theory (PPPT) claims that the rate of exchange between two currencies depends on the relative inflation rates within the respective countries. PPPT is based on 'the law of one price'. In equilibrium, identical goods must cost the same, regardless of the currency in which they are sold.

The main function of an exchange rate is to provide a means of translating prices expressed in one currency into another currency. The implication is that the exchange rate will be determined in some way by the relationship between these prices. This arises from the law of one price.

The law of one price states that in a free market with no barriers to trade and no transport or transactions costs, the competitive process will ensure that there will only be one price for any given good. If price differences occurred they would be removed by arbitrage; entrepreneurs would buy in the low market and resell in the high market. This would eradicate the price difference.

If this law is applied to international transactions, it suggests that exchange rates will always adjust to ensure that only one price exists between countries where there is relatively free trade.

An estimate of expected future spot rates can be made using the formula:

$$S_1 = S_0 \times \frac{(1+h_c)}{(1+h_b)}$$

Where:

S_0 = current spot rate

S_1 = expected future spot rate

h_b = inflation rate in country for which the spot is quoted (base currency)

h_c = inflation rate in the other country (counter currency)

Thus, a high level of inflation in an economy, relative to the inflation rates overseas will result in a depreciation of the currency. As a result of the currency fluctuation imports will cost more but it may be easier to export since goods will appear cheaper to overseas purchasers.

FUNDAMENTALS LEVEL – SKILLS MODULE

Financial Management

Specimen Exam applicable from September 2016

Paper F9

Time allowed

Reading and planning: 15 minutes

Writing: 3 hours

This question paper is divided into three sections:

Section A – ALL 15 questions are compulsory and MUST be attempted

Section B – ALL 15 questions are compulsory and MUST be attempted

Section C – BOTH questions are compulsory and MUST be attempted

Formulae Sheet, Present Value and Annuity Tables are on pages 14–16.

Do NOT open this question paper until instructed by the supervisor.

During reading and planning time only the question paper may be annotated. You must NOT write in your answer booklet until instructed by the supervisor.

Do NOT record any of your answers on the question paper.

This question paper must not be removed from the examination hall.

The Association of Chartered Certificate Accountants

KAPLAN

PUBLISHING

SECTION A – Objective test (OT) questions

1   The home currency of ACB Co is the dollar ($) and it trades with a company in a foreign country whose home currency is the Dinar. The following information is available:

	Home country	Foreign country
Spot rate	20.00 Dinar per $	
Interest rate	3% per year	7% per year
Inflation rate	2% per year	5% per year

What is the six-month forward exchange rate?

A   20.39 Dinar per $

B   20.30 Dinar per $

C   20.59 Dinar per $

D   20.78 Dinar per $

2   The following financial information relates to an investment project:

	$000
Present value of sales revenue	50,025
Present value of variable costs	25,475
Present value of contribution	24,550
Present value of fixed costs	18,250
Present value of operating income	6,300
Initial investment	5,000
Net present value	1,300

What is the sensitivity of the net present value of the investment project to a change in sales volume?

A   7.1%

B   2.6%

C   5.1%

D   5.3%

3   Gurdip plots the historic movements of share prices and uses this analysis to make her investment decisions.

To what extent does Gurdip believe capital markets to be efficient?

A   Not efficient at all

B   Weak form efficient

C   Semi-strong form efficient

D   Strong form efficient

4   Which of the following statements concerning capital structure theory is correct?

A   In the traditional view, there is a linear relationship between the cost of equity and financial risk.

B   Modigliani and Miller said that, in the absence of tax, the cost of equity would remain constant.

C   Pecking order theory indicates that preference shares are preferred to convertible debt as a source of finance.

D   Business risk is assumed to be constant as the capital structure changes.

5   Which of the following actions is LEAST likely to increase shareholder wealth?

A   The weighted average cost of capital is decreased by a recent financing decision

B   The financial rewards of directors are linked to increasing earnings per share

C   The board of directors decides to invest in a project with a positive NPV

D   The annual report declares full compliance with the corporate governance code

6   Which of the following statements are features of money market instruments?

1   A negotiable security can be sold before maturity.

2   The yield on commercial paper is usually lower than that on treasury bills.

3   Discount instruments trade at less than face value.

A   2 only

B   1 and 3 only

C   2 and 3 only

D   1, 2 and 3

7   The following are extracts from the statement of profit or loss of CQB Co:

	$000
Sales income	60,000
Cost of sales	50,000
Profit before interest and tax	10,000
Interest	4,000
Profit before tax	6,000
Tax	4,500
Profit after tax	1,500

60% of the cost of sales is variables costs.

What is the operational gearing of CQB Co?

A   5.0 times

B   2.0 times

C   0.5 times

D   3.0 times

8 The management of XYZ Co has annual credit sales of $20 million and accounts receivable of $4 million. Working capital is financed by an overdraft at 12% interest per year. Assume 365 days in a year.

What is the annual finance cost saving if the management reduces the collection period to 60 days?

A $85,479

B $394,521

C $78,904

D $68,384

9 **Which of the following statements concerning financial management are correct?**

1 It is concerned with investment decisions, financing decisions and dividend decisions.

2 It is concerned with financial planning and financial control.

3 It considers the management of risk.

A 1 and 2 only

B 1 and 3 only

C 2 and 3 only

D 1, 2 and 3

10 SKV Co has paid the following dividends per share in recent years:

Year	20X4	20X3	20X2	20X1
Dividend ($ per share)	0.360	0.338	0.328	0.311

The dividend for 20X4 has just been paid and SKV Co has a cost of equity of 12%.

Using the geometric average historical dividend growth rate and the dividend growth model, what is the market price of SKV Co shares on an ex dividend basis?

A $4.67

B $5.14

C $5.40

D $6.97

11 'There is a risk that the value of our foreign currency-denominated assets and liabilities will change when we prepare our accounts'

To which risk does the above statement refer?

A Translation risk

B Economic risk

C Transaction risk

D Interest rate risk

12 The following information has been calculated for A Co:

Trade receivables collection period:	52 days
Raw material inventory turnover period:	42 days
Work in progress inventory turnover period:	30 days
Trade payables payment period:	66 days
Finished goods inventory turnover period:	45 days

What is the length of the working capital cycle?

A   103 days

B   131 days

C   235 days

D   31 days

13 **Which of the following is/are usually seen as benefits of financial intermediation?**

1   Interest rate fixing.

2   Risk pooling.

3   Maturity transformation.

A   1 only

B   1 and 3 only

C   2 and 3 only

D   1, 2 and 3

14 **Which of the following statements concerning working capital management are correct?**

1   The twin objectives of working capital management are profitability and liquidity.

2   A conservative approach to working capital investment will increase profitability.

3   Working capital management is a key factor in a company's long-term success.

A   1 and 2 only

B   1 and 3 only

C   2 and 3 only

D   1, 2 and 3

15 Governments have a number of economic targets as part of their monetary policy.

Which of the following targets relate predominantly to monetary policy?

1   Increasing tax revenue.

2   Controlling the growth in the size of the money supply.

3   Reducing public expenditure.

4   Keeping interest rates low.

A   1 only

B   1 and 3

C   2 and 4 only

D   2, 3 and 4

SECTION B – OT cases

The following scenario relates to questions 16–20.

Par Co currently has the following long-term capital structure:

	$m	$m
Equity finance		
Ordinary shares	30.0	
Reserves	38.4	
	────	
		68.4
Non-current liabilities		
Bank loans	15.0	
8% convertible loan notes	40.0	
5% redeemable preference shares	15.0	
	────	
		70.0
		────
Total equity and liabilities		138.4
		────

The 8% loan notes are convertible into eight ordinary shares per loan note in seven years' time. If not converted, the loan notes can be redeemed on the same future date at their nominal value of $100. Par Co has a cost of debt of 9% per year.

The ordinary shares of Par Co have a nominal value of $1 per share. The current ex dividend share price of the company is $10.90 per share and share prices are expected to grow by 6% per year for the foreseeable future. The equity beta of Par Co is 1.2.

16 The loan notes are secured on non-current assets of Par Co and the bank loan is secured by a floating charge on the current assets of the company.

   In terms of risk to the investor, what are the riskiest and least risky sources of finance for Par Co?

	Riskiest	*Least risky*
A	Redeemable preference shares	Bank loan
B	Ordinary shares	Bank loan
C	Bank loan	Loan notes
D	Ordinary shares	Loan notes

17 **What is the conversion value of the 8% loan notes of Par Co after seven years?**

   A $16.39

   B $111.98

   C $131.12

   D $71.72

18 **Assuming the conversion value after seven years is $126.15, what is the current market value of the 8% loan notes of Par Co?**

A $115.20

B $109.26

C $94.93

D $69.00

19 **Which of the following statements relating to the capital asset pricing model is correct?**

A   The equity beta of Par Co considers only business risk

B   The capital asset pricing model considers systematic risk and unsystematic risk

C   The equity beta of Par Co indicates that the company is more risky than the market as a whole

D   The debt beta of Par Co is zero

20 **Which of the following statements are problems in using the price/earnings ratio method to value a company?**

1   It is the reciprocal of the earnings yield.

2   It combines stock market information and corporate information.

3   It is difficult to select a suitable price/earnings ratio.

4   The ratio is more suited to valuing the shares of listed companies.

A   1 and 2 only

B   3 and 4 only

C   1, 3 and 4 only

D   1, 2, 3 and 4

The following scenario relates to questions 21–25

ZPS Co, whose home currency is the dollar, took out a fixed-interest peso bank loan several years ago when peso interest rates were relatively cheap compared to dollar interest rates. ZPS Co does not have any income in pesos. Economic difficulties have now increased peso interest rates while dollar interest rates have remained relatively stable.

ZPS Co must pay interest on the dates set by the bank. A payment of 5,000,000 pesos is due in six months' time. The following information is available:

Spot rate   12.500–12.582 pesos per $

Six-month forward rate   12.805–12.889 pesos per $

Interest rates which can be used by ZPS Co:

	Borrow	*Deposit*
Peso interest rates	10.0% per year	7.5% per year
Dollar interest rates	4.5% per year	3.5% per year

21   What is the dollar cost of a forward market hedge?

A $390,472

B $387,928

C $400,000

D $397,393

22   Which of the following statements relate to purchasing power parity theory?

1   The theory holds in the long term rather than the short term.

2   The exchange rate reflects the different cost of living in two countries.

3   The forward rate can be found by multiplying the spot rate by the ratio of the interest rates of the two countries.

A   1, 2 and 3

B   1 and 2 only

C   1 and 3 only

D   2 only

23   What are the appropriate six-month interest rates for ZPS Co to use if the company hedges the peso payment using a money market hedge?

	Deposit rate	*Borrowing rate*
A	7.5%	4.5%
B	1.75%	5.0%
C	3.75%	2.25%
D	3.5%	10.0%

24 **Which of the following methods are possible ways for ZPS Co to hedge its existing foreign currency risk?**

1   Matching receipts and payments.

2   Currency swaps.

3   Leading or lagging.

4   Currency futures.

A   1, 2, 3 and 4

B   1 and 3 only

C   2 and 4 only

D   2, 3 and 4 only

25 ZPS Co also trades with companies in Europe which use the Euro as their home currency. In three months' time ZPS Co will receive €300,000 from a customer.

Which of the following is the correct procedure for hedging this receipt using a money market hedge?

A	Step 1	Borrow an appropriate amount in Euro now
	Step 2	Convert the Euro amount into dollars
	Step 3	Place the dollars on deposit
	Step 4	Use the customer payment to repay the loan
B	Step 1	Borrow an appropriate amount in dollars now
	Step 2	Place the dollars on deposit now
	Step 3	Convert the dollars into Euro in three months' time
	Step 4	Use the customer payment to repay the loan
C	Step 1	Borrow an appropriate amount in dollars now
	Step 2	Convert the dollar amount into Euro
	Step 3	Place the Euro on deposit
	Step 4	Use the customer payment to repay the loan
C	Step 1	Borrow an appropriate amount in Euro now
	Step 2	Place the Euro on deposit now
	Step 3	Convert the Euro into dollars in three months' time
	Step 4	Use the customer payment to repay the loan

The following scenario relates to questions 26–30

Ridag Co operates in an industry which has recently been deregulated as the government seeks to increase competition in the industry.

Ridag Co plans to replace an existing machine and must choose between two machines. Machine 1 has an initial cost of $200,000 and will have a scrap value of $25,000 after four years. Machine 2 has an initial cost of $225,000 and will have a scrap value of $50,000 after three years. Annual maintenance costs of the two machines are as follows:

Year	1	2	3	4
Machine 1 ($ per year)	25,000	29,000	32,000	35,000
Machine 2 ($ per year)	15,000	20,000	25,000	

Where relevant, all information relating to this project has already been adjusted to include expected future inflation. Taxation and tax allowable depreciation must be ignored in relation to Machine 1 and Machine 2.

Ridag Co has a nominal before-tax weighted average cost of capital of 12% and a nominal after-tax weighted average cost of capital of 7%.

26 **In relation to Ridag Co, which of the following statements about competition and deregulation are true?**

    1   Increased competition should encourage Ridag Co to reduce costs.

    2   Deregulation will lead to an increase in administrative and compliance costs for Ridag Co.

    3   Deregulation should mean an increase in economies of scale for Ridag Co.

    4   Deregulation could lead to a decrease in the quality of Ridag Co's products.

    A   1 and 4

    B   2 and 3

    C   1 and 3

    D   2 and 4

27 **What is the equivalent annual cost of Machine 1?**

    A $90,412

    B $68,646

    C $83,388

    D $70,609

28 **Which of the following statements about Ridag Co using the equivalent annual cost method are true?**

    1   Ridag Co cannot use the equivalent annual cost method to compare Machine 1 and Machine 2 because they have different useful lives.

    2   The machine which has the lowest total present value of costs should be selected by Ridag Co.

    A   1 only

    B   Both 1 and 2

    C   2 only

    D   Neither 1 nor 2

29 Doubt has been cast over the accuracy of the year 2 and year 3 maintenance costs for Machine 2. On further investigation it was found that the following potential cash flows are now predicted:

Year	Cash flow ($)	Probability
2	18,000	0.3
2	25,000	0.7
3	23,000	0.2
3	24,000	0.35
3	30,000	0.45

What is the expected present value of the maintenance costs for year 3?

    A $26,500

    B $18,868

    C $21,624

    D $35,173

30 Ridag Co is appraising a different project, with a positive NPV. It is concerned about the risk and uncertainty associated with this other project.

Which of the following statements about risk, uncertainty and the project is true?

    A   Sensitivity analysis takes into account the interrelationship between project variables.

    B   Probability analysis can be used to assess the uncertainty associated with the project.

    C   Uncertainty can be said to increase with project life, while risk increases with the variability of returns.

    D   A discount rate of 5% could be used to lessen the effect of later cash flows on the decision.

SECTION C – Constructed response (long questions)

1 PV Co, a large stock-exchange-listed company, is evaluating an investment proposal to manufacture Product W33, which has performed well in test marketing trials conducted recently by the company's research and development division. Product W33 will be manufactured using a fully-automated process which would significantly increase noise levels from PV Co's factory. The following information relating to this investment proposal has now been prepared:

Initial investment	$2 million
Selling price (current price terms)	$20 per unit
Expected selling price inflation	3% per year
Variable operating costs (current price terms)	$8 per unit
Fixed operating costs (current price terms)	$170,000 per year
Expected operating cost inflation	4% per year

The research and development division has prepared the following demand forecast as a result of its test marketing trials. The forecast reflects expected technological change and its effect on the anticipated life-cycle of Product W33.

Year	1	2	3	4
Demand (units)	60,000	70,000	120,000	45,000

It is expected that all units of Product W33 produced will be sold, in line with the company's policy of keeping no inventory of finished goods. No terminal value or machinery scrap value is expected at the end of four years, when production of Product W33 is planned to end. For investment appraisal purposes, PV Co uses a nominal (money) discount rate of 10% per year and a target return on capital employed of 30% per year. Ignore taxation.

Required:

(a) Calculate the following values for the investment proposal:

    (i) net present value   (5 marks)

    (ii) internal rate of return; an   (3 marks)

    (iii) return on capital employed (accounting rate of return) based on average investment.   (3 marks)

(b) Briefly discuss your findings in each section of (a) above and advise whether the investment proposal is financially acceptable.   (4 marks)

(c) Discuss how the objectives of PV Co's stakeholders may be in conflict if the project is undertaken.   (5 marks)

(Total: 20 marks)

2 DD Co has a dividend payout ratio of 40% and has maintained this payout ratio for several years. The current dividend per share of the company is 50c per share and it expects that its next dividend per share, payable in one year's time, will be 52c per share.

The capital structure of the company is as follows:

	$m	$m
Equity		
Ordinary shares (nominal value $1 per share)	25	
Reserves	35	
	——	
		60
Debt		
Bond A (nominal value $100)	20	
Bond B (nominal value $100)	10	
	——	
		30
		——
		90
		——

Bond A will be redeemed at par in ten years' time and pays annual interest of 9%. The cost of debt of this bond is 9.83% per year. The current ex interest market price of the bond is $95.08.

Bond B will be redeemed at par in four years' time and pays annual interest of 8%. The cost of debt of this bond is 7.82% per year. The current ex interest market price of the bond is $102.01.

DD Co has a cost of equity of 12.4%. Ignore taxation.

Required:

(a) Calculate the following values for DD Co:

    (i)   **ex dividend share price, using the dividend growth model**   **(3 marks)**

    (ii)   **capital gearing (debt divided by debt plus equity) using market values; and**
        (2 marks)

    (iii)   **market value weighted average cost of capital.**   **(2 marks)**

(b) **Discuss whether a change in dividend policy will affect the share price of DD Co.**
    (8 marks)

(c) **Explain why DD Co's capital instruments have different levels of risk and return.**
    (5 marks)

    (Total: 20 marks)

SECTION A – Objective test (OT) questions

1   A

$20 \times (1.035/1.015) = 20.39$ Dinar per $

2   D

Sensitivity to a change in sales volume = $100 \times 1{,}300/24{,}550 = 5.3\%$

3   A

Gurdip is basing her investment decisions on technical analysis, which means that she believes the stock market is not efficient at all, not even weak form efficient.

4   D

The statement about business risk is correct.

5   B

Increases in shareholder wealth will depend on increases in cash flow, rather than increases in earnings per share, i.e. increases in profit. If the financial rewards of directors are linked to increasing earnings per share, for example, through a performance-related reward scheme, there is an incentive to increasing short-term profit at the expense of longer growth in cash flows and hence shareholder wealth.

6   B

Both statements 1 and 3 are correct.

7   D

Operational gearing = Contribution/PBIT = $[60{,}000 - (50{,}000 \times 0.6)]/10m = 3$ times

8   A

Finance cost saving = $13/365 \times \$20m \times 0.12 = \$85{,}479$

9   D

All three statements concerning financial management are correct.

10   C

The geometric average dividend growth rate is $(36.0/31.1)1/3 - 1 = 5\%$

The ex div share price = $(36.0 \times 1.05)/(0.12 - 0.05) = \$5.40$

11   A

The statement refers to translation risk.

---

12 A

The length of the operating cycle is 52 + 42 + 30 − 66 + 45 = 103 days.

13 C

Risk pooling and maturity transformation are always included in a list of benefits of financial intermediation.

14 B

Both statements 1 and 3 are correct.

15 C

The two targets relating predominantly to monetary policy are controlling the growth in the size of the money supply and keeping interest rates low (2 and 4).

SECTION B – OT cases

16   D

The secured loan notes are safer than the bank loan, which is secured on a floating charge. The redeemable preference shares are above debt in the creditor hierarchy. Ordinary shares are higher in the creditor hierarchy than preference shares.

17   C

Future share price after seven years = 10.90 × 1.067 = $16.39 per share

Conversion value of each loan note = 16.39 × 8 = $131.12 per loan note

18   B

Market value of each loan note = (8 × 5.033) + (126.15 × 0.547) = 40.26 + 69.00 = $109.26

19   C

An equity beta of greater than 1 indicates that the investment is more risky than the market as a whole.

20   B

It is correct that the price/earnings ratio is more suited to valuing the shares of listed companies, and it is also true that it is difficult to find a suitable price earnings ratio for the valuation.

21   A

Interest payment = 5,000,000 pesos

Six-month forward rate for buying pesos = 12.805 pesos per $

Dollar cost of peso interest using forward market = 5,000,000/12.805 = $390,472

22   B

Exchange rates reflecting the different cost of living between two countries is stated by the theory of purchasing power parity.

The theory holds in the long term rather than the short term.

The forward rate is found by multiplying the spot rate by the ratio of the inflation rates of the two countries.

23   C

Dollars will be borrowed now for six months at 4.5 × 6/12 = 2.25%

Pesos will be deposited now for six months at 7.5 × 6/12 = 3.75%

24 C

Currency futures and swaps could both be used. As payment must be made on the date set by the bank, leading or lagging are not appropriate. Matching is also inappropriate as there are no peso income streams.

25 A

The correct procedure is to: Borrow euro now, convert the euro into dollars and place the dollars on deposit for three months, use the customer receipt to pay back the euro loan.

26 A

Deregulation to increase competition should mean managers act to reduce costs in order to be competitive. The need to reduce costs may mean that quality of products declines.

27 A

Since taxation and capital allowances are to be ignored, and where relevant all information relating to project 2 has already been adjusted to include future inflation, the correct discount rate to use here is the nominal before-tax weighted average cost of capital of 12%.

	0	1	2	3	4
Maintenance costs		(25,000)	(29,000)	(32,000)	(35,000)
Investment and scrap	(200,000)				25,000
Net cash flow	(200,000)	(25,000)	(29,000)	(32,000)	10,000
Discount at 12%	1.000	0.893	0.797	0.712	0.636
Present values	(200,000)	(22,325)	(23,113)	(22,784)	(6,360)

Present value of cash flows ($274,582)

Cumulative present value factor 3.037

Equivalent annual cost = 274,582/3.037 = $90,412

28 D

Both statements are false. The machine with the lowest equivalent annual cost should be purchased not the present value of future cash flows alone.

The lives of the two machines are different and the equivalent annual cost method allows this to be taken into consideration.

29 B

EV of year 3 cash flow = $(23,000 \times 0.2) + (24,000 \times 0.35) + (30,000 \times 0.45) = 26,500$

PV discounted at 12% = $26,500 \times 0.712 = 18,868$

30 C

The statement about uncertainty increasing with project life is true.

SECTION C – Constructed response (long questions)

1 **(a)** **(i)** **Calculation of NPV**

Year	0	1	2	3	4
	$	$	$	$	$
Investment	(2,000,000)				
Income		1,236,000	1,485,400	2,622,000	1,012,950
Operating costs		676,000	789,372	1,271,227	620,076
Net cash flow	(2,000,000)	560,000	696,028	1,350,773	392,874
Discount at 10%	1.000	0.909	0.826	0.751	0.683
Present values	(2,000,000)	509,040	574,919	1,014,430	268,333

Net present value: $366,722

Workings

Calculation of income

Year	1	2	3	4
Inflated selling price ($/unit)	20.60	21.22	21.85	22.51
Demand (units/year)	60,000	70,000	120,000	45,000
Income ($/year)	1,236,000	1,485,400	2,622,000	1,012,950

Calculation of operating costs

Year	1	2	3	4
Inflated variable cost ($/unit)	8.32	8.65	9.00	9.36
Demand (units/year)	60,000	70,000	120,000	45,000
Variable costs ($/year)	499,200	605,500	1,080,000	421,200
Inflated fixed costs ($/year)	176,800	183,872	191,227	198,876
Operating costs ($/year)	676,000	789,372	1,271,227	620,076

Alternative calculation of operating costs

Year	1	2	3	4
Variable cost ($/unit)	8	8	8	8
Demand (units/year)	60,000	70,000	120,000	45,000
Variable costs ($/year)	480,000	560,000	960,000	360,000
Fixed costs ($/year)	170,000	170,000	170,000	170,000
Operating costs ($/year)	650,000	730,000	1,130,000	530,000
Inflated costs ($/year)	676,000	789,568	1,271,096	620,025

(ii) Calculation of internal rate of return

Year	0	1	2	3	4
	$	$	$	$	$
Net cash flow	(2,000,000)	560,000	696,028	1,350,773	392,874
Discount at 20%	1.000	0.833	0.694	0.579	0.482
Present values	(2,000,000)	466,480	483,043	782,098	189,365

Net present value: ($79,014)

Internal rate of return = 10 + ((20 − 10) × 366,722)/(366,722 + 79,014) = 10 + 8.2 = 18.2%

(iii) Calculation of return on capital employed

Total cash inflow = 560,000 + 696,028 + 1,350,773 + 392,874 = $2,999,675

Total depreciation and initial investment are same, as there is no scrap value.

Total accounting profit = 2,999,675 − 2,000,000 = $999,675

Average annual accounting profit = 999,675/4 = $249,919

Average investment = 2,000,000/2 = $1,000,000

Return on capital employed = 100 × 249,919/1,000,000 = 25%

(b) The investment proposal has a positive net present value (NPV) of $366,722 and is therefore financially acceptable. The results of the other investment appraisal methods do not alter this financial acceptability, as the NPV decision rule will always offer the correct investment advice.

The internal rate of return (IRR) method also recommends accepting the investment proposal, since the IRR of 18.2% is greater than the 10% return required by PV Co. If the advice offered by the IRR method differed from that offered by the NPV method, the advice offered by the NPV method would be preferred.

The calculated return on capital employed of 25% is less than the target return of 30%, but as indicated earlier, the investment proposal is financially acceptable as it has a positive NPV. The reason why PV Co has a target return on capital employed of 30% should be investigated. This may be an out-of-date hurdle rate which has not been updated for changed economic circumstances.

(c)   As a large listed company, PV Co's primary financial objective is assumed to be the maximisation of shareholder wealth. In order to pursue this objective, PV Co should undertake projects, such as this one, which have a positive NPV and generate additional value for shareholders.

However, not all of PV Co's stakeholders have the same objectives and the acceptance of this project may create conflict between the different objectives.

Due to Product W33 being produced using an automated production process, it will not meet employees' objectives of continuity or security in their employment. It could also mean employees will be paid less than they currently earn. If this move is part of a longer-term move away from manual processes, it could also conflict with government objectives of having a low rate of unemployment.

The additional noise created by the production of Product W33 will affect the local community and may conflict with objectives relating to healthy living. This may also conflict with objectives from environmental pressure groups and government standards on noise levels as well.

Marking scheme		Marks
(a)	Inflated income	2
	Inflated operating costs	2
	Net present value	1
	Internal rate of return	3
	Return on capital employed	3
(b)	Discussion of investment appraisal findings	3
	Advice on acceptability of project	1
(c)	Maximisation of shareholder wealth	1–2
	Conflict from automation of production process	1–2
	Conflict from additional noise	1–2
	Maximum	**5**
Total		**20**

2   (a)   (i)   Dividend growth rate = 100 × ((52/50) − 1) = 100 × (1.04 − 1) = 4% per year

Share price using DGM = (50 × 1.04)/(0.124 − 0.04) = 52/0.84 = 619c or $6.19

          (ii)   Number of ordinary shares = 25 million

Market value of equity = 25m × 6.19 = $154.75 million

Market value of Bond A issue = 20m × 95.08/100 = $19.016m

Market value of Bond B issue = 10m × 102.01/100 = $10.201m

Market value of debt = $29.217m

Market value of capital employed = 154.75m + 29.217m = $183.967m

Capital gearing = 100 × 29.217/183.967 = 15.9%

          (iii)   WACC = ((12.4 × 154.75) + (9.83 × 19.016) + (7.82 × 10.201))/183.967 = 11.9%

    (b)   Miller and Modigliani showed that, in a perfect capital market, the value of a company depended on its investment decision alone, and not on its dividend or financing decisions. In such a market, a change in dividend policy by DD Co would not affect its share price or its market capitalisation. They showed that the value of a company was maximised if it invested in all projects with a positive net present value (its optimal investment schedule). The company could pay any level of dividend and if it had insufficient finance, make up the shortfall by issuing new equity. Since investors had perfect information, they were indifferent between dividends and capital gains. Shareholders who were unhappy with the level of dividend declared by a company could gain a 'home-made dividend' by selling some of their shares. This was possible since there are no transaction costs in a perfect capital market.

Against this view are several arguments for a link between dividend policy and share prices. For example, it has been argued that investors prefer certain dividends now rather than uncertain capital gains in the future (the 'bird-in-the-hand' argument).

It has also been argued that real-world capital markets are not perfect, but semi-strong form efficient. Since perfect information is therefore not available, it is possible for information asymmetry to exist between shareholders and the managers of a company. Dividend announcements may give new information to shareholders and as a result, in a semi-strong form efficient market, share prices may change. The size and direction of the share price change will depend on the difference between the dividend announcement and the expectations of shareholders. This is referred to as the 'signalling properties of dividends'.

It has been found that shareholders are attracted to particular companies as a result of being satisfied by their dividend policies. This is referred to as the 'clientele effect'. A company with an established dividend policy is therefore likely to have an established dividend clientele. The existence of this dividend clientele implies that the share price may change if there is a change in the dividend policy of the company, as shareholders sell their shares in order to reinvest in another company with a more satisfactory dividend policy. In a perfect capital market, the existence of dividend clienteles is irrelevant, since substituting one company for another will not incur any transaction costs. Since real-world capital markets are not perfect, however, the existence of dividend clienteles suggests that if DD Co changes its dividend policy, its share price could be affected.

(c)   There is a trade-off between risk and return on DD's capital instruments. Investors in riskier assets require a higher return in compensation for this additional risk. In the case of ordinary shares, investors rank behind all other sources of finance in the event of a liquidation so are the most risky capital instrument to invest in. This is partly why DD Co's cost of equity is more expensive than its debt financing.

Similarly for debt financing, higher-risk borrowers must pay higher rates of interest on their borrowing to compensate lenders for the greater risk involved. DD Co has two bonds, with Bond A having the higher interest rate and therefore the higher risk. Since both bonds were issued at the same time, business risk is not a factor in the higher level of risk.

Instead, this additional risk is likely to be due to the fact that Bond A has a greater time until maturity, meaning that its cash flows are more uncertain than Bond B. In particular where interest rates are expected to increase in the future, longer-term debt will have a higher rate of interest to compensate investors for investing for a longer period.

A further factor is that the total nominal value (book value) of Bond A is twice as large as Bond B and therefore may be perceived to be riskier.

Marking scheme		
		Marks
(a)	Dividend growth rate	1
	Share price using dividend growth model	2
	Capital gearing	2
	Weighted average cost of capital	2
(b)	Dividend irrelevance	3–4
	Dividend relevance	3–4
	Maximum	**8**
(c)	Discussion of equity	1–2
	Debt and recognising business risk is not relevant	1–2
	Time until maturity of bonds	1–2
	Different value of bonds	1
	Maximum	**5**
Total		**20**